Maxime Weygand

Maxime Weygand

A Biography of the French General in Two World Wars

BARNETT SINGER

McFarland & Company, Inc., Publishers
Jefferson, North Carolina, and London

LIBRARY OF CONGRESS CATALOGUING-IN-PUBLICATION DATA

Singer, Barnett.
    Maxime Weygand : a biography of the French general in two
world wars.
      p.   cm.
    Includes bibliographical references and index.

    ISBN 978-0-7864-3571-5
    softcover : 50# alkaline paper ∞

    1. Weygand, Maxime, 1867–1965.   2. Generals — France —
Biography.   3. France. Armée — Biography.   4. France —
History, Military — 20th century — Sources.   I. Title.
DC373.W4S56   2008
355.0092 — dc22 [B]   2008009009

British Library cataloguing data are available

On the cover: Maxime Weygand (Bettmann/CORBIS);
French flag ©2008 Shutterstock

Manufactured in the United States of America

McFarland & Company, Inc., Publishers
  Box 611, Jefferson, North Carolina 28640
    www.mcfarlandpub.com

Table of Contents

Preface and Acknowledgments

Prefaces should be brief, and acknowledgments more lengthy; but here I meld the two. I want first to say that I have tried to present a well-documented work here, using archival sources at the Service Historique de l'Armée de Terre, Vincennes, and colonial ones (Centre des Archives d'Outre–Mer) in Aix, along with some oral testimony, for the thorny subject of Weygand and Vichy in chapters 9 and 10, and in a way no one has done before. For the rest I have also used archival sources at the above-mentioned institutions, along with the Archives Nationales, Paris, and of course many printed primary and secondary sources throughout. However, even many of those haven't previously been used in works on Weygand. I have also had an entrée to Weygand's private papers, and particularly his lengthy, hard to read diary for World War I and its aftermath.

Writing about history is of course a humbling enterprise that one can never get totally right. If I haven't seen "everything" in the way of sources, I think I may also humbly say that doing, or pretending to do, such a thing sometimes brings too much in the way of historical trees, and too little forest.

Could more have been done? Certainly. But using the sources I have, and also analyzing much more deeply than has been done before Weygand's *own* copious writing, I have tried to do justice to an extraordinary personality here. As much as I consider myself a credentialed, university scholar specializing in French history, I've also tried to follow the path of Alistair Horne, Christopher Hibbert, A. J. P. Taylor, or D. W. Brogan in Britain, where, along with professionalism, amateurism (the love of doing) has produced a spate of readable, yet at the same time, solid works of history.

I must thank officials at the French archives noted above, along with those at the Bibliothèque Nationale in Paris and at libraries on this side of the Atlantic—the Library of Congress, and a number of other large university libraries, mainly in the East. The interlibrary loan service at Brock University has been exemplary, and I also thank Brock for a sabbatical permitting

1

sustained research. Finally, I give special thanks to the following: Marie-Martine Renard for permission to consult and quote from Weygand's papers, and Stéphane Allion at the army archives of Vincennes; Colonel Serge-Henri Parisot, who answered many questions, and gave me an unpublished manuscript from his time in the Secret Service in Morocco under Weygand; Professor William A. Hoisington, Jr., who kindly read the entire manuscript and critiqued an earlier draft of Chapter 10, on Weygand's proconsulate in Africa; Professor John C. Cairns, a long-time expert on the Fall of France in 1940, who gave me significant advice, and some confirmation (for Chapter 8); Professors Edward M. Coffman and John F. Sweets, who also provided readings late in the day, and some confirmation as well for my views (though obviously I take full responsibility for any infelicities here); V. L. Schmidt-Wilson for help with translations; and organizers of the "Empire, Borderlands, and Border Cultures" conference at California State University, Stanislaus, where I presented a paper on Weygand in March 2006. Memories of an ever supportive Eugen Weber, who like Weygand was a determined outsider with much to overcome, and of my late doctoral supervisor, David Pinkney, remain as well; and I like to think they would have appreciated some of what they read here. Last but not least, I warmly thank Katherine, and my daughter, Alexandra.

Introduction

Maxime Weygand is an important, yet often underestimated, figure historically, and his life and action in France's times of stress — particularly during the Great War and aftermath, then during the 1930s and World War II — continue to have much relevance. One thing is certain about Weygand: he was never an appeaser of the Germans, as so many associated with the French Right and Left *both* became after 1918 (the Right increasingly so from the mid–'30s). Weygand felt that only strength and firm, up-to-date military preparation, combined with subtle leadership, could dissuade, slow up, and hold off the Nazis. He believed that give the Germans, particularly the Nazis, an inch, and they might not initially take the clichéd mile; but ultimately, their appetites would drastically grow with the eating. And of course they did. Weygand and Churchill — who liked each other — were of the same mind in that regard. Both saw the Nazi menace correctly, and from early on; both saw too what Russia's Bolshevism would bring, and this almost from the creation. We should finally add that Weygand also beheld different swaths of the Islamic world up close, operating there and writing about it with great understanding, sense of complexity, and cogency.

History needn't be relevant to us, yet Weygand's example still is, due to the constancy of human behavior, and similar challenges people have faced. Had his repeated warnings during the 1920s and '30s — about the need for enhanced French unity, military preparedness, and adaptation to a new kind of war dominated by tank mobility and aircraft — been sufficiently heeded, the catastrophe of France's defeat in 1940 might have been averted, along with the horrid Nazi occupation that followed.

Our perspective gets us well beyond the older one of Philip Bankwitz, in the sole book on Weygand written in English (1967), and which seems to give to its subject with one hand, then take away with the other. Bankwitz's book is only a study, not biographical, and almost exclusively focused on Weygand's relations with the political realm in France after 1930.[1] Writing during the Cold War, when many in American academe felt their country had been too obdurate with Communism in its different varieties, Bankwitz especially took Weygand to task for consistent anti–Bolshevism, though denizens of Russia's communist empire would almost unanimously confirm his hostility a couple of decades after the book's appearance.

Bankwitz also seems unsure whether to credit caricatures of Weygand, making him a Rightist plotter against the French republic during the 1930s, or simply to call these crude exaggerations, as indeed they were. His tone and interpretations constantly shift. In fact, he can't be sure that he really likes Weygand, or is allowed to — this despite the fact that the aged general was kind to him and consented to interviews. Bankwitz was also trapped in the era of *French* history when he wrote — one that had just seen a messy dénouement to the protracted conflict in Algeria, and disobedience of some of France's greatest officers (including ex–Resistants). This also kept his warning light going about Weygand and the French army. And again, Bankwitz's focus is really but a study of Weygand after 1930, and from one optic only; in his prologue, he does very little with the Weygand of World War I. (To a lesser degree, neither does Weygand's last French biographer of 1989, the diplomat and tennis champion, Bernard Destremau.)[2]

Another lacuna in Bankwitz's book is scarcely his fault, given the nature of his work: he neglected Weygand's wonderful sense of culture, demonstrated in a host of tasteful, informative books, pamphlets, and prefaces, written particularly during the '30s, and then after World War II into the '60s. If membership in the Académie Française may sometimes seem a sinecure, Weygand eminently deserved his — much more than the man whose place he took there, Joseph Joffre. Weygand was a major and always interesting writer, including of military history, and his many books are full of factual and aesthetic surprises. Going through them, I kept having initial preconceptions revised considerably upward. All this is important, given that historians have recently learned not to separate the cultural quite so readily from the political or military; and here again is where this work goes beyond Bankwitz and those of his era who too neatly subdivided historical genres.

On the positive side, Bankwitz's book *is* well researched for its time, a standard in the field, and a good place to start. But it is also limited in focus, and diminished by ideological preconceptions, lack of empathy for its subject, and general outmodedness.

So we believe that we can add something significantly different here to a discussion of a singular and important French military figure. And that is not only due to interpretation; it is also owing to the fact that copious and revealing Vichy-era archives were closed to Bankwitz (given France's "50-year rule"), but can now be well sampled. Material found there indeed illuminates much that is crucial about Weygand in World War II. Destremau's 1989 biography did not utilize these archives either, which certainly confirm my view that Weygand was the best of Vichy, and in fact, what one might call an example of "Vichy Resistance."

Simply due to his military insights, skills, and culture, this French general elicited admiration from many greats — Churchill, Clemenceau, Franklin Roosevelt, generals Hubert Lyautey and Jean de Lattre de Tassigny, and Sir Basil Liddell Hart, to name but a few. Weygand's case remains important today, allowing us significant insight into the nuances of the still hot issue of Vichy versus Free France during World War II. Again, we affirm that he embodied a kind of "Vichy resistance"— much opposed to the collaborationism of a Laval or Darlan — and now getting more highlighting, if not yet enough, in the English-speaking world. I believe — with other observers, largely French — that right from the armistice of 1940, Weygand always kept "revanche" against the Nazis in the foreground; that he always felt France would come back for another round; that building the armistice army into the army of a turnaround, and giving nothing extra to the Germans, nor placating them in any way, were his *idées fixes* in this difficult period. Armistice agreements should *not* be renegotiated; bases in French North Africa, rail rights, and other things the Nazis demanded should *not* be vouchsafed, even in the breach. When French ministerial arms were twisted, stalling should become the order of the day. So Weygand believed, and at considerable risk to himself and to others who followed him, he put his money where his mouth was, demonstrating consistent bravery. If courage is one of the great human virtues, then Weygand was undoubtedly a virtuous man. In addition to noted admirers mentioned above, he also received heartfelt accolades from his son, Jacques, in a sensitive, informed memoir; and maybe that is ample confirmation that he was indeed what Jacques called an "être d'exception." If anyone knows a father, it is a son, particularly a smart, aware one, as Jacques certainly was.[3]

Highlighting this notion of "Vichy resistance," we must per force take some of the limelight here from a major French name, Charles de Gaulle, who has received too much of it. In fact, de Gaulle's antipathy to Weygand remained pathological until the end of his life, revealing an egomaniacal, petty, envious, credit-appropriating, and simplistic mindset. De Gaulle tried hard to erase from the slate of history figures like Weygand — loyal to France's chief of state for the first couple of years under Vichy, but who also countered the Nazis at every turn, worked well with the Americans, and then welcomed Operation TORCH. If not imprisoned in Germany, as Weygand himself was from November, 1942, many who worked with or under him went on to participate actively in the liberating campaigns of Tunisia, Italy, and finally, of France itself. These men included distinguished military leaders, such as future marshals Alphonse Juin and de Lattre de Tassigny. Thus, we not only revise earlier viewpoints on Weygand, like that of Bankwitz, but more generally, a Manichean division of good and evil in the France of World War II that still persists in certain quarters. A more limber perspective on the period has only recently become cutting edge in historiography — and was long overdue.[4]

Another reason for a new study of Weygand is that we now have more readily obtainable psychological knowledge than was the case even for Destremau in his 1989 biography — both general, theoretical knowledge, and specific knowledge of Weygand's thorny, and for a long time mysterious, origins that so impacted his adult life. In the burgeoning field of "borderland" research, it is perhaps time that we put more emphasis on what might be called "borderland individuals" — of which Weygand was emphatically one. We already know how important the peripheral backgrounds of Napoleon, the Corsican, Stalin, the Georgian, and Hitler, the Austrian were in their desire to make it to the centers of France, Soviet Russia, and Germany respectively, and to play dominant roles in those countries' (or empire's) fortunes. When it comes to Weygand, his "borderland" status was more psychological, given the truly unusual circumstances of his birth and childhood. And this had a great effect on his entire career, and also on the development of his exquisite taste and culture.

Owing to his background, Weygand clung to places in life that became sure for him, and that were in a sense homes, and which impelled him to serve his country so faithfully. His psychology was what helped make him a staunch defender of France, unwilling to grant any alteration to the armistice agreement with Germans he had already zealously countered in World War I and at conferences afterward. In the face of much opposition, he knew how to stick to his guns, averring what he felt was right. And he also knew how to bring out the best in others, creating thereby synergistic force and results.

The best example of the latter was Weygand's relationship with General (then Marshal) Ferdinand Foch — as his chief of staff during and after the Great War. However, Weygand's unquestioning idolatry of this flawed military leader constitutes perhaps his greatest character defect, one stemming, again, from the insecure conditions of his childhood. In his adulthood he made Foch a kind of talisman or lifeline. Did he also follow Pétain too faithfully in the next war? This is a more complex issue, and one which will be dealt with fully below. Weygand's policies in Vichy North Africa, including towards Jews and Arabs there, also require much nuance, and will be treated extensively as well. But onward to the genesis of a fascinating "Frenchman" — or *was* he, in fact, one?

1

The Formative Years

According to one psychologist, people who have faced insecurity and trauma in childhood "like to be able to predict, foresee, and influence events."[1] Given that Weygand had the mindset of an adopted child, and remained uncertain for a long lifetime about the identity of his real parents, it is consistent with literature on the subject that he would later search out (and find) "homes" and identities that seemed surer than had been available in a very unsure, painful childhood.[2]

Weygand's background remains nothing short of byzantine; however, the latest investigation on his origins, based on exhaustive archival research and interviews, makes it almost certain (as it couldn't be to his previous French biographer) that Weygand's father was Alfred van der Smissen, a dashing, brave lieutenant-colonel close to the Belgian royal house when he met Weygand's likely mother, and then rising to become a general. Weygand's most likely mother is Melanie Marie Zichy-Metternich, daughter (*no less*) of Austria's great foreign minister and chancellor and of Metternich's third wife, Melanie Marie Antoinette Zichy Ferraris. Based in Vienna, and enhancing her high nobility by marriage to a much older Hungarian cousin, Count Joseph Zichy, the childless Melanie seemed ripe for an affair when she met van der Smissen before and during the Franco–Austrian adventure in Mexico of the 1860s, where she went as a high lady-in-waiting to the Empress Charlotte (sister of the Belgian king). One *already* gets a sense of the extreme complexity in the Weygand etiology — including the fact that this somewhat Metternichian type was almost certainly the "coachman of Europe's" grandson! And that if indeed Melanie Zichy-Metternich got herself pregnant by van der Smissen, she didn't give birth to Maxime January 21, 1867, which was always considered his birth date; but more probably, and prematurely, in the summer of 1865.[3]

At all events, the boy of at least some royal blood (Hitler would derisively call him a "renegade Habsburg") was then protected by the Belgian monarch, and shunted to France, while his birth secrets were zealously kept, including from himself. The child first submitted to a strict upbringing by a widow, Virginie Saget, in Marseille — through to age six he actually thought he was her son, and that his name was Maxime Saget. Suddenly, at six, he was transferred to a rich "tutor," David Cohen, a Sephardic Jewish merchant with ties to Belgium's King Leopold II, from whom he received money that would help with the boy's elite, but demanding education. Cohen had separated from his first wife and was living common law (before divorce became legal in France) with Thérèse Denimal; and the boy's name now became an aristocratic variant of hers. He was henceforth called Maxime de Nimal, though cruel schoolchildren liked to poke holes in that moniker, ragging the vulnerable boy for having no real parents. His most likely ones, given above, remained absolutely unknown to him (and this through his entire life of almost 100 years). In sum, one of France's most important military figures probably didn't have any French at all in his origins; as well, he had already gone through two names at a young age, neither of which would last. But of course all know the paradoxes, the sometime gifts of having to overcome — best put in the Nietzschean adage that that which doesn't kill a person makes him or her stronger.

David de Léon Cohen was himself a mysterious, fascinating character with wide-ranging international business connections which, before reverses, reminded one somewhat of a Rothschild. He was born in Genoa, June 25, 1820, then was brought by his parents at a young age to Marseille (though his nationality was sometimes given as Spanish). As a young adult based in the French port city, Cohen mounted a business running vessels full of wool, wheat, skins, or arms, mainly along Morocco's coast, but with links also to the Italians, British, and Belgians, among others. His agents operated in Gibraltar, Antwerp, and many other far-flung places. When this enterprise encountered difficulties, he veered in different directions, such as Marseille director (1865) of The European Bank, founded in London a few years before. However, the bank's ensuing bankruptcy then intensified his own liquidity problems, though as the owner of several sumptuous homes, Cohen certainly had enough to weather that storm. For a time, he would make a comeback in the Moroccan carrying trade, and such reverses as he had experienced were due mainly to prevailing economic currents, events like the Crimean War, or the sultan of Morocco's inconsistencies. Cohen nonetheless remained a man to be reckoned with, and one possessing important connections. When it came to tutors, the young Maxime could have done worse.[4]

In lycées that were elite, but cold, demanding institutions, the boy compensated for his pariah status by losing himself in hard work — rather like the little Corsican who became iconically French, Maxime loved to read and learn, and what a marvelous culture he would put together. And not just a pedantic or parade culture; but rather, one that would give him deep, sensitive feeling for the entire history of France, along with its language, literature, and geography, intensifying a burning French patriotism. Due to his assiduous reading and taste, Weygand's spoken and written French would become that of a master.

In his youth, Maxime also became a convinced French Catholic, though he attended secular schools when anticlericalism was rife there. His conversion was facilitated by the visits of a chaplain, the Abbé de Bonfils; and freely choosing, this pariah-boy wasn't baptized until the age of ten (1877). But from then on, Catholicism became a lodestone for him the rest of his life, an orientation that would land him in much political trouble, especially during the divisive 1930s, when it seemed a convenient synonym for the Right. However, the vulnerable boy, then the man found comfort in taking his religion as seriously as all his life he would take his clothes, demeanor, positions, and military views. There were definite advantages emanating from those who provided for him at an early age. For one thing Cohen allowed him not only to become a fervent Catholic, but also to embrace an army career, the mention of which brought a derisive retort from a teacher at the Lycée Louis-le-Grand in Paris, when the teenager migrated to that prestigious institution.[5] The boy remonstrated strongly against the insult, and was ejected, only to obtain his baccalaureate at the less prized lycée of Toulon in the south of France. It was the post–1871 period of young Frenchmen thirsting for revenge against German invaders who had taken Alsace and part of Lorraine; and Maxime desired above all else entry into Saint-Cyr, the French officers' school, and then a career serving his country in the army.

The name game, however, hadn't quite run its course. Growing into adulthood as a short, slight, but resolute young man, Maxime de Nimal made it through the competition for entrance into Saint-Cyr as a "foreigner"[6]; but to become a fully French officer, the teenager required yet another pseudonym, and the one he would, in the event, make famous. David Cohen had a useful connection with an important politician of the moderate liberal stripe, representing Aix-Marseille. This Maurice Rouvier, a member of the French Opportunist party, bent an ear to Maxime's dilemma, stipulating that he required an actual, adoptive father of French citizenship (Cohen having been born abroad, and designated merely as a "tutor"). The man Cohen located to fill the bill was his accountant, François Joseph Weygand, a widower who accepted the deal solely for the cash it provided him.

So in 1888 an exultant young man, henceforth named Maxime Weygand, made it to his first French garrison at the foot of the Alps — and would now begin a glittering career as a French officer. Inside, however, he remained anxious — that is, when his high standards and ultra-busy life permitted it — that someone, *anyone* might detect his uncertain status, find out about this gotten-up moniker, and pierce a fragile personal edifice which had brought him the career he so desired. At any time an enemy might suddenly aim an arrow at Weygand's Achilles heel — his bizarre, nebulous origins; how fortunate, therefore, that his life was always so thronged (not least with two world wars to negotiate), because deep down, this was a perpetual concern inside of him.

Weygand's personality pluses and what some perceived as minuses all went back to this odd psychological background. From the time of his name change, Maxime became known for rigidity, determination, and stick-to-itiveness, and for doing military jobs the right way. That included riding well and indefatigably on the best mounts, yet later recognizing (in the way Picasso went from traditional to non-traditional art) when cavalry ought to cede to mechanized forces. Weygand was also a duelist of distinction, in the last European period when that still mattered to a gentleman. He was naturally aristocratic, but in the best way: strong, yet real, never letting himself devolve into decadence, and grateful always to have a chance at doing good for his country. From his superiors he received consistently high evaluations both in his first and subsequent garrisons. Topping his class as well at France's cavalry school in Saumur, he was made a captain in 1896, and existentially (like two later thinkers, Camus and Sartre, each fatherless from age one) wasted no time at all crafting a career.

That career required a suitable marriage, but for Weygand, so lacking in dependable family growing up, such a union couldn't simply be *pro forma*, as some then were. For this parentless only child of uncertain origins, marriage and family, like Catholicism and the military vocation, would have to become another home for him: and as it turned out, they did. In Marie-Renée-Joséphine de Forsanz, Weygand located the perfect match. On the other side, the Breton aristocrat Colonel, then General, Raoul de Forsanz was also seeking an officer of quality to wed his high-spirited but finicky daughter. From the start Renée could see only Weygand in her vicinity — perhaps because of the vulnerability she discerned in him (and which she apparently wished to soothe). Mademoiselle de Forsanz was half–Polish in origins via her mother, Hedwige-Marie-Antoinette Ciechanowiecka; and the Poles were of course a borderland people, both historical conquerors, but also conquered — by Germans, Austrians, and Russians. The long and short was that Renée would settle for no one but Weygand. Yet she was warned away from him by a number of people in her family, including her Polish grandmother; or at least, asked to think things out more soberly. Her father also did some desultory investigation in Marseille to learn more about this mysterious fellow and his background. All of which gave him pause. Renée, however, held firm, and the marriage was to take place in the fall of 1900; with, however, one more shoal facing this teetering psychological craft that was Weygand! For he now required an updated baptism certificate, the one he had still bearing the name Maxime de Nimal and needing (in order to make the marriage legal) hasty alteration to the name Weygand.

It hadn't been easy to get such a marriage off the ground; but where many today emphasize the outward forms of weddings, then don't make successes of their marriage, this union of rather inauspicious beginnings turned into a good one, giving a couple meant to parent together two bright, accomplished sons. Between Renée and Maxime, an invariably stable relationship developed, allowing each to be his or her best self. Weygand would be a no-nonsense father, mainly showing by the example of his own disciplined life. And the romantic, vivacious, nurturing Renée would always remain his perfect foil.

2

With Foch in World War I

During the period 1900–1905, following the Dreyfus Affair, Weygand's other "homes" besides marriage and family — Army and Church — were being dragged down, only to make a comeback nearer to the greatest war yet seen in history.[1] In the Belle Epoque before that lethal conflagration, Weygand became the top instructor of military exercises at Saumur's cavalry school. Then at home each night, he would continue working after dinner, with close studies that for him were neither a form of amusement nor dull duty. To many, including Weygand, war, a serious war, was increasingly becoming inevitable. So he felt that he had to learn carefully what such a conflict would entail arms-wise and strategy-wise. In 1912 he asked for a posting to frontier Lorraine, a region near Germany and therefore vulnerable. Anything but hidebound militarily, Weygand wanted to cry out what he knew of the machine gun's lethal nature — the determining fact of the trench conflict around the corner. As he would be before the next war with the Nazis, Weygand was obsessed by a lack of proper French arms to parry an ineluctable, muscle-flexing German menace before World War I; but simultaneously, he would always support the army and even its flawed leadership (especially under Chief of Staff Joseph Joffre at the start of this war, and the equally inept Maurice Gamelin for the next).[2] That was Weygand's psychology: fight for the truth, for what would help France and its people; but at the same time, follow orders.

A tragedy perhaps was that Weygand never became a commander under fire in this murderous, unprecedented conflict — a position he so craved, and which, given the death toll of the Great War, would doubtless have killed this courageous man. B. H. Liddell Hart (among other informed observers) saw it as a waste that, instead, Joffre would shunt Weygand to a staff position, as organizer and "refiner" for the impulsive, generalizing, and eruptive Ferdinand Foch.[3] Weygand wasn't supposed to last in that position; however, his loyalty, organizational abilities, tact, and trustworthiness made him, in the event, an associate almost married to Foch through this worst war in history — for five long years, along with several more in the demanding post-war era.

Like Joffre, Foch was too enamored of attacks against well-embedded machine guns, in which often fruitless, Pyrrhic enterprises he sadly hectored his more empirical British allies, including their first commander, Sir John French; however, Weygand could never be disloyal, and he wasn't. Inevitably, he would be criticized as Foch's minion, and as a fast-tracking careerist, when all he really sought was a position of command. Instead, he got rapidly promoted — to colonel in November 1914, and by the end of the war, to major-general, but all the while, remaining something of a military bureaucrat and/or diplomat.

On the positive side, Weygand learned from numerous conferences with English allies to admire the virtues of that nation and civilization, and not to become anything like the arch–Anglophobe that represented the worst of Vichy one war later. Militarily, he learned never to let France's guard down vis-à-vis its main foe through to 1945: the Germans. He believed always that they respected nothing but force. But as World War I went on, he also learned what wouldn't work operationally, and what might — and the human costs of any military plan.

Lieutenant-Colonel Maxime Weygand started his war service in August, 1914, with the 5th Hussars, under the Second Army led by General Noël Edouard, Viscount of Castelnau, dubbed (for his Catholic beliefs) "the fighting friar." Early on in Lorraine, where the offensive parts of Joffre's Plan 17 created numerous French graves, Weygand witnessed shell shock aplenty and at least some of the terrible heap of cadavers from already huge French losses. Rapidly, he saw how strong the enemy's artillery was. His recollections even on these first battles of the war are typically detailed. For Weygand got to do a lot of reconnaissance on a mare he called La Houzard, a horse that remained with him through to parades of 1919.

Already French military leaders were busy cobbling and re-cobbling together corps and armies, as the costly Battle of Morhange in Lorraine developed into a Second Army debacle — the same battle area of 1940, an eternal Franco-German crossroad. Along with big losses to the French First Army in Alsace, an enemy roll-up seemed very possible at this early point in the war.[4]

Counter-attacks were being hatched, but, as seen from the aforementioned steed's long life, Weygand would soon be removed from active duty in the field. Instead, on orders emanating from Commander in Chief Joffre, who had known Weygand before the war, he was summoned to meet General Foch near Nancy in Lorraine, where he also made a hasty visit to his family. At nearby Toul he was asked by Foch who — Lieutenant-Colonel Weygand

Left: Whether in war or peace, Maxime Weygand was always a serious man (Bettmann/CORBIS). *Right:* General, later Marshal, Ferdinand Foch: the man Weygand idolized and served faithfully during World War I and its aftermath (Bettmann/CORBIS).

or Lieutenant-Colonel B.C. Devaux, also summoned — had attained his rank earlier. The winner by three months was Weygand, and whether for that reason, or simply due to intuition, Foch selected Weygand as his chief of staff, but only on a look-see basis. It then developed into a permanent, gold-minted relationship. Like a dog, a formerly hurt dog, Weygand would remain ever faithful to General Foch, with the feeling well reciprocated.

And though de Gaulle later criticized him in the next world war for lacking command experience, Weygand did see and learn a good deal from the position he held under Foch during this protracted conflict. Immediately he was taken to command map rooms, as Joffre now ordered a retreat southward from the advancing Germans, who were descending from Belgium with Schlieffen-Plan precision and rapidity. At the side of Foch Weygand moved around a lot, until his superior was then attached to the Tenth Army, commanded by General Fernand de Langle de Cary. And Weygand's observations in memoirs long after the fact have the beauty of the artist a part of him remained (today's researcher can also find his drawings of military and governmental honchos in his musty private notebooks, and they too are marvelous).[5]

De Langle, who had been gravely wounded in the Franco-Prussian War, was certainly esteemed by his men, but they themselves had already been through hell, along with the Third, Fourth, and Fifth French armies; and Foch's assignment was mainly to cement liaisons between these armies, and to help protect de Langle's right. Among Weygand's great fortes was his organizational ability, and it would continually be put to the test — amalgamating or divesting armies and corps, given rapidly shifting conditions of this war. Already some of the top generals in charge of these contingents were horrified by all the losses and sufferings they had seen even in the war's first month.

Foch found it easy to be a perpetual moralizer and cheerleader of these soldiers, who kept having to enter dangerous battlefield situations. Better liaisons *were* effected, and the roads to some extent divested of the many refugees who clogged them (à la 1940). But far more than his boss, Weygand was the one who *saw*, ingested, and felt the tragedy unfolding for France's young soldiers being mowed down in such great numbers.[6]

Weygand was certainly surprised by Joffre's continuing southward retreat, but being so faithful psychologically to both Foch and the commander in chief, neglects in his memoirs the fact that the great General Gallieni was the one who finally sold its termination to Joffre — in the form of a counterattack in early September on German troops turning and offering their flank at the Marne. Nor would Weygand criticize Joffre's fondness for firing military talent like General Charles Lanrezac, admired even by the enemy for his subtle military ideas, but replaced at the head of the Fifth French Army in these early days of the war by Louis Franchet d'Esperey (a general the Brits would call Desperate Frankie).[7]

On September 4 the Foch "detachment" was now transmuted with reinforcements into a Ninth Army, as the Battle of the Marne dawned. A new Sixth Army under General Michel-Joseph Maunoury was rushed up to affront the German general Von Kluck's appetizing change of direction near Paris, while at first the Ninth was merely used to support the attacking Fifth. Weygand's memoirs are much more complex on all this than we have space to be here — a sense of military complexity that would stand him in good stead (*pace* de Gaulle) when he commanded in the next war. For Foch gave orders to a variety of generals under him during these fierce, lethal days of combat on the Marne from September 6 through 9. Improvisations were rife, and connections between armies maintained with great difficulty.[8]

Foch sometimes sent Weygand out to commanders in parts of the field who felt they could no longer remain in the fray; this was a kind of delegated cheerleading. But it did give Weygand real contact with battle realities. Some of the generals he met were already beginning to doubt the high command's leadership, and with reason. However, Weygand remembered how happy he was on the night of September 9–10 after the victory at the Marne, which, despite its great human cost, gave him a marvelous feeling of elation. Alsace and Lorraine would soon come back to the French fold, and the vistas seemed infinite![9]

But of course they were not; only vistas of endlessly, repetitively spilled blood through the rest of 1914, and then several more years on a trench-clogged Western Front. Weygand's continuing idolatry of Foch to the end of his life seems truly misplaced; for Foch now enjoined Entente cavalry to keep pursuing the Germans, even though they were getting decimated by the enemy's copious gunnery. The French could chase the Germans only so far beyond the Marne — to another river, the Aisne; and then came the enemy occupation of important French industrial regions, the race of rival entrench-ment north to the English Channel, and the beginnings of a stalemate France's military kept trying to end by hurling numerous bodies at German lines well defended by machine guns![10]

Once the Germans held behind the Aisne, this race to the sea was sim-ply an attempt by each side to lengthen its front, and simultaneously to turn the enemy's flank and break through. Instead, parallel trench lines soon stretched from Switzerland almost up to the Channel, and great battles in marshy Flanders would now ensue, with Joffre that October appointing Foch as his assistant, and overlord of all French armies in the North.

The prickly, self-righteous Foch soon ran afoul of commanders like the respected de Castelnau of the Second Army, who wished to retreat behind the Somme and avoid needless casualties. On this rift Weygand reveals him-self to be even-handed, conceding that de Castelnau was "a leader admired and revered by the entire army." And like Foch, he had sustained familial losses (two sons already dead in combat, and a third to perish subsequently).[11]

The division between Foch and de Castelnau never really healed; but there were many other intelligent commanders who saw the tragedy up close, and did not want needless engagements simply to kill off thousands more of their charges. In this regard, Weygand mentions, with equal admiration, enlightened figures like General Louis de Maud'huy and Colonel Pierre des Vallières.[12]

Key points up north in Flanders, not least what remained of Belgium in its western part, were now in trouble: should there be some withdrawal? Not according to Foch. Rallying the Second and Tenth French armies, and promising British and Belgian help, he got a reluctant, battle-tested de Maud'huy to his side for a hold-the-line policy, no matter the costs. In

Weygand's memory, Foch traversed some 800 kilometers in two days, animating all around him; but in these travels his chief of staff also observed a growing divide between the French leadership and the commander of Britain's Expeditionary Force, Sir John French, and constant efforts at reconciliation promoted by a Francophile Ulsterite, General Sir Henry Wilson.[13] Aided by Wilson, Foch finally convinced Sir John to hold on in the North. In point of fact, he bullied him, much as Joffre did—so that the B.E.F. endorsed questionable operations in this and coming years that would cost their own forces many young lives.

Foch's view was that Ypres was the key point in Flanders as a communications center for the region, and he also wanted badly to retain Dunkirk and Calais on the Channel coast. In the first month or so of the war the Belgians had helped the Allies by holding down the Germans, at least for a time; now in early October, 1914, they had to abandon besieged Antwerp and move westward, constituting another badly battered force that Foch rallied for more effort.

Suitably hectored, the Belgians agreed to defend against the Germans on the Yser river, and Foch, along with Weygand, kept moving about for more exhortations against retreat.[14] All of which constituted the background to the general Flanders campaign of autumn 1914, starting first with the Battle of the Yser, and continuing with the first (of several) at one of the most infamous battle sites of World War I, Ypres.

To be nearer these sectors, Foch had moved his staff headquarters (run by Weygand) from Doullens to Cassel. The Germans soon hit hard on the Yser, gained a bridgehead on the river, and began getting over it October 24. And Foch kept urging Belgian and French "resistance at any price."[15]

Just beyond the Yser Foch desired a new line of defense, including by flooding the Yser valley with sea water. By October 29 this flooding operation began, General Paul Grossetti's French assisting the reeling Belgians once more; and the stubborn Germans began withdrawal, leaving precious arms behind. Weygand—always knowing how to admire—took his hat off especially to the reluctant Belgians, spurred on by Foch, and by their own King Albert.[16] He also saluted the efforts of Grossetti, with an interesting description of that courageous, much-esteemed Corsican general. "This dynamo who feared neither bullets nor shells had one weakness—the fear of getting wet!"[17] After the war Weygand would visit Grossetti's native village, beholding both its bleakness, and its stubborn abodes dug into rocky cliffsides that had helped form the man.

Unfortunately, this war kept running from one costly engagement to the next, now with the first of several lethally celebrated battles at Ypres. And here Foch again overwhelmed Sir John French, who would have preferred to reinforce around Channel ports like Boulogne, rather than simply subscribe to a French offensive. Instead, the English were pushed into attacking on October 20–21, with French troops in support, but to no avail. The debut of the Battle of Ypres augured nothing but more losses. And Weygand remained a detailed, precise observer and chronicler of this continuing series of tragedies.

On October 23 Foch and his amanuensis mounted the tower of the old cloth hall that would later be much damaged at Ypres — scanning the entire battle terrain; and the poet in Weygand recalls "a sea of green against which numerous, prosperous villages stood out as large, light-colored blotches...." But he was also militarily realistic, and as he put it, the "site could delight an artist's eye, but it dismayed the soldier's.... In this farmland criss-crossed by irrigation or drainage canals, the water is the same level as the earth, and communications are hazardous; nothing favors conducting an overall operation here."[18] Such observations made Weygand an increasingly acute military theoretician, but one not yet possessing enough power to influence tragic events on the ground.

From October 26 to October 29 terrible fighting ensued, and German heavy artillery, combined with French and English inability to entrench, led to more appalling losses. Counter-attacks didn't work, especially when cavalry without sufficient gunnery resorted to the bayonet. Weygand remembers finding only the hand of an old cavalry instructor under whom he had studied; but, though much moved, he found Foch counseling the usual — to stay the sanguinary course. "Lack of concern, refusal to see things as they were?" Weygand would wonder.[19] But owing to his psychology, he couldn't bring himself to criticize this father-figure, even in retrospect.

Like the Belgians, the British fought bravely here, while Joffre brought up French reinforcements from around the hexagon; but all attempts to shore up the compliant English were, as Weygand remarks, no more than a "drop of water to put out a [raging] fire."[20] Sir John French and his tired charges were all for retreat at the end of October; while again, Foch urged them to stay put. Sir John, who obviously felt for his men, or those left, finally exploded, declaring that if he had to, he would go and get himself killed alongside them! And Foch, with Weygand observing the scene beside him, "stayed silent in the grip of a dramatically tense, drawn-out mental ambiance."[21]

Bloody fighting continued in Flanders through till November 10, and the French and British gallantly held down the Germans both at Ypres, and in surrounding areas. The latter finally began to end their assault on the 13th;

however, another enormous pile of Entente casualties here was what Alistair Horne has called (re the prolonged carnage at Verdun) the "price of glory."[22]

Foch and Joffre remained a mutual admiration society sold on the offensive spirit; while Weygand in his subordinate role as an organizer, but also as a silent observer, was quietly learning how to lead — and not lead — in war. He also honed diplomatic skills, meeting notables like England's King George V, visiting France after these murderous battles, or King Albert of Belgium.[23] And the Foch headquarters remained at Cassel until May 1915.

Here reconstitutions of armies, post-mortems and analysis went on, with the British still offering different views that went mostly unheeded by their senior allies. Joffre had already decided on large-scale offensives for 1915 along the Western Front, a year dubbed charitably "the sterile year," and which Weygand would call "that of the martyrdom of the French infantry."[24]

As offensive-minded as Joffre, Foch now felt that a long softening-up with artillery, before infantry went over the top, was the way to proceed in these trench engagements. It wasn't a significant enough variation on a hopeless strategic theme. With 300,000 of their soldiers already dead by the end of 1914, these high French generals should already have realized how deadly modern defensive firepower could be to such Napoleonic assaults.[25] But hundreds of thousands more would pay the ultimate price for this strategy — and Weygand? He continued to feel that he had to go along with the ex-professor of war, Foch.

Despite increasing English bitterness, there *were* openly Francophile Britons to cement inter-ally relations, especially Henry Wilson, who, unannounced, came often to see Foch and Weygand, invariably calling the latter "my little Weygand." Weygand was generally the one who could make Foch's views more comprehensible to figures like Wilson.[26] They got along well, but in fact, Wilson was hitching the British more firmly to a shaky cart indeed.

At the beginning of this fateful year of 1915, Foch saw his status changed from temporary assistant in the North to legitimate head of the Group of Northern Armies. And he would play a major role in preparing for offensives in Artois which, along with those in Champagne at another part of the trench line, were supposed to furnish the vaunted Entente breakthrough. Foch's urgent cheerleading continued, as he decided on a massive assault to take the crest of Vimy in the spring, with Joffre approving this refinement of his more general plans.

Meanwhile, the February offensives down the line in Champagne should have provided much needed caution. Joffre might continue hectoring — that enhanced French morale and inspiration would somehow break this trench stalemate; but Weygand's estimate of the first Champagne engagement was more realistic. As he put it, "along every part of the front we were faced with an adversary whose defensive organization was becoming more solid each day...."[27] The Germans simply wouldn't cede ground, content to remain behind ever stronger lines, sucker in the French, then cut them down in great numbers. And this would not change.

After all the losses at Morhange, on the Marne, at Ypres, and in the first Champagne offensives, there followed the great surprise of enemy chlorine gas, first used at the second battle of Ypres in late April, 1915. And here again, Joffre's empty memoirs should be contrasted to Weygand's realism and empathy concerning the terrifying effects of "a thick cloud, of pronounced yellow color..." that brought such suffering. These French, not to mention British and Canadian, troops, "half suffocated, surprised, and bewildered by a new method of attack," literally went crazy; that is, when they did not simply die agonizing deaths.[28]

How much the best laid plans of Entente mice and men were going sour. For with this use of gas the Germans had opened up the vista of unlimited warfare, heeding no conventions that might hold them back. The rules of the game had changed radically. Fearing more concentrated gas use, Sir John French wanted to pull back troops all around Ypres. And naturally the stubborn Foch felt that even a retreat of a few miles "would simply encourage the enemy."[29] On May 3–4 Sir John nonetheless withdrew to new redoubts, his anger with Foch only barely contained.

If employment of poison gas was breaking the rules of war, making it to some degree a war directed from laboratories, from the very start of this conflict there had been German atrocities aplenty. Recent scholarly literature shows that they indeed murdered many French and Belgian civilians, and also torched thousands of buildings, including cathedrals.[30] But the Germans could *also* wage more standard war, and adeptly; thus their bombardment of Dunkirk was yet another surprise for the French, just as Foch at his nearby headquarters was readying his big breakthrough campaign in Artois. Here at Cassel he still managed, however, to "enjoy an excellent appetite," as Weygand recalled[31]; and during these meals, one couldn't even talk about these significant battlefield developments.

Foch, however, wanted his *staff* busy as bees, and he had some good people working under Weygand, such as Commandant Pierre–Henri Desticker, the facile journalist-politician André Tardieu, and one Captain Réquin — with Weygand's recollected portraits of such aides again, marvelous.[32] On May 9, 1915, this Foch-Weygand team departed Cassel, selecting new headquarters at the chateau of Bryas nearer to the Artois theater. En route they heard loud artillery blasts — the first huge Entente attacks already in progress. Some of the armies involved succeeded in taking a first German trench line, then were typically annihilated en route to the second or third. The losses at hallowed sites like the dominant hill of Artois, Notre-Dame-de-Lorette, or in Foch's plan of trying to take Vimy Ridge, were appalling. Ultimately, Foch's charges took only nine kilometers of blood-soaked terrain. Then, on May 10 all attacks foundered, followed by a resumption from May 20 to June 10 of more terrific battles at villages around both Notre-Dame and Vimy. None brought any significant gain, and they truly pained Weygand, still working hard, but at the same time, waiting in the wings.[33]

One final French assault of mid–June petered out after several fruitless days, and so ended this truly infamous Battle of Artois. With some 100,000 men put out of commission in a month, Weygand felt that the price for this massive offensive had been much too high. He kept on learning, silently, painfully, steadily, as the war's holocaust of young lives continued.[34]

Along with poor results in Champagne during the winter, news of the disastrous spring offensive in Artois began bringing down the wrath of French politicians on Joffre; but again, Weygand, the former pariah, tried even in recollection to defend the commander in chief. Never having had a proper father, Weygand remained averse to criticizing France's great (if meretricious) father-figure of wartime. A propos, Weygand recalled having to write a speech on his succession to Joffre's seat at the Académie Française in 1931, and, in the same period, walking the lines of defense named for André Maginot, the French war minister of the late '20s and early '30s; and Maginot pointedly asking exactly what he might say positively about the ex-commander in chief![35]

That commander was, however, far from through with his decimation of lives, preparing more September 1915 offensives in both Champagne and Artois. Lord Kitchener's new armies were now on hand to swell effectives, and Joffre began discussing plans with subordinates, asking for their input and precisions. From Foch came the hardly new idea of trying to re-take the bloodied crest of Vimy. Whereas Philippe Pétain, a colonel in 1914 on the edge of retirement, but now a general heading the Second Army, was characteristically reluctant to lose more men, and said this wasn't the time for a grand offensive, only for more limited ones, and with restricted goals.

However, Joffre still held to the idea of large-scale operations in Champagne and Artois, and both General Victor d'Urbal, a decorated cavalry man heading the Tenth Army, and Pétain endorsed what was simply not in their hearts. And as Weygand notes, "I would conserve painful memories of these preliminaries to the September attacks."[36]

At least Foch's Artois was not the theater this time around that Champagne would be, nor quite so devastating. But as usual, Sir John French's every idea of alteration with his English forces was countered. Informed that the English attack should be south of La Bassée in conjunction with France's Tenth Army, General French decided that he wanted to operate *north* of it, leading to an inevitable argument with the stubborn Foch.

Once again, French tried to modify plans in mid–August, and this time brought down the wrath of his war minister, a soon-dead Lord Kitchener; and on August 22 at Joffre's headquarters of Chantilly, the British commander sadly ceded. During that summer, Joffre and Foch preached their usual message of morale, trying to enthuse troops for another round of inevitable slaughter. An initial artillery barrage started September 18, then came the opening of formal attacks in Champagne and Artois September 25, with gains minimal, losses again huge, and — to Weygand's consternation — the well-hyped breakthrough never occurring.[37] The English were now placing more hope in an October expedition to malarial Salonika in Macedonia, wishing to counter the Austrians and Bulgarians there.

All these costly offensives on the Western Front kept revealing the German character to Weygand — how thoroughly they dug in and replied defensively, and how loathe they were to give up any ground. It was a lesson that stuck with him when later he had to deal with the Nazis of World War II. Once totally behind something, this foe was simply not going to soften up. And as Weygand reminds us, and could have reminded Joffre, these most recent offensives *were* launched in late September — when persistent rain was normal, and certain to be a negative factor. Again, *pace* de Gaulle, Weygand continued learning a good deal in this war, but mostly from his own commanders' errors![38]

There was now much Gallic soul-searching following these 1915 disasters that had killed off so many soldiers. Foch himself began to realize that breaking through definitively was simply not possible on the Western Front — that a series of attacks with more defined goals was the better way to go. And Joffre was criticized ever more stridently by angry politicians, including war ministers like Joseph Gallieni, and later Hubert Lyautey, both distinguished imperial figures.[39] Weygand totes up the huge numbers of French dead simply from the September operations — over 30,000, including fine officers aplenty. His succinct, but apt conclusion? That "this experiment had carried a heavy price tag."[40]

Perhaps he was fortunate to be so busy as Foch's chief of staff and organizer; for undoubtedly, his heart would have been more repetitively torn by supreme command errors had he had time to remain in the field with soldiers, witnessing all the sufferings there. We get a good sense of Weygand's *actual*, quite bureaucratic, life during the war from the series of copious notes he took during the conflict — as well as after. I have consulted these notes in archives from April 27, 1915, onward, and Weygand's industry was astounding: large, detailed lists of various types of munitions, of horses, trucks, etc.; and questions sometimes provisionally answered concerning deployments, not only of French armies, but British ones. If Foch was a generalist, Weygand had a tremendous schooling by his side in empiricism and attention to detail, complementing his chief (as in a good marriage). For Weygand, schedules during World War I were everything. Besides exhaustive preparation for war maneuvers, even lunches and other meetings or conferences with the era's notables, especially during the latter stages of the war, were copious. Attack plans hatched at meetings were often shaped or altered according to what munitions could be procured — and Weygand was at the center of this activity. His opinions — especially on the difficulty of breaking German trench lines with offensives, or on needless losses — are sometimes proffered in these notes; but mainly, he served Foch obediently. However, he also learned to assess character — particularly when crossing paths on numerous occasions with the likes of Generals Haig or Pétain, both very different from Foch. Pétain, in particular, comes off in Weygand's jotted summaries of meetings as terse and practical, much more realistic about this bloodletting on the Western Front than was Foch, not to mention Joffre.

Frequently, Weygand understates in these private jottings; for example, on Joffre's insane September 1915 attacks in Champagne, "we have learned that progress is much less than formerly believed...."[41] By doing his job well and following orders, Weygand *was* climbing up the French military ladder; but he was also paying a price, given the necessity of keeping his qualms about poorly-conceived operations to himself. For the October 1915 attacks all one finds in certain Weygand diary entries is just the huge numbers of losses — French officers, dead and wounded, as well as non-coms. Appealing, however, if still underused was how (unlike more Cartesian generals), Weygand was always open to alternatives — pros and cons of aiming fire in certain directions, of using or not using gas, and the like.

Now commander in chief of all French armies, Joffre went on with his plans for 1916, hatched at a conference in Chantilly December 6–8, 1915, which high-ranking British, Italian, and Russian generals attended. But the British were angered by their own great losses in the Battle of Loos, their role in recent operations; and, having had to navigate between a critical London and the single-tracked Joffre, Sir John French finally resigned as commander of Britain's expeditionary force. He was replaced in mid–December by Douglas Haig, whom Weygand would come to know well.[42] Sir William Robertson was made Britain's chief of the Imperial General Staff, and Weygand admired this man whom he would also come to know up close: particularly his self-made ascent in his nation's army. Observing these Britons at repetitive close range, Weygand learned, thereby, about a country very different from France, yet so necessary to them militarily. Here again was where Weygand's World War I experience, and general taste and empathy, differentiate him both from General Gamelin of 1940, and from de Gaulle, later trying vainly to get along with Churchill. For Weygand the Great War was his key formative experience, and without his position running Foch's staff, he would never have rubbed shoulders so frequently with people who could teach him so much about other civilizations. (Nor would this utter outsider have ever gotten an eventual shot at the top position in the French army!)

On February 21, 1916, came the first German assault on Verdun, an appetizing target, given Joffre's prior removal of gunnery there. The extended battle for Verdun of course became the central part of World War I history during an even more appalling year than the previous one.[43] But another series of offensives up north on the Somme was also being spawned, becoming ever more necessary as Verdun month after month killed off so many young Frenchmen.

Weygand (whose geographical descriptions are again precise) and his superior, Foch, both knew the Somme landscape, and Foch's conclusion was that a big offensive there wouldn't work; something merely revealing French firepower would be much more appropriate. However, Joffre stuck to his general plan. Before the Somme he also made replacements that deeply saddened Weygand: General d'Urbal was ousted at the head of the Tenth Army, in favor of General Joseph Micheler, while General Emile Fayolle replaced General Dubois as commander of the Sixth. Weygand thought highly of d'Urbal, considering him tough but fair, and methodical; whereas a first look at his replacement over dinner with Foch gave him bad forebodings. As Weygand recalls, "[Micheler] was very tall and thin, with a Don Quixote–like physiognomy.... But there was something indefinable in the expression of his face, which despite the affability of his conversation, and camaraderie of his tone, did not inspire confidence."[44] Except when idolizing unduly (in the cases of Foch or Joffre), Weygand *was* a fine evaluator of military personnel; and indeed, when battle preparations came into play, and he had to deal with this Micheler, he found his initial fears confirmed — the man was, in fact, a querulous nitpicker, and emphatically no d'Urbal.

General Fayolle, however, was a different kind of army man. Fayolle had been at the "limit of age" before World War I, and, along with Foch and Pétain, a professor at the Ecole de Guerre before that conflict. He was then brought back into service during the war, and Weygand remained an admirer of this man who privately had no regard for Joffre as a leader, yet always did his duty. When it came to battle preparations, Fayolle wasn't afraid of voicing opinions, and always with requisite supporting evidence for his views. And he had that quality of courage in the field which Weygand perhaps esteemed more than any.[45]

Before the Somme offensive, both Foch and Fayolle agreed on the necessity of long, softening-up artillery barrages, and definitely nothing that smacked of a repeat of the Artois operations. Air reconnaissance was improving, and Foch used photographs provided by it to fine-tune his views. But plans kept being modified, and schedules hurried into action as Verdun snarled into a Pyrrhic stalemate that spring of 1916. Instead of the French being the majority army on the Somme, as originally envisaged, it would now be a larger British army — soon to endure its own holocaust (as Verdun was becoming for the French). And an ever more watchful and distrustful Parliament felt it should put leaders like Foch on the governmental carpet, asking pointedly what all this new planning would yield. Joffre too was heatedly questioned.[46]

The commander in chief nonetheless held his men, and much larger British effectives under Haig, to the fateful opening day of July 1, 1916, for this murderous Battle of the Somme. A preliminary week of barrage before that date only made the dug-in Germans more ready for a series of attacks that had lost any element of surprise they might have had. As is well known, English losses on the first day of the Somme reached an astronomical 20,000 dead, and some 60,000 overall casualties, revealing again how wrong-headed the high command had been about an engagement that was supposed to break the trench stalemate, but which continued on into the fall with little gain, and spiraling loss of life. The best Weygand concedes in recollection is that the Somme helped wear out the Germans at Verdun, which finally became an iconic, if costly, French victory that autumn of 1916. And while the Entente powers felt all but done by the end of this horrendous year, so too did a battered German enemy, its populace at home preparing for a "turnip winter."[47]

This had been the war's worst year, compounded by problems in a spent Russia on the eve of revolution, a German-occupied Rumania, the knockout of Serbia, and a clearly split Greece (between Venizelist Entente supporters, and Royalists leaning more to neutrality, or even toward the Central Powers). Ups and downs of a Franco-British expedition to Salonika, originally designed to save Serbia, became more and more costly. General Maurice Sarrail kept leading offensives northward into mountain country toward Bulgaria, then retreating back to the entrenched camp of Salonika, and — backed by elements of the French left at home — demanding more troops. He also took sides in a Greece on the edge of civil war. The British went along only with gritted teeth, while long desiring withdrawal from Salonika, a presence they felt only intensified manpower problems on the Western Front. Meanwhile, France's war ministers (Gallieni, Pierre Roques, and Lyautey), without regard for Joffre and his repetitive excuses, were now matched by the French government as a whole demanding military heads — preeminently, those of Joffre and Foch![48]

The upshot was the ouster of both from their positions of command, Joffre's blessedly permanent, while Foch's, as it turned out, was not. Joffre was made a marshal by Lyautey, then allowed to visit America, after it entered the war, putatively to enlighten Americans on military policy.[49] In terms of Foch, the process of downgrading had already commenced when Weygand was questioned in secret by General Maurice Pellé on his superior's possible physical problems, and putative outbursts with subordinates. Predictably, Weygand covered totally for Foch, proud that *he* had always gotten along perfectly with this often prickly boss. But in mid–December, 1916, Foch was nonetheless removed from his current posts, and "placed at the disposition of the Ministry" — which floored Weygand, as much as it might finally allow him to petition for his own position of command.[50]

In fact, Foch came out smelling like a proverbial rose, given that General Robert Nivelle, who replaced Joffre as French commander on the Western Front, immediately removed Foch from mothballs, giving him a kind of "study position" — to evaluate the possibility of a German invasion of Switzerland, and thence a more southerly incursion route into France. With a much attenuated staff, Foch chose to set up new headquarters at Senlis, and would Weygand come along? He felt, yet again, that he could not say no.

Foch's new position was a stroke of luck, in that he (and Weygand) could formulate conscientious reports on this Swiss situation, as well as on the German menace in Italy; but sometimes away on missions, and not part of the new General Headquarters moved from Chantilly to Beauvais, then Compiègne, they were not associated with the build-up for what became the disastrous Nivelle Offensive of April, 1917. Too much public debate on it, and criticism, allowed the Germans to figure out its plans in advance. Meanwhile, Russia in revolution was really falling out of the war, America was about to come in that April, Nivelle and Haig were at loggerheads before the attacks — and Foch and Weygand were on the sidelines, yet still in the active army. It turned out that Weygand had remained saddled to the right horse, as Nivelle's ballyhooed attacks on the Aisne and Chemin des Dames would become another French disaster, engendering, for the first time, serious mutinies.

On the eve of that operation, Weygand, along with Britain's chief of staff, Robertson, were off to Italy to meet General Luigi Cadorna, concerning plans for a possible Italian offensive against Austrian forces on the Izonzo River. (Count Cadorna would be a frequent visitor to conference tables that Weygand would draw in order to sketch rapid attendance, and he always appreciated the man's clarity and good manners.)[51]

At their meeting, Cadorna described a probable Austrian attack route in the Trentino, noting that for now, the Italians would remain on the defensive. Anything but simply an office man, Weygand got to view a variety of battle terrains here, and his tour of the Trentino and Carso astonished him, the latter especially difficult, mountainous country, where it was almost impossible to dig Western Front–type trenches. The tour on vertiginous roads came courtesy of one Colonel Abrici, who drove his limousine like an Italian racecar driver! Suitably briefed, General Robertson returned to London, Weygand to Compiègne to write up their reports.

Foch then followed with his own trip to Italy in early April, also meeting with Cadorna, and discussing eventual Franco-British help for Italian forces. While his superior was making these promises, Weygand was next sent to Switzerland, meeting with the Swiss chief of staff in Berne, a city brimming with foreign agents. Weygand and the Swiss general prepared a secret entente in case of a German surprise attack toward France, which would breach a perennially neutral country en route.

When Weygand returned home, the Nivelle Offensive was underway, with Haig's English opening the onslaught in rain and snow, and netting some 13,000 prisoners (April 9–14). On April 13 the French Third Army, followed by the Sixth and Tenth, began *their* forward activity, and the Germans hit back hard. French politicians turned stormy, placing a cautious, respected Pétain at the head of a General Staff that would henceforth carefully watch commanders in chief. A month later, after great loss of life and the onset of mutinies, Nivelle was forced out as commander in chief, and replaced by Pétain. The latter was the general French soldiers loved and trusted, and the only one who could calm these mutinies by a combination of rigor and reforms.[52]

But who would now replace Pétain as chief of staff, reporting on a daily basis to the war minister in Paris, and gaining thereby an entree into the French political world? None other than the formerly disgraced Foch, who had emerged from his problem-filled phase and near exclusion from the army in fine fashion. Nivelle was now the general in disgrace. However, Weygand did not simply damn this soldier and war leader. On the positive side, Nivelle's offensives had further worn down the Germans, and the bag of prisoners taken by both French and English (some 50,000) was considerable.

Regaining the Chemin des Dames was no small achievement, either. However, the idea of a big breakthrough was now definitively discredited in French operation rooms; limited-goal attacks with more restricted forces had become the preferred norm. Still, Weygand wondered whether a Joffre, maintained at the helm in 1917, could have ended the war that year with one more offensive in another sector. It was as absurd an assertion as any Joffre himself made.[53]

At all events, Foch was now chief of the French General Staff, with a complex administration to run. And as a newly-promoted brigadier general, Weygand stayed on board, henceforth involved heavily in political, bureaucratic, and decidedly *Parisian* tasks. To him, that milieu at first seemed quite foreign, and his dream of becoming a commander on the battlefields remained frustrated.

Conferences would now come thick and fast, and Weygand was a manically scribbling secretary at these — sitting beside the greatest military and political figures of his day, not only French, but British and Italian. Wherever Foch went, there went Weygand, and people began to esteem him as more than just his superior's alter ego.

The first major interallied conference was in London — Weygand's initial trip there — May 27–28, 1917. His drawings of the tables where dignitaries met remained his way of recording presences — and generally, on one side of the table, the British were clumped together, the French on the other. On the agenda in London was the problem of huge losses of British shipping at the hands of Ludendorff's unlimited submarine campaign that had just brought the Americans into the war; and also what to do about Salonika and Greece generally, given a revolt by the Venizelists there, and the king's ebbing grasp of his throne.

France's delegation included the leftist, rather utopian war minister, Paul Painlevé, Alexandre Ribot, the prime minister, and a future governor-general in French Indochina, Jean Decoux, among others. The conference was held at 10 Downing Street, and a somewhat awed and grateful Weygand found himself "in an excellent position to observe the world, so new to me, of the great and powerful."[54]

In this London meeting, England's Prime Minister David Lloyd George chaired discussions, and Weygand found him at once more Welsh-talkative than other Britons here, but at the same time wily as a fox. Beside Lloyd George were figures like Lord Curzon, the foreign secretary, Lord Derby from the War Office, Bonar Law, chancellor of the Exchequer, Admiral Jellicoe, and General William Robertson. Behind the prime minister, unobtrusive, but always shuttling papers to him, was Sir Maurice Hankey, a kind of gray eminence.

Prolix haggling around this and future tables is reflected in Weygand's copious notes — in the present case, on strategies in Salonika. Lloyd George flatly disliked the controversial General Sarrail's leadership there, which, according to Weygand, infuriated Painlevé, because that anticlerical war minister supported Sarrail, who was, among other things, a Freemason. After a break for tea, the group decided to send a new infusion of troops to Salonika in June, including French divisions which would occupy Thessaly, and help beef up the Greek army. And the Greek king would be forced definitively to abdicate, and to go into exile.

At the end of July another meeting featured the same dramatis personae, and this time discussion was mostly on the future of a much wounded Russia struggling for some sort of democratic framework under the leadership of Alexander Kerensky. Here Lloyd George was the optimistic Dr. Pangloss, figuring Russia would hold on in the Entente and never sign a separate peace with Germany! The French were more pessimistic, and of course would be proven sadly correct.[55]

Along with Russia and its queasy future, the scope of U.S. involvement in the war was also hotly, and increasingly, debated at these conferences that Weygand attended. There were a lot of jousts to come on just how the Americans should be trained, who ought to pay for transport of their troops, and how independent they should be.[56]

Pétain had meanwhile quelled the French mutinies, knowing how exhausted and blood-soaked France's army was, and how over a million young had already perished, trying to do the impossible. New rules stipulated that soldiers would henceforth be listened to, and that they would have more frequent leaves; and above all, that there would be no more massive, useless French offensives on the Western Front. Better to await the full arrival and readiness of the Americans.... More heavy artillery, and fine-tuning of aviation and tanks, the latter soon to make a successful debut at Cambrai in the autumn of 1917, would also help the French war effort.

Italy's Cadorna, whom Weygand saw a lot at conferences, had opened his own great offensives against Austrian troops on the Isonzo in May 1917; but he plainly required help, especially from the British — the only power on the Entente side with any vim left. However, Haig and Robertson were adamantly opposed to pouring troops into this theater. Meanwhile, Lloyd George, frantically trying that summer to halt his country's Passchendaele offensive, which would lethally snarl into swampy autumn mud, felt that aid to Italy might finally get the Austrians to sue for peace. Why keep breaking oneself on the impregnable Western Front? In the prime minister's view, Haig was too stubbornly one-dimensional, and Robertson a simpy chief of staff, unable to buck his commander, despite concerns of his own about the latest Ypres operation. As it evolved, a prescient Lloyd George would also see this "Flanders Fields" disaster as a progenitor of the coming Italian debacle that fall of 1917 around Caporetto.[57]

By that time, the Germans had come in to help the beleaguered, polyglot Austrian forces, engendering an Italian rout, and disordered retreat. Foch and Robertson now had to cobble together Entente troops for transfer there, and (along with Weygand) visited the country at the end of October. Foch gave his usual pep talks, trying to steady Italy's shattered nerves; and French divisions began arriving at the beginning of November, with British ones to follow. In Rome Weygand met with Baron Sidney Sonnino, Italy's minister of foreign affairs, another regular around upcoming conference tables. Visits to the Forum and Coliseum were ultra-rapid, if interesting to Weygand, and thence it was northward to Rapallo for the next Entente meeting, November 5.

Here the subject was developing a smoother inter-allied organization, in order to run a war that no one saw ending any time soon. Military coordination was the key word in the air, with the idea emanating most from Lloyd George, aware that he could not replace Haig and Robertson, who had deep political connections, including to King George V. Weygand found the British prime minister altogether too chirpy, given the Italian tragedy of that time. But the agreement of Rapallo, creating a Supreme War Council (SWC), was an important result of the conference.[58]

Military representatives to those SWC meetings would include Foch, Britain's Sir Henry Wilson, General Cadorna (partly to retire him from Italian high command) and soon General Tasker Bliss from the U.S. In December, on Clemenceau's advice, Weygand was designated to replace Foch, so that the latter could remain French chief of staff, yet have a "Fochian" representing him at these SWC meetings. And its headquarters would be right near Paris at Versailles.[59]

Foch continued to rally the Italians, as he had rallied English and Belgians in Flanders, and gradually they recovered from their disastrous retreat that had threatened even Venice. With French and English help, they now stabilized new positions. That fall of 1917 also saw Clemenceau take over at the helm of a French government entirely devoted to winning the war. Negotiation was not to the new prime minister's taste, and only reluctantly did he bend to the idea of this Supreme War Council holding monthly parleys. Weygand, as usual, had much staff work to do commandeering apartments near the Trianon palace in Versailles, and organizing much else. But he also got to meet privately with Clemenceau, finding "the Tiger" nobody's fool, especially when it came to vacillating politicians.

Military plans hatched for 1918 were about the same mix of real and aleatory as earlier war game preparations had been — and as usual, the coming year would present a number of unforeseen curves. Trying to create a unified command among the main Entente powers remained a key preoccupation at allied meetings in the early months of that year. It was also the year Clemenceau often left Paris to tour the fronts, rousing spirits à la Churchill in the next war. It was the year, too, of repetitive French arguments with Lloyd George, whose emphasis on defeating the Turks in the Middle East and liberating the Arabs was not that of Foch, Weygand, and company.[60] And perhaps best, it was the year that commanders in chief Pétain and Haig finally agreed that, given resources and manpower, keeping to the defensive was now the correct military policy on the Western Front. There was, however, much debate on just what form any allied campaigns ought to take here.

When it came to the new buzzword, "unity of command," Haig was most openly against it, while Pétain (and this shows over and over in Weygand's notes) was favorable in theory only, but cautious about how it might work out in practice.[61] With the other military representatives at their SWC conferences, Weygand batted out this issue, along with that of a "general reserve" of French and English divisions to be set aside for emergencies. But archival sources show that he took a key, more than theoretical, role as well in both the realms of strategy and coordination. His fine sense of geography in France or Italy, his practice in evaluating available materiel, and the fact that he was starting to be appreciated as more than just a Foch parrot, all played a role in his growing policy-making importance on the SWC at the end of 1917, and in the first few months of 1918. Weygand truly helped steady the Italians, predicting where Germans and Austrians might attack again, and at what time of year (given the state of rivers, mountains, and the like). He set agenda items for meetings, and his copious correspondence with Cadorna, Wilson, and Bliss, as well as other Entente generals, shows a man of authority and good sense, well aware of how depleted Entente forces were, and what now remained possible, and what didn't. The British would run things by him, and Weygand not only helped fine-tune their strategy, he was also a useful go-between — with correspondence to France's prime minister or Foch, and thence to SWC members. This was, in sum, a more important position for him than has been generally recognized.[62]

Meanwhile, allied coordination was growing stronger, and the idea of a general reserve more acceptable. One step led to the next here: the recently-created SWC designated a president of an Executive Committee, which would then supervise creation of this as-yet-uncreated reserve. And Lloyd George considered Foch the ideal president of that committee. By February 2, 1918,

Foch attained the position, and next day convened the Executive Committee to decide how many divisions the English and French might contribute to such a reserve. Haig remained as irked with this constantly implementing Foch as Sir John French had been with Joffre earlier in the war! Although they got along quite well with Weygand, Foch's moralism rankled the British, and they were still wary of having such a Frenchman over them, limiting their independence. In early March Haig complained to Clemenceau of Foch's erosion of his authority, while Lloyd George was assailed in the House of Commons for it. And was all this really necessary? Both Haig and Pétain found themselves together on advising caution; whereas Foch, in his indefatigable, almost priestly manner, kept fighting for his new obsession, unity of command, supported of course by Weygand.[63] At one point Foch threatened to resign as president of an Executive Committee with as yet no teeth; and his gambit worked — he was begged to remain in place.

All this Entente push and pull was then upstaged by Erich Ludendorff's massive attack on the British, March 21, 1918 — from Croisilles to the Oise River, aided by the foggy conditions of early spring.[64] Weygand's private notes from here through June still show no feeling of the war being near its end; instead, they reflect the sense of emergency wrought by Ludendorff's attempt to win quickly on the Western Front, before America's full impact was felt. Pétain had to help the now reeling English, and Haig kept frantically requesting more divisions from his ally. The Germans were attacking with overwhelming firepower, and after a few days believed they could drive a serious wedge between British and French forces.

Ever alert, Foch used this emergency to hector Clemenceau on the *immediate* necessity of command unity. And this time neither Haig nor General Hubert Gough, leading a battered British army, was in any mood to counter him, while Pétain was too preoccupied finding men to shore up the menaced British. For a brief moment, however, there was talk of Clemenceau heading up Entente operations! The English liked him, and as the later example of Churchill in World War II would show, some politicians could certainly be adept as military leaders. The plan called for Foch to then become Clemenceau's assistant![65] Predictably, Foch found the idea nonsensical, and when he and Weygand drove to the interallied conference meeting at Doullens of March 26, Foch felt that he was going to get a springtime surprise there. The English delegates (on one side of the table) whispered to each other, and the French to themselves; and meanwhile, one could hear the sounds of Ludendorff's guns drawing nearer. Amiens had been hit hard the night before; time, and Ludendorff's powerful armies, were pressuring the delegates convened here.

Direly, but tersely, Haig opened proceedings at Doullens, noting that the English were still holding north of the Somme, but having great trouble retaining their line south of that river. Pétain too was brief and to the point on how hard it was to muster enough military support for the British. A continuing fear of separation of English and French armies dominated the meeting. France's President Poincaré then stressed that the important town of Amiens must be held at all costs, and Foch proffered his usual generalities about giving up no French land whatsoever.

Then Clemenceau impulsively passed around a note, there were conferrals in small groups, and Weygand would later hear that the French prime minister (no great fan of Foch) merely broached the idea of that general becoming overlord for the threatened Amiens sector of the Somme Valley. But it was apparently the English there who felt this wasn't nearly enough. The bid-up text at Doullens then stipulated the following: "The British and French governments give General Foch the responsibility of coordinating the action of Allied armies on the Western Front. To this end, he will work with the generals-in-chief, who are invited to provide him with all necessary information."[66] At lunch, Clemenceau jabbed at what he considered Foch's pomposity, saying: "I know a general who is very pleased; he has finally found his situation."[67] And Foch's comeback was typically angry. As for Weygand, he thought the English worthy of praise — first for supporting the idea of a General Reserve, then the Executive Committee and presidency of it, and now for this final move at Doullens toward unified command.

Of course, much like Grimm's fishwife, Foch soon upped the ante, wishing to make his new authority even fuller; and on March 31 he wrote Clemenceau, asking for specific powers that would allow him real command. Clemenceau unexpectedly said yes to the idea, as did Lloyd George, and at the allies' Beauvais meeting of April 3, the Doullens text was altered, and Foch now possessed "strategic direction of military operations." He could do anything he wanted, not only to coordinate allied military action, but to conceive engagements himself. The only recourse commanders in chief Haig and Pétain henceforth had was to relate problems with Foch's directives to their respective governments. And almost as though it were still the Middle Ages, Foch was now talking of beating Ludendorff head to head![68]

In mid–April he received an actual title — "Head General of the Allied Armies in France." And at the beginning of May his authority included the Italian war effort, and soon after, Belgium's. Weygand all the while remained a full supporter of his superior, and his magisterial memoirs falter only when he buys into this head-to-head Foch-Ludendorff nonsense; as he put it, "they were two wills, two minds battling it out in order to seize the victory."[69] (All this quite blurring the situation of thousands of men still dying or being wounded in the field, not to mention the ever evolving role of technology, and that of the Americans in finally altering the lethal stalemate of trench war on the Western Front.)[70]

More sensibly, Weygand notes the large assignment Ludendorff had running operations in Eastern Europe, the Balkans, etc.; whereas Foch's directives were confined only to the Western Front. And those directives now poured forth profusely — with repetitive use of the words "tenir" (hold on) and "durer" (endure) aimed at the faltering generals Haig and Gough. Foch was back to what he loved best — peripatetic exhortation. However, fighting on the Western Front after March 26 remained hard and costly, including a back and forth tussle for Amiens in early April.

On April 9 Ludendorff began another thunderous assault on the English, with a view to breaking through and occupying the all-important ports of the Pas-de-Calais on the Channel. It was a massive, 20-division attack between the canal of La Bassée and that of Ypres, and again the English were legitimately panicked. Once more, Foch advised the old Dutch strategem of flooding land, and he also put together five divisions of French infantry and cavalry to help his beleaguered allies. Only by the end of April did Ludendorff's exhausted troops end this Flanders offensive, with the Channel ports still in Entente hands. Nor had the Germans succeeded in severing French and English forces, despite putting 126 divisions into the fight (90 in Picardy, 36 in Flanders). And again, Weygand magnanimously simplifies in laying it all to his boss: "The soundness of his diagnoses, his firm decision-making, the activity and energy he deployed to assure those decisions were executed, and his presence at threatened points attest to the full possession of qualities and military virtues which he had demonstrated in the first years of the war."[71]

Weygand, however, acknowledges the great losses still occurring, and the fact that the Germans had made significant territorial gains, approaching to within 60 kilometers of Calais, and remaining also on the outskirts of Amiens. With Ludendorff sure to strike again, everyone now agreed that the Americans needed to come faster into the fray, and with greater numbers: in March some 60,000 had made it over the Atlantic, and in April 93,000. Transportation was anything but sufficient for more, and with Foch pressing America's commander, Pershing, Weygand and his confreres at the SWC meeting in Abbeville May 1 and 2 spoke mainly of more U.S. involvement. Finally, the British agreed to provide ancillary ships to bring over more American troops. The result would be some 240,000 crossing in May, and 280,000 in June.[72]

Ludendorff still had a little time at his disposal, and was indeed ready to launch another series of attacks, this time against what he felt were vulnerable French forces, who had siphoned off divisions to shore up the British in the north. On May 27 a tremendous enemy shock wave hit French lines, and the Germans scrambled onto the blood-soaked Chemin des Dames, then crossed the Aisne. Pétain rushed up reinforcements to aid the battered French Sixth, and Ludendorff was himself surprised by how far the German advance had gotten, and how fast.

Now at his newest headquarters of Sarcus, Foch conferred often with Pétain — two very different personalities for Weygand to observe closely; and as the Germans reached the Marne river by the end of May, Pétain wanted the French government as a precautionary measure to leave Paris. But with American divisions coming in strongly for June, Foch was all for maintaining the status quo, and for limited but powerful counter-attacks; while Prime Minister Clemenceau also supported a warlike response at whatever the cost. There were, however, still squabbles with the English over *their* deployments, not to mention with the fresher Americans![73]

Literature on the sharp disagreements between Foch and America's General Pershing is extensive, and here again, one understands Weygand's need to follow his superior mainly without questioning; however, Foch's patronizing, and at times lethally callous, treatment of the American Expeditionary Force (A.E.F.) again reveals his character flaws. Kevin Stubbs argues that "Britain and France could not bear the thought of the United States winning the war and dictating the peace.... The French were a proud people, and Marshal Foch, commander in chief of the Entente armies in France, could not allow the upstart American general John J. Pershing to achieve the victory that had thus far eluded them."[74]

From America's entry into the war, Foch had been bullying Pershing to amalgamate forces and follow French directives; while the American commander fought back — in a series of protracted quarrels with Foch — for independence. After all, the U.S. was simply an "associate power," as President Wilson called it, not a full-fledged ally. During the meeting at Abbeville in early May, Pershing had to keep arguing his way into an eventual separation of armies; for now, some American units would be amalgamated with those of the Entente, some not.[75]

Thomas Fleming has provided the most strident indictment of Foch hurling sometimes green American troops into offensives conceived without sufficient prior intelligence, initially at the German positions of Belleau Wood, June 5, 1918, which, at great cost, American marines succeeding in controlling near the end of the month. Then came Soissons, where more significant American losses ensued that summer. To be fair, it was not only Foch, but also the French general Joseph Degoutte, and in the case of Soissons, the impetuous Charles Mangin, who impelled the Americans to attack without worrying about the thousands of casualties they would incur.[76]

The nadir of the Foch-Pershing relationship came after Allied commanders met at Foch's new headquarters of Bonbon, a chateau near Paris, July 24, 1918. The operational decision taken there was that American forces would attack the Saint-Mihiel salient, creating the possibility of a complete Allied breakthrough into the city of Metz and Lorraine generally — an idea both the American commander and General Pétain thought appropriate. Pétain even gave Pershing the idea of a diversionary thrust to confuse the Germans. But then Britain's commander in chief, Haig, a self-second-guesser since the slaughter of Flanders Fields, convinced Foch to alter the plan. Foch then bullied Pershing to water down this Saint-Mihiel operation that was conceived July 24, and was already well planned by Colonel George Marshall. Near the end of August a shouting match ensued between Pershing and Foch, raging on and off for a week. Pétain too tried hard to retain the original plan. When he and Pershing met August 31, they were minds and hearts in sync, both saddened by the new directives. Each, according to Edward Coffman, "thought that Foch overstepped his authority in attempting to dictate the abandonment of the secondary attack on the western side of the St. Mihiel salient." But as Coffman notes, "Pétain was more amenable than Foch, in part, because of his basic concern for his army" and great experience in the field, including at Verdun. All Pétain could muster in a meeting with Pershing and the obdurate Foch was to hold back the new Meuse-Argonne campaign until September 25.[77]

According to Stubbs, and it seems plausible, Pershing's preferred strategy of simply attacking the Germans with a half-million Americans on the Saint-Mihiel salient (German-controlled since September 1914) could have ended the war, and with fewer casualties and sooner than was ultimately the case. Stubbs argues that taking the fast-withdrawing Germans by surprise (which, in the event, occurred there) would have allowed the Americans to stream onto the Woëvre Plain, into the heart of Lorraine and the Briey iron basin, and not least, Metz, with its congeries of rail connections — and finish the game. Instead, what Fleming calls this "dangerous compromise" — another a priori rabbit coming out of Foch's strategic hat — was cobbled together: Pershing "would attack the Saint-Mihiel salient on September 12 as planned," but "then transfer the bulk of his 500,000-man army west of the Meuse River to attack through the Argonne valley on September 26 as part of the overall Allied offensive."[78]

Particularly with the end of the war now in sight, the assignment was

Generals Foch and John J. Pershing, American Expeditionary Force Commander, at Chaumont, France, in the latter stages of World War I. Quarrels over operational planning made their relationship a stormy one (CORBIS).

not only a large one, but another example of Foch's penchant for expending more lives than necessary in enterprises ignoring empirical data and limitations. (All providing additional lessons for his more thorough amanuensis, Weygand!) Simply the nocturnal transport of troops and guns from Saint-Mihiel, overlooking the Meuse River, west and north into the Argonne, would constitute a major undertaking. The two sectors were 60 miles apart, and 60 miles in that war was much different than in the next one. As Pershing put it, "our commitments now represented a gigantic task, a task involving the execution of the major operations against the Saint-Mihiel salient and the transfer of certain troops employed in that battle, together with many others, to a new front, and the initiation of the second battle, all in the brief space of two weeks." Moreover, rainy autumn weather came in for its predictable landing, and the battle in the Meuse-Argonne then slogged all the way through October, and into a foggy early November, even with an armistice right around the corner! The result? More than a million American soldiers, some lacking battlefield experience, others veterans moved from the successful Saint-Mihiel front, were sunk into this more forbidding sector of the Argonne forest. The eventual War Department count of dead U.S. soldiers in the campaign came to an astounding 26,277, and among those stunned and guilt-stricken was President Wilson himself.[79]

With the operation still going, Foch and Pershing were at it again in mid–October, Foch declaring that he cared only about results, and that he could not consider American losses, given what the French had been through in this war. He simply felt the Americans weren't doing enough; in a well-worn tradition starting with Joffre back in 1914 hectoring French and British soldiers to show more morale, his fellow Pyreneean, Foch, grew so irate that he wanted to move Pershing and troops to an unused front. After so much blood, sweat, and tears had been expended, Pershing again lost his temper.[80] And Weygand? His private notes and other sources show clearly that he respected Pershing and his views, and got along with him; but at such meetings he continued to defer to his boss. And that would continue after the guns stopped booming...

3

Armistice-Making and Peace Conference

From September, 1918, Weygand's notebook entries more and more concern terms of an impending armistice and Wilson's 14 points, as the tide (especially after Ludendorff's debacle in the last battle for Amiens August 8) was clearly turning. German war-weariness and instability at home, the American impact, the combination of a defensive-minded Pétain, penurious of men, and Foch finally transmuted into a more supple counter-puncher, together played a role in the impending termination of this prolonged conflict.

On October 3 Prince Max of Baden became chancellor of a more peace-oriented German government, subscribing to President Wilson's agenda as a basis for negotiation. At the end of the month Ludendorff and Hindenburg tendered resignations, and a mutiny in the German navy, and the threat of Bolshevik-style councils of German soldiers and workers, all showed a country that — having done the superhuman — was now falling apart. In this atmosphere the Entente debate was over an armistice versus unconditional surrender, and the former was selected.

Foch and his "completer," Weygand, played the key role in creating both its procedures and terms, though at frequent meetings they canvassed other politicians and generals for input. Their armistice terms *were* harsh, but given the devastation of the conflict, basically fair: two weeks after signing, the Germans must leave all occupied territory, and that included, from a previous war, Alsace and the parts of Lorraine they had retained. Their troops must also vacate the Rhineland on both sides of the river, and Entente soldiers would then garrison this crucial sector, with check points maintained at Mainz, Coblenz, and Cologne. Well before the punitive Treaty of Versailles, Germany was also to be significantly disarmed by the armistice (how ironic all this would become for Weygand in 1940!). The beaten country was forced to give up almost all its naval forces, including the totality of a once lethal submarine fleet; and from its land materiel, 25,000 machine guns and much artillery. It must also cede 5,000 locomotives and 150,000 railway cars, along with 5,000 trucks. Not to mention all its military aviation. It also had to endure a continuing naval blockade until signatures were apposed to a final peace agreement.

Weygand could not only recall to perfection this end-of-war atmosphere, but he could paint it even when he was nudging 90, and with such elegance and rightness, and a novelist's sense of observation, that the memorializer himself disappears, and the reader feels he or she is actually there. Weygand's book *Le 11 novembre* is fundamental reading here, though Destremau's biography does not mention it. Weygand first brings the reader back to November 7, 1918, and memories of Foch and the German delegation preparing to meet amidst an atmosphere of euphoria spreading like wildfire along the front lines — battered, grimy soldiers delirious from the possibility of the long war ending. Weygand deftly describes key members of the German delegation — Major General Detlev von Winterfeldt ("a flat cap covering his graying head, he wears with elegance a gray coat with velvet collar"), and the ill-fated parliamentarian, Matthias Erzberger, eventually to be assassinated.[1]

In the train that rolled along, Foch and other French army authorities wished to burn deeply into their visitors' psyches the terrible cost of the conflict. Erzberger, in particular — a man of the rear — was flabbergasted at the village of Tergnier, where "the train station was illuminated by torches whose flickering light gave its ruins an otherworldly look."[2] Weygand's book is punctuated by wonderful pictures, enhancing these prose memories. Along with the ruins of a 19th-century world, there was also in the air an impending post-war giddiness. "In the evening, foot-soldiers burned their last rockets, aviators their last landing lights, and along the front there was a drunken joy amidst a riot of brightness," writes Weygand.[3]

The next day the train reached the scene of the armistice agreement, an isolated forest clearing at Rethondes, chosen with care. Foch had rejected the idea of framing the agreement at Senlis near Paris, where his headquarters were now situated. As Weygand recalls — never having forgotten — "Senlis in 1914 had been odiously treated by the invading army. The mayor and some hostages, all of them innocent, had been shot. Most of the houses on the main street had been burned...." This is a significant passage, evoking the German system of "absolute destruction" in a way that now corresponds to Isabel Hull's recent book on the subject; but it was not simply colored by Hitler's subsequent, far greater brutality. Weygand had already felt this way during the Great War, and his memory of German methods then made him cry in the wilderness all the way through to 1940 — *not* to trust pacifism, and *never* to rely solely on defensive military arrangements.[4]

So Rethondes ... offering a contrastive calm in the Compiègne forest, compared to this singed Senlis. The "getting there," according to Weygand, had its effect on Germany's armistice-makers, having "traversed disorders created by their armies" and learned of the "systematic devastation" they had wrought. Of course "as good Germans," they wanted immediately to lessen the blows to be inflicted on them. On November 8, Foch had Weygand read out each article of the armistice in French, also translated into German, and Weygand clearly recalls the German reaction: "Their heads were held stiffly upright, their faces impassive, the German general's [von Winterfeldt] very pale, bore a painful expression" and became streaked by tears. "In its simplicity the scene attained the highest degree of *pathétique*...." The Germans seemed especially shocked by the imposed occupation of the Rhineland, and tried for "softening"— playing up the Bolshevik menace and extreme instability at home.[5]

Weygand had scribbled in his detailed diary on this period; but one gets the feeling that even without consulting it, he could still in the twilight of a long life recall at will this crucial period for France. The Germans had 72 hours to sign, and as all know, they did so in the early hours of November 11, 1918. After the conclusion of an armistice, Weygand's book then swings to the crazed, unhinged Paris atmosphere after news was received at 11 A.M. that day. He remembers flowers being hurled in abundance at Foch, and the two "principal artisans" of victory, Foch and Clemenceau, meeting on the Rue Saint-Dominique, and thence striding to see President Poincaré at the Elysée Palace. Cannon blasts saluted the war's end, and "in a matter of minutes, Paris put on its party clothes...." Rather like Flaubert recalling the 1848 revolution in Paris, Weygand remembered all this clearly long after the fact. "Flags of French colors and those of Allied countries came out of windows, were affixed on balconies, and in store windows. Cars, streetcars, and horses were decked as well in flags. The florists were overrun, flowers no longer bought in bouquets, but by the stem, and female blouses and all male suits must be decked out." An important French symbol — Joan of Arc — came to the fore, too, with many pictures displayed of that archetypal heroine. People were running in the streets to tell each other, faces lit up broadly, and Weygand makes his reader *feel* it all. The avalanche of happiness kept gathering strength, as "workshops emptied, the work day was ended, but with some wages doubled..."; and suddenly the capital's grand boulevards filled up with these rabid, liberated workers, men and women. Schools emptied too, children yelling "Vive la France!" and marching in the thronged streets, carrying French flags. In the Latin Quarter the great lycées and faculties also cancelled their classes. Music was heard everywhere, soldiers were carried by gleeful crowds, American and British soldiers were applauded, and by the end of this heady afternoon, the Place de la Concorde was "black with people." Parisians were now flocking to the Parliament, where at four P.M., Prime Minister Clemenceau read out the text of the armistice. The crowd impulsively sang the *Marseillaise*, and thousands, says Weygand, managed to get themselves right inside where Clemenceau was reading, stunning the place with exaggerated, insistent, repetitive applause.[6]

Memorializing was not of course the purview of Weygand alone; it became a national passion from the end of the war, and Weygand recalls the solemnity of the search for an unknown soldier, in order to console the bereaved without final knowledge of their lost loved ones. He discusses the consecration of the Arch of Triumph in Paris for that purpose. Napoleon had conceived the idea for this major arch on the Roman model after his victory at Austerlitz; but it hadn't been completed until the 1830s. In terms of events with national resonance, the *Arc* had thereafter hosted only the important funeral for Victor Hugo in 1885. Now at the end of World War I, the cortège

After arriving in Britain at the end of November, 1918, generals Foch and Weygand led a victory march through the streets of London (Bettmann/CORBIS).

following the ceremony of armistice in the Parliament had moving moments at a now numinous Arch at one end of the Champs-Elysées. A thousand war-mutilated, as Weygand says, led it off, and notable generals like Foch, Joffre, Pershing, and Haig on horseback were then acclaimed by huge crowds. There followed specialized regiments — Highlanders blowing bagpipes, troops from the English dominions, Italians playing their music, Japanese, Greeks, Portuguese, Rumanians, Serbs, Poles, et al. And with his deep patriotism even for the capital itself, Weygand notes how all were applauded by "the intelligent and sensitive Parisian crowd." The city then went wild to watch the French army itself march, led by General Pétain on a white horse, followed by other commanders, like "Fayolle, venerated by the entire army...." Weygand called this procession a "moving apotheosis..."; but of course such emotional high points can be the beginning of lower points — from summits one invariably descends.[7]

After the conflict came the search for a suitable tomb of an unknown soldier, and all agreed that it could only be placed beneath the religiously charged Arc de Triomphe. Weygand's own solemnity on all this was anything but feigned; he would ever be marked by the horrid slaughter of the war, and grateful to those who had given so much for the country he loved. Yes, "after such a painful struggle, where success would have been impossible without the self-denial, courage, spirit of sacrifice and perseverance of the combatants, it was fitting to praise this heroism, honoring the memory of those who had fallen without seeing the dawn of victory." And the worst was when family members could never find even a body. It was therefore "necessary to give these families a tomb where they could pray.... And right that this burial place should be without equal in its location...." The choice could only be Napoleon's Arch, for all this honor to the unknown soldier of France's greatest war in history "responds to a universal sentiment." In 1920 the search for unknown soldiers would begin at Verdun, where Sergeant André Maginot, badly wounded there during the war, came now as a member of parliament. Bodies were then dug up — one from Lorraine, one from the Somme, one from Champagne, one from the Chemin des Dames, one from Artois, etc.; and they were taken to Verdun's "chapelle ardente" in coffins. There Maginot spoke to soldiers, and in the night of November 10–11, the body of the "unknown soldier" (how they chose remains mysterious) was brought to Paris, eliciting another huge cortège up the Champs Elysées to the Place de l'Etoile. "At the head march veterans wearing their crosses and a forest of quivering flags follows ... the most blackened and hole-ridden of these standards recognized and acclaimed in passage." Pigeons flew out in four directions, the *Marseillaise* was sung, the Archbishop of Paris blessed the dead, and the masses then made a pilgrimage into the night to see the tomb. The Arch of Triumph henceforth became the "Altar of the Fatherland," and the flame there kept burning perpetually as a national sanctuary, maintained by veterans' associations.[8] For Weygand, this entire memory of the Great War remained anything but a once-a-year ceremonial exercise; but rather, his defining sense of France, and of what it needed to continue doing vis-à-vis potential enemies.[9]

In addition to being a memorializer who used that memory of World War I to buttress his views in later parlous times, Weygand could also be characterized as someone with a deep historical sense generally — and this again, due to a Burkean or Disraelian identification with his country's past. In fact, like those outsiders (Irish and Jew respectively, in a world of prejudice), Weygand had had much to overcome to reach the heights of Paris and nearby Versailles in this après-guerre era. A book he later penned on Louis XIV's palace, *cum* plentiful photographs, truly reveals that Burkean outlook. On the final page Weygand evoked the atmosphere of October 6, 1789: "The royal family had left the Palace, never to see it again. All the candles and oil lamps were extinguished. Great shadows veiled the Palace. Versailles was dying. Its mourning and profanation" — here he sounds especially Burkean — "would extend painfully throughout the entire 19th century...."[10]

However, Versailles, along with nearby Paris, was very much *alive* in early 1919; and Weygand was at the center of intra-national hagglings there that, for good or ill, would create a world and countries that still make headlines.[11] In the second large volume of his memoirs, which he wrote last, he really lets himself go with marvelous portraits of dramatis personae he saw often at the Peace Conference, and whom he had already seen numerous times during the latter stages of the war. Their traits, which he carefully sketches, and which helped make future history, stayed with him well after the next war they sought so much — but in dissonant ways — to prevent.

The French delegation naturally had Clemenceau at its head, supported by Stéphen Pichon, minister of foreign affairs, the well-known diplomat Jules Cambon, somewhat overwhelmed by "the Tiger," the facile André Tardieu, and Louis-Lucien Klotz, Clemenceau's minister of finance (whom his boss famously labeled "the only Jew who couldn't count"). From February Foch became a kind of sixth man on the delegation, heading a committee dealing with military problems, but invited only intermittently to meetings when such issues came up. He and Weygand were burdened at the same time by continuing dealings with German representatives over implementation of armistice conditions. The aforementioned delegation at the Peace Conference was basically at one with Clemenceau, recalled Weygand, and Foch would have to fight to get his points across. Louis Loucheur, who had done well

Time was a luxury at a pre–Peace Conference meeting, December 1918 in London, of (left to right) Marshal Foch, Prime Minister Georges Clemenceau of France, British Prime Minister David Lloyd George, Italian Prime Minister Vittorio Orlando, and Italy's Foreign Minister, Baron Sidney Sonnino (Bettmann/ CORBIS).

obtaining munitions at the end of the war as minister of armaments, was in Weygand's view less adept running the economic and financial side of things here; and on the whole, the French delegation (to a staff organizer extraordinaire) seemed less efficient than the British one. It also suffered from the fact that Clemenceau spoke good English and could therefore, according to Weygand, let that language dominate proceedings more than it should have.

He then sketches the English — starting with their chief representative, Prime Minister Lloyd George, formerly a stronger supporter of Foch, Clemenceau, and France. At the Peace Conference, the British prime minister became more of an open foe. Weygand was happy to find Sir Henry Wilson also on hand, now as chief of the Imperial Staff. But Lord Robert Cecil was a much tougher person to deal with when it came to questions of Rhineland administration. Weygand gives a fine portrait of the very tall Cecil slouched down in an armchair, with his head just popping up; and then when he spoke ever more vociferously, rising up and up, until he seemed to dominate the entire room! ("The effect," says Weygand, "was worth observing.")

He is similarly marvelous on the somewhat utopian Sir Arthur Balfour, who also seemed to look down on the rest, but whom Weygand loved hearing, "to such a degree was his language pure and his tone agreeable."[12] He also admired both the elegance and strength of the Italian delegation, led by Prime Minister Orlando and his right-hand man, Baron Sonnino — men who, again, Weygand had often seen before. And who, when displeased, stomped out of the Peace Conference proceedings. Weygand's diplomatic background in World War I, then at these complicated postwar joustings; his growing ability to feel individuals' characters and to gauge them; and his way of sticking deeply to subjects and tasks would all remain with him when the next world conflict presented its challenges — giving him deeper and more varied experience to draw on than could a mere general.

The *summa* of his portraits concerned His Majesty, President Woodrow Wilson! Weygand does not quite put it that way, but does evoke the idolatry of European crowds for the man, and how it all seemed to go right to Wilson's Calvinist head. His self-righteousness intensified, Wilson (in Weygand's view) took his prescriptions for a Europe in ruins as certainly as gospel; while the French underestimated how divided the U.S. was back home, ignoring the fact that the Senate would probably not back him up. This whole part of Weygand's memoirs is among the finest, saddest, and most enjoyable to read, and along with his private notes, treats the crucial seedtime of a new era of history, in which he himself would come to play major roles.

The actual workings of frantic peacemaking are too well known to go into at length, except that Weygand's unpublished notes on proceedings remain a fine source, increasingly revealing his exasperation while Foch's aide. Being such a careful secretary, at least on what he saw and heard, makes Weygand authoritative here.[13] We know how both he and Foch felt that Germany — potentially linked with a new Austria, which could push their collective population over 70 million — might easily recover, becoming a military threat again. They both admired and feared German affinity for hard work, and ability to endure wartime difficulties. Foch's obsession — or so it became — was to make the Rhine Germany's western boundary, to maintain indefinitely three Allied bridgeheads on the left bank (at Cologne, Coblenz, and Mainz), in order to compel payment of reparations; and (hopefully) to get a separate Rhenish Republic created as a buffer between France and its main European enemy. We know how Lloyd George and certain British generals opposed French "empire-making" in Europe, and how the idealistic Wilson placed all hopes in a League of Nations. Again, Foch was here only in a quasi-legitimate, advisory capacity, invited solely to meetings on military matters. Having attained the heights at the end of the war, he was now clearly angered at

At the Strasbourg cathedral of liberated Alsace, January 1919, securing lasting peace along the nearby Rhine remained a priority for General Weygand. From left to right: Marshal Joseph Joffre, Marshal Foch, Weygand, Field Marshal Sir Douglas Haig of England, America's General Pershing, and Marshal Philippe Pétain (Bettmann/CORBIS).

this limited role he was given to play at the Peace Conference, and kept trying to make it more comprehensive. As a kind of broker, Clemenceau was busy trading the severe version of the Rhineland for a military alliance with Britain and America, while not really trusting either to stay the course in a nebulous future; and none of this pleased Foch! Feeling persecuted, he drew ever closer to French military personnel in the Rhineland, especially generals Fayolle, Mangin, and Augustin Gérard, and became increasingly insubordinate.

With an ever supportive Weygand by his side, Foch haggled as well over the size of the future German army, and its character. He was eventually persuaded that 100,000 men would be sufficient for the keeping of order across the Rhine (an ironic figure, given Nazi armistice terms in the next war). In return for getting this reduced number of soldiers, Foch had to accede to a German term of service of 12 years, knowing that this would create the core of a well-trained army focused on revenge. Meetings involving his superior in Wilson's apartment or Clemenceau's office did not please Weygand, either. To the rest, Foch seemed more and more a single-tracked interloper, hectoring the Council of Four, and going over their heads not only to army men, but to France's President Poincaré and to the media, for which Clemenceau harshly rebuked him. Weygand recalled bitter Foch-Clemenceau tiffs of the time, including one occasion when the French prime minister told the generalissimo that he was no longer the center of the world — the war was over! At a later point he tried to get Foch to fire his associate, or at least muzzle him — because Weygand had himself become too much of an angry guard dog. Loucheur also averred that "it is Weygand who pushes Foch."[14]

The watering down of Allied occupation provisions — the group at Cologne to last only five years, at Coblenz ten, and Mainz 15 — was the coup de grace for Weygand's superior. After terms of the Peace Conference were delivered to the Germans in June of 1919, Clemenceau stopped Foch's continued dickerings with Rhenish separatists, transferring to other positions his support system there (Fayolle, Mangin, and Gérard). To which Foch responded by not attending the signing ceremony at Versailles June 28, and predicting that this "peace" would be only an armistice for 20 years — here of course he proved to be on the money. And Weygand kept backing him without reservations.[15]

In so many ways World War I and its aftermath remained formative events in Weygand's life, memory, and actions. One reason was his close relationship with the British in this period. As he admitted, he hadn't really known the English before 1914, possessing only an image inside of the country's strength on the seas, in its empire, etc. Not until 1917 did he traverse the Channel and first view with poetic feeling the cliffs of Dover, en route to a conference in London. As seen, he then, and on numerous future occasions, met with people like Sir Henry Wilson, Viscount Edmund Allenby, Viscount Alfred Milner, Lloyd George, Haig, Robertson, Churchill. They became Weygand's associates and interlocutors — sometime enemies, but also friends, and important personal windows on England. In a still classic book, Marc Bloch would argue that a key reason for the French defeat in 1940 was lack of personal relations between the two great allies; however, Weygand kept from World War I something deep inside when it came to England, and was not typical of so many French who became mostly hostile toward that country.[16]

However, the fractious atmosphere at the Peace Conference *also* played a role in Weygand's continuing estimate of the English. As seen, their leaders differed from the French when it came to keeping the Germans down, and away from a potential second round. To Weygand, he and Foch were on one side, the Brits on the other; and while Clemenceau certainly sympathized with the tougher French line, he knew he had to cede somewhat to the "Anglo-Saxons." As Weygand would recall, "there is no doubt that the spirit of co-operation between the two countries which was so remarkably in evidence during the first world war lost something of its magic the moment the Armistice was signed. And we could truthfully say that up to the outbreak of war in 1939 it was never so strong again as it had been." Weygand kept good memories of the English alliance with France during the Great War, but viewed après-guerre Britain as a country that began sliding away — to him, one of the chief reasons the Nazis would be so emboldened during the appeasement era of the '30s.[17]

Weygand's recollections of World War I and the peace conference following remained also the memory of his role by the side of Foch. The full biography he eventually penned on his mentor, appearing in 1947 (there was an earlier, shorter work on him in the late '20s), is, as usual for Weygand, tastefully written; but it doesn't compare to his own memoirs, and isn't near to being objective. The book continues to make of Foch a far greater and more perfect figure than he was. And this again was due to Weygand's supreme gratitude — of a vulnerable outsider getting inside, and to the top of his country's military-diplomatic structure. Quintessentially French, Foch himself seemed to accept a man whose own "Frenchness" — particularly in a more ethnocentric era than ours — was fragile, given the faultline at its base.

His biography thus fudges on his superior's a priori sententiousness, his over-reliance on the lessons of Napoleon, applied to offensives a technological century later; not to mention his stupid apothegms about French will and morale being the necessary additive to overcome the German foe. Like Joffre, Foch had sermonized far too long, greatly underestimating the destructive defensive power of machine guns combined with barbed wire and trenches — and this to the tune of many young lives lost for dubious military reasons.[18] The irony is that shorn of Foch, but somehow given a position commensurate with his military acumen, Weygand would himself have been a better commander and war theorist, except perhaps in the last stages of the war, when Foch had somewhat altered his outlook. A person's strengths can simultaneously be his weaknesses, and Weygand's strength of fidelity was, in the case of Foch, a weakness, too. Like so many who look to mentors (particularly those from such odd psychological backgrounds), Weygand didn't realize that he himself had exceeded Foch militarily — that *he* was the more organized, empirical, and supple one, and more caring, too, about soldiers in harm's way.[19]

In sum, Weygand retained that unquestioning idolatry long after it was necessary — though he became in most regards a truly mature adult. His preface to the first volume of his memoirs, running through World War I, shows this continuing Foch-idolatry. In his first line he declares: "The idea of leaving a remembrance of the eight years I had the honor of spending by Marshal Foch's side has always seemed a vital duty to me." Weygand goes on to note that in this first volume (written after volume three), "I wish that these more personal and direct memories may complete the image of a leader admired and revered by all who had the inestimable privilege of working with him, and who were able to know and admire the power of his mind, his intrepid character, the depth of his patriotism, and the purity of his soul." A few lines further he calls Foch "not only the central figure, but also the raison d'être, of these memoirs...."[20] True, Weygand had wanted above all else to command a cavalry unit in the war, and had not *sought* the appointment with Foch; it had simply happened. His pleased superior then grew into the accomplished, attentive father Weygand had desperately wanted, and on whom he could model himself, while engaged in an arduous climb up the Disraelian "greasy pole." As he put it, "Since I began serving with General Foch, I felt his confidence in me growing, and I began to hope that by dint of hard work I would succeed in giving him what he had every right to expect from his chief of staff."[21] The way Weygand puts it makes of Foch the legitimate Olympian entitled to demand anything from this most *illegitimate* aspirant trying to merit his trust.

Of course on a mundane level Foch did help make World War I the time when Weygand was rapidly promoted to colonel and thence to the various rungs of general, and to the diplomatic heights as well. But with or without such promotions, he would have done too much for Foch — taken too many notes in his private notebooks, produced overly detailed reports, prepared munitions gathering and the like super-minutely, and so on. More generally, Weygand was *always* a man who did too much — and not merely for Foch. He had to do more simply in order to feel that he was acceptable! And this remained the case as he prepared to meet new challenges of the 1920s.

4

"Finding Himself" in Poland and the Middle East

After a protracted war and imperfect conclusion to cacophonous peace-making, Weygand finally got a chance to influence a conflict on his own, this owing to the newly-formed Poland's tangle with Communist Russia in the throes of its civil war. Weygand's posting to Poland, along with one a few years later to the Levant, would reveal him at his best — the kind of firm, yet enlightened leader that France would badly need in 1940, and not get until it was too late.

Weygand had already possessed a vivid feeling for Poland's complicated history and the weight of its longtime imperial masters (Germans, Austrians, Russians), partly due to his wife's origins on one side. He was also aware of the differences between Poland's two most prestigious, post-war political personalities: Marshal Jozef Pilsudski, actually of Lithuanian ancestry, and a socialist military figure imprisoned in Siberia five years by the Russians, and therefore vengeful toward that colossus to the east; and Ignace Paderewski, a renowned musician from Austrian Galicia, who (rather like the Italian Mazzini) cared only for Poland's own *risorgimento*. Weygand describes a luncheon after the war with his wife, Paderewski and his spouse, and the eminent French philosopher Paul Valéry, also on hand with his wife. He noted how even Valéry deferred to Paderewski's wide-ranging, never-boring grasp of diverse issues past and present. (Being the man who signed the peace treaty for Poland, Paderewski was obviously better known to Weygand than Pilsudski.)

Weygand realized how fragile this new, liberated Poland was, with its eastern frontier only temporarily placed on the "Curzon Line," which Polish irredentists were not pleased to accept. Meanwhile, a fledgling but tough Communist Russia wished to teach Poland a lesson, and invade them from the east. By the spring of 1920, having defeated major armies of the White side in the Civil War, they seemed ready to do so; and so the Poles chose what another small country, Israel, would choose in 1967 — a preemptive strike. At the end of April Polish armies drove toward the Ukraine — under Pilsudski as both military chief of staff and head of state. Nearing Kiev in early May, they embraced a huge, varied landscape, and found that they had bitten off more than they could proverbially chew. In fact, they hadn't thought ahead — particularly to the difficulties of the Pripet swampland — and Weygand, himself so attentive to geography and deployment of enemy forces, would always reprove this light-hearted, ill-conceived sortie, which then conditioned such a strong Bolshevik response.

For Trotsky and the Russians were now roused to counter-attack, and by mid–May found themselves easily mopping up the Poles on their territory. By the beginning of July their advance back toward Poland was becoming a dangerous rout for a young, headstrong, but now quite panicked country. The former invaders were ejected from Kiev and the Ukraine, and an Allied conference at Brussels July 2 — featuring Weygand's usual copious notes — debated aspects of a now pressing, post–Peace Conference problem. By mid-month the Poles were frantically begging the Allies for help, and Lloyd George considered Weygand the best person to dispatch in order to provide them military counsel. Foch also supported the idea with enthusiasm.[1]

The enemy, however, was redoubtable — including military leaders like Russia's great tank innovator, Mikhail Tukhachevsky, and General Semyon Budyonny, a one-time Cossack peasant who knew how to exploit an enemy's weak spots with maneuvering cavalry and raking machine gun fire. And they were definitely on a roll, taking Vilna July 15, and Grodno a few days later. On July 21 France's Prime Minister Millerand dialed up Weygand, informing him that both the French and British governments wanted him to lead a delegation to Poland, and soon. France's delegation would include a renowned diplomat, Jules Jusserand, not quite Weygand's cup of tea, and to head the British delegation, Lord Edgar D'Abernon, who truly was.[2] For someone who so understood martial realities, Weygand knew people equally well, and those he could trust.

With directives from his government, especially on how to procure an eventual armistice in Poland, Weygand left France. He was this time given leeway to prove himself militarily, as he had never been able to prove himself before. Arriving in Warsaw July 24, he met with General Paul Henrys, a Lyautey alumnus from the Algerian-Moroccan theater, and head of France's military mission of some 400 officers here (including Charles de Gaulle). These French had been working to improve the Polish army, and despite the fact that armistice negotiations had begun, the Poles were now talking of fighting hard against the Russian advance toward their greatest city, Warsaw. Weygand was more cautious and, as always, more empirical; with the right planning, and the right leadership, and a real effort at unifying Polish factions, they might have a shot — but nothing seemed certain for this shaky new power.

Adept (as with Foch) at promoting synergism, Weygand from the outset knew that he would have to proceed carefully in his dealings with Pilsudski, as prickly as his old master, and more vain. Weygand — ever a quick study — soon saw how poorly organized these Polish armies were, and how bad communication between their branches was. They did have some adept generals, such as Josef Haller, formed before World War I by the Austrians, and Dowbor Musnicki, an alumnus of the Russians; but Weygand realized that three different military backgrounds from the pre–1914 era (Austrian, Russian, German) impeded unity within the Polish ranks. For instance, the Austrian army had allowed Poles to reach high officer status, while the Russians and Germans mostly hadn't. And there were bitter rivalries — especially between Pilsudski and Haller. So Weygand immediately worked at bringing these leaders more together, in order to exploit what he considered the courageous potential of average Polish soldiers, who needed only to be well led. He was the same peripatetic Weygand here that France would finally call on to revive its forces in 1940; the Polish situation, with fierce Russian Communists bearing down on Warsaw, constituted a valuable dress rehearsal.

To be sure, Weygand benefited from the prestige of the French army following World War I, and from his prior association with Foch. He also benefited from British support, in the form of his chief assistant, the celebrated Major-General Sir Percy Radcliffe. All this made it easier for him to heal divisions among the Poles. Another trump card he and the Poles possessed was potential disunity among the Russians; only a minority of convinced Bolsheviks were keeping the rest in check with the same kinds of threats toward them and their families that would remain standard down to Gorbachev. Like Churchill, who understood what Bolshevism would lead to well ahead of most, Weygand also took these Russian Communists seriously; and it was a valuable course to take *in situ*.

At one point Pilsudski asked Weygand to head the French military mission; but reluctant to backbite, he demurred, asking that General Henrys, a fine officer, be kept in place. At another point Weygand was offered an active general's role leading the Polish army, but said he preferred to stay within himself as an omnipresent military counselor. He remained his usual thorough self — starting days early, getting briefed by Henrys and a variety of liaison officers, then finding out all he could about a landscape which he came to know exhaustively, and the state of the Polish army, which required much rallying.

He did not, however, simply enthuse, but also gave pointed advice on where counter-attacks ought to be mounted — especially along a line on the Bug river, and how bridgeheads on the Vistula ought to be attained to defend Warsaw from imminent attack. His detailed recollections have the ring of authenticity, and in them one feels oneself in the hands of an acute, detailed, but never boring military master.

Fights back and forth on the Bug ensued during the first week of August, and Soviet desertions increased. Meanwhile, the fortification of Warsaw — with trenches, barbed wire and the like — went on apace. Weygand inspected every inch of the area, and kept inspiring the 30,000 Poles who went to work on them each day, aided by French military engineers; while Poland's armies were being supported by infusions of Allied armaments. More volunteers, more animated officers to replace those who weren't right for their positions augured well; and Pilsudski then went out to the countryside, leading counter-offensives from south of the city, and leaving Weygand in charge back in Warsaw.

Ever one to work in tandem, Weygand never insisted on his own unadulterated ideas; but instead, bent his prescriptions to Polish proclivities, especially to those of Pilsudski. He had had a schooling in personalities of this sort, and how sad again that he never really got to promote such synergy with British allies before and during the next world war.

In this smaller, more restricted conflict, the tide began turning, and suddenly Polish forces under Haller, General Wladyslaw Sikorski, fighting hard at the head of the Fifth Army, and the rest were working well both on their own, and in support of other operations. Weygand now witnessed vociferous displays of Polish patriotism, and saluted Pilsudski's overlordship of offensive operations in the countryside, because nobody in his estimation could have led such attacks more effectively.

Meanwhile, the battle of Warsaw began on the afternoon of August 13, leading to the departure of most ambassadorial personnel on trains Weygand commandeered for the purpose. He, however, remained behind, and with some optimism now, was moved even during thronged prayer services in the threatened city.[3] However, he was not simply an emotional imbiber; instead, his detailed recollections of the various armies fighting the Russians truly reveal his military acumen, though he and Pilsudski nearly sundered at certain points. Weygand deftly sketches the duality in the marshal's character that perhaps mirrored the duality of a frontier people itself (conqueror and conquered, oppressor and oppressed throughout its history). As Weygand put it, "This eminently gifted leader and patriot was also affected with a suspicious and unhealthy vanity, and perhaps did not pardon me for the role I had been playing...."[4]

But the French general knew how to reduce discord, and the Poles started winning decisively, taking many prisoners (some obviously hoping to leave dictatorial Russia). Sikorski's Fifth Army alone eventually netted some 20,000. Certain Russian soldiers were chased right to the German frontier, and some crossed to elude the pursuing Poles.

Weygand believed that the resulting Polish victory, and the preservation of their country, was very significant, given that it would keep the Russians out of Europe for another two decades, allowing the French and British to focus on other matters besides Soviet expansion. Back safely in Paris, the general reported to France's war minister on what many considered an improbable turnaround, then went to his place in Brittany, also visiting Foch in that region. Seeing ahead, Weygand remained wary of a Poland that would always be stuck between two potentially great powers, Germany and Russia, and with borders that weren't easily defensible. This was not a fashionable worry in the slightly tipsy atmosphere of 1920; but some 20 Augusts later, he would have his prophetic fears sadly verified.[5]

Weygand's achievement in helping keep a new Poland free from Soviet empire-making would, however, do him paradoxical harm in France, as the fissure between Left and Right widened considerably there during this decade and the next. Such an atmosphere made Weygand a figure to be pigeonholed and critiqued from one side of the ideological spectrum, especially by French Communists. Simplistically, he was categorized as a hidebound Catholic and conservative, and one who, in an era of pacifist hopes, seemed overly wary of both Germans and Russian Bolsheviks. Due to this primitive picture, Weygand would pay repetitive prices in the divisive atmosphere that growingly claimed his country.

Meanwhile, historiographical debate on just who ought to be given majority credit for the Polish turnaround in Warsaw began, continuing long after that period. Some considered the victory quite simply unfathomable, and as Norman Davies sums up, "The 'Miracle of the Vistula' in August 1920 is as exceptional in the modern history of Poland as in the career of the Soviet army. Once, and once only, the Poles emerged victorious in single-handed combat with the forces of their great neighbour."[6] Given the lack of Polish planning, Davies himself wasn't sure (in that book) why they won, procuring an armistice in October, followed by a formal treaty with the Russians in March 1921. But in an earlier work, Davies echoes the more recent viewpoint of Thomas C. Fiddick: that despite the heroics of Pilsudski and Sikorski, and to some degree of Weygand, the principal reason for the victory lay on the Soviet side. In Fiddick's optic, the Soviets were then in the process of softening the rigors of War Communism after the ravages of civil war, with

Lenin's New Economic Policy and a resumption of modified capitalism taking hold.[7] In fact, Weygand needn't be given majority credit for this great comeback victory; but at the same time, his rigor, thoroughness, organizational verve, and ability to inspire certainly contributed. That dedicated anticlerical, Clemenceau, put it well, and fairly about an obvious Catholic and the right-hand man of his great opponent at the Peace Conference: "Dangerous but valuable," said the Tiger of Weygand. "And having one rare quality — the ability to do his work without talking and without having it talked about. He went to Poland. I don't know what he was up to there — but whatever there was to be done he did it. He put everything back in its right place."[8]

Another great contemporary, Churchill, believed that this Marne-like recovery *did* have a lot to do with Weygand. Churchill's feeling for Weygand is obvious when he writes: "At the head of Marshal Foch's '*famille militaire*' stood a soldier of subtle and commanding military genius veiled under an unaffected modesty.... France had nothing to send to the aid of Poland but this one man. He was, it seems, enough." Churchill believed that propaganda which later inflated the role of Weygand in Poland was largely due to the British, not to Weygand himself, who "characteristically declared, both publicly and privately on all occasions, that it was the Polish army which did the work. The reader may choose either explanation, or both together."[9]

The two main English figures with whom he worked in Poland were indeed almost Weygand press agents! Major-General Radcliffe wrote in a letter from Warsaw that "Weygand most modestly disclaims any credit for the recent successes, but I am certain that both from the technical and moral point of view he has made just all the difference. His tact, loyalty and firmness have been beyond praise and I have the greatest admiration for him in a most difficult situation. Pilsudski is said to have admitted that he had learned more about war from Weygand in a fortnight than he had acquired in 6 years campaigning!" As for Lord D'Abernon, he noted that the Poles naturally emphasized Pilsudski's role in the victory, but "I am sceptical about it myself, believing rather that the military success was due in a large measure to the sober methodical method of Weygand in organising Polish resistance...." D'Abernon then gives a lavish character portrait of Weygand as "the ideal soldier, precise, hardworking, firm in opinion yet modest, brave yet prudent, believing intensely in discipline, method, and organisation, but neither stereotyped nor deficient in resource."[10]

In the early '20s Weygand was given new missions, continuing his reciprocal appreciation of Englishmen he met at conferences, such as Sir Harold Nicolson. He was also saddened by the death in this period of his former associate, Field Marshal Sir Henry Wilson, an Ulster M.P. murdered by two I.R.A.

Between England's General Haig and King George V (left to right), and with Foch on hand, too (far right), General Weygand in Belgium, 1922, discusses battles of World War I. Weygand had deep feeling for England, and for English notables he knew well; but he also felt relations between France and Britain cooling during the early '20s (Hulton-Deutsch Collection/CORBIS).

members outside his home in London. Along with Foch and Nivelle, Weygand traveled to England for Wilson's funeral in June, 1922. In October he had a cordial lunch with D'Abernon, discussing German intransigence, the Turks and the Chanak crisis, the future of Russia. But a general cooling of Franco-British relations due to different points of view concerning Germany continued, especially with a French invasion of the Ruhr in January, 1923, to force payment of reparations. From 1922 onward, Prime Minister Poincaré had been considering this eventual occupation, contacting Weygand about it. Then, when the crisis came to a head at the outset of 1923, many in France wanted Weygand to go there as high commissioner, with quite a press campaign in his favor. In typical fashion, however, Weygand refused to take the top position in the Ruhr, since that would mine French personnel already in place. Another problem was a series of catfights occurring between pro–Foch and pro–General Degoutte camps within Poincaré's administration. Quite simply, Weygand wished to avoid this political crossfire. The gimpy veteran, now war minister, Maginot, then decided in tandem with Poincaré to post him elsewhere; and it was an appointment that turned out eminently suitable.[11]

Weygand's nomination as high commissioner of the new mandate of the Levant (Lebanon-Syria) stepped on no military toes; for General Henri Gouraud, who had spent several demanding years in the position, had had quite enough of it. However, in this future cauldron of the Middle East, Weygand — with his intelligence, thoroughness, and *courtoisie*— became an enlightened proconsul, presaging what he would later accomplish in French North Africa during the Second World War.

Before assuming his post, the general did undergo some separation anxiety; for apart from his month or so in Poland, he had been at Foch's side almost nine years, and — à la Disraeli unleashed from Lord Derby — would finally be on his own, and in a more exigent position than the Polish one of 1920. The Weygand who was almost superstitious about Foch recalled that the marshal remained "present in my mind and heart. Never would I act without wondering if he would approve of me." He also sent Foch an emotional letter on how much their long association had meant to him. On his side, Foch was also reluctant to part with Weygand, noting that "it was not without many heartburnings that I let him go, but I had not the right to clip his wings."[12]

This post-war mandate had devolved to France owing to a presence in the Levant going back to the period of the Crusades. Its main impact had begun during the 18th century, with both Catholic missionaries and traders coming to the region. Before World War I, France was the strongest European power in an elastic Syria, with important investments in banking, utilities, rail and other transportation, and tobacco cultivation (with cotton yet to take off). It also had significant commercial ties with greater Turkey generally, and ideas of controlling the Mediterranean if and when that imperial power collapsed. The Sykes-Picot agreement of wartime then prescribed an eventual divvying up of the Ottoman-controlled Middle East, with Syria-Lebanon to come under French control at the end of the conflict.

However, as the war drove to its close, the British under General Allenby helped place Sherif Hussein's son, Feisal, in power there. During the Peace Conference the issue went back and forth, and finally the British, themselves a new mandatory power in Palestine to the south, agreed in September, 1919, to leave Syria. At the San Remo conference of April, 1920, France officially received its Levantine mandate, then under Gouraud's tenure proceeded to eject a pan–Arab Feisal from the region (by late July). The French Mandate began in earnest September 1, 1920, and the Lebanese, finally vouchsafed a

"Greater Lebanon"—after four centuries under the Turks—were happiest with this colonial presence; while Syria's Arabs were less so. Gouraud, another Lyautey alumnus, and still vigorous, though one-armed after a wartime shell explosion in the Dardanelles that had also broken his legs, left Weygand something considerable on which to build. He had made France respected here, defeating foes wanting to strong-arm the region into a greater, more unwieldy Arab "nation," one that would have featured the same inter-clan or religious conflict seen in today's Middle East.[13]

Weygand rapidly learned about the complex situation that had obtained under his predecessor, including budgetary problems, and the many ethnic or religious issues (status of Armenian refugees, Persians requiring the same privileges as under the Turks, prohibition of alcohol importation into certain regions, tax exemptions, and the like). From one general he received advice to the effect that with Muslim Arabs of the Levant, neither threats nor apologies were useful, as they indicated weakness. He knew that Syria could easily become a center of pan–Islamic propaganda, ginned up by Egyptians and pro–Feisal British.[14] As usual, Weygand worked well with those who knew more than he did in a variety of areas. He also placed on his staff one long-term associate, Lieutenant Roger Gasser, son of a French soldier killed near the end of World War I. The new high commissioner knew how to form a team, and began work almost immediately. One says "almost," because on board ship toward the Middle East, the poet inside emerged, and he kept abandoning dossiers to get out on deck and enjoy what he beheld.

Arriving in Beirut May 9, 1923, the general was impressed by a stunning panorama of mountains and seascape—and in recollection, again pours his art into painting the scene. But realism quickly took over, as it had done for Lyautey in Morocco of 1912 (where he was still resident-general). Weygand was coming to an area of much strife since the Turkish defeat in World War I. He knew that Gouraud's era had been plagued by France's attempt to weld historically important Cilicia (north and west of Syria) to the mandate, making it a locus of Armenian safety and independence. After an exhausting guerrilla war, the area remained with Kemalist Turkey (by the Treaty of Angora), and the French packed up in October 1921, leaving the Armenians, in particular, embittered.[15] But even in Lebanon, where Weygand was based, anarchy punctuated by plentiful robberies was endemic. Almost immediately, the high commissioner went into action, altering a justice system that had made executions into long waits (including for the French president's imprimatur). Instead, Weygand now relied on Lebanese judges who could more promptly hang criminals, showing their bodies in public as deterrents. A bit queasy recalling all this, Weygand noted that suddenly French prestige went up, and that Arabs in their *souks* began seeing a kind of miraculous power in this energetic French official.

In positions of this sort, Weygand would always be a person to move around and see things directly, never just a retailer of theories from the vantage point of an office. So he soon took the high road between Beirut and Damascus, carefully observing the variety of landscapes, peoples, clans, and religious orientations he encountered en route. Like the port of Beirut itself, the Middle East's finest, this road too had been built by the French back in the 1840s. Stirring descriptions of what he saw make Weygand's memoirs in this section sparkle, especially on his first look at Damascus itself. Here the exhilarated general opened his window at dawn to admire an unforgettable light over the city, a profusion of Arabian Nights minarets, and the many fine, deceptively peaceful gardens there. Perhaps without quite realizing it, he was already becoming — if for a short time — another adept French proconsul in the lineage of Louis Faidherbe in Senegal, or Gallieni of Vietnam and Madagascar. Like them, Weygand had both art and science in his soul, was an able administrator and military thinker, but much more as well.[16]

As noted, he worked adeptly with other quality personnel who smoothed his path here, such as the French delegate Ernest Schoeffler — "an experienced administrator of calm, sound judgment, an upright, conciliating character, marvelously knowledgeable about the business of the state of Damascus."[17] So vulnerable himself, Weygand always had and would retain (except in the case of the sur-idolized Foch) a healthy admiration for those who made France better both at home and abroad.

Of the four states created in the French Mandate, Damascus and environs was the one with closest and fiercest ties to the wider Islamic world of its day, particularly Egypt. Some in Damascus still aspired to captain a united Arab entity, and this pan–Arabism made the future capital of Syria and its hinterland very different from Lebanon, where protection of equal rights between Christians and Muslims was much more of a priority.

The Sunnis of Damascus were so numerous and powerful that they scared the Syrian Alawites of the mountains, who were therefore given their own state and autonomy; not to mention the Rif-like Druzes, a small Islamic sect looking to Palestine and the British for help against a Sunni majority — and the possibility of getting *their* own state, which ultimately they did.

Even among Sunnis, certain ones aspired to Syrian independence at the head of a greater Arab "nation"; while others were growingly content with the protection and economic amelioration France provided here. (That included its role as an increasingly adept facilitator of religious pilgrimages to Medina and Mecca, via modern transportation.) The Alawites manifested no such ambivalence — they totally bought into the idea of French protection, and Weygand was certainly willing to give it to them.[18]

He was, however, less impressed by Aleppo (head of its own state) than by Damascus, though he saluted a marvelous French delegate and troop commander there, General Gaston Billotte, eventually to be a tragic part of Weygand's frantic attempt to impose order in France of May 1940. In the Aleppo region, Billotte had supervised the construction of roads and schools. He also retained a firm military presence here, but in the Gallieni tradition, was also supremely enlightened. "A great worker, demanding of others as he was of himself, General Billotte was a veritable leader," Weygand would recall.[19]

The high commissioner himself combined empirical realism in inspection tours with a certain idealism, taking Mandate prescriptions very seriously: in fact, he kept a copy of those directives in his desk, and when at his office, would open a drawer each morning to consult them. His Burkean cast of mind, making him aware of the gradualism of history's long sweep, and the vicissitudes that had been so prominent here, made him agree with the idea of only progressively leading peoples of the Levant toward full independence. That idea would later be denigrated as paternalistic; now, as we witness much instability in the Middle East, the mandate view may yet return to historiographical respectability.

However, Weygand was quite outside these later sarcasms and ironies; to him, France could be a true symbiotic facilitator here, and like French administrators before him in Algeria or Tunisia, he felt it imperative to do more — and in a fairer way — than had prior masters of the Levant, the Turks, who had concentrated more on what they could draw from these provinces of a once-gigantic empire, rather than on what they could give. Not that Weygand harbored illusions on the French task: any proconsul in the Levant would have to deal with bitter sectarian and even family rivalries, and with the necessity of priming the economic pump in a part of the world not yet known for gushing oil and billionaires. Like the great Lyautey, but without his theatricality, Weygand also knew how important externals were to winning Arab allegiance here. Gouraud had been a penny-pinching bachelor, and Weygand found his Beirut residence not up to the standards necessary to make an impression on a populace so taken with appearances. Weygand was not put off by a bumptious race track nearby, which would be a problem only on Sundays, the day of the races; worse was the fact that he found no view at his residence — and this in a city of views![20] His residence seemed so dowdy that he immediately planned extensive alterations, in order to please the many visitors he would soon get there.

The general ran a budget that had to provide cash for many things; but

watching his francs, he made suitable rooms for friends, for his wife to enter-
tain in when she arrived, and for regional notables who soon streamed in to
meet with the new high commissioner. It wasn't long before Weygand detected
a certain psychology here. He found these "Orientals" ultra-courteous and
full of flattery — but as Napoleon had observed, flattery often went together
with calumny. That meant plenty of behind-the-back critiques of Weygand's
associates, putatively never good enough to represent an august France here!
In addition to these critiques, Arab notables also had an indefatigable way of
never taking "no" for an answer: if they desired something, they kept on pushing for it, without admitting defeat.[21]

Weygand certainly played the card of post–World War I French prestige, and also of France's history in this region. He learned that the word
"Franc" was still used in names here, and that the memory of the Crusades
was important not only for Christians, but for Muslims too, particularly in
Lebanon. Compared to the tyrannical Turks, rumor had it that the French
had long been comparatively fair administrators. And there were still tangible reminders of that prior French presence, such as Crusader castles like
Beaufort.

Though it did him little good with anticlericals back home, Weygand
was also able to feel how Catholic missionaries and educators had kept French
influence going here through the 19th and early 20th centuries. And on current travels in the region he was definitely emboldened by hearing numerous
cries of "Vive la France." The many newspapers in Lebanon and Syria of the
era (though with circulations often under 2,000) were largely Francophile,
even when considered fanatic. There was even admiration for this energetic
high commissioner emanating from dailies of the wider Arab world.[22]

Material problems, however, and the finite nature of his budget provided
limits on what Weygand could accomplish in this region of the Middle East.
Aviation, still in its childhood, needed beefing up here; as for France's navy,
it was also small, but an important element in French prestige, in a time when
the arrival of any boat was a significant local event. Despite the many needs
he had, the general enjoyed being in charge, going head to head with the
British, with Sharif Hussein, and really, with any group or person who would
weaken the mission France had here.

Nor did he wish to change political structures in any significant way.
Gouraud had created "Greater Lebanon" — cradle of a fragile Middle Eastern
country still in existence; and Weygand was happy with that creation. However, he felt that the Syrian Federation of the states of Damascus, Aleppo,
and Alawites wasn't working nearly as smoothly. In Lebanon the French were
adept at exploiting and maintaining a balance between the roughly half of

Lebanese who were Muslims and the half who were Christians, led by the numerous Maronites, formerly Orthodox, then Catholic, yet still retaining a patriarch with whom Weygand dealt. This was the religious Middle East, and *pace* anticlerical Leftists at home, Weygand as a polished Catholic notable could appeal to Levantine inhabitants partly for that reason. And there were French Catholic institutions to build on here, such as the prestigious Jesuit university in Beirut, with faculties of medicine, law, and engineering, and a teaching hospital soon to be built. Its rival was the American University of Beirut that took a sometimes simplistic point of view when it came to the imperial French.

Weygand was adept at filling out political institutions in the Mandate, habituating inhabitants to being run by their own elites, and with elections to their own representative institutions. But seeing that the Syrian federation wasn't really working, he then had the courage to plan the amalgamation of the states of Damascus and Aleppo alone as a Syrian state, while the Alawites would remain under a French governor. Weygand's idea would be to get the Syrians en route to taking responsibility for their own nation-in-the-making, rather than orienting themselves toward a more nebulous pan-Islamic entity, where — as he presciently saw — they would end up under another dictatorship. Meanwhile, a small state of the Druze Djebel would come under another enlightened French governor, Captain Gabriel Carbillet, aware of both their pride and independence, but also their penchant for clan conflict. Carbillet would remake their finances and judiciary, and in the short run, provide real order in a region where the proclivity for disorder was so ingrained.[23]

Weygand played a key role in rapid economic transformation here — promoting the building or improvement of roads and rail, and especially the enhancement of cotton production that fairly zoomed upward, along with wine and fruit exportation. He knew which towns had problems getting water, and which wheat-raising areas required it, and which rivers needed courses changed. Irrigation projects over huge expanses, dikes, and the like were conceived during Weygand's period here. And to fuel the economy, better banking and credit sources were put in place as well. Syria had long been a commercial crossroads, and French personnel of the time were hopeful that its links to Iraq, Persia, and points farther East would be strengthened.[24]

But though a good, practical administrator, Weygand was also enlightened in the cultural sense. Like the greatest of French proconsuls in previous eras, he grew to love the entire region, taking a special interest in archeology projects that enhanced knowledge of ancient history and languages. In fact, he resembled a Jefferson in his omnivorous interests. And when his wife arrived in the fall of 1923, the high commissioner's residence became a lively place for not only dinners and balls, but theatrical and operatic productions.

Weygand did get one time out with a trip back to France, but was unable to see political handwriting on the walls there. On his return, he enjoyed a trip to the Holy Land in Palestine, visiting Jerusalem in concert with British authorities, and Nazareth, and becoming very moved. But given political vicissitudes in France, all good things would inevitably come to an end for him in this part of the world. A new Cartel des Gauches (coalition of the Left) government in France placed ideology first, and on November 29, 1924, working at his desk after a brisk morning gallop, Weygand received a call from an associate, asking whether he had heard the news: that General Sarrail would be replacing him as high commissioner of the Levant. It was a stunner. Everyone — even on the Left — knew how able Weygand had been in this position; but he would now be recalled to the metropole, and after the stability he had wrought here, it was a slap in the face, a dash of cold water, indeed.

Many in the Levant protested, some wished to telegraph the French government, but Weygand dissuaded them. He had had 19 months at his post, and was sad to see the end approach. But sore at heart or not, one had to stay in line and obey; that was ever his way. After a flurry of final visits, Weygand got on the boat December 5, recalling sadly: "The day of departure had arrived. I was about to leave these lands to which I would forever feel attached.... The country was in order, and progressing, and France was better armed and more respected here than ever before."[25]

Muslim and Christian delegations, from both Lebanese and Syrian regions, thronged the port, mourning Weygand's departure; and soon the Cartel des Gauches would see the error of its ways, as the situation in the Levant rapidly devolved toward chaos. Weygand's successor, the controversial Sarrail, nominated partly because he was an anticlerical Freemason and sometime socialist, irritated inhabitants of the Mandate, and helped usher in a Druze revolt. The result was an eventual French bombing of Damascus itself, and predictably, Sarrail didn't last long as high commissioner, and was soon ousted from the position. "If it ain't broke, don't fix it" remains a cliché people too rarely heed in history!

5

To the Heights of Hampered Power

Weygand's next position of the mid–1920s was very different from his previous one — in fact, it couldn't have been more different. He now became director of the Centre des Hautes Etudes Militaires (CHEM) in Paris, created by Joffre in 1911. It was a post where, in theory, Weygand would instruct and thereby nurture new talent, producing officers with a sense of evolving military realities. The telling nickname for this institution was the "School of Marshals." Weygand was also placed on the French War Council (Conseil Supérieur de la Guerre); but in neither function could he really use his clairvoyance[1] — especially about the need to mechanize the French army, and to hatch independent tank units, light and heavy, eventually operating in concert with aircraft. The Germans began learning these lessons, much at variance with lessons of the last war; while Weygand's hidebound and ever more pacifistic France didn't want to, preferring the defensive doctrines of Pétain and of the Cartel politician Paul Painlevé. The latter sold the idea of a fortified "Maginot line" — already adumbrated in Conseil de Guerre meetings of 1922 — to the war minister assuming that position again at the decade's end, and for whom the line was then named. And Weygand didn't dare backbite someone as clearly patriotic as André Maginot. However, he knew, he saw, and he wrote about the need for supple, offensive instruments and doctrines of war. Never, however, would his entreaties sufficiently persuade.

A Paris courting Weimar Berlin during the Briand-Stresemann era of the middle and late '20s, while Germany's military was girding for a rebound via secret contacts with the Soviets, did not please Weygand. How much better off he had been in the Levant! France's army was at a low, non-respected ebb when he took his instructional position, and remained that way through the balance of the decade. The Briand-Kellogg Pact (1928), outlawing war as a policy, is the well-known apogee of this rose-colored outlook of the period before Hitler's accession to power. Surveillance of German arms limitations was coming to an end, as was Allied occupation of the Rhineland itself. The honor system was replacing all this vigilance. And in 1928, a law on French military service pared it down to only one year — Weygand calling repetitively for double that.[2]

Meanwhile, Pétain was becoming an aged commander in chief, one who had refused the *cumul* of being chief of staff as well — the latter position too bureaucratic for his taste. But the hero of Verdun was also tiring of his own position, and nearing age 75, thinking of a return to private life. In talks with the chief of the General Staff, General Eugène Debeney, they together worked up a plan of Weygand succeeding Debeney as French chief of staff in January, 1930. Then, after a year, Pétain would leave his position of vice-president of the Conseil Supérieur de la Guerre, one that made him designated commander in chief in time of war. (The president of the Conseil was the war minister, but there merely as a figurehead.) Weygand would then become France's commander of wartime operations, should they, in fact, be necessary, and inspector-general of the army. Pétain didn't like some of Weygand's ideas, yet knew him well, and admired his overall military talent and character.

So with Debeney's approval, Pétain made his choice, at the same time knowing enough about the political world and its divisions to breast his cards — that is, until the right moment. The moment arrived with a Center and Right–dominated parliament in place near the end of the decade, and especially when André Tardieu became prime minister in early November, 1929, and Maginot, the war minister: for both these political figures knew what Weygand could do in such a responsible position.

Unlike Pétain, however, Weygand would have been ideal as *both* chief of staff and designated commander in wartime, and there would have been thereby, less possibility of division at the top of France's military structure. A precedent for such a move went back to the period of World War I, and Maginot definitely favored giving Weygand such a heavy, but at least unified, series of responsibilities. However, Tardieu knew that he had to keep elements of the Left from criticizing unduly in Parliament and in the press, and decided definitively to split the two functions, ratifying Pétain's original plan: Weygand would become chief of staff for one year, assisted by the intellectual, vague, and vacillating General Maurice Gamelin. Then, in 1931, Gamelin would become chief of staff when Weygand was transmogrified into vice-president of the Conseil Supérieur, and generalissimo for future war.

There was quite a press to-do anyway, particularly over the fact that Weygand had so distrusted both the Germans and Soviets during the '20s. On January 3, 1930, he nonetheless took over as chief of staff in Paris, while

The always impeccable Weygand in army hat, uniform, and medals stands beside Marshal Foch's widow and two daughters, mourning the generalissimo's death in March 1929, at funeral services held beneath the Arc de Triomphe in Paris. It was now Weygand's turn to attain France's top military positions (Bettmann/ CORBIS).

awaiting political confirmation that month. And predictably, parliamentarians of the Left, especially on the far Left, were vociferously sardonic about the appointment.

Weygand, however, did receive approval, and at the dawn of the '30s, an infinitely more demanding decade than the previous one, was catapulted to the top of the French army. Quite improbably, as a once despised pariah still worried inside about his origins, Weygand was now chief of France's general staff! And in that post he would get along well with Maginot — that is, in the short time that talented war hero remained alive. Weygand was also happy to get close again to the interesting Tardieu, whom he had known well in wartime, but who had split with Foch during Peace Conference meetings over the Rhineland.[3]

Had he cared less for his country, and for his army, Weygand could legitimately have permitted his ego to be massaged by this appointment, even despite its limitations. He might well have basked, and rested on his laurels. Instead, he found his military ideas for France — correct ones, it turned out — countered at every turn. His supposed "Rightist" intransigence, and Clemenceau-like fear of another German round, met with repetitive derision on the Left, whether Communist, Socialist, or moderate liberal. Clemenceau had himself been a politician of the Left, but a militarily realistic one. Passing away at the end of the utopian '20s, he now left a vacuum.

In the position he had been given at the beginning of 1930, then the vice-presidency of the Conseil Supérieur de la Guerre a year later, Weygand continued to endure the slings and arrows of sizeable elements in both the media and the Chamber of Deputies.[4] They kept deriding him as too anti–German and anti–Soviet; too anti–Republic (to which, however, Weygand was always faithful); too Catholic; and simply too strident and demanding of vigilance, along with sweeping military change in France.

Examining the French army, and its preparations for another possible conflict, Weygand beheld many insufficiencies, and came to realize that once in tandem with Gamelin from 1931, he would be linked to an intriguer and compromiser, who would go along too easily with the disarmament mania of that period. But at the same time, Weygand remained incapable of working against his colleague, and instead, simply kept trying to be heard against the din of a still strongly pacifistic France of the gathering Depression era. Tanks, oil supplies, a two-year law replacing one-year service — these became, to many, his tiresome iterations. Weygand not only knew how badly the French army needed overhauling, he was also worried about the effect of low births during World War I, and the resulting "hollow classes" to come during the late '30s. His sole consolation was working with War Minister Maginot, with whom he would tour frontier regions and military installations; but this fine partnership lasted only two years, for Maginot's time left on earth was brief, indeed.[5]

Weygand's private life meanwhile remained a stable one; his sons had turned out well — the oldest an engineer and reserve aviation officer, the younger one a bright officer in Morocco, awarded the Legion of Honor, and with a personality and verve all his own. When he needed to relax *en famille*, the general went out to a place in Brittany that he owned, some five kilometers from the Foch country home near Morlaix.[6] Like Churchill, Weygand was also busy balancing close attention to pressing, present-day concerns with a wide-ranging historical-literary sense of the past. Perhaps it would always take one who really knew and felt history to intuit what was crucial in the present, and near future.

Weygand's biography of Louis XIV's great commander, Henri de la Tour d'Auvergne, Viscount of Turenne, first appeared in 1929, though translated

Marshal Pétain and America's General Pershing attend dedication ceremonies of the Marine Monument near Meaux, France, September 10, 1932. Memories of the Great War weighed heavily, and for some French military thinkers, *too* heavily (Bettmann/CORBIS).

into other languages during the '30s; and his feeling for the subject again reveals the outsider's propensity for getting into the very insides of France's past (rather like Napoleon, who also admired Turenne). In his work on Weygand, Bernard Destremau sees some likening here of Turenne to Foch; but my view is that Weygand more centrally identified aspects of his *own* military self in the great commander of the 17th century (without, however, spelling that out). In 1657 Turenne was appointed Colonel-General of the Cavalry in France, the military branch in which Weygand had cut his own teeth professionally. Then as Marshal-General of the king's camps and armies, Turenne grew into not only a strategist of the first rank, starting in the War of Devolution during the late 1660s, but also, like his biographer, a wonderful organizer. Turenne wanted French soldiers to have good apparel (it was the age when uniforms were just becoming standardized), equipment, and food, and — no Falstaff— regular pay as well. Like Weygand himself, his Turenne was a man who was both disciplined but generous to soldiers, and forgiving of faux pas on the battlefield when chance intervened to trump their courageous actions. Turenne's manner, says Weygand, was "at once firm and kindly," and because he walked the walk militarily (ultimately paying with his life during Louis XIV's invasion of Holland in the 1670s), his men willingly followed him. Turenne was also a diplomat of distinction — well acquainted with the English, the Dutch (when at peace), the Spanish, and other foreign powers. As Weygand declares, "he had friends or personal representatives everywhere. He was in correspondence with all the leading men in Europe." Turenne's diplomatic qualities included "insistence upon exact information, discretion, [and] prudence...." Weygand could easily have been describing himself here, especially near the end of World War I and through the Peace Conference. And like Weygand, Turenne did not hunger for money, and in fact, died poor, despite his place at Versailles and two houses he had in Paris. "In the army," says Weygand, "his simplicity was in strong contrast to the luxurious living of other commanders" and his "private life gives an impression of dignity, sincerity, modesty, loyalty, and generosity."[7]

Was Weygand projecting here, or using his outsider's enthusiasm to make Turenne perhaps larger than life? Or was he employing his own taste and growing sense of self to get at the essence of one of France's military greats? Both assertions perhaps have truth to them; but Weygand was a true historian, not some bureaucrat manqué with the right degrees.[8] We haven't space here to show how innovative Turenne was in his military strategies of the 17th century; but in similar fashion, Weygand was himself busy adapting to the new in this regard, and one can see why he, like Napoleon, could so easily identify with this towering figure.

For both his military and literary resumé, Weygand was rewarded by election to the Académie Française in June 1931, taking the late Joffre's seat by a unanimous vote of 34 Academicians. A reception followed next spring, and, having picked out his sword to go with the traditional green costume of the Académie, Weygand was feted by notables, including Marshal Lyautey, who offered him his sword in the company of Jules Cambon and Jules Jusserand of the French ambassadorial corps, current government ministers, assorted royalty, and from his summer roosting area in Brittany, mayor, priest, presidents of the veterans' society and of the Chamber of Commerce.[9]

However, the current rough and tumble of politics at the dawn of a divisive French decade was much more irritating than ceremonies associated with the Académie! Weygand's impeccable attire and *hauteur* of mien annoyed more rumpled politicians of the time; so also did his constant desire for specifics, and precise answers relating to issues of national defense. Like Churchill admonishing André Maurois in the mid–'30s that airplanes ought to become the sole preoccupation of his writing, Weygand was obsessed as well with planes, tanks, and the lunacy of arms limitations in this last, pre–Hitlerian period. He also fought a losing battle to unify commands, and especially, to have the air ministry subordinated to a generalissimo of other forces, and part of a coordinated series of forces, rather than a separate component.[10]

During the year he was France's chief of staff, Weygand vigorously promoted "mechanization"—especially getting firms like Renault and Citroën on board in the manufacture of tanks. And he would go out to supervise the fortifications to be named for Maginot, believing, however, that good possibilities for defense should *always* be combined with powerful, flexible offensive capabilities. But would this happen in his country?

Not if it was up to a more pusillanimous Gamelin, who took over as chief of staff, and in that position remained politically correct when it came to international disarmament, a holdover idea from the '20s. These two generals (Weygand and Gamelin) couldn't have been more different, and emphatically devolved into an odd, but not symbiotic, couple at the French military summit. It especially irked Weygand that as vice-president of the Supreme War Council from 1931, and designated commander for wartime, he had more of a bureaucratic load but much less actual power than in his previous position. At first he tried to appear at the General Staff offices a couple of days a week to report and liaise; however, presences at the other end weren't reliable, and he subsequently gave up on that. He had also to fight to promote deserving soldiers, and maintain the Office of War Materials that he had put

Left to right: Generals Gamelin and Weygand — typically quarrelsome — in a photo of September 1931, as French War Minister André Maginot, holding canes, Air Minister Jacques-Louis Dumesnil, a visiting General Douglas MacArthur, and General Louis Gillaumat look on (Hulton-Deutsch Collection/CORBIS).

in place under a Jewish colonel, Bloch-Dassault. There were also war games to attend in different parts of France, and visitors to meet, including General Douglas MacArthur, America's new chief of staff, a courageous soldier in France during World War I, then a supporter of Billy Mitchell's innovative ideas concerning war from the air, and warning that France had better stay strong and militarily current.[11]

But the disarmament conference of 1932 still found many proponents, and a new leftist government under Lyon's mayor, Edouard Herriot, coming to power in the May 1932 elections, brought much sympathy for a position Hitler would soon render passé. The war minister in Herriot's cabinet, Joseph Paul-Boncour, was no Maginot, and big cuts in the military budget followed, partly due to the onset of the world-wide depression (though it was a more gradual economic downturn here than in the more industrialized U.S. or Germany). The minister of war who then replaced Paul-Boncour, assuming office the month and year of Hitler's appointment as German chancellor (January 1933), was Edouard Daladier, a Radical-Socialist from the south who wanted to continue cutting in the army, and also to ease Weygand right out of his position! The "bull of the Vaucluse" would change and recognize military realities later in the decade; but in this era he was on quite another path, and in the not so long run, obviously the wrong one. This should have been confirmed that same year (1933)—when Germany under a now forthright, dictatorial leader strode out of both the League of Nations and the disarmament conference in November, then announced it would rearm without limitations. Weygand could now see what Nazi military thinkers saw—that tanks to move all over the place, making obstacles like rivers no longer important, had become the strategy of choice, and that restricting these wonderful instruments of war to a support of infantry was not. He did manage to put together the first Light Mechanical Division in France, but much more remained to be done.[12] Innovations would be agreed to on paper, but then Parliament niggled on credits and applications, factory owners were loathe to convert operations in anything but a haphazard manner, and even farmers criticized Weygand for abandoning the horse. Nor did it help that there wasn't just one kind of person to get used to at the War Ministry; during Weygand's tenure in the two top French military positions from 1930 to 1935, there were no less than ten ministers of war (and 16 governments)! And getting along with Gamelin as chief of staff remained a trial. From this general, Weygand could feel no real approbation for his innovative ideas, and their years of so-called "collaboration had not brought us closer." One rare foreign minister of mettle, Louis Barthou, seemed to be a hope when it came to vigilance vis-à-vis the Germans; but in 1934 he was murdered in Marseille, along with the Yugoslav king, on a visit there.[13]

That was the year a scandal and its aftermath, involving a naturalized Russian Jew, Stavisky, and including the firing of Prefect of Police Jean Chiappe, brought on severe Rightist riots in Paris (February 6, 1934). These, in turn, helped spawn the Popular Front idea on the other side of the ideological spectrum; but in this crisis, symptomatic of a kind of civil war atmosphere in France, Weygand didn't get his feet wet politically, though some thought he did have governmental ambitions. However, he simply wouldn't dabble that way; he was no politician. More of a problem to him was being chained to the inferior Gamelin, and weighed down as well by the military ideas of the popular Pétain, who after the crisis of 1934 became France's war minister, averring (wrongly) that the Ardennes forest wouldn't be a meaningful sector in a future conflict. Weygand already knew how dangerously misguided such conventional wisdom in the army was, predicated too much on the experience of World War I; but he was hamstrung by his intense need to remain loyal, ever his psychology. He did talk, and with authority, in the

Conseil Supérieur about "preventive war"; but even during the later Phony War era of 1940, with France on the brink of annihilation, that concept would remain the butt of much sarcasm. The media, Gamelin, large sectors of Parliament — all these fora of opposition together constituted a lot for Weygand to overcome in a position of putative influence.[14]

When Weygand reached retirement age in January, 1935, and with no war yet to lead in, his opposite number Gamelin was rewarded for his massaging, cozening ways by not only becoming Weygand's successor as generalissimo in time of war (and vice-president of the Conseil Supérieur) on January 21, 1935; but also retaining the chief of staff position, and that of inspector general. What they hadn't given a fine military thinker, they were giving to one who — despite any revisionists who care to differ — was of a decidedly lesser quality.

Gamelin was certainly bright: he had topped his class at Saint-Cyr, and was a bookish man with a taste for difficult philosophers, such as Henri Bergson. But he was more skilled at public relations, especially with politicians,

America's Chief of Staff Douglas MacArthur, flanked by General Weygand in dark tunic and General Gamelin in light one, at an army meeting in Reims during the early '30s. Did MacArthur know that Weygand was much the greater French strategist and general? On the far left is General Henry Ford, and beside Weygand on the far right is General Jules-Antoine Bührer (Bettmann/CORBIS).

than at being a forthright, innovative military leader — and this would never change through to the fateful year of 1940.[15]

After one last report on the poor state of France's army and military preparations, Weygand was eased out of the Conseil Supérieur — and the army itself. Or at least into a kind of semi-retirement, with the proviso that he might be recalled if needed in more parlous times. Against significant opposition, he had left much on which French rearmament programs could continue to build; but what he had lived for seemed gone ... or was it?[16]

6

Recharging Batteries as Military Historian

There were now other, more artistic aspects of himself that Weygand had time to cultivate — and did in a whirlwind of sustained lucubration and published output during the next several years through to 1939. Some of his best work came out while Hitler was running from one gain to the next — remilitarization of the Rhineland, annexation of Austria, dismemberment of Czechoslovakia, en route to his Polish demands, which finally forced a weary, divided France and Great Britain to bring on another world war. In his shorter books that were almost pamphlets, Weygand showed himself to be a first-rate essayist on problems France was enduring in these demanding pre–World War II years; in the longer ones, he was a wonderful, clear, and again, Churchillian book writer, especially in the field of military history.

First, Weygand got to travel simply for pleasure, finally able to wend his way down to recently-pacified French Morocco, in order to visit his Legionnaire son, Jacques, who was posted there. Weygand and his wife made their trip in leisurely fashion, so that all senses could be aroused, and he thoroughly enjoyed himself en route. The visitors went directly south to a country that was nearing a terrible civil war, Ortega's invertebrate Spain. It was still, however, an hospitable, warm Spain that could thrill the general — and did. With awe he examined Phillip II's Escorial, imposing lair of the great Catholic Reformation monarch; the Prado museum; the sunny, smiling cities of Cordova, Grenada, and Seville.

The couple finally reached Gibraltar, and there he met with a British commander he had known in World War I. And thence across the water to Agadir, which he loved; in fact, he loved Morocco, period. And he found his son's superior to be of high quality — a battle-hardened alumnus of World War I and North African wars, tough, but fair, and naturally aristocratic.[1] In this part of Morocco Weygand enjoyed the Sunday scrum of the market, where he could distinguish Moroccan Berbers from Arabs, and savor the riotous hawking of fabrics, jewelry, and the like (reminding a reader of street scenes in a soon-famous movie, *Casablanca*).[2]

This was a quite stable, still optimistic, and, to a degree, pioneering French Morocco, and less divided and hopeless than the home front, to which Weygand now had to return. There, his new position was as an administrator in the Suez Canal Company. This post, along with weekly meetings he attended as a member of the Académie Française, constituted something of a waste for him; but then, he had already had much good fortune (given his background) even to get where he was.

In Egypt, when he first arrived on a trip there as a Canal administrator, Weygand met with key Muslim notables, including King Fuad, who had already admired the general's order-making in the Levant. Here, Weygand could represent an august France, impressing by his own precision, courtesy, and general deportment, important to Muslim notables of that period. Weygand's marvelous two-volume work on Fuad's distinguished ancestor, Egypt's Viceroy Mehemet Ali and his sons, had already been commissioned by the Egyptian monarch, pointedly designating Weygand for the job; and having begun research some six years earlier, the general finally had time and energy to bring the enterprise toward fruition. Mornings at home he would work on it, and in the afternoons, used Paris libraries; and when completed, the work was appropriately dedicated to Egypt's king. How Bernard Destremau's most recent biography of Weygand (1989) could have ignored this absorbing, well-researched piece of history is unimaginable. But the splendid, informative result again shows that Weygand should not be underestimated as a writer of history — especially given the complexity of this swath of the Islamic past. Weygand was never one to shirk his homework, and along with being characteristically thorough, never one to bore. In other words, it is still worthwhile, given what we need to know about the Islamic world, to pick up Weygand's two oversize volumes, with a fine supporting collection of 19th-century art, revealing the wide variety of garb donned by warriors and religious people of the time. (Especially numerous here are wonderful works by Carle Vernet — the romantic passion for *outre-mer* a large stimulus to European artists of the 19th century.)[3]

But Weygand as historian is every bit equal here to these romantic sketchers. Himself an outsider who appreciated dignities created and held onto with difficulty, especially in the turbulent Near East, he could feel his way adeptly into his thorny, but always interesting, subject; and in the process, the artistic historian disappears, and the reader of the '30s, and even of today, is back in this fascinating, topsy-turvy era of the 19th century — one, however, bearing similarities to today's Middle East. If Weygand knew the Germans, he

also came to know the Islamic/Arab world as well, including its many variations; and it would stand him in good stead during the coming war in North
Africa. His close military analysis of battles amply shows his acumen in that
regard, too. We must therefore treat this splendid work in some detail.

Weygand's first chapter is on Mehemet Ali's early life, and he begins in
Hegelian fashion: "There are, in history, men who bear in themselves the des-
tinies of a people and sometimes of several peoples." And he ranks Mehemet
Ali right up with the Alexanders, Napoleons, and Peter the Greats — world-
historical "shapers of humanity."[4]

He then sketches the background of a figure who, like the author, had
much to overcome. Born in a small town east of Salonika in 1769, this Alban-
ian from Ottoman Macedonia did not seem likely to become "a new
Ptolemy."[5] A la Weygand, Mehemet Ali was raised in a difficult family atmosphere, with a father dying young, and a brother to avenge (the Turks having
decapitated him). His greatest influence came from one of his father's friends,
who saw his potential. And the boy was no softie, learning to procure taxes
for this adoptive father-figure, including by throat-cuttings. Weygand frankly
sees his subject as Machiavellian, but at the same time, naturally noble.

His adoptive father made Mehemet a good marriage with a wealthy
divorcée, a union producing five children, including three sons. Then, before
Napoleon's arrival in Egypt, the young man worked in a desultory fashion
trading tobacco as "a kind of unspecified bureaucrat, as many are in the Middle East, at once military and civilian, half officer and half trafficker."[6] (Weygand's culture and experience showing simply in this description.)

Mehemet Ali then came to Egypt in 1801, where Napoleon had defeated
the reigning Mamelukes, but was now losing to English and Turks. At first,
Mehemet took on the French, though ironically, he would later require their
aid and protection. He had come from a hinterland to a complex milieu Weygand now delineates clearly for the reader. Arab invasions of the seventh century, the use of slave troops, Mameluke cream rising to the violent top: it is
a dizzying landscape, and quite a canvas for the author to fill. By their toughness Mamelukes became *beys* under the Turkish sultan, and their military tactics obviously fascinate Weygand, though from the 13th to the 19th century
they had scarcely evolved: "Disdaining enemy fire, they fought only on horseback ... throwing themselves in disorder against the enemy from the first contact...." If they won, it was quickly, and there ensued nothing like modern
humanitarian conventions, but rather wholesale slaughter. If they didn't win,
they ran![7]

The author goes on adeptly to Ottoman decline, and the squabbles of
factions busy exploiting Egypt's *fellahs*, while the latter showed the typical

resignation and inability to revolt that still obtain in Middle Eastern populations under diverse oppressors. Weygand distinguishes between Arabs anchored in one place, and those of tents who migrated constantly to live off plunder.[8] He paints languid, often corrupt Copts working under *beys* in Egyptian cities, and Syrian, Greek, or Armenian minorities in commerce; and above, the Mamelukes uncertainly, but still wantonly, running the show. Full-page Vernet drawings of them show his subjects passionate and romantic in their gowns, with knives always at the ready.

The Turks then tried to polish off these Mameluke *beys*, and amidst this turbulence, Mehemet Ali aligned himself with the right people, rising high in Cairo, the second city of Islam after Constantinople, as Weygand tells us. He became chief of police of the palace, even as the English under treaty with Napoleon left in 1803, permitting pillagers freer rein. Alliances between pashas, the Turks using now one, then another, and playing off rivals; the Mamelukes still playing *their* role; and Mehemet Ali somehow gaining power in this furious wasp's nest — it probably reminded Weygand somewhat of divisions in his own place and time. And of the tragedy of weak French leadership, contrasted to that of a forthright Mehemet Ali, who in July, 1805, became pasha or viceroy of Egypt.[9]

As the Ottoman representative here, he now felt strong enough to destroy the Mamelukes, and the French began backing this creator of order, while the British supported a rival. Meanwhile, migrant Arabs from places like Libya streamed in, backing one side or the other, mainly to plunder. The Turkish sultan also gave Mehemet support, but "the 'Porte,' irresolute in its designs and veiled in its schemes," was as fluid and vacillating a support system as any entity here.[10]

Weygand's history never stops fascinating, for no sooner was one group (the Mamelukes) brutally dominated by his main figure than another threatened. The next warlike situation to claim the pasha's interest was presented by the Wahabis, who had recently rebelled and taken holy cities of Arabia from the declining Turks. These Wahabis were fierce Islamic puritans refusing to bow before anyone but Allah, believing they were the only true interpreters of the Koran. Iconoclasts founded in the late 17th century, they loathed what they considered ersatz Muslims, and were now depredating parts of Iraq, Hedjaz, and the holy city of Medina, and Mecca itself — destroying numerous sanctuaries and monuments; but no purer than today's Osama, they also grew rich attacking caravans of pilgrims, or pirating in the Persian Gulf. The worried sultan in Constantinople now needed the energetic Mehemet Ali to stem this religious (or anti-religious) tide.

Tied down at home, the viceroy decided to dispatch one of his sons

(Tusun Pasha) with an army to make alliances in Arabia, and hopefully liberate Mecca. But those troops were decimated by disease, and at one point totally surrounded by Wahabis, and anchored for safety in one small part of Arabia. However, a tough Wahabi chieftain died in April, 1814; and as usual, Weygand's description of the weak son, Abdullah, who followed him is to be savored. There now ensued (from 1816 to 1818) the progressive defeat of these marauding Wahabis, spearheaded by Mehemet's oldest and toughest son, Ibrahim.[11] European drawings of the time show a handsome, resolute man, now leaving Cairo with his forces in September 1816 for Medina. And Weygand, the Catholic, can feel this religiosity rarely absent from Near East warfare — the invader praying at each shrine en route, while braving sandstorms, and with the usual array of health problems scourging his troops.

As is still the case, allies began streaming to the stronger side (Egyptians under the Turks); and despite eye disease and searing dysentery, their victories continued. Finally, the weak Abdullah was himself snared, and taken in December 1818 to Constantinople, where the sultan had him promptly decapitated, and his headless body displayed.

Amidst such Machiavellian mafias, Mehemet Ali had risen higher; no longer simply Egypt's viceroy, he was now honored in the Islamic world as liberator and protector of its holy sites.[12] Weygand then details his next fora of expansionist warfare — Nubia and the Sudan, providing a detailed geography lesson on regions down the Nile and Red Sea, the influence of the Sahara, and so on. He also tells us what people worked at, and how black slaves were traded by Arabs. The viceroy's main reason for heading an Egyptian contingent to invade Sudan was that, like Candide's Eldorado, it sounded like a land of riches. And he needed badly to replenish his treasury, despite launching a lucrative Egyptian cotton crop to feed Britain's hungry textile factories. Weygand also notes another practical consideration — that he could lure fellow soldiers with a penchant to conspire to an area where dysentery and malaria would take their inevitable toll.

On Nubia and its desert Weygand continues with complexities he never shirked — concerning geography, people, armaments, and the like. Mehemet's third son, Ismaïl, was dispatched with an expeditionary force here to win Nubia, their initial successes confirmed when they sent 1,200 pairs of ears home, in the way fedayeen on Israel's borders were rewarded for such ear trophies. Onward they went to conquer le Sennâr, eight months a desert, as Weygand tells us, but "as soon as the rainy season arrives ... the double action of heat and humidity blankets the country with riotous vegetation." He also informs us that the Sennârese religion "was Islam mixed with fetichistic practices, their language a corrupted Arabic, their type a composite of the surrounding populations, Nubians, Hallas (Abyssinians), and Negroes."[13]

Looking for riches in this part of Africa was a perilous enterprise, and in addition to troops succumbing to disease, advertised riches never panned out — "the mirage kept fleeing before the seekers of gold...."[14] And when Ismaïl tried to shake down a religious notable, he and retinue invited to a festival were cooked in return — kept inside at sword's point, while fire and smoke suffocated them to death. Finally by 1824, the future Anglo-Egyptian Sudan was at least partially in the latter's grasp: eastern Sudan, almost up to Darfur, scene of recent horrors, had become Egypt's tributary. And this entire part of Africa had brought more brutally-conscripted soldiers to Mehemet Ali's forces.

For virtually the rest of this exciting first volume, Weygand discusses the creation of a modernized Egyptian army under the viceroy's leadership, using European methods and materiel. But his second volume remains equally insightful and dramatic.[15] He begins with Mehemet Ali's next idea of dominating Greater Syria (1831–1833), an area Weygand obviously knew. Other Ottoman pashas in Syria and Palestine were then at odds, whetting the viceroy's appetite, not only for the *pashlik* of Saint-Jean d'Acre (Akko), which was denied, but also for those of Tripoli, Aleppo, Damascus, and Jerusalem. He also envisaged economic gains — plentiful timber for a budding Egyptian navy, and the lucrative Syrian trade with Asia Minor — and would impress Arab Muslim, Maronite Christian, and Druze soldiers into ever more powerful armies.

Using quotations from such as Napoleon, Weygand delineates the great geographical differences between Egypt, developing historically in the Nile valley, and a Syria of hills and mountains, and with much smaller rivers. He gives good detail on the viceroy's considerable expeditionary force, buoyed up by Arab auxiliaries and under the command of his able son, Ibrahim, and with huge amounts of baggage. Despite a cholera attack back in Egypt, the naval convoy of troops (aided greatly by French experts) went well. Conquests began with Gaza, which — thanks to Napoleon — no longer had walls to deter invaders. Next came Jaffa, then as now a stirring town on its hill overlooking the Mediterranean, and with a good "military reputation: built as an amphitheater on heights partially bathed by the sea, it was surrounded by a wall with towers and forts."[16] Ibrahim's men swept in from the sea, and the taking of the town both by water and land was child's play; then it was off to nearby Jerusalem, which again yielded easily. And "thus Egypt's viceroy became the protector of both Christ's tomb and the Wailing Wall venerated by the Jews!"[17]

Here, as in parts of Syria proper, both Christians and Jews were happy for the incursion of forces promising more tolerance, and release from oppressive Turkish taxes. Ibrahim's large army then reached Akko November 27, 1831, and again, Weygand offers a fine description of its situation: "Saint-Jean d'Acre had for the most part, conserved the same silhouette as in 1799, offering the form of an irregular pentagon, with three sides washed by the sea; the other two, better fortified, constituted a land redoubt."[18] And he tells us that a Frenchman, Phélippeaux, had put up the bastions here — which made a takeover harder for Ibrahim's besiegers. In a six-month attempt to do so, much of the Egyptian force perished, and as Weygand could feel by experience, survivors had a tough time adapting to the relative rigors of a Levantine winter, compared to Egypt's.

The Ottoman sultan then threatened Mehemet, urging him to call off the siege; and when this was refused, enjoined all Syrian pashas to fight the invaders. Quickly, the Turks now rallied a tremendous army, marching it toward this theater. Meanwhile, by March Ibrahim's charges had begun breaching the walls of Akko, and "his inflamed harangues, delivered in a resonant voice, had considerable impact."[19]

The defenders, however, rallied, and there were powder explosions, and great losses to the invaders. The sultan began playing off pashas and denounced Mehemet Ali religiously, to no avail. Chased away and leaving much equipment, Ibrahim made it to Tripoli April 5, executing notables there who had helped the other side. He then chased Pasha Osman across Lebanon and up the valley of the Orontes, and to Baalbeck, site of Roman ruins in the northern Beqaa valley. As Weygand reminds us, Baalbeck, equidistant from Damascus, Beirut and Tripoli, and on a key trade route, had always been strategically crucial.[20]

Massing forces there, Ibrahim sent another group back to Akko for a fuller try at investment. And by May 1832 there were more breaches made in its walls, and the kind of destruction a CNN generation thinks only a contemporary phenomenon: "In the city, with tightly packed houses and narrow streets, projectiles had smashed into terraces, demolished many dwellings, decimated the population." All through the night of May 26–27, Egyptian artillery wrecked an old fortress town "under an avalanche of projectiles," and the scaling of its walls began in earnest.[21]

In response, the Turks unleashed a terrific counter-attack *cum* explosive mines, and the place became such a wreck that even Abdullah's palace there was gone. Both sides were on the edge of giving up; but then Ibrahim found another way into the city, and won the day. Amazingly (and it still would be), he allowed the top people there, including Abdullah, to live as Egyptian prisoners. And in the ruined city Ibrahim found lots of arms, but also thousands of dead, some from plague-like disease. And lest we think all this quaint war-fare by today's standards, Weygand estimates the use of some 50,000 bombs there, not to mention about 200,000 cannonballs, "a considerable number for the era."[22]

Egypt's viceroy now had a glittering reputation, and the nerve to con-front the sultan of Turkey himself! And this impending David and Goliath confrontation resonated deeply for Europe's romantics, particularly in a bored France. The sultan wouldn't bend to the new power, so Mehemet Ali impelled his willing son and army deeper into Syria, where people flocked to what seemed a compelling force.

Not that the other side stood pat, as the sultan declared open war, nom-inating a rival Pasha Hussein as head of Egypt, the Sudan, and Crete. The Turkish military had been subject to much reform, but were European meth-ods instituted by such as the great von Moltke (mastermind of future Pruss-ian wars) useful here? Weygand, the military theorist, had his doubts.[23] At least Pasha Hussein was a resolute, brave man; however, the sultan stuck him with a westernizing co-director of the armies, another named Mohammed, and the rivalries of a diarchy were, again, something Weygand knew well in his own era! An army required one man at the top, and this the Egyptian foe had; not to mention a battle-hardened quality, due to much experience in the field.

Mehemet Ali now urged his son forward toward the *pashliks* of Damas-cus and Aleppo. In June, 1832, Ibrahim was en route to Damascus, an impor-tant Islamic city, but lacking good walls, making it an easy prey. Several of his spread-out armies then headed for Aleppo, while the Turkish army began swarming from another direction. Their Mohammed knew how significant were the defiles of Beylan as an entry point into Syria — and from experience, so did the author. The Turks progressed toward Antioch, and the two sides would finally meet in a classic battle at Homs. Weygand describes better defensive ramparts here than in Damascus, but Mohammed's Turkish troops also extenuated by forced marching, disease, and hunger. And Ibrahim's soldiers nearing Homs July 7, earlier than the Turkish side had envisaged.

Here was a tremendous force of some 30,000, and Mohammed in a strategic quandary: should he retreat, or confront this strong Egyptian army? Weygand felt that withdrawing toward Aleppo would have made most sense — given the possibilities of linking up with Hussein's armies there. But Mohammed decided to fight on the spot; and even then, as Weygand says, he should have "solidly clung to Homs and to the gardens which bordered it to the south. The Turks, valiant soldiers," as Weygand knew from World War

I, "have always excelled at fighting from behind obstacles." Ever mindful of terrain, the author pointed out that "the situation of Homs, closing off the valley, would have allowed him to fall back gradually to Aleppo, giving troops from Antioch time to arrive."[24]

Instead, Mohammed pushed his troops at dawn into the countryside outside town — three lines of a heterogeneous army. With Napoleonic intuition, Ibrahim could now decide how to deploy on the various wings, and again, one feels Weygand's passion for military strategy here. One can only précis his sophisticated analysis — of Ibrahim's center affronting the enemy head on, while maneuvering cavalry and infantry to turn its left, and using "a powerful diversion" to scramble the Turkish right.[25] Use of the surprise element — hallmark of great commanders — worked well, with tremendous Egyptian artillery blasts met, however, by brave if disorganized Turkish ripostes. The Ottoman center now buckled, as did its right, and all disordered attempts to counter-attack came to nothing.

At night Mohammed galloped away to Homs, leaving desertions and total disaster among the Turks. Can one think of anything but France's own *déroute* four years after Weygand described all this? Losing some 100 dead, Ibrahim's forces had won a smashing victory.

And Weygand allows himself to divagate — on what makes a poor military leader versus a good one. Most centrally, Mohammed had neglected that key word in armed conflicts — location! For he had dropped his left "without support or backup, completely hanging in the air. He didn't even think of seizing the edges of gardens south of Homs, which would have permitted effective flanking fire against an enemy pouring out from the ruined hamlet...." What a contrast Weygand draws between the unempirical Mohammed, and Ibrahim, who "had perfectly discerned the maneuver imposed by the terrain and the enemy's situation." And Ibrahim was on the wave of the future, presaging "modern war, based on flexibility, power, rapid action, and the effect of surprise, [all] bringing a decision."[26]

When on July 9, Ibrahim's Egyptians marched into Homs, and thence toward Aleppo, they gathered numerous prisoners into an ever greater army. Hussein moved rapidly to Aleppo, trying to organize in the face of disorders there. But the "Alépins" wouldn't support the Turks, nor were reinforcements from the sea feasible. The Turks' best ally was the pitiless sun scorching Ibrahim's troops, and especially cholera, wreaking its Crimea-like horrors.

But at top speed, Ibrahim's men then bore down in the direction of Antioch — with two columns approaching via different directions. They arrived July 28, and Weygand knew the landscape Ibrahim encountered: "Before him rises the Amanus, a branch detached from the Taurus and constituting a wall nearly 1800 meters high. The Beylan gorge, which slices it, links the plain of Antioch and the gulf of Alexandretta, and in a more general fashion, Syria with Cilicia."[27] Weygand knew this as an historical route of conquest — of ancient Egyptians and Assyrians, Cyrus' Persians, Alexander's Greeks, Hadrian's Romans, Arabs, and Christians.

Exquisitely, he sketches the possibilities of remaining on the defensive here — that is, for a Turkish army now hunkered down in the marshy port of Alexandretta, and with rearguard above Beylan on the Amanus escarpment.[28] Unfortunately, Pasha Hussein did not seize those possibilities, in part because his chief French military engineer and advisor had been left sick back in Aleppo, where the Egyptians took him prisoner.

Yet again, Weygand is finely detailed on the deployment of Turkish left, center, and right, and how, once more, Ibrahim made apt military moves. In the morning of July 29 he assaulted, his enemy here anything but dug-in Hezbollah with sophisticated arms, or women and children used as human shields, as in 2006.[29] A Homs rerun rapidly developed — the Turk center and right buckling, the left again turned; and another disorganized frenzy of flight ensuing. Versus 2500 Turkish casualties, a mere 20 perished on the Egyptian side. And to Weygand, Hussein before Beylan was no more strategically able than Mohammed had been outside Homs three weeks earlier.

On July 30 Ibrahim's charges took over Beylan, then in Alexandretta found a treasure trove of cannonry and supplies, which the Turks had brought in by sea. Rather like the Prussians' coming prospect of pushing to Vienna (1866), Ibrahim might now have marched on Constantinople itself. In his case, Bismarckian restraint was no brake; however, diplomacy of the roused European powers was. Russia, wanting the Ottoman Empire to remain its quasi-vassal, and the British, wishing to use this sick Turkish Empire *against* Russian expansion, both feared the new juggernaut; while King Louis-Philippe of France, countered by a young generation inspired by such exploits, was all for moderation as well. Due to these Great Power pressures, an aging Mehemet Ali now needed to throttle his son, and it was a sad dilemma, given a weak Turkish army beset by disease, desertions, and ethnic revolts. Weygand knew well how diplomacy could over-trump battlefield gains, making them ephemeral.

The sultan now tapped one Pasha Rashid — fresh off victories at Missilonghi and Scutari — to run a huge army of some 80,000 soldiers; but Weygand notes sensibly that numbers aren't everything. As with Polish forces after World War I, the problem here was "lack of cohesion, due to very different origins and kinds of training."[30] Rashid had been effective against guerillas; how would he do, asks Weygand, against organized regiments? True, the

Egyptian side was itself augmented by irregulars — captured Turks, Bedouin or Syrian Arabs, etc.; but with two precious months to convalesce and cohere. Part of this Egyptian army had to occupy newly-conquered Syria; and so Ibrahim would make do with some 27,000 soldiers against Rashid's 80,000. It behooved him, therefore, to get a jump before General Winter arrived on the plateaus of Anatolia.

With father still trying to bridle son, Ibrahim learned of Turkish incursions forward into the passes between Adana and Konia, and moved into the mountains toward Eregli, an old frontier fortification of the Byzantine Empire. He sent two armies on two different routes, and Weygand's superb narration and analysis continue.

In Eregli several weeks, Ibrahim then regrouped forces, still needing approval for a final move forward into Anatolia. Mehemet Ali wanted to hold back this steed-like son, while the latter argued that any retreat would merely seem like weakness to the enemy. So Mehemet bent a little, allowing him full steam ahead to Konia; but no further.

Yet again, Ibrahim split armies to take two routes, so often seen in Napoleonic campaigns; and Weygand is his usual detailed self on columns within those armies and ill-conceived sultanic instructions, removing Rashid's best strategic card: to lure the invader deeper into Anatolia, where winter would surely have weakened soldiers used to hotter climes.[31] The sultan, however, wanted an immediate engagement, with Konia the focal point. His hand forced, thither marched Rashid's forces in mid–December 1832, and Ibrahim decided to give battle outside the fortified town — on a plain flanked by mountains on one side, and swamps on the other. Ibrahim again hoped to use the surprise element, striking at the Turkish left. However, his opponent, Rashid, was also fond of alacrity. And again, Weygand's passion for military history continues to keep his reader riveted.

Rashid himself commanded the Turk left, knowing its weakness; while his center and right were headed by other pashas. A mid-day skirmish where the Turks advanced into fog, shooting wildly, saw Ibrahim reply with the luck of a short break in the murk, so that he could see exactly where his foe was deployed. He could then choose the right time to unleash his artillery. While the Turks lost bearings in the soupy fog, Ibrahim adapted, bringing men in from all lines, then decimating the enemy's cavalry, and pushing it toward inhospitable swamps. He then wheeled to barrage Turkish infantry on the plain from three different sides — and they gave up. The coup de grace came when the vizier Rashid, galloping to help his left, was captured. Finally, the Turkish right was defeated too, and sent running to the mountains; and by nightfall, Ibrahim had won another smashing victory.

Weygand again analyzes the reasons for this outcome at Konia — noting how good defense and offense must combine (a lesson for those in his own country afflicted with the "Maginot mentality"); and how one must always use the environment to one's military advantage. He felt that with lesser forces, Ibrahim had both planned and adapted well here, and for those reasons, won.

The victor then stayed in Konia roughly a month, departing January 20, 1833, and with an occupying battalion left in place there. He wished to keep chasing, but news of the Konia victory had resounded throughout Europe, and the powers would tolerate no further adventurism. For there was now a possibility that Ibrahim could topple the sultan himself, making his father the new one. And neither Russia nor England could countenance such an occurrence. Already Nicholas I, most military of tsars, had rushed troops to Scutari outside Constantinople. And so, by a Russian-brokered treaty of May 4, 1833, Mehemet Ali made do with semi-overlordship of Syria, and the territories of Hedjaz and Crete.[32]

Weygand goes on to describe this Syria under Egyptian rule from 1833 to 1839, showing that it was better administered than either Turks or regional Arabs could provide. Christians and Jews there were particularly grateful for less onerous taxes, as well as relative toleration. But there were revolts in Palestine and Syria, and only by the end of the decade did the occupier have them in hand. Especially tough were mountain peoples, preeminently Druzes, who greatly valued their independence. The whole Syrian occupation cost Mehemet Ali much treasure and many soldiers, making the sultan of Turkey think again of revenge.[33]

His idea was to reassume a dominant role in Arabia, move toward Syria, and possibly retake Egypt itself! Revolts in Arabia aided the Turks — the Bedouins on the move again, along with the Wahabis. Nothing, as usual, was holding still in this part of the world. Forced out of Yemen, Egypt now retained only a shaky hold on the holy cities, and an optimistic sultan determined on a new round of war in 1839.

The Turks duly approached the Syrian frontier from different directions, crossing the Euphrates in May 1839; and on the other side, the Egyptians, with a strong emplacement at Aleppo, let the enemy be drawn in deeper. The big powers urged the Egyptians to remain firmly on the defensive. But as they advanced, the Turks were promoting Syrian-Lebanese revolts, which Ibrahim could not abide. So despite European admonitions, his father allowed him to attack back on June 11, 1839; and the French government sent an envoy to give a personal warning. This Captain Callier arrived in Aleppo June 26, just as Ibrahim was winning another of his hallmark victories against the Turks at Nizib.

Weygand's analysis of that victory takes into account the historiography, making Nizib "most glorious of all victories won by the Egyptian armies," and which some even likened to Napoleon's Austerlitz.[34] But in the author's view, it was not nearly the victory Homs or Konia had been, and signs of decay now seemed present in an army that had won too often and too easily.[35]

Again, a headstrong Ibrahim wished to chase the Turks back into Asia Minor, but Captain Callier and Mehemet Ali together provided oedipal throttles. And France's romantic youth at home became ever more angry at their government! It was a combustible situation, which again Weygand sketches beautifully.[36]

It was time for the powers to get involved, preeminently an irate England. On July 15, 1840, Britain, along with Russia, Prussia, and Austria, agreed to the London Convention, by which Mehemet Ali would retain hereditary rule in Egypt, and administration for life of Akko and hinterland. In return, he must withdraw from the rest of Syria and Lebanon. Ali wouldn't accede, so Austrian and British naval forces blockaded the coast of the Nile Delta, and struck at Beirut; and in late November 1840, Mehemet Ali gave up Crete and Hedjaz, accepting hereditary rule of Egypt, still quite a gain within the Ottoman Empire. Both he and his great son, Ibrahim, died near the end of the decade.

What then were the overall lessons for Weygand? One was that the right kind of military leadership could still work in a divided, Nazi-menaced France. Others were associated with history's customary vicissitudes, and the effects of great-power interference. At the least, Weygand had put much passion and determination into one of his greatest books, too generally neglected. And given King Fuad a wonderful present commemorating his distinguished ancestors.

7

Regaining French Themes

In response to contracts he received, the French general continued writing furiously, and in 1937, two important essays on France's parlous present appeared in book form. Both showed how he could use facts to generalize with column-like verve on issues that then mattered, and which still do. One was titled *Comment élever nos fils?* (*How to Raise Our Sons*),[1] where Weygand emphasized that education was fine, but if only bookish, and not *éducation* in the wider French sense of creating a complete person, incomplete.

In this book-pamphlet, he first sketches his France vis-à-vis dictatorial states like Nazi Germany, Fascist Italy, and a more mysterious Soviet Union. His initial cliché nonetheless remains true: that a country's youth is its future. However, Weygand was loathe to enter the old optimist-pessimist debate, whereby some declared French youth of his time the best contingent ever, others the worst. Strongly, but sensitively, Weygand instead delineates a younger generation in France that was extremely vulnerable, and which could go in many directions, depending on how it was led. For education (as his Latin-reared generation knew) indeed meant "leading out." Weygand conceived of France as a long-simmering project of centuries, and he did not believe that astonishing technological changes were automatically making its people better — far from it. Better education therefore remained crucial.[2]

In terms of classroom instruction, Weygand wanted it to be more patriotic, knowing that in his day both the French Left — drawn to pacifism — and a growingly defeatist Right were making that anything but certain. He looked back nostalgically to the period after the 1871 German defeat, when anticlerical makers of a new compulsory, secular school system in France could at the same time push patriotic teaching at least as much as their Catholic rivals.[3] This was no longer the case in his France of the '30s.

The author moves on to indict formulaic teaching, and cramming for the baccalaureate, which only a minority then obtained, but which was less than ideal, he argues, for the creation of an elite. In chapter 3 (they are short ones), he goes on to the almost complete lack of physical education in France, pointing to the country across the Channel as a saner model.

The next chapter looks carefully at other youthful generations abroad, especially in a now menacing Germany. There Weygand discerned tremendous unity and purpose; and while not at all desiring France to become totalitarian, he showed that what was being passionately inculcated in Germany's young could only spell future disaster for his country — that is, without corresponding French alterations in its educational system.[4]

H. G. Wells' famed line about modernity being a race between education and catastrophe also begged the question: what *kind* of education? Only education making more pacifists? Or thousands of curved-over bookworms? Weygand himself feared impending catastrophe, but his plan for educational improvement was anything but what a Bloomsbury intellectual would have predicated in that domain.

A fuller book-pamphlet, appearing in the same year, was on the subject the general knew best — national defense: *La France est-elle défendue?* (*France: Is It Defended?*).[5] Buttressed by facts, and written with his usual ease and clarity, this extended essay was also cogent for its day, soon translated and published by the Germans, who were obviously paying attention.

Weygand's initial chapter returns to the aftermath of France's pyrrhic victory of World War I — and Foch's attempts to detach the Rhineland, versus the impermanence of Anglo-American guarantees against German rearmament. Then, in fairly short order, came the evacuation of occupying troops five years early from that borderland near France; the false lure of Genevan disarmament conferences, and of a weak League of Nations; and under the Nazis, "rearmament in broad daylight, succeeding rearmament in secret," followed by remilitarization of the Rhineland.[6]

In the next chapter, Weygand skillfully analyzes national defense systems abroad, especially in renascent Germany, using precise statistics: 850,000 soldiers in Germany's active army, and a valuable corps of reservists and veterans, along with completely renovated materiel; a new, ever more powerful air force; and huge factories operating round the clock, where just the one making Junkers fighters or bombers employed some 15,000 workers! The author adeptly summarizes varieties of aircraft the Nazis could deploy, and their always evolving creation of new prototypes that, more rapidly than in France, would then become standard.[7]

He then sketches the forces of Mussolini's Italy, and of Stalin's U.S.S.R., more of "an enigma," and soon to suffer from massive purges of army personnel. Weygand's statistics return to a more reliable state when it comes to Great Britain, where he signals recent military improvements, particularly in aviation; however, he is more dismissive of armies in Central or East European states of the "Little Entente."

The main emphasis here is on France, and that subject constitutes the rest of this small book. And Weygand's tone is less dire than one might expect. He is especially optimistic about the rapid growth of a French fleet which could benefit from port use in far-flung parts of its empire, such as Dakar, Casablanca, and even Saigon.[8] In the army, a two-year law had belatedly replaced one year under the colors, due to the problem of the "hollow classes"; and materially, he points with pride to the extensive Maginot line of fortifications.

The big problem remains France's lack of unity, along with too much reliance on this "Maginot mentality," ignoring a simultaneous need for mechanized, rapid offensive forces to attack proactively, before the Germans inevitably skirted fortressed soldiers. An "attaque brusquée" by the Nazis was, in Weygand's view, certain, and he knew that they would execute it at the location and moment of their choice. Was France really ready for such an occurrence? The author did not feel that it was, and mostly due to a defeatist, resigned mentality, not to the state of its arms, despite their obvious deficiencies. He is especially prescient about the Germans taking out French planes on the ground, and massing wide-ranging panzer forces for a rapid incursion, both of course to occur in 1940.[9]

Industrial delays and the too slow implementation of defense projects certainly constituted significant problems in France of this era; but worse was lethal devaluation of the military itself, and a consequently low amount of career soldiers, well-trained aviators, and specialized technicians. Weygand approaches the end of his essay with a plea for unity; but of course his pamphlet, however easy to follow, was not to create that unity in a France on the edge of another great conflict.

Book contracts continued to chain the author to his desk, and such essays must have been a welcome relief from far more sprawling projects. One of the latter, following his marvelous work on Mehemet Ali and sons, was no less than a history of the French army, one it took Weygand three years to complete. And characteristically, he put much effort into this encyclopedic, superbly illustrated, and truly astounding *Histoire de l'armée française* (1938). Though emphatically a man of the present, Weygand also shows himself here to be much more than a de Gaulle intellectually, and more akin, yet again, to that English politician-historian, Churchill.

From the book's beginning, the reader lingers on the conflict between Gauls and Romans — a dim French past Weygand had made his own. Even on the Gauls, he is his usual detailed concerning ethnicities, institutions, and

kinds of arms employed. But he also indulges his philosophy of history, and
aware of current French decadence, illuminates it in crisis-filled periods even
of that long Gallic past. He knows how peoples slip, and how conquerors then
see their way open to shattering victories.[10] Providing diagrams of defensive
or offensive alignments, the general highlights Caesar's military/organizational
genius, but patriotically sees virtues in his rival, Vercingetorix. As he puts it,
this "young chieftain had everything to captivate and inflame nations avid
for the glory of combat. He was 20 years old, handsome, and exceptionally
courageous." And though finally losing in regions like Burgundy and
Provence, at least he had "the soul of a leader."[11] For Weygand, all this again
offers lessons — and from the very dawn of the creation of a French army.

When he reaches the Crusades, the author draws again on his own personal experience of the Middle East. During the First Crusade of 1096–99,
"the march to Antioch across barren plateaus caused unspeakable suffering
and huge losses for the conquerors. Deprived of water and provisions, they
were forced to live on cactus and crushed aloe, and almost all their horses
perished."[12] He reminds us that the Arabs had so often benefited from other
civilizations, including with Byzantine-built fortifications at Antioch. When
he writes of places like Damascus and Aleppo, you feel Weygand's earned
authority. And he typically salutes distinguished enemies, such as the "skilled,
noble" Saladin, a Kurd born in Tikrit, and a key human reason for the Crusaders' loss of Jerusalem.[13]

But despite all the botches and losses, including of leaders like St. Louis
IX, Weygand reveals his French-Whiggish optimism when it comes to what
remained from these Crusades: "Both from a religious and moral point of view,
they positioned France as the 'eldest daughter of the Church' and carried the
renown of French knighthood far and wide."[14] The French had also learned
militarily from skilled foes, something Weygand considered crucial in his
own time. "To their Muslim adversaries, the Crusaders owed another sort of
progress. From the first contact, they had had to suffer from their tactics, at
once aggressive and prudent, from their hails of arrows shot from a distance,
from their encircling maneuvers, and their skill in slipping away and conceal-
ing themselves."[15]

The result? Better French cavalry tactics, lighter packs, and significant
improvements in the building of castle-fortresses. Finally, Weygand sees here
"precursors of a colonial policy already bearing the French trademark."[16] The
outsider's fierce French patriotism remains vividly apparent throughout the
entire book.

His parts on the vicissitudes of English invasion and occupations during
the Hundred Years War again highlight techniques, but also personalities, and

the ever-present seductions of decadence. Weygand remains a fine, indefatigable historian here — his work well enhanced by sumptuous color paintings. He is not a simple moralist, yet much of what he treats historically remains relevant to France's situation of the 1930s.

In the run–up to a prolonged war between England and France, the author contrasts two medieval kings and systems, with the French decidedly inferior in both departments. England's "Edward III, in all the vigor of youth, was only 25 years old. But he had already been matured by ten years of rule, by responsibilities and tests," writes Weygand. Edward may have been "a lord of handsome allure" but beneath, there lurked a "strong personality — ambitious of conquest, secretive, and of a reflective, enacting mindset...." Against Edward's resolve shown in the first invasive battles of this long conflict, "France, softened by a recent efflorescence of civilization ... and avid for enjoyment and pleasures, appeared an enviable prey, and all the easier a target, as it was weakened by the irregularity and insufficiency of its fiscal resources ... and by rivalries that on the battlefield, had created an even wider gulf between nobles and commoners."[17]

Weygand goes on to a detailed, but never dull account of military techniques, where the English also led the way. Yeomens' bow and arrow use that helped them win great battles is contrasted to heavily-armored French cavalry without ability to maneuver (leaders having forgotten lessons of the Crusades); and in general, "the Frenchman, less robust and athletic" than the Briton, wasn't at all ready for this full-scale invasion of his territory.[18]

Ever the military distinguisher, and knowing that no modus operandi could simply be repeated in battle, Weygand contrasts the hail of arrows that won for the English at Crécy in 1346 with refined techniques a decade later at Poitiers, another devastating victory. At the latter venue, the French put more emphasis on infantry, but English cavalry maneuvers this time helped turn the tide. By 1360 a victory-laden England held huge swaths of France, and the French king was imprisoned in England, to be returned only for a massive ransom. It was one of those classic low points in the history of both the French army, and of the country.

Yet the French *would* rebound, under a young king, Charles V, "already educated by events, meditation, and study."[19] This ruler would improve French discipline, pay, and recruitment, and against English pillagers, defenses became more effective via better castles and fortified churches in country villages.[20] Once more, personality could sometimes save the day. And again, what a canvas to fill! The reader is stuck here in these vicissitudes of an extended conflict, yet Weygand, already a man of 70, has so much farther to go in his treatment. Indeed, additional French low points would ensue just in this

Hundred Years War, until the ultimate rebound wrought, in part, by one Joan of Arc. Then came the ultimate irony of 116 years of combat yielding the English but one French port town, Calais!

Weygand then segues to the artillery revolution at its dawn near the end of the Middle Ages, and again, we have plentiful and fine illustrations of bombards or cannons. But he does not ignore social history — recruitment problems, desertions, and the like. And he makes one realize that, as much as Louis XIV's era of the late 17th century was perhaps the most important seed-time of the modern French army (not least via uniforms that were finally standardized), the 18th century which followed also saw a host of important military reforms, with laws Weygand carefully treats, and technical innovations that lasted.

The author shows adeptly that this pulling up of national socks was a constant in French military history. For instance, after the disaster of the Seven Years War (1756–1763), leading to the loss of French Canada, along with significant reverses in India and the Caribbean, "our setbacks led to a frenzy of research: we kept on asking questions, experimenting, and translating German regulations...."[21] In other words, just as France would be inspired by German techniques after 1870, and as Weygand in his own day knew that Nazi deployment of aircraft and tanks was the way a new war would be fought, so the French after 1763 drew in part on the innovations of Prussia's enlightened despot, Frederick the Great. Weygand again seems to be emphasizing that in the military realm, one should *always* learn from competitors and enemies.

He correctly identifies that whole Indian summer period before the French Revolution as a spawning time of France's armies, techniques, and armaments that would soon spread Revolutionary ideals abroad. Just as he admired Louis XIV's fortress maker, Vauban, he now reveals his great esteem for Jean Baptiste de Gribeauval's reconstitution of French artillery before the Revolutionary and Napoleonic eras. Gribeauval had been a French lieutenant-colonel, then a general of artillery in Austria under its redoubtable empress, Maria-Theresa, during the Seven Years War. In this conflict between rival Habsburgs and Prussians, he was imprisoned by Frederick II, who nonetheless recognized his genius, making him a German field-marshal, before returning him to France. Back in his own country after the disaster of 1756–1763, "he was then given responsibility to reform French artillery." And the always thorough Weygand provides a lot here on calibers, angles of shooting, and the arsenals that turned out new artillery pieces so useful to Napoleon, himself a poor boy educated under teachers like Gribeauval. The bottom line? Here was a significant military innovator, one who (not unlike Weygand) had bucked trends and much French opposition in his time; and therefore, "one could not praise the name of Gribeauval too highly...."[22]

As the author then navigates the many vicissitudes of the Revolutionary period and its wars, one is still amazed that a man of his age could keep going with such readable thoroughness, not allowing ideology to cloud his assessment of French military achievements of the time, nor those of its leaders, such as Robespierre's right-hand man during the Terror, Saint-Just. With a fine David painting of the latter opposite his page on this figure, Weygand notes: "Saint-Just was certainly the representative [on the Committee of Public Safety] with the most efficacious influence. Lacking pity, even for his friends, he decreed and had the death penalty applied for looting, unauthorized absences, collusion with foreigners...." Weygand knew of the drownings of priests, the destruction of churches, and all the other horrors wrought during this dictatorial, anticlerical era; yet he *also* saw the Terror as a necessary part of French military progress. In fact, "one must acknowledge ... that these rigorous measures, although too frequently summary and unjust, did re-establish obedience."[23] Disastrous for Catholics, the age of the Terror had at least kept France together in the face of formidable foes (Austria, Prussia, and England).

The author's introduction to the age of Napoleon, portrayed sweepingly in chapter 8, is beautifully nuanced. And it again reveals his perhaps unwitting Hegelianism: that is, how the right person could incarnate France militarily, and thereby, an entire era. As he writes: "From the time of Bonaparte's appearance on the scene, his history and that of the French Army would dovetail. To follow the 20 years of his life as imperial leader is to see him make the forces of the Revolution his own, to be present at the birth of the 'Grande Armée,' and witness of its triumphs, then of a growth not proportionate with the resources of an exhausted France, and of successes ever more dearly bought." And finally, "when an imbalance between ambition and the possible was wrought," one sees this "genius succumb to the sheer number of his adversaries, the lassitude of his military leaders and of the entire country, leaving in his wake a trail of glory, and lessons that several generations would permit to fall into oblivion."[24]

Is Weygand not telling the reader that even Foch, not to mention Joffre, of World War I had been too enamored only of one part of Napoleon's strategy, his penchant for rapid offensives, and that they had ignored the downsides, when applying his techniques to a conflict ruled by machine gun, barbed wire, and trenches? Thankfully once more, this is a more mature Weygand shorn of his mentor, and of a sur-idolization that had once gone too far.

He salutes the little Corsican's greatness at his apogee, and *precisely* because there was anything but one Napoleon; rather, an improviser, a military creator, and a reactor of genius. This is the Napoleon of Austerlitz (December 1805), not only an intuitive, mercurial inspirer, but also thoroughly scientific, precisely calculating rates of marching, how long forces could remain in combat, etc. And at the same time, a marvelous organizer and delegator. Rigidity of the Joffresque kind comes out in these pages as a shoal to be avoided by French military thinkers — truly the wrong way to imitate Bonaparte at his famed apex.[25]

In his parts on Napoleon's decline and fall, including the sweepingly pathetic Russian campaign of 1812, Weygand draws attention to the ungainliness of ever more massive forces, and increased French resort to foreign troops, the majority when it came to the disastrous campaign mounted against Tsar Alexander. This is the Weygand who had warned France after World War I that it must not adapt to a low birthrate by looking ever more to colonial subjects for its armies.[26]

When it comes to those French imperial armies and conquests that grew exponentially in the 19th century, starting with the takeover of Algeria in the 1840s, the author has yet another vast canvas to fill, and does so here as revisionists are starting only now to do again — pointing to the great idealism of French ventures in North Africa, Indochina, and the like. Individuals who made France's huge colonial empire (still intact when Weygand was writing) were "impelled by their taste for adventure or by the simple accomplishment of their duty in these distant lands where the flag was to be protected, or to be raised higher.... At every step of the colonial conquests, there is reason to admire the heroism, understanding, and humanity of these pioneers of overseas France."[27] With marvelous illustrations of uniforms appended, Weygand has much to do describing the dizzying variety of French colonial battalions or regiments. On the various outfits largely made up of the indigenous, he especially salutes the *tirailleurs sénégalais* (Senegalese sharpshooters), and their celebrated pluck during World War I. There are labored descriptions too of Indochinese corps, of those drawn from French Madagascar, etc. And again, Weygand remains a detailed distinguisher. On troops from Madagascar, he notes that "the value of the Malgache fighter presented the same differences as the two principal types in the population: the Hovas — more civilized, sedentary, and less resistant; and the Sakalavas — cruder, more adventurous, and more robust." But on the whole, he shows real admiration for these foreign forces.[28]

He then moves on to a French North Africa he would soon come to know well — and its Algerian Arab troops, its Berbers, and so on. On the legendary Lyautey of Morocco, he points especially to the quality of his wonderful aides like Henrys, Mangin, and Gouraud, who came to prominence during the First World War, and whom Weygand had known personally. His conclusion to that part: "For a century, the French army, during long periods of peace when it could have softened up and lost its vitality, had the privilege of seeing theaters of far-off wars open up to it, acting as the fermenting agent for an ideal, and for the most noble military aspirations."[29]

Weygand contrasts to that idealism and large imagination displayed in colonial fora the limited horizons and views of the French military at home before the Franco–Prussian War (1870), confronted by a more effective German foe: "On one side, very pronounced preparation, boldness of conception, and prudence in execution; on the other, neither preparation, boldness, nor prudence.... The German generals demonstrated initiative, decisiveness, and solidarity," everything that Weygand valued in military leadership. Whereas, in that disastrous contest of 1870, "the French high command was passive, obeying orders to the letter, and lost when faced with the unforeseen."[30] Yet comebacks had always occurred throughout the long stretch of French military history; and what followed the debacle of 1870–71 was what Weygand called (in the next chapter's title), a "Military Renaissance."[31] Was it too late now to promote yet another one in France?

In this handsome, magisterial volume, Weygand had been focusing on periods when France had previously fought for survival — the Hundred Years War, the French Revolution, and so many others. He wasn't simply being an archivist: he was saying, in effect, that France had *always* had to fight for existence, and that his own era was little different. In fact, he concludes with a sketch of the army of 1938, emphatically against de Gaulle's idea of a professional, smaller force, *or* of one that might lean too heavily to the use of colonial troops. The nation must still be in arms; morale, as in the golden era of French patriotism during the Revolution or before World War I, must return; but this man who had already given his country so much knew that he alone couldn't fix the serious problems France now faced. He simply hadn't the clout, and certainly not as a too-repetitive, righteous-sounding voice in the wilderness, a military Jeremiah. Maxime Weygand had spoken out and published a good deal; but would France, *all* of it, listen, and better, act? Was there even sufficient time left?

8

Hurled to the Top Against the Nazis

In 1939 a still under-employed Weygand headed a mission to Iran, Turkey, and Rumania, as a notable esteemed and valued by people he met there; but saddened that the latter two countries didn't see France as a viable ally, opting instead for vague agreements, and mostly for neutrality. They too could see the handwriting on the wall in his country.

So here was this mostly unheeded military figure in retirement and past the age of 70, critical of French army doctrine and preparation, but *also* staying in line — patiently so, hoping still for a position of command. Some of that hope was justified owing to his distinguished past, which had allowed Weygand both to be retired for limit of age (January 21, 1935); but also to be "retained on the active list without limit" — in case. War clouds were of course gathering now, and on the eve of a new conflict in Europe, August 30, 1939, he suddenly received a shocking communication from General Gamelin: he would recommend to Prime Minister Daladier that Weygand now be given supreme command in the Eastern Mediterranean, constituting a return to what the general loved, and centered on an area of the world he already knew, the Levant of Lebanon and Syria. Would he take it? He most certainly would — happy to be back, but conscious at the same time that he had not really followed army developments in over four years, and that yet again, he would need to learn a good deal in a hurry.[1]

In a way, however, this re-entry into service became a half-measure, and tragic for France, because, ensconced in that sunny clime, Weygand would be removed from the mainstream of what soon became called the Phony War in France; too removed, in other words, to see how wrongheaded was the current strategy in Western Europe emanating from Chief of Staff Gamelin. En route to his post, Weygand did meet Britain's number one in the Middle East, Archibald Wavell — a general he respected; and still mindful of the two-front experience of World War I, which had tied down the Germans (and with

Weygand inspects British troops at Sandhurst's Royal Military Academy in mid–May, 1939, on the eve of another world war that would see him "hurled to the top" of the French army; but in truly dire circumstances (Hulton-Deutsch Collection/CORBIS).

Russia no longer an ally), both took seriously the idea of welding together the Balkan countries, relying especially on Turkey, and forming an active Eastern front against the Nazis.

In the Levant, Weygand no longer combined the offices of high commissioner and troop commander; he now possessed only the latter. The former function was split off, happily so, for he got along with Gabriel Puaux, its current holder. But his efforts at rallying the Balkan nations and the Turks still eventuated in only imprecise agreements: mindful of how rapidly the Nazis had crushed Poland during the first weeks of World War II, they felt essentially that being too clearly in a comparatively weak Allied camp might make *them* more appetizing. And certainly in the Eastern Mediterranean, and the Levant itself, French forces seemed quite weak even to Weygand.

From the summer of 1939 an expeditionary force was created there, and oriented toward a rapid strike via Turkey into the Balkans. Given a combined Anglo-French fear that the Nazis would come this way next, Weygand considered the World War I strongpoint of Salonika crucial once more. Much of his correspondence in 1939–1940 is on the hypothetical, and what were really war games: making this army more modernized and technical, filling it with fighters specialized in mountain warfare (such as *spahis*), spiffing up rail connections to Central Anatolia — all presuming the Balkans *could* become an active theater before a Nazi invasion of France. Sadly, this was Weygand's customary thoroughness turned in the wrong direction. Interminable missives between Weygand and Daladier or Gamelin, or local commanders, on how to integrate Senegalese sharpshooters or North African troops into regular troop detachments here; how to employ local Arabs in the occupying force necessary to keep order back in the Levant; or on how to procure both mechanized battalions, and mules, horses, and the like, all seem mostly misdirected today. Weygand put 100 percent into his job, but this was really the wrong job, the wrong theater. The crucial one was back home on the German and Belgian frontiers. And Weygand was prevented from understanding that theater, tied down here with much bureaucratic work — tables and tables of personnel to review, a bulging correspondence even on the procurement of locomotives, or weekly reports to digest on the state of the Levant's Arabs, which by today's standards was a calm one, according to French authorities.[2]

However, Weygand was anything but office-bound in his position. He was often out touring to check on battalions of great diversity, and to alter their composition. He also inspected corps specializing in anti-tank warfare, aviation units, or outfits earmarked for protection of the borders and seacoasts. He kept a close watch on incoming boats bringing all sorts of military gear and gunnery, and in sum, did anything but sit still in his Near Eastern bailiwick.

On a visit to gray, *drôle de guerre* Paris in December 1939, Weygand begged authorities for more sophisticated arms dispatched to his region of operations, particularly aircraft. He was mostly disgusted by the tergiversating complacency of politicians who would one day become his Vichy nemeses, especially Pierre Laval. But he *was* wrong at this point in thinking that the Balkans would imminently open as a front, while a stalemate not unlike that of the First World War would prevail at home. That notwithstanding, Prime Minister Daladier now wished that he had selected Weygand early on for the top position of command in France, rather than agree to the maintenance of Gamelin. In the capital, Weygand attended a full slate of meetings with this prime minister, other cabinet members, and ambassadors, and with the chief of staff; procured some of his requested arms; saw his family briefly; heard with gratitude that his old associate from 1920, General Sikorski, wanted to place a Polish brigade in Syria; and en route back, saw notables in places like Ankara, then tribal leaders in the sun-struck Levant itself. He was, however, frustrated, and at one point contemplated a final resignation, little knowing that at the end of March, 1940, France's new prime minister, Paul Reynaud, now wished to oust Gamelin and place Weygand in the supreme position of command. It turned out that Reynaud (who also held the Foreign Office appointment) was far from the only one.[3]

Back in Paris again on the eve of the Nazi invasion, Weygand beheld an atmosphere of resigned weakness, including fatally low manufacturing of needed munitions. His meetings with Gamelin and officials in the Air Ministry revolved around the Finnish situation, Weygand's own reiterated need for men and materiel in the Eastern Mediterranean, and generally, around hypothetical war games. French plans, for instance, to bomb oil wells of the Caucasus were only studies, and nothing those with power wished to implement. When he left the capital after this second trip home, April 12, returning to the Middle East, Weygand had a feeling of foreboding inside; his childhood had taught him to sense catastrophic changes looming on the horizon — and the collapse of Allied forces in Norway, the imminence of drier, more tank-friendly weather on the Franco-German frontier, it all added palpably to that ominous feeling inside.[4]

But when on May 10, 1940, the Germans surged into France and the Low Countries, Weygand was still kept almost completely in the dark, owing partly to poor communications with the Levant, and partly to the character of Gamelin. He was sent only nebulous, misleading generalities about the possibility of rapid collapse on the Western Front. Gamelin's first telegram to Weygand, received May 11, painted a rosy picture of Allied plans (moving the B.E.F. and top French troops up to Belgium's Dyle River, predicated on the last war), in order to repel the invasion. News of the fall of Rotterdam on May 13 gave Weygand a somewhat better picture of how dire things really were back home; and when he heard on May 16 that the Germans had traversed the Meuse, France's last frontier against a blitzkrieg offensive, he realized the gravity of panzer divisions about to have their way with flat French plain country of the north, supported by marauding aircraft. Gamelin had ignored tips even from the enemy, and they had easily traversed the Ardennes gap between Belgium and the Maginot Line. Succeeding with Operation "Scythe Cut," these no-nonsense Nazis were now arcing up toward the Channel to pincer French and British troops belatedly rushing west, when Weygand received a strange telegram May 17 — finally hearing that things were indeed serious at home; but with specifics still withheld. The telegram simply ordered the general's immediate return to Paris.

Something important seemed afoot — and he did receive news of

Reynaud arguing in his cabinet, to the effect that Weygand was now at this eleventh hour, a better choice as commander in chief than Gamelin, something which of course should have been realized years earlier.[5] But there were still no concrete details offered when Weygand took the fastest plane available out of Beirut at 5:15 A.M. on May 18. His plan was that with one stop in French Tunisia, he could then reach Paris by nightfall. However, hard winds in the teeth of the aircraft forced a detour to refuel in Egypt, and a layover in Tunis for the night; and Weygand (with time now an ebbing luxury) could make it to Paris only on mid-day of May 19, a Sunday in the capital. Thanks to Gamelin's wan meretriciousness, and to that poor standard of French communication, which outdid the English or German norm, Weygand still knew little. He had trusted the army and its hierarchy, yet it took courage and even abnegation to say yes to the top job proffered him that Sunday in a meeting with Reynaud and Marshal Pétain. Observing generals sagging dejectedly around him, meeting with the ineffectual Gamelin May 20, and with the government obviously in panic, Weygand could now gauge the real situation, and tried quickly to ascertain just what divisions and arms had been lost — this from army personnel that he knew, and whom he trusted not to mince words.[6]

What may fascinate the historian is that a mature soldier so focused on being up to the minute during this national catastrophe was also inside — however briefly — the vulnerable little boy wondering again what General Foch might have done in such a predicament. And whether Foch would now support his current actions.[7] Because Weygand knew that action was now of the essence. And he knew too that, unlike Gamelin, previously hunkered down without radio communications in the Vincennes fortress, he badly needed to get out to the rapidly altered "fronts" and see for himself what had happened here while he was across the Mediterranean.

Immediately, he put forth measures to keep civilians off major roads during the day, in order to facilitate military movements. He also resorted to old "75s" from World War I to strengthen anti-tank maneuvers. And over the prime minister's objections (fearing his new commander might be killed), Weygand opted immediately to go north, in order to locate his key generals and against real odds, keep the king of Belgium and his country fighting alongside the French and British. He promised a trip of only 24 hours. On May 21 at 7 A.M., he was out at Le Bourget airport, scrounging for any plane that would take him; and one was indeed found — duly fired upon en route by German aircraft, but at a courageous patriot who disdained death. This trip finally brought the new commander in direct touch with the disaster — copious bombs from the air exploding and machine gun fire well-nigh constant, and desperate refugees still clogging the roads. Even when he had landed some 20 kilometers from Béthune in Artois, finding a functioning telephone became a major operation. This was indeed a national emergency. But Weygand wanted badly to reach top personnel of the British, Belgian, and French commands, not at all easy to locate in the smoke and disorder of this lightning invasion that was going all Nazi! That he couldn't link up with Lord John Gort, the B.E.F.'s commander in chief, and soon to craft a Dunkirk retreat, would constitute, in the short run, a source of anger, and later, a great regret. However, Weygand did make it to historic Ypres, where he met a despairing King Leopold III of Belgium, who wouldn't accept retreating and fighting to the west in order to cover a proposed Franco-British offensive southward. Weygand wanted alacrity, but in fact, wasn't well informed on the problems of his general plan: to close the "panzer corridor" by a downward thrust on a southwest line between Bapaume and Cambrai, and one northward from the Somme — supported by the RAF. In theory, the enemy would be sandwiched in between. However, the Belgian king and his advisers had sensible objections — that leaving their relative refuge on the Escaut River for a nocturnal retreat amidst thousands of refugees, and to doubtful positions on the Yser, would mean the loss of even more of their country, of Ostend and other parts of the Channel coast, along with precious ammunition. Weygand then met with General Billotte, commander of France's First Army, and an esteemed alumnus of Syria; but Billotte seemed clearly wounded in spirit. Together they discussed these adaptive offensives, but Billotte felt that the French, battered by their retreat from the Dyle, couldn't negotiate such operations. Even on the defensive, they were only just holding tentative positions. Right after the meeting, Billotte then got into a bad automobile accident, which put him in a coma, and within days, brought his death. Despite obvious depression, he was the one general who might have maintained cohesion with British and Belgian allies. Now all seemed to be conspiring against Weygand, including Gort arriving to his summons only after his departure; had they met, perhaps Gort would have succumbed to the general's verve and feeling for the English, keeping his forces more powerfully in the game, and altering an evacuation plan he was soon to sell Churchill. Some argue, however, that he played ball too *long* with this overly ambitious "Weygand Plan," and that he should have pushed the Dunkirk withdrawal on Churchill earlier than he did.[8]

With the contemporaneous Nazi capture of another top French general, Henri Giraud, whose troops had been mis-employed by Gamelin, there was nothing auspicious in the North. Not that Weygand had time to rue; he was focused entirely on acting in the present. The only use he made of the past was to appeal to all sons of the Great War *poilus* to now give their best. He saw how pounded and almost out of commission the Calais airfield was, then took a complicated trip back to Dunkirk, eluding the Nazis, and thence traveled by torpedo boat across the Channel toward Dover, and back to Cherbourg, with no German mines blowing him to smithereens, as might have happened. En route, he spoke with as many French soldiers as he could about this grave situation on ground and air, and he had now seen enough for himself of the omnipresent chaos — summaries he had first received in Paris far underestimating how extensively the Germans and their untrammeled speed had made, and were still making, a mockery of every French position.[9]

Weygand nonetheless rallied his French response, based to a degree on previous Gamelin orders, against combined Nazi use of panzers and air pulverization; and it included a hesitant compromise by the Belgians the morning of May 22 — withdrawal to the Lys River for covering operations, but no further. Just back from his trip, Weygand then had a meeting with Churchill and Reynaud in Paris, slated for one P.M. May 22, and leaving him no time even to shave. Churchill and the English generals there appreciated Weygand's youthful vivacity, but the leaden atmosphere at the fort of Vincennes seemed much as it had been under Gamelin. The French commander's sole desire was to counterattack these marauding Nazis — something that should have been done a week earlier — using what remained of the French First Army and B.E.F. from the north; and a new, beefed-up group coming up from the Somme. In reality, too many Allied tanks and too many aircraft were already gone — disabled, destroyed, or sometimes simply unfindable. Orders that were sent didn't always arrive (the Belgians, for example, remained confused about their next steps for the next several days); units that were supposed to be full divisions were anything but. Crowded roads greatly intensified these military problems, making mobility something one could discuss only on paper; and Weygand (still lacking firm data) was undoubtedly overstating his case for these offensives that simply could not be mounted, but which kept Churchill a little longer in the optimistic dark![10]

One problem was the lack of a secure base of operations at Arras, where the British were now fighting desperately, impressing Rommel by their fierce ardor. But on May 22, Nazi forces were already getting west of the town, and the British by the next day were readying an evacuation. This really doomed Weygand's offensives to be launched from that area. However, a long-term benefit of the Arras fighting was its status as one of several holding actions that ultimately made the low-odds Dunkirk operation the success it would become. For at Arras, even the go-ahead Rommel was given pause by how well the British were fighting, adding to Hitler's general, and still mystifying, panzer "pause" plan.[11]

On May 24 came Lord Gort's first pronouncement on withdrawal from Dunkirk, presaging the end for Britain's war effort in France. It came against the background of British and French squabbling while defending nearby Boulogne, allied cooperation worsening by the day. British evacuation from the besieged city began unilaterally, before the French even knew about it. A more important Calais seemed, on the face of it, easier to hold, given marshland and numerous irrigation ditches there, and strong ramparts. Here, indeed, the B.E.F. fought to the death to support their allies, as "the last major sacrifice that Britain was going to make in that lost cause," according to Michael Glover. From May 25 the British knew the war in France was essentially done, and defense of Calais only continued into the next day as a holding action to slow up and kill off enemy soldiers oriented now toward Dunkirk.[12]

Weygand, meanwhile, had continued on as Gamelin's peripatetic antithesis, often traveling two or three hundred kilometers a day to get the French metronome aligned with the Germans'. He still wanted a two-pronged offensive, but by May 25 this was definitively in limbo. Talk of an armistice had already surfaced at certain meetings, especially given that French forces were now grossly outnumbered and outarmed. The Dunkirk operation was soon going full throttle, and rapidly had to take priority over any major southward — or northward — movement of troops. Weygand was at first against the evacuation plan, but the crucial nature of Dunkirk only became exaggerated when adjacent ports fell — Boulogne May 25, Calais the next day. Then in the midst of the Dunkirk operation, Leopold III — having seen enough of his troops slaughtered on the Lys — decided to remove Belgium from the war, doing so May 28. No more aid could be had from that ally, either; disdaining an armistice, his country had fully capitulated.

The Dunkirk story has been told and retold, but remains one of the most stirring actions of World War II: suicidal fighting and the disappearance of entire regiments in rearguard "perimeters" supporting the operation, as well as wholesale SS executions; nerve-wracked, often wounded soldiers wending their way to the coast and patiently awaiting conveyance; ships and beaches strafed relentlessly from the air; men shedding their arms to avoid overloading boats; ghastly drownings of exhausted, cramp-wracked swimmers; engineers hastily constructing jetties; great RAF sacrifices in the air, and spirited French resistance at Lille (where Weygand gave up 35,000 as prisoners) — the story still fascinates, especially in Hugh Sebag-Montefiore's recent, masterly account. All manner of boats to remove troops — from ferries to dinghies — allowed the operation a chance at success well beyond initial estimates of 45,000 possibly making it out: but success for *whom*? Only after the Belgian capitulation did Weygand cede to the idea of any of France's forces exiting along with the British (May 29). But of course that had to receive English assent, and on May 31 in Paris the French commander stood up forcefully to Churchill, persuading him to take more French servicemen along with his own (about 165,000 men already out, according to the British prime minister, but at that point, only some 15,000 French). Weygand also kept pushing to keep the operation going when the British wished to end it — and thus, it persisted into the early hours of June 4, amidst continuing murderous fire from land, sea, and air. The fact that over 100,000 French got out was not least among Weygand's achievements during this debacle that soon became the Fall of France.[13]

French courage — of soldiers fighting in the rear of this massive maritime enterprise and surrendering there — certainly played a role in the Dunkirk operation's legendary success. But there had also been linguistic misunderstandings on the beaches, and enhanced Anglophobia as a result. The government in nervous Paris, meanwhile, remained inconsistent and confused, and Weygand was now concentrated on moving southward to hold his bridgeheads on the Somme. There were still frequent and vain French requests for more British air support; however, Churchill and his generals had now logically committed everything to defending their own island. France's military leaders knew they were essentially done; yet on June 5, Weygand announced the Battle for France with a plea to all French soldiers — that they must fight as fervently as they could along the new "Weygand Line."[14] If Reynaud had once seen him as a hope, that politician was now only intermittently supportive, and among the rest in the cabinet, ideas of capitulation were taking firmer hold. Yet through to about June 7 there was much gallant fighting by revivified French soldiers, slowing up the Nazis' advance. Even if belatedly, they were now being directed by a leader who inspired.

Then, as the Weygand Line on the Somme and Aisne was breached, and the French blew up bridges in cities like Rouen, the Germans prepared to cross the Seine, the last real line of defense before Paris. Their inexorable armored units, pounding, ubiquitous aircraft, and waves of infantry were simply too much for these disorganized, badly equipped defenders. And the Italians looked certain to come in as well against France, as they did June 10. A grateful Weygand — anything but a Joffre — kept thanking French troops for these last, brave efforts in the field. But as the Germans began crossing the Seine, he felt a huge gulf between himself and the militarily less realistic Reynaud. He simply did not want to varnish the situation with colors of false hope for a government now rushing out to Tours in the west of France.

Weygand had made what still seems a sensible decision — to call Paris an "open city," considering it ill-advised to emulate the resistance of 1870 there. This time it would lead to the destruction by a murderous foe of a monumental series of beauties nothing could replace — and as much as anyone, Weygand cared about the layered past on Parisian streets.[15]

Churchill now demanded a prompt meeting of the Supreme War Council, and on June 11 through the morning of June 12, he and his entourage met French leaders at their new General Headquarters of Briare on the Loire. Weygand offered no hope for holding the line before Paris, yet asked that every available British plane be dispatched to France, which England's prime minister refused. He did try to rally Weygand's spirits, and those of an effaced Reynaud, evoking the spring of 1918 in France, and how a rebound via land operations had then occurred in similarly dismal circumstances. But Weygand knew how different this conflict was from the previous one. Churchill also said that if the French could make it to the spring of 1941, there would be 20 or 25 British divisions to help them out. No Pollyanna, Weygand grew angry with such proposals, realizing how vague they were. The British, in turn, became irritated with France's refusal to permit bombing of Italy from southern French bases (stemming from Reynaud's fear of reprisals on cities like Marseille).[16]

With Paris now a dead cert for German occupation, Weygand still covered his army, refusing to blame his soldiers or even the former shaper of policy, Gamelin, who had made obvious errors leading up to the catastrophe. Reynaud's vicissitudes were, however, a major problem at this point. For the French prime minister could at times talk earnestly, if unfactually, of a Breton redoubt, or fighting on in North Africa; and at others, of simply giving up. He and other key politicians had already managed to interfere a good deal with Weygand's command. Too many cooks were spoiling what remained of a bad broth, as Weygand began focusing only on procuring a relatively suitable armistice with the Germans. His soon-opposite number, Charles de Gaulle, newly promoted by Weygand to brigadier-general, had just come into the government as under-secretary of state for defense. And suddenly he revolted oedipally against the army's big bonnets, including the commander in chief! Like Reynaud (and well connected to the latter), de Gaulle went all over the lot with ideas to elude a now ineluctable debacle. He was not one who could easily obey, and this the commander in chief (with his history of loyalty to those outranking him) could not abide.

Anything but grateful, de Gaulle backbit Weygand plenty, trying to get General Huntziger on side to replace him, and making personal, unauthorized overtures to Churchill. However, Weygand was too preoccupied with selling the idea of an armistice (before more French land was lost, not to mention lives) to watch his back. His son Jacques argues that he was *never* good at that anyway, and Weygand's wife would also try to warn him about human duplicity; but right now, too much was urgent to expend energy bringing such as *le grand Charles* into line.[17]

On June 12 Weygand was summoned to Tours, and after a trip at first delayed by a throng of refugees, the road became easier to travel once the bulk turned southward to what would become the Unoccupied Zone. When he met with cabinet members at the Chateau de Cangé, he was simply flabbergasted by Reynaud and several other ministers deferring any idea of an armistice. Where was the *time* for this delay going to come from? Reynaud at first hoped that Churchill's imminent arrival might bring him something from across the Channel, and he was also busy framing a wire to America's President Roosevelt, with the idea that that still-isolationist nation would come into the war — fast. Both were examples of magical thinking; but another reason to keep fighting (proffered by politicians shielded from chaos and suffering in the field) was that *any* armistice was bound to be abhorrent, and that France would lose its fine fleet in the process. Weygand said he wouldn't allow that to happen, arguing instead for an empirical, flexible stance; in other words, for seeing exactly what the Germans might be willing to vouchsafe, then acting. However, only Pétain and two other ministers in the cabinet supported this stance. Say what one wanted, both Weygand and Pétain had had distinguished military records. Both — but moreso Weygand — knew the realities of continuing the struggle in Brittany, or in Africa, and how chimerically the prime minister was speaking, given the state of France's army. The commander had witnessed first hand the lack of materiel and disarray in what remained of French forces, and was astonished that these politicians didn't seem to care about men dying in a lost cause each day, overwhelmed by a far better-equipped enemy.

Late in the afternoon of June 13, Weygand was back in Tours — Churchill, flying again with considerable bravery, had now arrived there; and instead of a collective meeting, the British prime minister first had a tête-à-tête with his French counterpart at the city's prefecture. Here Reynaud declared that France would keep going, surprising his own, non-consulted cabinet, and of course Weygand. German divisions were now approaching Chartres, and while in Tours, the commander in chief received a message that they would certainly reach Paris next day. This is the point when Weygand presciently suggested that the French fleet be transferred *immediately* to North African ports — and again, wasn't heeded.

Meanwhile, rumors flew aplenty, and there was one announcing a French

Communist coup in Paris (the kind of rumor frequently heard in the besieged capital of 1870); and Weygand briefly took it seriously. Some were saying that the red flag was now aloft over the prime minister's Hôtel Matignon, and that the influential French Communist, Jacques Duclos, reigned at the Elysée. A quick call from Minister of the Interior Georges Mandel to Paris' prefect of police promptly quashed this canard. But was Weygand simply being an hysterical anti–Communist? Especially given the fact that France's Communist Party, once courageous in opposing the Munich accord, was then made illegal by Daladier's government after the outbreak of war — for following the Soviets, partnered with the Nazis and benefiting in Eastern Europe. Or that the French party's secretary-general, Maurice Thorez, had deserted his army unit to camp almost the entire war, as it turned out, in the Soviet Union![18]

Amidst the din of such rumors, and contradictory views swirling among cabinet ministers, Weygand was trying to force the government to tell French soldiers why they must continue fighting and dying. He also reminded Reynaud that the Roman Senate had stayed in *Rome* when barbarians once poured in to that great capital. Government figures thinking of running to North Africa would invite more Nazi gobbling of France, the general averred; and they would be pursued there, too. Now and then, Weygand examined the leather case he had kept with him since 1918, once bearing Foch's armistice terms. And he wondered briefly again how Foch would handle the present crisis, then remained with his own *idée fixe*: to try and preserve the most he could of France, its empire, and its army via another armistice.

On the fateful day of June 14, Weygand was back at G.H.Q., while the Germans entered Paris that morning. The same day he received official news of the government migrating south from Tours to Bordeaux. And to that city Weygand was summoned — this time in a message emanating from Pétain. He arrived the afternoon of the next day, with a stiff neck owing to a minor car accident, and first met privately with Reynaud, who was talking in panicked tones of the Dutch and Belgian monarchs, and how their countries had capitulated. Speaking to this elected official, Weygand saw no analogy at all, and was furious even at the idea of capitulation. He had learned from childhood not to give things away without fighting; now he was applying that lesson to the military, political, national stage of France. More bad news arrived — that the British (as was natural at this point) would no longer follow French military orders. Having endured a last tragic sacrifice in France — of the legendary 51st Highlanders division — all they wanted now was to effect evacuations from ports like Le Havre and Saint-Nazaire. Sir Alan Brooke was the B.E.F.'s new, no-nonsense commander, and easily convinced Churchill on this pullout policy.[19] The evening of the 15th Reynaud also turned the screws again, declaring that his ministers *all* desired capitulation, and that such a request must come from the army, and specifically, from its commander! To which Weygand, barely mastering his temper, refused again — another significant legacy to both his country and the many living in its empire. Why should the government flee the onus of its own misguided policies? He not only told that to Reynaud, but to cover his back, repeated it to President Albert Lebrun.

The military's General Headquarters had now moved to Vichy, and thence Weygand traveled that night. French fighting (and retreating) still went on, but all commanders in the field now desired an armistice, especially before refugees completely disaggregated what was left of a coherent army. A peripatetic Weygand flew back next day at 10 A.M. to Bordeaux, relaying this collective wish, and that of soldiers ranking below the generals. Reynaud's flip-flops were, however, at an end — word reaching Weygand of his resignation, and Reynaud's own recommendation that the president ask Marshal Pétain to form a new government. Of course the chameleon (or was that simply weak?) Reynaud knew well that Pétain supported an armistice, not capitulation.[20]

Once Reynaud resigned June 16, the request for an armistice under Pétain's new government became a foregone conclusion. The former hero of World War I would not buy Churchill's hasty idea for an Anglo-French Union, in return for all French warships somehow reaching English ports. Almost immediately, the Marshal called for Weygand as his minister of national defense; and Weygand felt that he must accept the position, in order to supervise the creation of an agreement preserving as much as possible for France. He would also continue on as commander in chief until the end of hostilities.

Weygand quickly used his added clout to quash the appointment of a clearly defeatist Pierre Laval as foreign minister, instead recommending a graduate of the Ecole Polytechnique, and veteran of World War I, Paul Baudouin. Laval had already tried to blackmail Pétain — he would come in to the government *only* with the foreign minister's portfolio; but at this juncture he ceded. In the midst of a catastrophe Weygand had once more done something important; however, this was to be but the first swallow of a long summer trying to counter the arch-appeaser, Laval.

On June 17 at 9 A.M., Weygand got right to work detouring a monster order of U.S. aircraft (including 93 Northrops, 50 Curtises, and 100 Glenn Martins) to Britain. Never would he be an Anglophobe; nor would he ever desire even a smidgen of enduring collaboration with the Nazis. He also diverted France's uranium to the English, and neither of these acts were of small importance in that nation's own fight for survival. As for the French fleet that Weygand had wanted dispatched June 13 to French North Africa, he was now going to require luck to protect it in an armistice.

The Germans were still mopping up in the French provinces, and demands for the end of fighting (except in the isolated Maginot Line) multiplied. France's Army of the Alps was, however, prepared to affront the invading Italians, even as south-marching Germans soon began inflicting a trap door crunch from their rear. In big French cities not yet occupied, mayors like Lyon's Edouard Herriot demanded no destruction of bridges, and an "open city" approach mirroring that of Paris; and mayors of smaller cities and towns followed suit. From Morocco, resident-general and military commander Charles Noguès telegraphed the government, concerning *his* fears of France losing North Africa. Ironically, Weygand's policy would preserve it from the insatiable, methodical Nazis — but few knew that in these confused days.

By June 18, still working frantically, Weygand got the entire cabinet to agree that if the Germans took over the French fleet, there would *be* no armistice. For the general there were implacable *sine qua nons*; and his mindset, so different from Reynaud's, much less Laval's, now came in handy, as did his prestige from helping craft an armisticed end to the last world war.[21]

Through Spanish intermediaries, the Germans replied to a French query, declaring that they would indeed be willing to negotiate an armistice (this in the early morning of June 19). But there would need to be negotiations as well with the Italians. The French got back to the Spanish, signaling their willingness to proceed, and choosing their armistice delegation — General Charles Huntziger, a commander in the field whom Weygand admired, heading it up; and a handful of others on the committee, including General Henri Parisot, father of Serge-Henri Parisot, and fresh from a position of seven years as military attaché in Rome, to dicker with the Italians. The main French delegation (affronting the Nazis) was spirited to the same area of France where the armistice of World War I had occurred, and there received German terms. Over a bad connection Huntziger reached Weygand, who first asked him for an overall impression. "Very harsh" were Huntziger's words (and indeed, reading through the German articles gives exactly that impression today).[22]

Weygand's amanuensis, Captain Gasser, wrote down as best as he could what was dictated. The Germans would retain the final text of the document, making their complicated demands hard for the French to digest and to respond to by the deadline of June 22 at 9 A.M. Nazis developed rules, then held to them; and Weygand knew this psychology well. The thoroughness of everything the foe wished to take from the fallen French, both now and potentially, was mind-boggling, and a challenge to anyone but the thorough themselves — which Weygand and his chosen associate, Huntziger, certainly were.

As noted, Weygand's private notebooks contain all the German ideas for revision of Foch's armistice terms of November 1918, and his "no's" to many of them. The Germans were more Machiavellian in their responses of June 1940, and even more obdurate. On the French side this time, there were hopeless queries: for example, asking that Paris be considered part of an eventual unoccupied zone. The Germans replied that conditions on the ground would dictate that — and that they would need to wait and see. It turned out to be a request with no possibility of accommodation. Another major area of concern was French aircraft that the more tough-minded like Weygand and Huntziger did not want used against England. Military aircraft *were* to be delivered to German authorities, but the French asked that they not be employed for warfare; and after discussion with Marshal Goering himself, the response elicited was that once disarmed, these planes would remain under German surveillance, but not be placed in combat. To which of course they could always reply "unless".... The Nazis were certainly ones for legality, or the appearance of it, even when treating the ghettoes of the East; but in actuality, a fluid, ever more savage legality. It is also clear that few Germans at this point gave the British much chance of staying in the war, one reason for such softness as there was in this nonetheless very tough agreement.

The fleet was the specific purview and obsession of Admiral Jean-François Darlan, who had become chief of staff of the Navy under Léon Blum in 1936, and was now minister of marine in Pétain's government. But no matter how much he would later placate the Nazis, Darlan also wanted the French fleet kept from their hands as an instrument of war. So again the French stood firm here — and the Germans agreed (for now) that once hostilities ended with France, that navy would not be used for combat; however, final dispositions were still to be ironed out with a Permanent Armistice Commission headquartered at Wiesbaden, which could bring revisions. In other words, here was another slim reed (made, however, a little more resilient by Darlan's secret resolve to scuttle his ships should the Nazis make their grab).

It was long easy to believe that the courageous ones of 1940, in addition to de Gaulle, were the 26 French deputies and one senator who tried to sail on the *Massilia* for North Africa, starting their trip June 21; and who were unfortunately apprehended several days later, after the armistice was signed. The group included Daladier, and a few deputies of Jewish origins, such as Jean Zay (half–Jewish, in actuality), and a more conservative Mandel, both to be murdered later in the war. However, there were other forms of courage — even at the initial point of armistice-making, not to mention in succeeding months and years — necessary to confront figures like General Wilhelm Keitel, and the Nazis generally.

Leaving out the genetic in Weygand, perhaps it took the outsider, as he had been, to understand and really see inside cultures as they were. One swath of his *Recalled to Service* is very apposite here — on the Germans, particularly of this terrifying era. Weygand was referring both to the armistice, then to interminable cat and mouse debates with Nazi authorities that followed, as they tried unremittingly to alter and take more than what the armistice granted. He was also writing of the orders he gave other French officers to hide all the arms they could, which would cost a number of them (such as General Aubert Frère) ghastly imprisonment in Germany, and in quite a number of cases, their deaths.[23]

Responding to critiques that he might have been endangering his countrymen by countering the insatiable Nazis at every turn, here is how Weygand recalls his rebuttal:

> The German, we said, only respects those who make a stand against him. He despises the resigned, and to accept molestation without protest is to invite fresh exactions. The German, whose only law is his own interest and who means to dominate everywhere, is concerned nevertheless to seem to be acting in accordance with justice. Thus, to allow him, through silence, an appearance of justice is to give him the principal satisfaction demanded by his hypocrisy.... Finally, most surprising thing of all, the German wants to be loved whatever he does. Why should he not be, after all, if he "correctly" demands only what he is allowed to believe to be legitimate? Thus, in making no public protest against injustice, we should become accomplices in it and slip little by little into enslavement.[24]

Lest Weygand appear in this remarkable passage simply a hortatory coach on the sidelines, that philosophy would henceforth be seen in his doggedly thorough, courageous actions during ensuing months and years. As for the armistice, in the end, the French did, uncertainly, retain their navy; got a roughly two-fifths swath of their territory unoccupied, mostly in southern France, even if it took time for the Germans to depart major cities like Lyon, Saint-Etienne, or Clermont-Ferrand; and were permitted an army of 100,000 soldiers, ostensibly to keep order in the country, but in fact, to become the kernel of a secret army of revenge that would be a main Weygand preoccupation. Better, the French empire would remain intact too, if always vulnerable. And the Nazis, feeling that they were to a degree "had" in these armistice negotiations — or, oxymoronic as it sounds, too kind (despite massive amounts of infrastructure, materials, and foodstuffs that they *did* take, and huge costs to the French) — wanted very soon to revise armistice terms heavily! Weygand's mettle would rapidly, and repetitively, be tested.

Signature of the armistice in the same railway car of World War I, and in the same forest clearing of Rethondes, amidst German hoopla, and *diktat* statements in reverse on how Germany *hadn't* caused World War I, and *had* been traduced at the end of it: all this was mere insult added to injury. On the evening of June 23, French negotiations for an armistice with Italy then began in a more relaxed atmosphere, with this more leisurely foe getting a much smaller part of France to run in its Southeast, and armistice control commissions in North Africa (with the Germans soon to come down and, as was their wont, improve on the job). France would not agree to total demobilization and disarmament in North Africa and the Levant — for fear of losing their colonial subjects; while simultaneously, they were too weak, as Weygand understood, to continue the fight militarily from the other side of the Mediterranean.[25] Signatures apposed, fighting was completely over June 25, the outnumbered Army of the Alps having repelled the Italians; and the surprised holdouts of the Maginot Line finding it harder yet to surrender.

Weygand of course received much *a posteriori* criticism for helping craft, then for accepting this armistice agreement; but one can no longer accept uncritically the old, one-dimensional view — especially from Americans — that something "out there" could have been tried after Paris and much of France had fallen. William L. Shirer, writing in the "America superior" mode of a not yet riotous part of the '60s, before publishing at the end of that decade, took Weygand to task for ignoring General Noguès in Morocco, to the effect that North Africa could provide a military base against the Nazis. According to Colonel Serge-Henri Parisot in 2006 — unlike the sentenced Noguès (after the Allied invasion of 1942), an "official Resistant" who also knew North Africa well — this idea was "parfaitement utopique." All such estimates ignored the state of France itself: its capital occupied, its people clogging roads in the millions, holding on to mere shreds of a former existence, and themselves overwhelmingly favoring an end to hostilities.[26]

Noguès' worry was that due to the armistice, the Germans would take over French North Africa; but precisely because Weygand and his associates got what they did, and the general then put his life on the line holding the Germans to it, this never materialized. Had there been a premature attempt at an armed uprising in North Africa, all of France would likely have been occupied, and much property and many people destroyed in the process. North Africa would surely have fallen into the German grasp as well. Weygand always said that it was better to hold what one could, and patiently prepare the ground, including for what became the Allied invasion of November 1942. This is obviously in line with William Langer's more contemporary (that is, nearer to the events), and less "20/20 hindsight" viewpoint.[27] Of

Formulation of a Franco-German Armistice of 1940, in the same railway coach, and at the same site in the forest of Compiègne where Marshal Foch and General Weygand had presented terms to the Germans in November 1918 (Bettmann/CORBIS).

course, the debate will continue among historians. But who, as of June 22, 1940, could then foresee the British staying alive? Or the Russians eventually provoked into war with the Nazis? The armistice *was* a tough one, even a diktat; however, the French fleet never did fall into German hands, about two-fifths of France retained some autonomy, there was at least a French government that did not need fully to collaborate, and there was no *gauleiter* to run the show as brutally as he liked. Most crucially, the French empire remained an empire, and therefore, a potential launching pad for a comeback.

The most prestigious opponent of the armistice was Charles de Gaulle, believing that France's Marne recovery of World War I could have happened again in this conflict, but from across the Mediterranean. Unfair to Weygand, and not bothering to distinguish between the words "capitulation" and "armistice," de Gaulle was critical of the commander in chief in his war memoirs, and Weygand wrote an elegant, intelligent riposte in a book he published during the mid–1950s.[28]

De Gaulle pointed to Weygand's supposed surprise at what motorized warfare could wreak, when as seen, Weygand had long been warning of

France's need to go down that strategic route. However, the most important chapter in Weygand's book-length rejoinder is on de Gaulle's idea of continuing the fight in North Africa. Foch's old World War I staff man is very specific on the lack of arms, war industry factories, and soldiers (many having been transferred to the mainland) then in Afrique Française du Nord (A.F.N.). He is also much more specific than the generalizing de Gaulle on the time element and its exigencies. Reynaud had only begun talking of a North Africa operation from May 29. By that time, as Weygand correctly notes, "the situation ... was so tense that days, even hours, had their value...." From the optic of his important military positions of the '30s, Weygand knew how much actual preparation time would have been necessary to reinforce A.F.N. sufficiently, so that it could become an immediate war theater. And the English? Their vague promises notwithstanding, they had their own fish to fry, and couldn't have been of much aid transporting up to a half a million men across the Mediterranean; they had already *had* their Dunkirk. Weygand declares pithily — and correctly — that de Gaulle failed to factor in "the forces — their quality, proportion, distances, [and] the weather"; and therefore, his rapid suppositions simply reveal "an impardonable légèreté."[29]

One final problem was also gravely underestimated by the same generalizing de Gaulle who got under the skin of Churchill and Roosevelt in wartime, and probably for similar reasons. And that is, again, how the Germans would have responded to the French government's maladroit attempts at continuing hostilities in North Africa. Given their alliance with Italy, the Nazis could easily have rushed into French Tunisia via Tripoli, Weygand avers, using naval and air bases on Italian Sardinia or Sicily. Given Franco's wish to expand the small slice of Morocco he held, and to stay on the Nazis' good side, they could easily have entered A.F.N. from that direction, too, as indeed they later planned illegally to do after the armistice. And the British at Gibraltar were utterly weak at the time. All this the preachy, vague, and compared to Weygand, less literarily tasteful de Gaulle seemed to ignore. There is little doubt that Weygand is correct in his aphoristic summation: "To transport the struggle to North Africa in June 1940 would have meant losing it."[30]

It *is* true, however, that the armistice would rapidly and legitimately have constituted a disaster had Weygand and his best associates not then proceeded to fight almost daily, and with much bravery and industry, to hold to everything in it, and not grant the coveting Nazis anything more. Some of this again remained Weygand's psychology going back to his early years. Stand up to the Germans, yes; but *don't* revolt against established authorities in the French army or at the head of the political system. That included his old World War I colleague, Pétain, whom Weygand admired militarily, but whom he considered less adept politically. This quality of obedience was pure Weygand — and as stressed, a habit learned (for survival) in his childhood, and in the army. He had already done many things he would have liked not to do; he wasn't in the world of journalism (Shirer was a media man who actually witnessed the armistice, but as a protected American, then had somewhere safe to go). Nor was he safely ensconced like de Gaulle in Britain. Weygand simply couldn't dissert on these matters from some comfortable position of shelter![31]

9

Countering Germany as Vichy Defense Minister

Marshal Pétain had made Weygand defense minister June 17, but he didn't occupy the position for very long — a matter of eleven weeks only, including as Vichy's minister of national defense, once the German-approved government chose that spa town as its supposedly temporary headquarters. (Too many bigger cities in the south had problems precluding their selection.) There was a scramble for space at Vichy, but the big hotels basically worked as locations for ministries, including Weygand's at the Hotel Thermal. Amidst near unanimity in France for giving Pétain extensive powers as head of the French state, there were, however, big divisions even in Vichy's early days, with the self-made businessman-politician, Pierre Laval, and Admiral Darlan on a more appeasement-oriented flank; and Weygand emphatically on an opposite one. Weygand's obdurate stance vis-à-vis constant German demands for armistice alterations, and his attempts to repel those demands both with public protests, or ones made through proper channels to armistice authorities at Wiesbaden, increasingly brought him opprobrium in Vichy meetings, especially from those who considered a German victory inevitable, along with a formal peace. As defense minister, Weygand also fought the heavy-handed absorption of parts of Alsace and Lorraine that had once been under the Germans before 1914, and from which many inhabitants were to be thrust out, including young men sent unwillingly to Nazi war theaters. He opposed German revisions in the North of France, isolating certain parts, particularly near the Channel, and placing them under totally military occupation. And the sad dismantling of French machinery in countless factories, or of military hardware sent to Germany for its use, another phenomenon that went well beyond the armistice, raised Weygand's public ire; as did German destruction of certain French academic libraries or laboratories (such as at the Collège de France), or wholesale pilfering. Not to mention the steep increase in occupation costs which simply bled the French; the miring of nearly 2,000,000 prisoners of war in anything but temporary stalags; and transmogrification of the demarcation line between Occupied and Unoccupied France into a kind of Berlin wall, if with unusual vicissitudes. All these things had to be fought, then fought again and again. Weygand's own precision, thoroughness, and dogged ability to confront were supremely tested by this Nazi foe.[1]

But the German demand that rankled most, and was most serious, given the precariousness of France's empire, arrived on the defense minister's desk July 16, 1940—from the head of the French armistice delegation to Germany, the Alsatian General Huntziger. It was a copy of a letter sent by Hitler to Marshal Pétain, demanding Nazi use of eight air bases in French Morocco, including all hangars, with more roads and runways to be constructed entirely by French construction crews, and with a German military commission supervising. The document also stipulated German takeover and employment of the railway from Rabat to Tunis—in other words, of a transportation lifeline spanning French North Africa. Not to mention use of key French North African ports, and those on the southern coast of France! And French merchant marine ships to transport Nazi personnel to all these places, and with German escort vessels to ensure these French crews stayed in line. The Germans also wanted all meteorological stations placed at their disposal, and other installations too, whence they could transmit messages. All this constituted much more than just an entering wedge when it came to Nazi infiltration of an empire Hitler had left intact in the original armistice. Among many, François Charles-Roux, a career diplomat now in Vichy's Foreign Ministry, was stunned by these proposals signifying "military occupation of our North Africa, and Germany's use, for its military needs, of our Mediterranean coast and of our merchant marine in the Mediterranean"—truly "colossal demands!" And ones clearly showing that no German agreement could be taken as final, and that Nazi appetites of the period remained infinite. In his own letter to Weygand, General Karl von Stülpnagel, president of the German Armistice Commission, framed all this as an ultimatum that had simply to be obeyed. Nothing daunted, the irate defense minister immediately stomped over to see Vice-Premier Laval, and in meetings with that figure, Darlan, Foreign Minister Baudouin, and Finance Minister Yves Bouthillier, forced through a response of absolute rejection, leading the government to stonewall these demands, if in language resembling that of La Fontaine's flattering fox! The letter of refusal to Hitler, drafted by Charles-Roux and ex-ambassador to Berlin and Rome André François-Poncet, then redone by other experts, was full of flowery, courteous bowing to German greatness. And allusions to French compliance with the letter and spirit of the armistice. If a majority of Vichy's inner council supported this policy of a deaf ear, there is no question that without Weygand's adamant stance, things would have gone rapidly worse for the French empire and unoccupied south. The general's actions here typified his courageous brand of "Vichy resistance."[2]

So did his use of the Mers-el-Kébir tragedy of early July, when the British sank elements of the French fleet anchored there, and with great loss of life. Weygand did not know until after the war that there had been a third alternative proffered by the British, and which might have saved those lives — i.e., that the fleet take off for the safety of Martinique in the Caribbean; and here he would later blame admirals Darlan and Gensoul for keeping their stubborn counsel on the matter.[3] But out of bad came a certain good. The charmed life of France's empire in World War II, operating under an Axis shadow, continued in part because Weygand impelled his Direction des Services d'Armistice (D.S.A.), which he placed under General Louis Koeltz, to demand revision of provisions on disarmament and demobilization of French troops in North Africa. Now, it was pleaded, that empire needed to stay strong against the British and other possible sources of incursion! In this demand for more troops in Africa, the French would also benefit from a misguided Anglo-Gaullist attempt to wrest Dakar from Vichy in September. The result was that the French received more and more of what they wanted, if not *sub specie aeternitatis*. At the same time, Weygand *also* tried to soften Britain's blockade of goods it feared would land in Nazi hands, but which intensified French suffering.[4]

Defense of the empire — the only trump card left in the French deck — was among Weygand's key concerns while at the Defense Ministry, and profuse official correspondence he maintained on the subject shows this well. For openers, the D.S.A. (under his ministry) negotiated with Germans and Italians to assure a certain amount of airplane service between metropolitan France and Algiers (Algiers-Marignane return flights three times a week), Tunis (one per week), Oran (one per week), etc.[5] And always proactive, Weygand kept demanding current, precise information on the different parts of the empire, maintaining a large correspondence with Vichy's colonial secretary, Henri Lémery, a mulatto from Martinique slated, like Weygand, not to last long in his position. There were many documents where Lémery would indicate "possible claims" or "vague possibilities" when it came to Italians, Spanish, and especially, the Germans. In one letter to Weygand of August 21, 1940, the colonial minister showed his differences from the proactive defense minister, noting that "a study on probable requirements of Germany and Italy concerning our colonial domains" was hard to provide, given that "we are not in control of events." As for a "considerable work" that Weygand had demanded on the economic, military, and political attributes of the colonies, again, Lémery pleaded difficulties of execution. To which Weygand replied sharply, declaring that "the goal I am pursuing is to prepare for *discussions* with our adversaries, when the time comes, and for the best *defense* against their demands." Hence, he felt, the French government must know everything in advance about the value of its colonial territories, without of course advertising any of that to the Germans and Italians, "in order not to arouse appetites which they perhaps do not yet have!" Much documentation on the colonies — including precise, extensive tables — followed. When it came to keeping the empire from Axis enemies, Weygand would remain a dedicated anticipator, one who countenanced no excuses from those he set working on the problem.[6]

In addition to Germany, the most fearsome threat to the French empire, Fascist Italy, had long set sights on certain parts, especially Tunisia, owing in part to a large population of Italian settlers there, as well as its resources and strategic location. They were also hoping to make incursions into the Algerian province around Constantine, as well as French Somaliland, and African territory south of Libya down to the lake of Chad. And if Spain's Franco was off and on about trying to gobble French Morocco, he was certainly encouraged in that aim by Il Duce. In the New World, meanwhile, Brazil made claims on French Guyana, while others saw French Caribbean islands such as Martinique and Guadeloupe as potential prizes. The vulnerable mandates of Syria and Lebanon also aroused appetites, while the Germans, who desired complete revenge on 1919 peace-makers, could feasibly envisage a potential take-over of French Togo and Cameroon, formerly their African colonies.[7]

One part of the empire that presented more than the usual amount of complexities made Weygand's ministry resort to an elaborate balancing act through that summer of 1940: French Indochina, now threatened by a new imperial power of increasing ferocity and means, the Japanese. Here his responses were not typical of the way he dealt with the Germans, but in this case, perhaps all that he could muster. The story began at the time of the armistice, when the governor-general of Indochina, General Georges Catroux, bowed to Japanese pressure, allowing them a control commission in the north of Vietnam (Tonkin). In good French proconsular tradition, Catroux did this on his own. The fledgling French government at Vichy then fired him from the position, replacing him on July 20 with Admiral Jean Decoux, commander in chief of France's navy in the Orient, and, despite French weakness, inclined at all costs to stand up to the Japanese.

In short, France had yet another redoubtable foe on its hands, particularly after the Japanese Control Commission took up residence in Tonkin, June 29. French Foreign Minister Baudouin then decided to open bilateral negotiations between Vichy and Japanese government authorities. This was partly due to Decoux' firm attitude, wishing to retract concessions made to this foe — who, like the Nazis, possessed a gargantuan appetite for territory. In early August, Arsène Henry, French ambassador in Tokyo, reported a Japanese ultimatum, in which they demanded passage through Tonkin for their armies, and takeover of certain French air bases in Vietnam.

Unlike in his dealings with the Germans, Weygand felt himself to be the new kid in town when it came to these issues, and he sought expert advice from authorities like General Bührer, chief of staff of French colonial forces, on how possible French defense of Indochina really was against a Japanese military incursion. Weygand's instinct was, as usual, to stand firm, and Bührer supported him, hoping that over 100,000 French soldiers there, and some 100 airplanes might serve as a deterrent. But Foreign Minister Baudouin was becoming a more appeasing force at Vichy, with Weygand's strong voice and ideas increasingly outnumbered, and out-talked. So negotiations began in earnest, with the French willing to allow the Japanese to send supplies through Tonkin en route to China, while in return, there must be no encroachment on French colonial territory. This muddy picture became muddier when the Chinese indicated that were this to happen, *they* would then attack southward into what is now North Vietnam to inhibit a Japanese advance by that route. Meanwhile, Decoux in Indochina, calling frantically for arms, remained strong in defense of *his* series of colonies or protectorates, just as General Charles Noguès would in Morocco.

The archives are replete with correspondence on this threat to Indochina, involving Weygand and his ministry. A typical document he sought and received was penned by Bührer, August 12, 1941—"Note on the Possibilities of Defense of Indochina and Particularly of Tonkin," stamped "secret." Bührer felt that the French could defend themselves here *only* if the Germans and Italians allowed them the freedom to do so. Reading this report, one gains a sense of the complexities simply of this theater that far away in Vichy, Weygand had somehow to try and unravel. Japan desired a serious foothold in French Indochina, both for economic reasons, and as "champion of a yellow Asia"—which for the moment, the U.S. was mostly inhibiting in this part of the world. Bührer, perhaps hoping against hope, felt that English, American, and Dutch aims in the region ought to allow them all to stand firm in common—"for maintenance of the status quo." Weygand certainly wanted to move more arms to Vietnam, but transports had to be OK'd with German and Italian armistice commissions, and these were notoriously dilatory—which was probably the main reason Weygand inclined (against his instincts) toward negotiations. At least in those, the French would try valiantly to retain the most they could get, as evidenced by a typical telegram sent to the Defense Ministry from Arsène Henry in Tokyo (August 21, 1940): "Despite a long discussion, it was impossible to reconcile our points of view."[8]

Weygand ardently desired American aid for French Indochina, but again, Foreign Minister Baudouin raised a caution light on a mission sent to Washington in order to buy war materials for use there. As Baudouin told Weygand in a letter of August 13, 1940, "Suppose these arms purchases from the U.S. were possible, they would risk alarming Tokyo, and in my opinion, the danger of nettling Japanese sensibilities is not worth the strengthening of our defenses expected from such acquisitions." Baudouin mentioned the contrary view of the colonial minister, who felt that the German and Italian armistice commissions would let all this pass, and that going to the States for military aid was the sole way to buttress French Indochina; however, Baudouin considered it unlikely that the Reich, with its links to Japan, would allow such American acquisitions to go through. Oddly enough, the same sorts of arguments would be heard even when the U.S. became more of a belligerent, and when Weygand crafted economic-military accords with them in North Africa (see next chapter). Instead of concluding firmly here, Baudouin ended by throwing the ball into Weygand's side of the court, asking him what *he* thought of the matter![9]

Weygand's response, typically stamped "SECRET," was dated August 20, 1940, and even as Decoux kept calling for arms before the onset of the rainy season, seemed to incline to Baudouin's optic, averring that such purchases at present did seem risky. As Weygand put it, they could "kindle Japanese susceptibilities, and in addition, never be delivered!"[10]

Negotiations dragged on until their conclusion in the next month, with the Japanese gaining an ever stronger foothold in French Indochina. Meanwhile, the outgunned Weygand was becoming persona non grata in his important position at Vichy. The opposite number he rankled most in council meetings due to his obdurate tone and policies was Laval, whose know-it-all manner and willingness to placate the Nazis Weygand openly despised. Their continuing wrangles were what finally doomed his position at the National Defense Ministry, which he was certainly using as a springboard for an army of resistance and revenge.[11]

On the other hand, Weygand all along possessed certain credentials to remain a top player at Vichy. He had had a long history of dealings with Pétain. And from the beginning, he was positive about some of the main changes instituted by the government, including (with certain misgivings) its July 10 constitutional streamlining, producing an important executive function for Pétain, who assumed previous functions of both prime minister and president, and more. Weygand knew, however, that Pétain was old, and that some delegation of authority was necessary; hence the idea of a vice-premier — but unfortunately for the defense minister, the super-ambitious, pro-German, anti–British, and fundamentally untrustworthy Laval was designated there. This was not at *all* what Weygand desired. Nor could he endorse the "dauphinate" idea of an heir to Pétain, who would again be that wily and, in Weygand's view, spineless Laval (and later on, an equally repellent Darlan). In sum, Weygand was not suspect on the grounds of opposing some form of movement back toward traditionalism. Most everyone in France during this era of shock — and of varying stripes — went through a good deal of soul-searching after the defeat; and a document Weygand wrote and gave to the government itself emphasized a return to family, God, and country, a better education system, a higher birth-rate, an end to embittered relations between employers and workers, fewer naturalizations of foreigners — in other words, much that would be embraced by Vichy. In this document, Weygand did not use the term "national revolution" — that came from elsewhere. He also said nothing directly about Jews, but did mention pernicious Masonic influence before the war, and that of capitalism, and of widespread materialism and pleasure-seeking. However, figures well to the left of Weygand had their own ideas of fundamental changes after the "strange defeat" — Marc Bloch, André Gide, and many others coming easily to mind. The great catastrophe had engendered in all but the most cynical ideas of pulling up national socks in some way, shape, or form.[12]

However, Weygand simply hadn't much time to generalize on such ideas or ideals. He was mostly kept busy with detail — starting with getting his new ministry staffed, as well as locating infrastructure and the like to put in place at Vichy. He was also in the top class of ministers who needed to attend meetings every morning at 11 A.M. (the others being Darlan, Laval, Baudouin, Bouthillier, and Raphaël Alibert). And except for Laval, no other minister had the prestige to readily broach issues not on the agenda. For Weygand, armistice haggling remained a key preoccupation, and as seen, an exhausting, repetitive one. Issues like obtaining medical supplies, getting wounded soldiers out of camps, allowing certain generals to cross from one zone to the other (often next to impossible), using certain bridges, setting up proper communications between zones, trying to whittle down enormous German requisitions of cash they wanted delivered on precise dates each month, allowing certain sectors of French infantry to have grenades or mortars were not only concerns for the Defense Ministry (Bouthillier too courageously protested the financial bleeding of France). But many *were*, and Weygand was constantly in touch with Huntziger, France's representative in Wiesbaden, trying to keep rapacious and strict German authorities from asking for more, much more, and at the same time, from reducing French rights and comforts once taken for granted.[13] And in all this, Weygand kept having to oppose other Vichy ministers in an increasingly incendiary atmosphere — on subjects both of great importance, and ones that seemed nonsensical to him. Examples of the latter were the ideas of trying members of the Third Republic political class for the defeat (genesis of the Riom trial), or of founding a single party. Weygand's *idées fixes* were much more practical and pressing, such as encouraging the stockpiling and hiding of French arms, which would cost a number of idealists who followed his directives their lives.

Another was giving the secret service free rein to continue spying on the Axis, which Weygand did without reservation, and again, in the face of opposition. The Service des Renseignements (SR) under the thorough, cultivated Colonel Louis Rivet was allowed to move its installations down to the unoccupied zone, and a new Bureau des Menées Antinationales (M.A.) within it allowed perfect cover for their continuing activities. This bureau was to watch for pro–English or Gaullist maneuvers against Vichy; in practice, Weygand impelled it to help early Resistants, or at least look the other way, and to use its new installations in the south to provide the English detail on German military plans. Over the opposition of Laval and Darlan, Weygand fully supported the tracking of Axis activities via this newly-created M.A. — with spies extraordinaire like Paul Paillole given their own sub-cover in an ersatz Travaux Ruraux (T.R.) branch of the Agriculture administration, with its most important location in Marseille. (A good place to be if one needed to leave precipitously for North Africa!) T.R. was earmarked for "offensive counter-espionage" against Axis authorities, including the Abwehr, and buttressed by the use of 30 tons of archives it had somehow spirited to hiding places, including in the cheese cellars of Roquefort! From T.R. there was much linkage to British intelligence via conduits in Portugal and Switzerland, among others; and from the time of Vichy's beginnings the British code people at Bletchley Park also received a good deal from French signals intelligence, due in large part to support from Weygand, who helped Colonel Gustave Bertrand move his cryptanalysis section to a chateau in unoccupied France. According to J. F. V. Keiger, Bertrand "continued to help the British in cracking the Enigma codes until German occupation of the southern zone in November 1942."[14] British authorities would acknowledge this information emanating from France under Weygand's tenure in the Defense Ministry as a prime source of help during the Battle of Britain. The French S.R. was also ahead of the herd with intelligence of divisions between Germans and Russians in 1940, prefiguring Germany's invasion of the Soviet Union. Shadowing the Abwehr, they tried to warn the Soviets well in advance of the invasion on June 22, 1941, and had they been heeded, the war might have been shorter.[15]

Keeping this copious espionage going was onerous, requiring secrecy to which Weygand lent himself unstintingly, using the power of his position. There was a pressing need for extra-budgetary money, which he procured on his own initiative from the Finance Ministry, until the activity was made more official in late August, 1940. And Weygand ensured that even if he departed his position, this spying on the Germans would continue — in part owing to the intuition of spooks like Paillole that Weygand *would* be imminently turfed, and that therefore, everything must be routinized as quickly as possible. Another trump card for an institutional legacy was Weygand's influence on Huntziger, who would indeed become the next national defense minister, as well as minister of war, and continue, if with less obsession, along Weygand's path in support of the secret services.[16]

The scope of Weygand's position as defense minister was quite simply immense, and as usual, he gave 100 percent in the position. But cacophonous political wrangling became impossible for Pétain to put up with as September hove into view, and the issue that finally impelled the marshal to make a move was the illegal Nazi absorption of Alsace and the Moselle department of Lorraine. On August 7 the Germans named Joseph Burckel *gauleiter* of this department in Lorraine, and Robert Wagner *gauleiter* for Alsace. Suddenly Nazification *à la polonaise* ensued — edicts against use of the French language, a hunt for Jews, and impressment of young men drafted as *malgré nous* ("in spite of ourselves") into the Wehrmacht. Weygand's strident protests merely intensified an already existing antipathy between him and Laval. Finally, Pétain essentially said a plague on both houses, deciding to settle Weygand in another position of authority, well removed from Vichy.[17]

The former defense minister would now be given a supreme position in Africa, where he could rally the population, promote unity, and form a suitably armed military. And for some time at least, he could also skirt the nettlesome Lavals and Darlans back home! For the purpose, Pétain created a new combined post of delegate general and commander in chief of forces in Africa, and it was an offer Weygand could scarcely refuse, especially from a man he still respected for having steadied the fractured French army of 1917. Pétain's decision became public September 5, 1940, and the Defense ministry, amalgamated with that of War, then devolved to Huntziger. There were other alterations to ministries and ministers the next day, including the appointment of a clearly collaborationist Admiral René-Charles Platon at the Colonial Ministry, replacing Lémery. According to observers like Charles-Roux, this was in part the triumph of Laval, able to control the press in his new position as minister of information, and of Darlan. With Weygand's departure, the government had lost its strongest, most consistent anti–Nazi voice.[18]

On the day of the "purge" (September 6), Weygand took a last ministerial flight to inspect French regiments and arms — his 86th since August 29! In a period when aircraft flights were anything but automatically safe, Weygand had thus flown over 80 times in little more than a week, showing his typical courage.[19] And this one, in fact, ended badly, crash-landing near Limoges, and banging him up to the tune of a half-dozen cracked ribs. The accident, and his need for recuperation time, then kept him from flying off to Algiers right away, as he was supposed to do. After surmounting with his usual stoicism the resultant pain, and stomaching with difficulty imposed convalescence time, he finally made that trip on October 9, 1940 — to a post allowing Weygand more scope for useful action than anything he might have procured in the ever more poisonous nest of vipers that was Vichy!

10

Anti-Nazi Proconsul in French Africa

Once landed in North Africa, Weygand — like FDR after his first inauguration — wasted no time. In many ways, this was the summit of an outsider getting inside, and making policy — the position that even more than that of high commissioner of the Levant eminently suited him. As commander of military forces in Africa, and superior of other authorities in its colonies and protectorates, Weygand had the power to be an order maker *ab initio*, and meant to use it. Finding associates he could trust, he brought along his son Jacques, who helped Weygand fill out a staff he did not wish to bloat unduly. As his secretary general in Algiers, he received a distinguished official and graduate of the Colonial school, Yves Châtel, and they worked well together — Châtel yet another admirer of Weygand. Much of Châtel's experience had been in French Indochina, and some thought part of him had remained there in opium-perfumed memories! However, Weygand appreciated Châtel's "mental alertness, his experience of men, and his administrative capabilities...."[1] Jacques thought that Weygand's chief of staff ought to be a military man with fire in his belly, General Alphonse Juin; but Juin had been imprisoned by the Germans at the end of May 1940, and was still incarcerated, though from the moment he set foot in Africa, Weygand demanded his liberation. At Vichy, General Huntziger also thought of Juin as Weygand's top military aide, especially to fill in when the general was away on one of many projected tours. A grateful Weygand wrote Huntziger that "no one seems better qualified to occupy this post ... according to what I know of him, than General Juin." Nothing if not gutsy, given that Hitler more and more came to detest him, the new delegate general pushed the Germans for Juin's release, and Vichy authorities stayed on it until Juin was freed in June, 1941.

By then, Weygand had his top military aide in one Colonel de Périer, henceforth chief of his military staff, and a real find. Neither had known each other before de Périer was called to Algiers, but they worked well together all the way through Weygand's era in North Africa (while the liberated Juin would instead be appointed commander of forces in Morocco). Weygand's staff of some 20 people included his son Jacques, an old associate, Major Gasser, as his private secretary, and under each military or administrative leader in the various branches or *bureaux,* a clutch of three or four trustworthy people to assist them ably. The staff gradually filled out with new appointees, all ratified by Huntziger's War Ministry; and with new creations, such as Weygand's blandly-named "Section d'Etudes" (Study Section) supervising the hiding of arms! According to Emmanuel Mönick, who became secretary general in Morocco, and got to know Weygand well, the new proconsul was a fine designator of personnel, and delegator. He was a careful listener, and one who inspired those around him; but at the end of the day, a person who made tough decisions on his own. Weygand of course had a massive African canvas to work with — and overwhelming tasks at hand. Being a seasoned, sensitive diplomat, Mönick could tap into those feelings of awesome responsibility that weighed on the general's shoulders.[2]

In his new position Weygand proceeded both carefully and quickly. Even where he chose to live with his wife was a significant decision, by a man who hated to pamper himself while so many other French were suffering. He also didn't want to outshine a somewhat uppity governor-general in Algeria, Admiral Jean-Charles Abrial, a heroic figure during the Dunkirk evacuation, and naturally distrustful of Weygand's new "supra" position. So Weygand and wife chose as their abode an old Arab villa near Fort Lempereur in El Biar, with a view of Algiers' harbor, and whose last official resident was Governor-General Edouard Laferrière in 1898. This meant much labor, some done by Weygand himself, when he had the time, in order to make a viable house and garden out of this "Gone with the Wind" ruin. Repairs were completed by March 1941, and to such standards that after Weygand's forced departure, General Juin would live there, and then no less an eminence than de Gaulle, chortling snidely at his rival who had made the place so liveable.[3]

When there, Weygand had many meetings and visits, and remained an early-to-rise kind of man, and one who did plenty of homework at night. A bit of Sunday ping-pong with Jacques, who came with his wife to dine that day, broke the work routine; but it was rare. As for Madame Weygand, she headed the Red Cross down here, expending much energy to ensure that packages from a better-fed North Africa made it to undernourished France.[4]

Weygand of course felt the need to get around the empire, assessing the status quo, and suggesting improvements, and this he did from the beginning. He was fortunate to have a large, somewhat untrammeled mandate far from Vichy — with its fall-out from Montoire in October 1940, Pétain's tussle with Laval culminating in the latter's dismissal in December, the short era dominated by Pierre–Etienne Flandin, then Darlan coming to full power. How much better to be removed from such internecine quarrels, and to have liberty of implementation in a vast area where one could make a difference. Until Darlan's staggering *cumul* of offices (including the Foreign Ministry, Interior, and, by August, Defense), and his growing tightness with the Germans, which weighed too heavily, Weygand had much room for maneuver.[5]

Concerning his wish to see French Africa, Weygand felt that Algeria could wait, as there he would be in daily contact with its governor-general and staff. Tunisia was thus first on his list of visits, and he flew there on October 15. Weygand knew its resident-general — Admiral Jean-Pierre Esteva — and had much esteem for him; but as with Abrial, there was some discord that Weygand put to the fact that Esteva had been head man on his turf before creation of the general delegation. (Esteva's later career during the Nazi takeover of Tunisia, and in the purge atmosphere after World War II, would be a tragic one.) As for Morocco, its resident-general, Noguès, was again esteemed by Weygand, as one formed in the Lyautey lineage, and with all the martial, administrative, and human qualities necessary for such an important post, not least in wartime. However, Noguès too had monarchial tendencies (and after becoming the Americans' "No-Yes," was another who would pay in the post-war ambiance). Suddenly the highest political, economic, and military authority in North Africa, Weygand would obviously have to employ much finesse with such dignitaries. It was not only the two residents-general and Algeria's governor whom he had to cure of "l'esprit de chapelle"; but also their bureaucracies, which Weygand immediately began to centralize, and render more efficient, breaking down centrifugal tendencies which had become a liability. He also simplified policy on North African currencies, which were henceforth linked and could not be exported, helping to keep living costs relatively stable. It turned out that Pétain could not have picked better for this demanding new position.[6]

In the first three months Weygand was in Africa, nothing daunted by his previous mishap in France, he took to the air repeatedly to observe situations on the ground. His son provides a dizzying list of the general's stops, if not in order: Tunis, Oran, Rabat, Casablanca, Fez, Dakar, Saint-Louis, Aoulef, Gao, Bamako, Abidjan, Lomé, Ouagadougou, Cotonou ... and on it went! For 40 of his first 80 days in the new position, Weygand found himself teetering around the continent on airplanes. And he did so not only to be empirical and learn, but to rally inhabitants on the need to view the armistice as merely a springboard to *revanche*. As Mönick notes, Weygand was a one-man "dissipator of all fears."[7] Mönick, however, saw the paradox here: that this man whose own childhood was so aleatory, and who still sought God's help, could nonetheless impart much strength to French Africa of wartime.

One thing was certain: Weygand would again be no Gamelin. Just as he had gone right out to the French provinces in May 1940, he now wanted to see everything and everybody first-hand. As an example, his hour-by-hour travel agenda on a trip that fall of 1940 to Algeria's department of Oran combined an effort to see not only all requisite notabilities, but much else, too. Starting with a 7 A.M. air departure from Algiers and arrival an hour and a half later at La Sénia, Weygand would be a whirlwind, including a stop at Oran, then at Mers-el-Kébir, visits of ships, back to Oran, then on day two Tlemcen, then smaller places, including industrial facilities, back to Oran for a day at the prefecture; and on day three an inspection tour at the Foreign Legion training base of Sidi-Bel-Abbès, onward to Mascara, back again to Oran; and on the fourth day, to Mostaganem, Nouvion, Noisy, and thence, a return by plane to Algiers.[8] The more he became acclimated, the more Weygand's questions on these trips became pointed, and precise. In Algeria he combed places as different as the desert outpost of Colomb-Béchar on the Moroccan border, and the mining town of Kénadsa, where he encountered a mix of notables, army officers, schoolchildren, and miners; but more than that, the spirit of a roused populace out to see a celebrated soldier from France. Weygand inspected the coal mine there and railroad construction, which "not only interested the General, but provoked his enthusiasm."[9]

We have a fine memoir by Georges Hirtz showing the considerable impact of such tours. A veteran of administrative positions in North Africa, Hirtz had then gone into the army, and after the German victory, and demobilization, was sent to oversee this mining operation at Kénadsa, the most important site of coal deposits in French North Africa. Hirtz' task was to organize some 8,000 miners — a mixed bag of Algerian Kabyles, Lorrainers, Moroccan Arabs or highland Berbers, etc. He also had to supervise the improvement of rail service to shunt the coal to bigger towns or ports.

Weygand's visit of January 6, 1941, is highlighted in Hirtz' memoir, especially the general's curiosity, élan, and thoroughness. Weygand was happy to learn that coal production had been going up steadily under Hirtz' tenure, but he was more probing and less satisfied than other visiting dignitaries. As Hirtz recalled, "the general delegate is a questioner. He quickly inspires confidence by the pertinence of his interrogations, and the piercing clarity of his comments." Almost immediately, Weygand stressed the importance of coal for making fuels that were so needed (and lacking) in North Africa. He also emphasized the need to improve rail transport that could connect lands between Casablanca and Tunis and improve the North African economy. And he stressed to all here that this enhanced economic activity *would* help France rise up again. "The armistice is only a temporary, forced halt," Hirtz recalls him saying; and unity and confidence here would facilitate a French recovery, so "the essential was to hold on until the U.S. was able to enter the game...."[10]

The effect of all this on Hirtz, not to mention his miners, was palpable. He had been thinking of jumping to the Gaullist side, but now saw a leader with another way — a more patient one. Weygand's strength of purpose was infectious, and Hirtz henceforth felt that "here is where everything had to start again, under a leader who knew what he wanted, and exactly where he was leading French Africa." Weygand, in turn, appreciated how well Hirtz had been able to organize this beehive of activity out in the Algerian *bled*. Later, when he added the position of governor-general of Algeria to the others he held, he would have Hirtz transferred to his staff in Algiers.[11]

A note by the prefect of Algiers March 8, 1941, concerns Weygand's subsequent tour to Palestro, Dra-el-Mizan and Michelet, where he kept asking questions and demanding real answers, including about availability of food for Muslims there. If he didn't obtain adequate responses, he immediately revealed his displeasure. As the prefect wrote, "the General in Dra-el-Mizan interrogated the Mayor on this point, and the latter's vague replies appeared to provoke irritation in him." At the "mixed commune" of Palestro Weygand was received by the mayor, sub-prefect, and other notables, as well as government functionaries and army veterans. He told the town's mayor and justice of the peace to "clamp down pitilessly on the black market," then gave the same message to other authorities about reporting infractions. Before leaving Palestro, Weygand insisted on visiting its dock facilities, where he was especially interested in how grains were being apportioned by the month to feed people.[12]

In radio addresses, such as of February 1, 1941, Weygand also showed his FDR quality, rallying inhabitants of French Africa and telling them to support each other, and to avoid divisions or cynicism. The task was made easier by a widespread preference for France, rather than Nazi Germany as a potential new imperial power. But that France needed to show confidence, and from the beginning, its delegate general in Africa clearly advertised that he would be a real leader. The effect was felt by many.[13]

Weygand had obviously had much experience as an administrator, at least since his position running Foch's staff in World War I; and so he dealt conscientiously and firmly with a wide variety of issues related to finances and the economy, security, and how police and other functionaries were carrying out their duties. He never suffered fools gladly, nor would he side-step the smallest of problems. These are treated in numerous letters he sent authorities at Vichy to demand even such items as duplicating machines. Weygand also received, commented on, and made decisions related to copious correspondence from the two residents-general and Algeria's governor; for example, a letter from Noguès May 17, 1941, discussing a request from one Colonel Boeuf (Jean Sermaye in the literary world) wishing to traverse French Africa, which would then lead to an extended literary report — and which Weygand permitted.[14]

Before he himself became Algeria's governor in the summer of 1941, Weygand wrote a lot to Admiral Abrial on security needs in important areas such as the Oranais, full of Spanish immigrants and therefore, coveted by Franco's Spain. He had to deal with railway workers' and other unions, and with the many people soliciting government work. He had to attend many public functions, and preside over numerous meetings or conferences, such as one of April 23, 1941, on the provisioning of North Africa (harvests, exports, kinds and numbers of livestock, soap factories, trade exchanges, peanut and other oils, and the like). The second major topic there was the supplying of French North African needs by the U.S. Number three was Imperial production and finances. Only two days later came another meeting at La Maison d'Agriculture in Algiers for the Society of Algerian Farmers. Weygand took a keen interest in all these pressing issues, and tried to make policies based on what he learned.[15]

Most important, he wanted those below him running various administrative branches in North Africa efficiently, which would help keep this immense part of the empire out of enemy hands. France might have the lost the war on the mainland, but here, nothing would be allowed to slip under a demanding delegate's radar. In police reports he didn't want ersatz information, only the real thing. Thus on March 10, 1941, in a letter to Abrial, his "Object" was: "Periodic Reports of the Departmental Police of Oran." A copy he had received of the bi-weekly report of February 15–28 from the superintendent of Special Police in that department was "completely insufficient," failing to inform the reader about Oran's economic situation, the morale of the indigenous, activities of political parties, and foreign propaganda. He enjoined the governor to pass on these criticisms immediately; in a similar manner, he demanded monthly reports of value from military officials in North Africa, ones that were both substantive, yet to the point. From Weygand there would be no *mañana* mentality, nor mincing of words when the administrative hierarchy didn't come up to snuff.[16]

Government functionaries must provide not only good reports, but come to meetings on a precise schedule. In his letter of March 19, 1941, to Abrial and the residents-general of Morocco and Tunisia, his "object" was: "Monthly meetings of civil servants and personalities of the different North African countries." Weygand's rationale was that the smooth, unified operation of economic and administrative activities in North Africa necessitated meetings of such personnel each and every month in Algiers. He made it clear that, depending on the availability of transportation, they would always occur between the 15th and 20th.[17]

Institutions like the *chantiers de la jeunesse* (youth camps) to regenerate young people physically and militarily in the metropole were intended to help form an army of *revanche* down here, and Weygand took them seriously. So did the man dispatched to run them in Algeria, Colonel A. S. Van Hecke, a veteran of the Somme and an ex–Foreign Legionnaire, who had also worked with Weygand in Syria some two decades earlier. Van Hecke found that the general had not changed an iota when it came to doing a job. Both wanted this new institution to be centered firmly on fighting another day against the Germans. In Van Hecke's view, administrators like Châtel or Esteva seemed much more wan than Weygand about standing up to the Nazis. Weygand's hatred of the enemy was easy for him to spot, and he even considered it "violent."[18]

Being appointed as Algerian governor-general in mid–July 1941 merely made Weygand's panoply of assignments more demanding, as did the general tightrope policy he was following. He had to evaluate many propaganda and intelligence reports, for example, concerning Morocco, where some were "preparing the atmosphere with a view to eventual intervention of the English and Americans in this protectorate," which deep down, didn't displease him, providing the time was right and the ground prepared. The fact that Weygand opened impressive contacts with the U.S., including economic ones, helped increase Allied prestige, and when American boats arrived in Morocco with material on board, the population thought it a "providential importation." Still, more and more looked to "Gaullist and Anglophile elements," as in the region of Marrakech. Events of the time in Syria (first favoring collaborationists and the Nazis, then Gaullists and the English) were also changing minds, while the entry of Russia into the war seemed of smaller moment here.[19]

However, Weygand's popularity, including as Algeria's new governor-general, remained genuine and widespread, according to authorities taking regional or local pulses. A typical report of August 9, 1941, noted: "The nomination of General Weygand as Algeria's governor-general was the main event of the past two weeks in the entire colony. Both the French and Muslim populations openly expressed real satisfaction in private conversations, as well as in the press." In improvised demonstrations too, there seemed to be real enthusiasm for the delegate, such as at one of July 25, 1941, outside Algiers' Winter Palace, "where the crowd of natives demonstrated its attachment to the person of General Weygand."

The same report again noted little change in perceptions of exterior events, such as Russia's entry into the war, though most Europeans canvassed seemed to hope the Nazis and Soviets would wear each other out, "with France hopefully benefiting." But there were real fears concerning the recent French-Japanese accord that might loosen French control of Indochina, constituting the beginning of the end there. Economic trends? Not bad overall, but the indigenous suffered "especially from the shortage of material needed to make their clothes." In terms of propaganda, those on the extreme collaborationist Right (which Weygand loathed), like adherents of the Parti Populaire Français, did best in the Oranais, and were starting to win over pro–Nazi natives there. On another flank there were also Communist tracts, especially again, in the Oranais, where a Spanish-Communist organization was operating in this heavily Spanish region. The French parties were starting to affect the indigenous, too — as usual, revolutionary developments started at the top. But "the state of mind of the Muslim population is on the whole, very satisfactory." As for Jews, they were following with more assiduity Russia's war against the Nazis, and listening more to English radio. However, the application of Vichy's statutes (on which more below) was keenly felt, and Jews also complained that they weren't getting enough charity from their own. Oddly, some were apparently ginning up Muslims, to the effect that Pétain wouldn't last, and that the English would win, and that therefore a French Popular Front government would return. On the Muslim radical side there was, however, some antisemitism, combined with anti–French feeling, producing tracts such as one noting proudly: "France is on its knees before us" and ending with a "HEIL HITLER." There is a pile of other such bi-weekly reports Weygand and those in his office had to digest — most of them as detailed as this one.[20]

The archives bulge even with long lists of government functionaries under Weygand, especially when he became Algeria's governor-general. This meant many precise, careful meetings with them. It also meant quite a number of hirings. Weygand and people in his office had to pore over long "Aptitude Tables," showing diplomas, marriage and children status, and other items relating to personnel for the departments of Algeria in question.[21]

As in Bugeaud's era of the 1840s, there were numerous requests from people on the mainland wanting badly to reach this comparative paradise. A letter of August 13, 1941, to His Excellency General Weygand (followed by

all his position titles), emanated from one Michel Korsakoff of 3, Rue Clu-
vier, Nice — a self-described naturalist, member of Lyon's Linnaean Society,
and of the Natural History Society of North Africa, and a former officer in
the Russian Imperial Guard. Korsakoff said he had lived in France since 1922
and now wished to come to Algeria to collect specimens. He mentioned previously published brochures on colonial fauna, and other trips that had contributed to his work. The same file contains all sorts of other letters and
telegrams sent to Weygand's office, asking for positions or favors. There are
even supplicatory letters addressed to Mrs. Weygand. One such handwritten
missive is from Marie-Louise de Neuville (September 24, 1941), a former head
nurse in Algerian hospitals. Writing from a village in the unoccupied Allier
of France, she informed Mrs. Weygand that her father was an army officer in
Algeria, that she herself was born and had many friends there, and that she
wanted to come back as soon as possible. In addition, she said she spoke Arabic, and knew the Muslim world well. And she had once been Madame Weygand's neighbor in France! The final emphasis is on her patriotism, and the
fact that she hailed from an Alsatian family with great devotion to France.[22]

Other kinds of requests reaching Weygand's office included those to
attend funerals of Muslim notables; or by workers on railways and in other
functions, who wished to be transferred, or to receive early retirement. One
sent to Weygand September 24, 1941, from Albert Weiss, Dock Manager for
the Descartes Grain Cooperative in Algeria, mentioned a "disastrous" financial and lodging situation (although his position certainly seems enviable for
the time). Many, including Muslims, desired letters of recommendation from
Weygand's office. Many Algerians also asked the governor for leniency, due
to having run afoul of the law. One such letter to Weygand's office, September 12, 1941, is from a Muslim notable, Bacha Mohammed, who worked for
the Postal and Telegraph Office at Burdeau (near Algiers), and wanted help
on a case for which he seemed loathe to provide detail. An even more curious letter of August 31, 1941 (listing all of Weygand's titles), is from one Sayah
Meziane ben Seddik, who admitted to repetitive problems with the law, but
desired a fresh start. He informed Weygand that he had turned over a new
leaf, but was nonetheless on the point of being interned again; and a police
note of September 23 appended to this original letter mentioned his seven
prior condemnations — four for thefts, three for parole infractions. Weygand
was warned not to give in to the man's blandishments — but all such affairs
required reflection, and decisions.[23]

They also required both thoroughness and alacrity, qualities the proconsul demanded from everyone working under him. He simply would not be a
passive figurehead here. Instead he wanted all political and economic reports

sent in copy form directly to his office. This information, he wrote in a circular, "permits me to follow from day to day the political and economic situation of the Colony." But incomplete documentation in any domain remained one of his bug-bears. At one point he fumed that he required punctual reports from prefects of the Algerian departments of Constantine and Oran, and hadn't received them on time, not to mention those from the Southern Territories and from Oran's chief of Special Police.[24]

As in Lynn Case's old book using prefectoral reports as a guide to Second Empire opinion, such reports that Weygand *did* receive in Algeria provided a lot on what people were thinking — which was of crucial importance to him.[25] They were to be bi-monthly, and not to be slim in any category. For example, that of the prefect of Algiers, September 26, 1941, on the "general situation in the department of Algiers" from September 1 to 15, 1941, had various lengthy sections. Under Section A — Moral Situation of the European Populations — the prefect offered estimates such as the following: "The German-Russian conflict is a major subject of all conversations" and some denote "the Reich's weakening, and want a general uprising in occupied countries." They also keep up hopes by listening to foreign radio, he said. But the majority of the population "is mainly concerned with material interests, such as pay, always considered inadequate, and getting food supplies, becoming more difficult every day." He adds information on syndicalism in the department, different political stripes, and so on. Then comes Section B, "Moral Situation of the Indigenous Populations," and the atmosphere mostly seems fine, despite the odd sign proclaiming "Down with the French." As for Part C, "Moral Situation of the Jewish Populations," their hope for an English and Russian victory seems widespread. Some antisemitic tracts have been distributed in Algiers, and authorities are trying to learn the authors' and distributors' identities. And for Part D the prefect remains typically exhaustive on Foreigners, and Foreign Propaganda. On F (Economic Situation), he goes carefully over the current state of harvests, salaries, food supply, and special shortages in Algiers — of potatoes, coffee, tomatoes, beans, and the like.[26]

Weygand had additional sources of information on the state of this and other parts of Africa, one being the Second Bureau's summaries emanating from their Muslim Affairs Section. These reports for 1940–1941 show that good harvests played a great role in the maintenance of French governmental stability, and that in Algeria, Morocco, and Tunisia they were indeed good (due to rainfall and other factors, with forecasts for upcoming ones also propitious). They show as well, that Muslims in rural areas were not much seduced by radicals, and worried more about their day to day well being. Extremists had more impact in the big cities. Projects like the building of dams or planting of olive trees also helped enhance the authority of Weygand and his subalterns.[27]

Two subjects in this era require our special focus in order to evaluate the delegate general's (and commander in chief's) policies in French Africa. One is the question of why he did not simply jump to the Gaullists in 1940–41, and the answer revolves around the fact that Weygand still considered de Gaulle a dissident, and one lacking requisite horses. Weygand believed that with most of France, including Paris, still occupied, the military ground was not yet firm enough for a rebound from that side. In November 1940, de Gaulle's elegant aide, General Catroux, formerly governor of Indochina, had sent Weygand a letter enjoining him to bolt from his Algiers base. On February 24, 1941, de Gaulle himself wrote a typically off-the-top missive on the subject, in which "I urged Weygand to seize the latest opportunity which was being offered him to resume the struggle." There were other Gaullist communications sent via emissaries in order to influence French Africa's delegate general and commander in chief; but Weygand wouldn't budge, and — especially when Darlan spied on him continually — would have found it increasingly difficult to do so, even had he wanted to. The main factor was loyalty, and the fact that Weygand was far more patient and deliberate than de Gaulle, shown in his opening-out to the Americans. Weygand felt that he was taking a more realistic, less dangerous route toward the same goal desired by *le grand Charles*. De Gaulle seemed only to be bringing fratricide to certain parts of the French Empire, and the fact that he didn't sufficiently prepare for serious military enterprises was seen in the abortive attack on Dakar in September, 1940, which he had hectored the English into joining, and which not only made Weygand continue to distrust him, but also his own British patrons.[28]

So many officers who cut teeth around Weygand would make Gaullists look good militarily later in the war — when the time was more propitious. And de Gaulle in this era had no monopoly on anti–Nazi courage; in fact, he himself took fewer risks than did Weygand. Nazi ire was already well focused on the delegate general's stubborn refusal to consider armistice alterations, and as early as December 12, 1940, co-terminous with a secret Nazi "Plan Attila" to occupy all of France, Hitler had Marshal Keitel send Admiral Wilhelm Canaris, head of the Abwehr, an order to get Weygand liquidated! (Italy's Marshal Badoglio also had a plan in the works to eliminate both Weygand and Morocco's resident-general, Noguès.) Canaris fortunately convinced Keitel that this was not the right moment for such a move. One can certainly admire the pluck of many who joined the Resistance under the Gaullist standard; but again, there were other kinds of courage and risks being faced in this comparatively early stage of the war.[29]

When it came to affronting Gaullists, Weygand had great help not only from residents or governors general in North Africa, but also from a burly, fascinating character who became Vichy's governor-general (and/or high commissioner) for French West Africa, remaining in the position until 1943. Weygand's ideas were exactly the same as this Pierre Boisson's: no more disorders in what remained of French Africa. Gaullists had already taken over in French Equatorial Africa by nothing more than "palace revolutions" — in colonial areas less important strategically and economically than French West Africa. They were also governed differently, allowing easy coups. But for the rest, containment now became the policy of choice, and Boisson seemed the right man for this assignment, having already won spurs in leading a vigorous, well-organized response to the Anglo-Gaullist invasion of Dakar, September 23, 1940. Lest one consider him merely a loathsome fascist, what Boisson accomplished was pure Weygand. He so impressed the Germans that he could maintain order in French West Africa that he was able, thereby, to keep *them* out. At the same time, he derived a rationale to beef up an army that later contributed to France's liberation. To do this in a huge area of millions of square kilometers and some 15,000,000 inhabitants (henceforth eschewing revolt), and with the English also improving subsequent relations, was no mean feat.

But then Boisson, a strong, stubborn Breton, was no ordinary man, having toughened himself on the red-hot anvil of trench warfare in World War I. Part of Joffre's insane offensives in Artois of 1915, he sustained a foot wound that put him in the hospital for two months. Back in the Arras sector in May, his infantry battalion was decimated, but he made it through, as he did again in mid–June. Then came the death factory of Verdun the following year, where this time Boisson — answering Pétain's call to hold the line — bought it dearly. After surviving on the defensive, he led a forward assault of June 6, 1916, into enemy positions, and was badly wounded in the hand and chest; yet as highest-ranking French officer, he continued on, taking prisoners, while fast losing blood. Then in a counter-attack, a German grenade exploded into his already damaged leg. When he regained consciousness, the limb was almost severed, and in German captivity, a surgeon amputated to the knee. Boisson was subsequently allowed to regain France as a useless *mutilé de guerre*.

But after a distinguished colonial career in the '30s, he was strong enough to affront the Germans in a second world war, and as with Weygand, his equation of Gaullist disorders with Nazi incursions in French Africa remained intact. Boisson first met the delegate general for several days in late October, 1940, on Weygand's initial tour of Afrique Occidentale Française (A.O.F.). From then on, Weygand fully supported Boisson. Not that they

were identical; Boisson hailed from a secularist background, and had served
the Leftist Popular Front in Africa with distinction, enacting their reforms.
But the two now had the same aims: to keep A.O.F. economically viable,
including by a huge trans–Saharan railway that couldn't be finished in
wartime; to repel the Axis, which Boisson did — only one German official
briefly allowed in Dakar under the cover name René Martin, then ejected; to
beef up the armistice army, which again occurred dramatically (by summer
1942, the number of well-armed soldiers in A.O.F. having risen from 15,000
to 125,000); to await the right moment for a comeback (and indeed, Boisson
would place French West Africa in the American camp right after TORCH);
and not least, to keep *Gaullists* from making the Axis more than a menacing
shadow in Africa, using French quarrels as their pretext for invasion. Thus in
Boisson's bailiwick, branches of Weygand's Second Bureau kept watch on
Gaullist and other dissidents in this vast federation of West Africa, including, in names then used, Niger, Mauritania, Soudan, Dahomey, Upper Volta,
Guinea, and the mandate of once German-held Togo. There were branches
here also of organizations like Menées Antinationales. There were, as well,
purges of Gaullists and/or Freemasons in administration, but Ruth Ginio
estimates that only some 40 persons were affected, despite early Vichy laws
abolishing Masonic "secret associations" in France. Those laws were then
replicated in A.O.F., but government replacements often came from the same
republican backgrounds. More numerous were Freemasons no longer allowed
to be members of a society or to attend meetings. Liquidation of their property in A.O.F., as elsewhere, also brought considerable cash into government
coffers: money directed, however, to the "Colonial Budget for War Veterans,
Mutilated, and Pupils of the Nation" (the latter having lost a father in the
war, of which A.O.F. had many).[30]

Like Weygand, Boisson was in much touch with ministries at Vichy,
particularly Platon's Colonial Ministry. He was constantly being enjoined to
cable back urgently — on budgetary matters, aviation, tractors, wives wishing
to rejoin husbands in A.O.F., refugees there from Alsace-Lorraine, dams on
the Niger, nurses hired to fight leprosy, rubber importation and ricin prices —
the list was endless. Permits to transport explosives or for civilians in different
parts of French Africa to acquire hunting rifles were subject to much correspondence back to Vichy. When Platon wished to discuss matters personally
with Boisson, all else must be dropped. The colonial minister sent the governor-general in Dakar a typical telegram, January 30, 1941: "Circumstances
make direct contact between us indispensable (stop). Beg you to come Vichy
at the soonest ... for stay approximately 48 hours." Vichy simply could not
be ignored, either by Weygand, or by "mini–Weygands" like Boisson.[31]

Often, however, the route went from Boisson's demands, particularly in the realm of hirings or security needs, to Weygand, and thence to Vichy. Without *Weygand's* power, Boisson's in A.O.F. would have been much diminished. One of Weygand's telegrams sent to the Colonial Ministry at Vichy, November 30, 1940, shows this process well: "I insist that satisfaction be given to the demands for personnel formulated by the High Commissioner, and especially for security personnel. There is urgency!" Other Weygand telegrams to the ministry asked for prompt execution of economic demands — for more fuel, both to use in A.O.F. and, in the case of Senegalese peanut oil, for transfer to North Africa; for the ratification of rice exports from Saigon to Dakar; and much else. Weygand also asked the Colonial Ministry to support Boisson's anti–German measures, forbidding the docking of German liners at Dakar, and any other activity that might provide Nazi inroads into A.O.F. As well, Weygand had the larger African picture in mind when he suggested what could and could not be sent from North Africa to A.O.F., in both the realm of armaments and munitions, and that of goods.[32]

Vichy, however, remained the ultimate authority, and thus, A.O.F.'s governor-general also had to follow new laws regarding Jews there. A few firings of Jewish government, financial, or engineering personnel consequently ensued. But given that the entire Jewish population numbered in the hundreds down here, the problem was not as significant as elsewhere. This, however, segues us to the *second* important subject where Weygand's policies require careful evaluation: his comportment toward North Africa's Jews, whose population was *far* larger than in A.O.F., numbering over 400,000! The subject of course falls within the larger, complex, much-debated one of Vichy France and its Jews during World War II. It is a subject that sometimes seems prey to simplifications, and from such an optic, it is easy to fault Weygand in this regard during his North African proconsulate. However, his hard, obsessional work to hold onto the empire and keep it from the Nazis' grasp *also* greatly helped Jews of the Maghreb survive during this terrifying period.

It needs to be stressed that France had long been a protector in North Africa (as it was in the Levant) — its use of the term "protectorate" for both Morocco and Tunisia not merely ironic.[33] In Algeria, which was a special case, being both colony and a part of France, the push to grant Jews citizenship from the time of Napoleon III had come to fruition during the Franco–Prussian War with the Crémieux decree (October 24, 1870). Of Jewish origins, and minister of justice under the Provisional government that followed the Second Empire, Adolphe Crémieux' edict gave him great renown among Algerian Jews; while at the same time, arousing antisemitism in European *pieds noirs*, and Arab envy, especially given the sharp increase in Jewish population, due to immigration from neighboring Tunisia, France, and later, Eastern Europe. This explosive situation in Algeria was seen in antisemitic, largely European riots there during the Dreyfus era of the late 1890s, incited by the socialist journalist and Algiers mayor, Max Regis, an adherent of Edouard Drumont, author of *Jewish France*, who also became an Algerian deputy. Thousands cheered Regis and Drumont, and many participated in boycotts of Jewish merchants, doctors, and lawyers there.[34] After disturbances ebbed, there were later ones, including pogroms of the mid–1930s in Constantine. All of which constituted a mitigating factor in the Crémieux decree's later abrogation under Vichy, and which cannot be attributed to putative antisemitism in Weygand, given that he was between positions when the measure was formulated.

Many on a farther, more virulent Right than ever occupied by Weygand had already pressed for the decree's termination in the late '30s — especially the Parti Populaire Français, ardently hoping for deportation of the over 100,000 Algerian Jews. Once Vichy was in place, the main creator of the Crémieux decree's cancellation was Marcel Peyrouton, minister of the interior, and an ex-colonial administrator in North Africa. But there was pressure from Pétain as well. Legislation of October 7 and 11, 1940, ended naturalization possibilities (with few exceptions) for Algerian Jews; and if Weygand went along, he did so because he still worked for the French state, and in part too, because one of his concerns in North Africa was to maintain good relations with the Muslim population, which had long envied this special status. As Louis Berteil notes — and he was in North Africa during Weygand's tenure: "This measure was unjust, but significant in its effects. Everyone knows that Muslims in countries where important Jewish communities exist only accept their presence if they are servile and pay tribute. Egalitarian cohabitation can subsist solely through the imposition of force by a powerful occupier." And France had long been that powerful, yet generous imposer; now, "bringing Jews down to the condition of the indigenous constituted for the Arabs satisfaction of their traditional hatred of Jews, conciliating them to the Vichy government." And of course Vichy had a serious competitor — the Nazis — *also* trying to win over North Africa's Arabs, and make them revolt.[35]

One already sees that the subject of Weygand and the Jews of North Africa is more complex than the two cursory pages Destremau vouchsafed it in his 1989 biography. He did, however, defend Weygand from charges of being antisemitic, citing a lunchtime conversation where the general apparently disdained such talk, averring that "I was raised by a Jew and don't allow people to calumny them in front of me." Destremau lays this attitude in part to Weygand's Catholicism, the healthiest kind, in his view, and which he likens (without evidence) to that of the most decent French churchmen of wartime, such as Archbishop Saliège.[36] But one thinks too of a Clemenceau remark in this context — that even among Jews, there were few free of anti-semitism; and to impute a certain perfection to Weygand here strikes one as naïve, particularly given the regime for which he worked, and the period.

However, despite impressive scholarship, the old, pathbreaking views of Marrus and Paxton in *Vichy France and the Jews* also strike one now as somewhat over-simplified. These scholars argue that Vichy took measures against Jews that outpaced those of the Nazis, but among others, Susan Zuccotti's more recent treatment sensibly qualifies, declaring that most were in part implemented to placate, keep autonomy, and anticipate, generally following the lead of earlier German edicts in the occupied zone. Ignoring the Nazis in France of World War II was simply not a real-world possibility.[37]

None of which is meant to defend Vichy's policies in this domain. There is no defending the rough camps for Jews and other undesirables in France that had their counterparts in North Africa, where some 7,500 in 1942 were interned, a number that had diminished from the previous year, when Weygand was still there. In Algeria some of these camps were pure work camps, with Leftists from Spain and other refugees who would have suffered back home represented. Others, like the one at Bedeau in the South Oranais, concentrated Jewish soldiers. Living in desert tents and other extreme conditions, camp internees were subject to hunger, in some cases (in others, food was satisfactory), and to beatings from Foreign Legionnaires who administered them. Their numbers included Jews from different parts of Europe who had enrolled in the French army before the defeat, and now paradoxically, found themselves safe from the Final Solution through to liberation later in 1942, or in the case of Tunisia, '43. One such internee was a 22-year-old Austrian Jew, Kurt Fleisher, who had left a doomed Vienna of 1938 for France, then joined the French army. He went to Algiers in October 1940 as a member of the Foreign Legion. In fact, Fleisher owed his life to the fact that, due in good part to Weygand, the French empire remained safe from Nazi tentacles; back in Vienna, or even occupied Paris, his fate would not have been so fortunate.[38]

More difficult is the problem of the severe Jewish statutes originating on the mainland, and which had an equally harsh effect in Algeria up to the November 1942 Allied landings. The first such German measure against Jews in Occupied France occurred about a week before the initial one promulgated by Vichy October 3, 1940. That said, one certainly winces at the zealotry in these first statutes of "purification" crafted by Vichy ministers, preeminently Raphaël Alibert, a lawyer and one-time professor of constitutional law, who became French minister of justice in July, 1940. And in zealous implementation, Minister of the Interior Peyrouton certainly matched him. Signatories of this first statute of Jews, October 3, 1940, included (in addition to those ministers) Baudouin, Laval, Huntziger, and of course Pétain; but not Weygand — again, he was permanently out of the government at Vichy. Broad definitions of who was Jewish, a law that sought to eject most Jews from the French army's officer corps, as well as from journalism, the theater, cinema, government service, etc.; and a measure of October 4 allowing prefects to lock up any foreign Jews in their departments showed that Vichy meant harsh business, indeed.[39]

On October 18 the Germans formulated their second decree for the Occupied Zone, forcing Jews to inventory personal property, and hand in the lists at police stations. Confiscations, including of valuables like furniture, art, and jewelry, would follow, along with forced selling of Jewish businesses, or closures. As in the rest of Europe, this was how the Nazi vise closed ever more tightly, and Vichy followed with an October 25 decree removing ordinary Jewish soldiers from the army, and now dismissing Jews in teaching and the like — with great impact not only economically, but emotionally to those used to an open society. On April 26, 1941, the Germans one-upped Vichy when it came to their zone — Jews could no longer work in banking, insurance, real estate, or transportation there.[40]

With a second Vichy statute for Jews, this time Darlan's baby, of June 2, 1941, there was a great reduction in Algeria of Jews in education, especially as teachers, but also as students, and a severe *numerus clausus* (generally 2 percent) when it came to professions like law, medicine, architecture, or notarial work. As on the mainland, there were also wholesale firings of Algerian Jews in the arts, cinema, and the like.

But while there was some antisemitic glee at the local level, all this really emanated from metropolitan France. And Weygand fought openly anti–Jewish administrators in Algeria, such as Governor-General Abrial, if not *only* for that reason. He also fought against Xavier Vallat, a World War I veteran who had lost an arm and leg in the conflict, and headed Vichy's "Commissariat général à la question juive" (CGQJ), created March 29, 1941, partly because the Germans desired a department of Jewish affairs in occupied France. Vallat visited Algeria in mid–August of 1941, pressuring Weygand on "aryanization" of property — by now a Vichy policy — and which he wanted under his own control. It is clear that when Weygand launched a "Service algérien des questions juives" (Algerian Service for Jewish Questions) on August 14, 1941, he was following a lead prescribed by Vallat's organization of similar name at Vichy. Despite his best efforts to oppose Vallat, aryanization of Jewish property in Algeria then fell under that official's control; and there were certainly local volunteers to help enthusiastically with confiscations. However, the process only got going in December 1941, after Weygand's departure, and mainly affected the richest Algerian Jews, while generally skirting smaller tradesmen. It then persisted only to the November 1942 Allied landings.[41]

If aryanization of property in Algeria never had much time to work, Jewish statutes were certainly onerous there, with a *numerus clausus* on Algeria's Jewish children in schools of first 14 percent, then 7 percent, showing an increasingly tough trend. Nonetheless, Algerian Jews, led by Maurice Eisenbeth, the chief rabbi of Algiers, protested vigorously. Eisenbeth would have had much less impact in metropolitan France, owing to his Polish-Jewish mother, and the general situation there. In Algeria he spearheaded the opening of private establishments, largely on French models, in order to compensate for ejection of students from public schools. Secondary sources agree that Jews became more united in Weygand's wartime Algeria (and beyond) than was possible in France of either part.[42]

The effect of Jewish statutes in Algeria can be seen in cases like that of the future intellectual André Chouraqui, whose parents found themselves suddenly in dire economic straits. Their son, formerly a student at the lycée of Oran, and at higher institutions in Paris, was no longer able to continue in law, scrambling to find other employment. But bad as conditions in Algeria were, they became much worse in the metropole, and Chouraqui remembered Weygand's resolutely anti–German stance, and protection thereby, of Algeria's Jewish population.[43]

Memories of Jewish life in smaller Algerian towns, like Sétif, during World War II again indicate a better quality of life than in many parts of France, including in the realm of food. One also reads of antisemitism in the ordinary population here, making Weygand's protective authority again necessary. As one Rosette recalled: "They [Gentiles] were just biding their time.... They couldn't wait for the Germans to come to town." Another man qualified: "I don't call them pro–German. I'd just call them anti–Jew, that's all."[44]

As for the notorious yellow star, the first hints of it in Algeria came long after Weygand's departure both as delegate and as Algerian governor-general. His successor as governor, Châtel, was according to some, about to order some 100,000 yellow armbands *cum* star in the fall of 1942; but the Allied invasion soon after trumped that possible Algerian concession to the Final Solution. As for implementation of a *Judenrat*-type organization — quite early on, there had been a Vichy-imposed census of some 115,000 Algerian Jews — it also came after Weygand's departure in the form of L'Union Générale des Israélites d'Algérie of 1942. This again mirrored the Union Générale des

Israélites de France, or UGIF. The measure in Algeria was not officially published until days before the Allied landings, and never went into operation. And for all these things Châtel would pay after the war.[45]

In sum, the problem of Jews in Algeria through to the November 1942 liberation is a difficult one, as is evaluation of Weygand's role there; but the fact that few Algerian Jews were actually deported and murdered by the Germans can in part be laid at his anti–Nazi door. Regarding expropriation, Arab radicals and/or terrorists of the '50s and early '60s, who became the country's leaders, outdid Vichy when it came to both fleeing, propertyless Jews, and *pieds noirs* more generally.[46] Being comparative shouldn't exonerate, and Weygand certainly enforced Vichy's purge atmosphere to a degree (especially against groups like Freemasons); but one must also remember the context of this horrendous period.

When it comes to Morocco under Weygand's stewardship, but a protectorate run by a resident-general in tandem with the sultan's *makhzan*, we come to an area where the Jews of wartime suffered distinctly less than in Algeria. The region benefited from a wise resident-general, Noguès, who had taken the position in 1936 and following in Lyautey's tracks, respected both Jews and Arabs, including the sultan. Because Morocco was a protectorate, there was no Crémieux decree to revoke here. Despite lobbying pressure from the Alliance Israélite Universelle, Lyautey (resident-general from 1912 to 1925) had opposed granting wholesale citizenship to Jews; France had entered Morocco partly to cure an anarchic situation of intra–Muslim civil war, and did not want to arouse resentments seen in neighboring Algeria. Succeeding residents-general concurred, and only a minority of Jews living there were able to become citizens.[47]

During World War II, Weygand did nothing to force Noguès and other Moroccan authorities to be stricter in applying anti–Jewish measures; through to the November 1942 invasion, such legislation was applied only in a tepid, ambivalent, dilatory manner. Noguès was a key figure here, but so were other enlightened French administrators, such as Roger Thabault, director of primary European and Jewish education in Morocco from 1929, until replaced in November 1941 (the month of Weygand's own forced departure). Thabault fought hard against the first Jewish statute, and also to keep Alliance Israélite Universelle schools in Morocco, which he had often inspected. He also pushed to get fired Jewish teaching personnel into those schools — and the price (despite Noguès' support) was antipathy even from erstwhile friends, and opprobrium when he visited Vichy. Thabault, however, had some success, and Vichy continued to subsidize Morocco's Alliance schools in wartime![48] An equally important aide to the Jews was Morocco's Sultan Mohammed V, also reluctant to back antisemitic measures here. Again, Weygand never pulled rank on such authorities, as he could easily have done.

Besides Jewish statutes bringing a *numerus clausus* that affected some students, but comparatively few careers (a takeoff in the number of Moroccan-Jewish professionals yet to come), there was also the threat of expropriation and economic aryanization that never materialized here. Nor did the policy of expelling Jews from European quarters in cities like Rabat or Casablanca, and sending them back to restricted ghettoes (*mellahs*). Vallat plumped hard for this measure, but we have seen how Weygand opposed him sedulously. Authorities in the protectorate like Noguès and the sultan also disagreed with forced evacuations, and through to the Allied invasion, the policy remained a dead letter.

One could argue that Weygand was a kind of hero to Moroccan Jewry, as most feared German authorities ensconced at Anfa (a rich part of Casablanca) or Fedala far more than the French, and Weygand kept these plotting Nazis at bay, while preparing the ground via contacts with the Americans for North Africa's ultimate liberation. One Jewish memoir after another salutes French authorities trying to hold the line in Morocco.[49] And oral memories of life in Rabat for a then-young Jewish girl cite no overt persecution by the French. Orli K. recalls being six or so at elementary school, and seeing photographs everywhere of Marshal Pétain, who had "the aura of someone impressive." The schoolmistress would have pupils rise and extend their right hand — showing that one was devoted to the French leader.

But the wholesale firing of Jewish personnel, as was the case in France, and for a time in Algeria, did not touch her school. Two of Orli's teachers were Jewish, and both remained in their positions. One was of Sephardic origins, the other Ashkenazi, originally from Alsace, Orli supposed. She "wasn't nice," and quite often would single out Jewish girls in class, making them rise, then harangue them, to the effect that they might soon have to return to the Jewish quarter. (Orli's father was an accountant working for a company that exported grains to France, and being well off, the family no longer lived in the *mellah*.)[50]

Weygand stayed closely in touch with Noguès on such issues, as he did with Tunisia's Esteva; but in that protectorate too, Jews were no real target, finding life mostly unaltered under Vichy, and under *beys* who had to watch their own flanks for radicals wanting to oust them. Italian armistice commission authorities here were also more relaxed than the Germans would have been, though as seen, Mussolini had long coveted this part of French North Africa. After the November 1942 landings in Morocco and Algeria, German forces would rush into the protectorate, and for roughly six months its situation became far more dire than it had been under a Weygand-Esteva tandem. "As Jews stood looking on in silence, the Arabs were taking to the Germans like fish to the water, shouting with joy...," one witness recalls. Requisitions, imprisonments, beatings, and deportations followed.[51]

Again, evaluating Weygand's comportment on this issue remains difficult; yet bluntly to call him an "antisemite," or to aver that he reveled in Jewish tribulations of the time would be simplistic. Weygand was a soldier/administrator in a French regime that had been overwhelmingly approved in Parliament, and felt he had to follow at least something of its lead. And he certainly worried about arousing Muslim resentments against Jews, wanting no disturbances that would provide pretexts for Axis interference. As well, he had no liking for the Popular Front heritage, which also conditioned his actions in a Maghreb where many Jews had been on the Left, as in metropolitan France.[52] But on the whole, North African Jews were well served by having such an obdurate anti–Nazi in power, given monstrosities then occurring in Europe. Assessing the status of over 400,000 Jews of the Maghreb under Weygand (117,646 in Algeria, 89,360 in Tunisia, and about 200,000 in Morocco, according to the 1941 census), Esther Benbassa considers their "situation ... not at all comparable to that of their co-religionists in metropolitan France...."[53]

As for North African Arabs, how well Weygand did with that large sector of the population is another difficult subject, depending partially on the historian's viewpoint. I am one who takes seriously the "France of notables" that has now largely disappeared, and which played a significant role in the maintenance of their empire. In those not-so-distant days there were also strong *Muslim* notables in North Africa, who respected Frenchmen of the sword, such as Weygand, despite the 1940 defeat. At the same time, there were also the stirrings of Arab-Muslim radicalism and rejectionism, which would come to lethal fruition in the next decade.

In this period such radicals were often at one with Nazis they hoped would finish off an already wounded France. Their anonymous letters are abundant in colonial archives: for example, one sent to Weygand's office in July 1941, noting fervently: "Thanks to Hitler, France is now paying for the injustice it has inflicted on [Algerian] Arabs since 1830." There was of course no mention of the many benefits brought to a region previously under the Turks. This Muslim radical considered Hitler an ally — only the German dictator and Algeria's Messali Hadj could, in his exaggerated view, "save the indigenous from French slavery." He added an epithet that remains sobering in today's multicultural world: "An Arab will always remain an Arab." In other words, the polished boots and well-knotted ties of a Weygand simply couldn't seduce such people into embracing ideas of French grandeur. Instead? "Let us love and admire Chancellor Hitler" and remember that "eternal France is unworthy of existence," he wrote.

More serious was a note from the Director of General Security in Algiers to Weygand, July 21, 1941, discussing a death threat on the delegate general's life contained in two recent letters. Authorities believed they knew the person behind these letters, but he was on the run and couldn't be located. The letters were found in Blida, and again, one praised Messali Hadj and Hitler, according to a report from Blida's gendarmerie. Typed parts of one sent July 17 show that the writer had recently heard of Weygand's nomination as Algeria's governor-general, declaring that "we don't need Governors." He then announced that the general would be imminently assassinated! The time mentioned was five P.M., July 21, and the writer also urged Weygand to show his wife the letter. The second epistle of July 17 extolled Hitler as well, hoping that he would completely devastate France. These letters — and many others like them — are important not only as sources of antipathy to Weygand or to colonial France, but also as evidence that the Marxist orientation of the next decade's strongest Algerian terror group, the Front de Libération Nationale, may have been a fair-weather development. Previously, Nazism was considered more central to liberation here.[54]

However, the lion's share of what we have in the archives for wartime is from Muslim notables of North Africa, and definitely pro–Weygand; for instance, a poem written in Arabic by one Sheik Mohamed Zouani Ben Sidi Mbarek of September 1941, commenting on the delegate general's previous arrival in Africa: "Welcome, O WEYGAND, o pure son of France [unintended irony!]. Welcome to you, who in battle, made a name for yourself among the brave." Weygand's assistant governor-general, Châtel, responded September 29, thanking the man for his devotion. Here was an individual example among many, showing adherence both to Weygand and to the France that he represented. There were also collective manifestations, including a "Demonstration of loyalty to the General in Chief, Governor of Algeria, by the native populations"— reported on by the police commissioner in Algiers, July 25, 1941. The report noted a "sizeable crowd of native people estimated at some 7,000, gathered at five o'clock this evening at the Place Lavigerie to express loyalty to the person of the General in Chief, Governor of Algeria." Even if manipulated by notables, "the enthusiasm of the Muslim population was intense...." There was much sustained applause in response to speeches, including one by Weygand, and fervent singing of the *Marseillaise*. And "it was significant that this crowd of Muslims was composed of humble workers, small tradesmen, artisans, old soldiers, and retired government employees. The Mozabite colony was well represented, and I did not notice the presence of the usual politicians."[55]

It is no exaggeration to posit that Weygand's successes vis-à-vis North African Arabs (and to a lesser extent, Kabyles) were almost as remarkable as those he had keeping the Axis at bay. He made even a weakened France respected by his discipline and military aura, and people mainly felt they should toe the line. As one French government functionary told Louis Berteil prophetically (seeing ahead to the savage conflict of the '50s): "I know the Arabs well, I've lived with them for 60 years, and those of Birtouta are no worse or better than elsewhere; but if they're keeping tranquil right now, it's because they fear General Weygand: wait a little, they will quickly be buying arms to throw us out the door!" In this period Weygand's toughness was certainly a deterrent. For example, when he heard of an army revolt among Algerian sharpshooters in January 1941, he leapt up from the barber's chair, where he was getting a haircut, and promptly stopped it, with Muslim notables helping deliver up the ringleaders. It was the last such mutiny of the war in Algeria. Weygand also kept Messali Hadj, a former Stalinist once incarcerated by Daladier, and now pro–Nazi, behind bars. But at the same time, he exhibited a certain laissez-faire toward North Africa's Muslims, especially when it came to black market trading. He also forced through a raise in their salaries of some 10 percent, while cutting work hours; and Berteil recalls Arabs streaming from their *douars* to be comparatively well paid in larger towns, then using leisure time back home to spend and live well.[56] At once bad cop/good cop, particularly in an Algeria he came more and more to run, Weygand maintained stability in a region that would later be full of anarchic divisions.

But his main obsession was keeping the empire strong and safe from the Axis, allied with his desire to resuscitate an army here that would eventually help defeat it. These views clashed with those of collaborationist Vichy policy-makers, especially as Darlan took greater control. Weygand hoped to have more success with Pétain, and in a long missive to him of January 4, 1941, on the "Situation of Military Forces in French Africa," he began on difficulties of creating a viable army in North Africa, given restrictions of the armistice commissions. He then furnished the marshal a precise sense of French and indigenous troop numbers needed to bring that army up to fighting capability. On the important matter of materiel, a concern that kept surfacing during his tenure, Weygand stressed the lack of submachine guns, grenade-launchers, and mortars; and of light trucks, motorcycles, and all-terrain or combat vehicles, etc. One-third of what *did* exist left North Africa as part of Germany's reparations agreement. Weygand also mentioned critical shortages of spare parts and the metal to create them. Unwilling to wait, he asked "that these shortages be made up without delay, because the training of motorized units is paralyzed here ... with only a part of A.F.N. forces now ready for combat." Another of his preoccupations was protection of extensive coastlines here. At present, he told Pétain, he had only 33,000 men to defend a seacoast of over 2,000 kilometers. He also wished to form "an elite black army" in West Africa, but knew how difficult it would be "in the dry season." On the issue of military aviation, his tone is also dire, yet clear, with emphasis on the large problem of fuel shortages. Nonetheless, "if recommended solutions are rapidly carried out, the African Army will be able to fulfill any assigned tasks by the first of April."

Here Weygand's psychology clearly placed naive, filial hope in his superior; when in fact, Pétain was much handicapped by age, Nazi spies around him, and a need to temporize or delegate. Thus the marshal sent a copy of Weygand's missive to Darlan, who shunted it to General Huntziger, who framed a stolid response to Weygand January 20, 1941, on letterhead showing his capacity as commander in chief of French land forces, as well as war minister. Concerning army numbers, Huntziger noted that his government had kept trying to get imprisoned officers freed, and to enroll others who were demobilized, and to add former members of the Foreign Legion. In Part II, relating to materiel, he began with submachine guns, declaring that "very few of these weapons exist in the Metropole." French negotiators had kept asking the German armistice commission for manufacturing rights, and to the latest letter sent in that regard, no reply was as yet received. Essentially the same was true for munitions, with demands still being sent to the armistice commissions for rights of manufacture. But beyond his quibbles on each detail of Weygand's shopping list, Huntziger's general tone also shows a contrast between a more divided, defeatist Vichy, and the proconsul's go-ahead North Africa.[57]

Of course behind Huntziger was Darlan, wishing himself to stonewall wherever possible, as in a first reaction of January 17 to Weygand's original missive, sent to Pétain. For instance, on the issue of the naval air force, Darlan felt that it was "inopportune to modify this organization...." The *real* kinds of things he and his ilk were working on, especially after he came to full power in February as vice-president of the Council and Pétain's new heir, are seen in a confidential letter of March 28, 1941, sent to him by Admiral de Rivoyre, Head Secretary of Naval Coordination. The letter followed a conversation de Rivoyre had had with Darlan March 12, giving his plans on lines that had been previously discussed. These treat the development of French Africa that would "open perspectives of French-German collaboration," and the report of 56 pages is focused mainly on *German* needs. Commodities that would be useful to the Nazis include different kinds of wheat, wool, wood, skins, and oils. His mineral list includes manganese, zinc, cobalt, coal, copper, and iron, and he notes where more research is needed to develop production. He then treats the possibilities of developing roads and rail in this empire, and expansion of radio, telephones, air facilities, and the like, all to be aided by German participation. And all *for* the Nazis and their "new Europe," not (as in Weygand's optic) to facilitate a French comeback. Had he seen this document, the delegate general would doubtless have fumed, but he already knew how different his posture was compared to those at Vichy who were ready to invite the foe into the store everywhere, giving him at least part ownership![58]

When Weygand had to choose economically between helping North Africa in the short run by aiding Germany and Italy via exports, or doing what it took to keep U.S. supplies coming in, his sympathies invariably lay with the latter. Lengthy studies he himself commissioned on zinc, phosphate, lead, and so on in North Africa's mines *also* warned businessmen here never to deal directly with the enemy. They must always first contact North African governmental authorities. Weygand was more than willing to fight for research money or machinery that would help extract minerals, but never to aid Axis powers and alienate the U.S., which might then cancel *its* contracts to bring in supplies for French North Africa.[59]

The infamous Paris Protocols of May–June 1941 showed how much Weygand diverged here from Darlan and the rest of Vichy's bureaucracy (increasingly staffed with the admiral's choices). Since June 1940, Weygand had not altered his desire to "keep rigorously to the stipulations of the armistice, carrying out its inescapable requirements but opposing every violation of its clauses, every overstepping of them, every encroachment...."[60] And the latter line understates the courage it took to do so.

The late Professor Bankwitz, no more than middling in his admiration of the general, nonetheless calls the Protocols which Darlan and the Nazis formulated during May and negotiated into June, 1941, "the major crisis of Weygand's rule...," and one which he resolutely confronted. On paper "the Germans obtained military, naval, and economic concessions which gave them virtual control of North Africa...." The fact that this was stalled in practice — except for Syrian bases vouchsafed the Nazis, which by July were taken back by English and Gaullists — was in large measure due to Weygand. He traveled to Vichy for cabinet meetings on June 3 and 4, and as Bankwitz notes, "brought all of his dramatic pressure to bear on Pétain and the cabinet." And he had a united front of colonial officials alongside him — both Boisson and Esteva also summoned, and completely supporting Weygand. "As a result, the

Marshal Pétain (left), head of the French state, and Admiral Jean-François Darlan on a Vichy boulevard in World War II. Weygand courageously opposed Darlan's negotiations for more extensive collaboration with the Nazis in the infamous Paris Protocols of May–June, 1941 (Hulton-Deutsch Collection/CORBIS).

French government temporized by drawing up a list of counter demands to be fulfilled by the Germans before the Protocols went into effect." These were so huge, including French control of both metropolitan zones and no more demarcation line, that the Germans simply backed down. Weygand had bought time — important time — which worked also because the Nazis would soon be preoccupied with Russia and other significant war theaters. They certainly wished to use Dakar militarily, and especially, Tunisia's Bizerte as a base for the Afrika Korps; but that would have to wait. Bankwitz concludes that "Weygand cannot, of course, claim the entire credit.... The result, however, of both Berlin's problems and Weygand's obduracy was that Darlan's collaboration did not, after all, bring about a war between France and Britain allied with the United States." Quite the reverse, in fact; more than any French military or political figure, Weygand kept Gallic North Africa intact, thereby facilitating the Anglo-American invasion to come.[61]

Back at his post, the general still had elaborate balancing acts to per-
form when it came to military versus civilian needs in North Africa, and this
never abated. For instance, Algerian wine was earmarked for the mainland,
but some — shades of contemporary concerns — might also be used to furnish
what a rejuvenated, mechanized French army badly required here, a ready fuel
supply. Presiding over a Conference on Wines September 10 and 11, 1941,
Weygand made the prime subject of his opening remarks "transforming a
million hectoliters of the last harvest into fuel." He then opened the floor to
problems this would entail, but still wanted vinegrowers to proceed as best
they could with the first million hectoliters distilled. Some pleaded lack of
time, lack of money, lack of available hands; however, Weygand emphasized
that to keep getting more American aid, French authorities here needed reliable shipping to transport commodities. And due to fuel shortages, "delays
in boat departures of sometimes 10 days" were a real problem. Algeria especially needed more gas derived from its plentiful vineyards; yet Weygand still
believed there would be plenty of drinkable product left over for export to
France. He felt that the U.S. might be able to supply roughly one-half of
French fuel needs here, and weighing different points of view, drew out from
those present what it would take to get the other half. In the end he wanted
something solid and unanimous to emerge from the conference. And he got
his wine-producers to agree on prices, and people from various government
branches to assent. At the close of proceedings, Weygand thanked all present
for "a fine spirit of conciliation...."[62]

As long as he could, Weygand pestered Darlan and other authorities in
Vichy to obtain what was needed for the defense of North Africa. His detailed
reports on lack of readiness kept coming out — he was never one to take no
for an answer. One such report of March 15, 1941, and another to Darlan of
October 27, on "Defense of North African Coastlines," equally emphasized
deficits of arms and men. These seascapes were still prey to an Axis *coup de
main*, said the latter report, and Weygand ranked Tunisia's most vulnerable
(prescient, given the later German invasion), then Morocco's, and finally Algeria's. Bizerte was particularly appetizing, but then, Darlan knew this — the
delegate general referring to copious prior correspondence on the subject.
"Months pass," he said, "and Bizerte is virtually undefended."[63]

Another Weygand letter to Darlan of May 21 was typically clear and
tough-minded on his concerns: modernizing and improving a resurgent army,
despite foot-dragging armistice commissions. Weygand noted that to "complete formation of a North African Armistice Army ... that is, even without
demanding any advantage, but only the strict application of the imposed diktat," required volunteer soldiers who had been waiting several months for

travel authorization to North Africa; arms and munitions from France that had long been requested; more combat vehicles, and the like. Knowing, however, to whom he was writing, Weygand noted the possibility of British attacks, and the necessity for better air defenses; but between the lines (and from repetitive use of the word "diktat"), one sees who the real enemy is here.[64]

To the end of his North African reign, the delegate general dueled with the admiral on these matters. An undated Darlan letter (simply given as September 1941) was dispatched to Weygand, showing how testy he was getting with him, referring to his letter of September 19, where "you have again drawn my attention to the danger represented by progressive German and Italian infiltration into North Africa." More, "you added that you considered this danger as capital, and asked the Government continually to support you in the war of details that you must undertake in order to thwart all these maneuvers." Darlan assured Weygand, hypocritically so, that Vichy was entirely behind him in the protection of French North Africa, and "against the extra-conventional activities of Axis representatives." But then on October 28, this defense minister, among his other positions, wrote Weygand on their sole difference — a major one: "In the domain of hypotheses, I will emphasize only the priority that there is in general, reason to accord the *English* threat...."[65] Case closed...

In two areas Weygand far exceeded legal limits in countering the Axis, contributing thereby to his eventual fall at the hands of the Nazis, who pressured Vichy ministers on it. One was camouflaging arms and other materiel well beyond Armistice Commission restrictions. In Africa, Weygand still encouraged and supported such activity to the fullest, inspiring subordinates in the same path, using his "Section d'Etudes." For him the empire was to be a launching pad, and this required an army with suitable and copious arms. When he was finally "chopped" in November 1941, Weygand and associates had worked so fast that the amount of materiel covered up there, and available for another day, was impressive. A swelled military had much more firepower than would have been the case had someone else occupied his positions. Under different guises, including the necessity of "policing," he had increased French troops in strategically crucial North Africa from the initial 30,000 allowed by Italian armistice commission authorities, and some 110,000 then permitted by the Germans, to circa 180,000. At his departure, that army could dispose of trucks roughly double the number there were supposed to be. Ditto in almost the same proportions for artillery, with shells and infantry munitions about five times their theoretical amount. Weygand's administration had hidden with verve machine guns galore, cannonry, tanks, and the like — in forests or on farms, in grottos or reserve officers' buildings. There were, as well, thousands of tons of camouflaged aluminum, nickel, and other minerals, which the German military-industrial complex so coveted. Not to mention vital radio and radar equipment spirited from the Nazis, medical supplies — and the list went on. Weygand's military associates, such as Juin and de Lattre, who would shine in France's liberation, did so in part because they were legated the wherewithal. Ships were continually bringing in clandestine arms cargoes, to the point where "in 1942, when moving again to the Allied side, General Juin could dispose of thousands of rifles, millions of cartridges, and equipment of all kinds."[66]

The other domain where Weygand went well beyond the acceptable was in intelligence-gathering, fully supporting agents of the empire trying to counter the Axis. He was well seconded by Commandant Henri Navarre, head of the Deuxième Bureau in Algiers, and from early 1941, Lieutenant-Colonel Jean Chrétien, who became head of all intelligence in North Africa.[67] French coastal installations tracked movements in the Mediterranean of Italian and German shipping, giving that information to the British, who were then able to torpedo a goodly number of enemy ships bearing war materials. Weygand also organized French surveillance of armistice commission personnel, who were in theory simply monitoring the agreement's provisions, but actually using their positions in North Africa to infiltrate, and to fire up opposition Muslims, and engage in outright espionage. These commissions and consulates became foci for a variety of German or Italian visitors — diplomats, engineers, financiers, and even priests — who did double-duty as spies. Concerning the main enemy, Jacques Weygand puts it well: "To justify this infiltration, all pretexts were good for the Germans: some called themselves liaison officers, others claimed to be looking for deserters who had taken refuge in the Foreign Legion, still others baptized themselves buyers, while some claimed to have come here to maintain burial places of Germans who had died in North Africa. In reality, all were spying, insinuating themselves, corrupting."[68]

As for Italian armistice authorities, those in Algeria made elaborate inspection tours and sent profuse correspondence, warning of their need to be alerted to *any* French troop changes, movement of munitions or artillery, or even of horses. From his base at Algiers' tony Hotel Aletti, Colonel Alberto Vinaj, head of the Italian Control delegation for Algeria early in Weygand's period there, was especially punctilious. One of his most comical letters has as its "object" *Movimento quadrupedi*. This missive of November 20, 1940, translated from Italian into French, noted that he had just learned that morning of 1500 horses being sent from Oran, Algiers, and Bône to Marseille, and warned that he *must* be "informed within opportune time of any movement of men, animals, or materiel." He rhymed off earlier French transgressions — transfer of an artillery corps to Tunisia without his approval, and of a group of Foreign Legionnaires; and now these animals! The French, however, enjoyed baiting these Italian authorities, and Weygand's stern measures for hiding materiel (including edicts of death for loose-lipped soldiers) certainly exceeded the strictures of figures like Vinaj! There were also Italian frontier squabbles with the French, for example, on the Saharan border of Algeria and Libya, where French authorities invariably played innocent.[69]

When the Nazis supplanted the Italians as armistice watchers in Morocco at the end of January, 1941, Weygand knew he must preempt rigorously. In the spring of that year he created a division within the Service des Renseignements (S.R.) to track these German authorities in Moroccan cities. He also maintained gutsy restrictions on their comportment in public. This meant, for instance, that (unlike in the movie *Casablanca*) German military men could not wear uniforms in public, or at least while Weygand occupied his position.[70] But more than just physical tracking was necessary to counter the foe, and this led to a complicated system of radio intercepts, phone taps, and amplified microphones placed in residences or offices occupied by Axis personnel. General Antoine Béthouart, who later became a right-hand man to de Gaulle, was recruited by Weygand to oversee the operation in Morocco — this in addition to being commander of troops in Rabat, then Casablanca. Cooperation of employees in the Postal and Telegraph Office was thorough, and Italians were paradoxically more suspicious about all this than the less psychological Germans. (The Italians were *also* more fearful in Algeria or Tunisia, when the French secret service engaged in sexual blackmail, bomb threats, and even beatings of their personnel, all actively or tacitly supported by Weygand.)

As for these Germans in Morocco, Weygand remained firm on keeping them isolated — forbidding French officers from shaking their hands, or eating with them, and enjoining the secret service to keep both French and Muslim-Arab civilians away as well.[71] The S.R. branch in Casablanca that tracked the Germans via phone taps and the like was called the Bureau de Coordination de Casablanca (B.C.C.), and an unpublished manuscript by Colonel Serge-Henri Parisot, who became its head, reveals much more to these French (reporting back to the resident's office and to Weygand's) than does the great American film of that time.

The main foe here was the German K.I.A. (Kontroll-Inspektion in Afrika), supposedly monitoring the armistice, but faking the French delegation (D.F.A.M.) at every turn, and wanting much more, right up to a takeover of Morocco (so the listenings and decipherings told). This "Plan Felix" fell apart only because of French prudence, unexpected German reverses in Russia and Egypt, Franco's recalcitrance, and the surprising Allied invasion of North Africa.

Prior to late 1942, little of that seemed in the cards, and French intelligence-gathering was therefore serious business, if hampered by rivalry among different intelligence organisms, or by the D.F.A.M. Parisot's listening and deciphering officers were gung-ho patriots, most escaped from the Germans. With real courage, they planted microphone devices in phones, and tracked K.I.A. members, and those of the Control Commission of the Luftwaffe, the German Land Army, etc. They also countered German propaganda with Arabs, and watched scum in the business world who profited by dealings with the Nazis that went well beyond armistice limitations. Profits could easily be made from export of minerals, coal, textiles, and many other things in Morocco that the Reich desired. One intelligence coup of this new organization came when 200 tons of leather goods (illegal to export) were to be brought by a French businessman to the Spanish-Moroccan frontier, where a man from Hamburg would meet him. But when the telegram announcing date and time for the rendezvous was placed at the Casablanca post office, a French secret serviceman came up a few minutes later, and in a German accent said it was the wrong date — it should be put down as ten days later. Much anger ensued from the empty-handed meeting that followed!

These Germans of wartime Casablanca lived in commandeered villas, hotels, and apartments, largely in the classy Anfa section of the metropolis. But even while living in style, the German consul himself remained part of a plot to inventory pretty well everything in Morocco (not only French troop emplacements, but post offices, and even art), prior to the Nazi version of eminent domain. Hitler may have been impulsive, but at gradually turning the screws, the Nazis of wartime were thorough, deceptive planners, including here. And beyond North Africa, they had designs on the rest of French colonial Africa, too. All this makes the period of Weygand's powerful positions on this continent a crucial one.[72]

Supposedly few in number, German personnel in Morocco had *great* material advantages — transport planes, trucks, and so on at their disposal, and with no fuel shortages to worry about. They also had much contact with the home base. And they had plenty of money with which to buy informers. On both sides information was regularly peddled here — by cafe waiters, restaurateurs, or chambermaids. However, the scene in *Casablanca* of a French woman dating a German, then impulsively singing along with the *Marseillaise*, is not far-fetched. Outside of the Parti Populaire Français, or foreigners like "Dollar," an East European tennis teacher in Casablanca working for the Germans (and collared by the organization Weygand spawned), most French here were anything but pro–German.

Microphones to amplify the spoken word were installed by secret service "workers," fixing German telephones by first breaking them, then putting in the gizmos; but had the "Boches" discovered these devices, it would have meant capture of these agents, egg on the delegate general's face, and probably the takeover of Morocco, and even Algeria. And it was hard to keep such things secret, given babblings of even Allied agents. According to Parisot, the latter lacked finesse and, especially in the American case, were "children" one couldn't trust entirely. (Parisot was warmer to Gaullists, particularly military ones, rather than the parlor variety "who poured oil on the fire while remaining in their slippers.") But in sum, this well-run French spying organization was yet another Weygand feat during his period here.[73]

When it came to intelligence coups, the manner in which he allowed the U.S. spying access in French North Africa was perhaps his greatest, pre–TORCH legacy. We have alluded a number of times to his close relationship with the Americans during his period in A.F.N., but must now give the issue fuller treatment. From the start, Roosevelt trusted Foch's old sidekick, and according to his special legate, Robert Murphy, "one reason why the President hoped for anti–Nazi action in French Africa was because General Maxime Weygand had recently been appointed Delegate General there ... Roosevelt could not believe that this honorable old soldier would tolerate indefinitely French subservience to Germany...."[74] The president's trust was vindicated, particularly when he made Murphy his supreme authority in the Maghreb, and mutual admiration between him and Weygand transpired from the beginning of their relationship.

However, the way in which the Murphy-Weygand accord got off the ground, and the Americans developed an ever more burning idea of liberating French North Africa, was not at all predestined; rather, it resembled the progress of a battered salmon making it through many miles of hurdles to spawn. The idea of America supplying the French and helping them resist the Axis in North Africa had originated simultaneously with the French diplomat Mönick, and with a Briton, David Eccles; but also in part with a bohemian, tasteful idealist from Virginia who had made a career in the U.S. Foreign Service, and saw more of the world (including the Arab world) than almost any American of his century. Yet this James Rives Childs fortuitously found himself in Washington during the early stages of the war. To get the idea by the State Department, and especially influential skeptics like Herbert Feis, director of international economic affairs, was difficult; but perhaps due to his own background, the president knew how to bypass patrician bureaucrats and run with an idea he liked. Mönick then became Murphy's first contact. Meeting at Rabat in a fragrant nocturnal garden, the two hammered out ideas on how America might overcome Britain's blockade and get supplies to French North Africa; after which they shared a bottle of champagne. A key American fear was that its much-needed tea, gas, or sugar arriving on French ships might be rerouted to the metropole, and thence to the Germans. Mönick's idea was that American consuls and vice-consuls should be permitted to supervise unloading and distribution in ports like Casablanca. He felt sure — and was proven correct — that America would soon be in the war, and was therefore the wave of the future. It was also fortuitous that Admiral William D. Leahy had become American ambassador to Vichy, and that as another Weygand fan, fully supported these démarches. In 1941 Childs was then made U.S. consul in Tangiers. Having attended the Sorbonne (after Harvard), written a book on Restif de la Bretonne, and learned to esteem all things French, this Gallophile continued to impress on the White House how important the budding Franco-American agreement was — which then impelled the president to strike a committee of investigation on French North Africa and speed the process, not least to what ultimately became Operation TORCH.[75]

However, Weygand *also* played a major role in this growing relationship with the Americans. Murphy first met the general in Rabat in late December 1940, and with Weygand discussing his empire's pressing needs, bent an already pliant ear. Those talks then eventuated in the Murphy-Weygand Accord of February 26, 1941, but not without difficulty from Vichy. The marshal wished to sign, but fearing the Germans, Darlan was typically antipathetic, while Flandin went back and forth that winter of 1941, when the issue was being discussed. So the accord was simply initialed by Murphy and Weygand in Algiers, with Murphy then given a permanent position in the city where Weygand was based. Murphy never wavered in his view that A.F.N. would find it easier to "retain its relatively independent status if it received moderate economic support from the United States."[76] But neither he nor Roosevelt would have plunged the U.S. in this direction — given British, German, and Vichy distrust, along with that in the U.S. departments of State, Treasury, and Economic Warfare — without the *ad hominem* sense they had of Weygand. And Weygand was himself eager to play ball with this benefactor, stressing the empire's great need for food and pharmaceuticals, basic equipment, and especially gas. Not to mention arms for the new, beefed-up army of *revanche*. In the delegate general, Murphy felt instinctively that he had an appealing, trustworthy partner.[77]

Implementation of the accord signed February 26, 1941, included unfreezing of French funds in the States to pay for this vital economic aid; but it then went off and on "at the whim of every pencil-pusher in Washington." It also took careful negotiation with the English for their blockade to be relaxed, permitting certain boats to bring American goods into A.F.N. ports. And the Nazis were predictably angered, while simultaneously fearful that an impoverished North Africa would be more vulnerable to the British. The accord then became more fragile with the hatching of the Paris Protocols, rendering both Germans and blockading British more obdurate. Later, more deliveries were made, due in part to the U.S. Treasury ceding to Murphy's growing clout. In the Americans, Weygand had found the right source for aid, spurning intermittent English overtures of military and other cooperation. As Martin Thomas notes, these "British could not [yet] lend enough material support to preclude a Germano-Italian descent upon French North Africa." Better to work with the U.S., especially when an enigmatic businessman, soldier, and spy, Colonel Robert Solborg, began giving a decidedly military flavor to the agreement — which he also helped sell to Roosevelt.[78]

An important turning point for execution of the accord came with Hitler's invasion of Russia, the Americans now feeling that the preoccupied Germans would be less likely to move on A.F.N., particularly Morocco, where their armistice officials and consulate had a foothold. The Americans could now envisage the delivery even of fighter planes to the French here. But to get any supplies through the English blockade, Weygand had to agree — and did so whole-heartedly — to allow American intelligence inspection rights in French harbors, again, to ensure that nothing would be sent to a German-infested metropole. Weygand gave the Americans carte blanche, including in the creation of 33 "vice-consuls," really intelligence experts from the Office of Strategic Services; and secondary sources agree that this intelligence access significantly helped the U.S. in the coming success of TORCH. Meanwhile, as Chantal Metzger notes, simply "from a practical point of view, American economic and humanitarian aid was of great utility." Great quantities of tea, coal, cotton goods, sugar, medicine, and the like — much of it delivered on credit — significantly enhanced the situation of the average North African, while many metropolitan French suffered from shortages. As delegate general and commander in chief, Weygand had helped make not only Bogie's Casablanca, but the entire Maghreb a comparative refuge.[79]

Concerning this forthright proconsul, was there a final straw that snapped the German camel's back? In actuality, there was a series. Murphy and Weygand renewed their accord in July, 1941, and the Nazis permitted it for three months only, but with misgivings, due to intelligence they felt was being passed to the U.S. In fact, well trained as those American agents were, and popular in North Africa, some also helped undermine Weygand's position by indiscretions. (It didn't help that Weygand had pampered them with courier service and permission to employ secret codes, and basically given them a good deal of leeway.) The Nazis certainly envied this treatment, desiring the same for their own consular officials.[80]

In tandem with German pressure, another central reason for Weygand's fall was his ever-worsening relationship with the powerful Darlan. François Lehideux, Vichy's minister of industrial production, considered them completely opposite personalities, especially when it came to dealing with the Germans. Weygand's position in North Africa became less secure from the time he opposed the collaborationist Paris Protocols in the spring of 1941. He was too openly vociferous both for Darlan, and for the Nazis, and his arrests and/or expulsions of Axis spies in North Africa merely intensified this resentment. In September the Germans menaced Darlan directly concerning the maintenance of Weygand at his post. In October Darlan sent a sharply negative reply to a Weygand report on the continuing need for U.S. help, averring that such aid could only push the Germans into an invasion of French Africa. Then on October 17 Darlan told Pétain that he had just seen Otto Abetz, the Reich's ambassador to France, and been told in no uncertain terms that Weygand's position had become unbearable to the Germans, due mainly to his relationship with the Americans, which harmed the cause of collaboration. Pushed by General Keitel and Hitler himself, Abetz wrote Pétain a firm letter on the necessity of ousting Weygand from his position. Support for the Germans came also from Jacques Benoist-Méchin, a cultivated collaborator at Vichy's Foreign Ministry, and a Germanophile close to the Nazi ambassador. Benoist-Méchin wouldn't forgive Weygand for his opposition to the Protocols, and his relationship with the "Anglo-Saxons." A third prominent anti–Weygand figure at Vichy was Pierre Pucheu, minister of the interior (from August 11), formerly a self-made businessman, and later to die by Gaullist firing squad (de Gaulle unwilling to pardon his wartime hunt for Resistants that also included an attempt to save hostages from Nazi execution). Meanwhile, Pétain continued stalling both the Germans and this coterie of ministers, but only for a short while. He certainly knew that the Nazis could make one pay for prolonged disobedience, including by executing innocent civilians.

However, Weygand himself dug the final shovelful of his North African grave during centenary celebrations in early November for the inception of Algerian sharpshooters and *spahis* (native cavalry) corps. Delegating planning to General Joseph de Monsabert, Weygand saw his crew in Algiers put on quite a show. After a picturesque parade at the hippodrome of Caroubiers, featuring a colorful variety of costumes and standards, there was thunderous applause, and Weygand was saluted by several thousand indigenous veterans wearing medals, whom de Monsabert had brought in from their villages. But to observers present, these *spahis* and *tirailleurs* (along with Foreign Legionnaires and representatives from other outfits) seemed to be not merely commemorating, but looking forward — to revenge. An Italian armistice official on hand wrote the secret service in Rome on this French army in Africa that seemed too full of itself. Nor were German consular and armistice officials in the front row amused, quickly informing the Fatherland, where eminences like Goering already reviled Weygand.[81]

Rumblings in French dailies, such as a front-page spread in the *Journal de Rouen* of November 11, 1941, told readers that Weygand's position in Africa was now tottering. On November 15 Marshal Pétain was given a sealed envelope emanating from the German General Staff, with a note inside urging him to recall the delegate — now. Pétain kept his counsel, and next came direct pressure from an irate Abetz in Paris. On November 17 Weygand was ordered to Vichy, and Colonel Van Hecke, set to defect to the Allies, tried ardently to keep him in Algiers. He also worked on Weygand's son Jacques, and his wife, but Weygand would not be dissuaded from staying in line. (Did the general fear for his other son and family in occupied France?) Whatever the case, he made the fateful trip, and next day before Pétain and Darlan, was told that emanating from Hitler himself, the Germans wanted him immediately out of Africa. Nor would Vichy allow Weygand even on a temporary basis to regain Algiers for goodbyes, and to collect his effects. He was considered too popular for that. Pétain then signed a decree terminating the position of delegate general in Africa; it would be replaced with separate positions of military command and a permanent General Secretariat for North Africa. The Weygand affair elicited protest from quite a number of career soldiers in France, but Pétain declared that he had been pressured for a long time by the Nazis, and finally had to cede. Behind closed doors with Leahy, however, he "said the decision had caused him great pain, that his personal views did not count.... He [even] repeated twice, 'I am a prisoner.'" Pétain added that the Germans had promised "in event of refusal to occupy all France ... and to permit the native population to die of hunger." Meanwhile, Darlan fairly gloated — in his view, such a "megalomaniac" as Weygand should never have been given this position in the first place![82]

If no megalomaniac, Weygand certainly *had* been a real proconsul, caring deeply for all North Africans, including Muslims, and implementing reforms that helped them. These included the building of new housing projects to replace rat-filled, disease-prone shanty towns. It included aid to runaway children shining shoes in the streets, whom he tried to place in greater numbers in schools. And it included regular wartime procurement and distribution of coffee, so prized by inhabitants of the Maghreb. Weygand also fought ultra-fascists like Doriot's P.P.F. tooth and nail, and edged out Admiral Abrial as governor-general because the latter was no reformer and remained pro–Darlan. Quite simply, the delegate general had been a whirlwind of activity, of conceptions and inceptions. Weygand was not only the best of Vichy in North Africa; in many ways he really wasn't Vichy at all.[83]

Yet he basically followed whatever orders came from above. All that ensued now was his termination from all African positions, and soon, the loss of liberty itself, except to write — there was nothing else to do while he was henceforth under surveillance in the south of France at a hotel in Grasse, then at Cannes. So he began what was certainly proper to a man of 75, his memoirs, starting with the recent, searing events of 1939 onward that became volume three. But while Weygand could now focus on his past, many still considered him a man of the present, and Vichy was inundated with letters of protest — from North Africans of all social classes, Europeans and Muslims alike, vigorously protesting this recall. Remaining behind in Algiers, Madame Weygand, too, was mobbed by well-wishers, until she, son Jacques, and members of Weygand's staff were able to board the *Lamoricière* December 2 for Marseille — an old ship that would go down with much loss of life its next time out! Even then, people on the quais cried out in force, hoping against hope — "Vive Weygands" resounding to deaf official ears. As Jacques Weygand says poignantly, this was no au revoir — it was "an adieu for us, and we would never again see Africa."[84]

Well into 1942, there was continuing evidence of the departed Weygand's popularity there, especially as a military figure so appealing at the time to Arabs devoted to their own leaders. One of those Muslim notables was Amédée Froger, mayor of Boufarik, a World War I veteran, and later murdered by his own during the Algerian revolt of the '50s. As head of the Municipal Council of Boufarik, Froger put through a deliberation in a meeting attended by three assistants, and 15 other councilors, of whom the majority had Arab names. Six were absent. The deliberation ran as follows: "At the moment of General Weygand's departure from Algeria's governor-generalship, the Boufarik Town Council, in its meeting of December 6, 1941, acknowledges the eminently French task he brought to fruition in Algeria, as in the African empire, rallying all hearts and energies under his unchallenged authority...."[85]

In early January (3 and 7), 1942, Châtel, Algeria's new governor-general, sent letters to Weygand in France, noting regrets over his departure expressed by town councils at Ténés and Marengo. On January 9 his missive to Weygand included a laudatory original in Arabic concerning the delegate's period in North Africa, emanating from one Mohamed Racin. A letter of January 29 to Weygand included mention of regrets by the Municipal Council of Sidi-Moussa, as well as a telegram from the president of the Chamber of Agriculture of the Department of Constantine, saluting the legacy of a man "who retains an unshakeable right to our admiration and gratitude...."[86]

Prefects generally culled such information and relayed it upward with their own comments. Thus the prefect of Algiers called one of these pro–Weygand deliberations (from the town council of Tizi-Reniff) "the saddened and emotion-filled expression of regrets concerning his departure from Algeria...."[87] On February 2 the prefect of Algiers addressed to Châtel's office "the text of two motions in which the members of Palestro's Town Council express their faithfulness and complete devotion to General Weygand, and communicate their sentiments of deep thanks." Extracts from a municipal council deliberation for Palestro showed its composition to include a French mayor, but also Arabs such as Bakir Saadi, Ali Moussaoui, and Abdelkader Belaid. (There was one female member, a Madame François.) In that deliberation, the council focused on a lineage of notability, with Châtel as "worthy continuer of the work undertaken by General Weygand...." Like the others, this motion was approved unanimously (January 10, 1942).[88]

On February 13 Châtel sent Weygand a deliberation from Algiers itself, "by which the city council expresses its gratitude to you for the work you accomplished in Algeria." (This from their meeting of February 3.) Some also wanted to name squares or streets for the departed Weygand, and the prefect of Algiers related one such demand to the governor-general, March 20, whereby the mayor of El-Biar, "reflecting the views of most of his administered, requests authorization to name the main town square 'Place Général Weygand.'" Referring to the general's visit here, "M. the Mayor of El-Biar wishes to emphasize that his stay, and the active goodness of Madame Weygand left a very profound impression in this community." The prefect endorsed the demand, but Châtel's reply of March 31 cited Weygand's previous injunction (while in Algiers) against naming streets or squares for him; this said, Châtel too supported the idea, as long as the mayor wrote directly to the general for his consent. And exactly as in Algeria, much adulation in neighboring Morocco and Tunisia for the departed delegate general was also denoted by the War Ministry's *deuxième bureau* reports, with no reason to be biased in favor of Weygand![89]

The same issues that had been Weygand obsessions still obtained in this era preceding the Anglo-American invasion of November. One report by a General Buffin, after his trip to North Africa of April 13–25, noted his inspections of troops, meetings with military leaders like General Juin, and continuing shortages of everything Weygand had always sought. Buffin spoke to another general about a motorized drill near Tunis, and the man said he could follow the itinerary by seeing all the broken-down vehicles en route, or those simply rolled into ravines. Lack of gasoline remained a big problem, and alcohol used in its stead had to be doubled in dose to work. There was still a shortage of requisite weaponry, too, and authorities receiving this report penciled in various places, "to be modified." Another document of May 30, 1942, emanating from the Defense Ministry, treated "security stocks in North Africa" and also seemed dire on this once-central Weygand concern. It noted the toughness of the Nazi Armistice Commission (C.A.A.), regarding "the feeble quantities of gas which Germany allocates to us each month...." The report's writer feared that even those allowances might be entirely eliminated. There are precise lists here of reserve stocks, and the usual wishful thinking expressed that repeat demands *might* work with German authorities who impeded deliveries of fuel for planes, etc.[90]

Other documents of the post–Weygand era treated the ever-present problem of Nazi propaganda with Muslims in North Africa, such as a detailed, secret report of the War Ministry's Bureau M.A., May 11, 1942. Such documents and others show Vichy's continuing precision in exhaustive lists relating to different branches of the military; but what was also needed were figures like Weygand to *do* something with such information.[91]

If Châtel was more appeasement-oriented than Algeria's former governor, the man who followed as North African military commander felt himself totally in the master's lineage. This was the future Marshal Juin, a *pied noir* who had shown his mettle in the era of Lyautey, and was now anti–Nazi to the core. From the beginning, General Juin stressed that he would perpetuate Weygand's heritage, even after suppression of the General Delegate's position, and splitting off of command of French Northwest Africa and parts to the East. Simply as commander in chief of the former, Juin retained much power. And from the beginning he emphasized to Darlan (in a letter of December 12, 1941) that he would remain a Weygandian. Juin's idea was to stay strong in North Africa, including for fear of Muslims being swayed by the enemy. In this long missive he goes on unabashedly: "The morale of the Army of Africa which General Weygand remade, by personal prestige and his oft-repeated slogan 'The Empire will be defended against all comers,' remains high: this despite fears caused by his departure, and the feeling we all share of the inadequacy of our means." Bluntly, Juin emphasizes who the true enemies remain for his "Germanophobic, Italophobic" troops, and also mentions numerous Anglophiles among civilians here.[92]

Juin retained even Weygand's staff in Algiers, except for the head of the Second Bureau, Navarre, whom Darlan transferred. In his opening statement to that staff, Juin declared emphatically: "Gentleman! The seance continues." Which, he said, "signified my wish to continue in the tracks traced out by General Weygand." This, however, did not preclude bumps in the road, such as being sent later that December on a disagreeable, forced mission to Germany, where — in theory — Juin was to procure more troop allowances for North African defense. In practice, he met a recalcitrant Marshal Goering in the sumptuous, but somewhat terrifying headquarters of the Luftwaffe in Berlin. To Juin, Goering was "a sort of living Buddha, playing compulsively with the numerous rings on his fingers and smoking many cigars" lit for him by another officer. Juin broached the need for loosening Italian armistice restrictions, so that the French army could become stronger in Tunisia; but Goering's sole preoccupation was allowing Rommel's Afrika Korps the possibility of withdrawing into this French protectorate from neighboring Libya. *That* would be real collaboration, an idea Juin found repugnant.[93]

Safely back in Algiers, Juin continued along the Weygand path, criticizing Vichy plans for decentralization of North African military authority, and plumping for his own overall control, despite some autonomy granted to Tunisia. With one vigorous czar at the top, troops and materiel could be rushed without undue debate to areas in crisis, he said. He also kept emphasizing the lack of fuel for French military needs, and the need for more cables and transmission equipment for his secret services, as well as copper, lead, cement, and so on, especially to help build up defenses at ports like Bizerte. He favored North African business itself manufacturing critical equipment, such as batteries or generators. And he continued to fine-tune Weygand's defense plans for the coastlines, linking up with the troop commander in Tunisia, de Lattre de Tassigny. All this again, *not* to counter English or Gaullists, but the Axis. In a typical letter, Juin wrote Darlan ("commander in chief of all Land, Sea, and Air troops"), August 24, 1942, on Weygand's old concerns about protection of these North African seascapes, particularly along the Atlantic. France still required naval forces over and above those allowed by the armistice commissions to protect Morocco's *littoral*, and Juin emphasized that "the idea isn't new. In October 1941, I had the opportunity as Supreme Commander of Troops in Morocco to submit similar proposals to the General Commander in Chief of North African Forces [Weygand], and also to the D.S.A. No follow-up came from these propositions, the D.S.A. having considered it pointless to present them to the German Armistice Commission, which in that era, systematically refused all requests concerning Morocco." Among other things Juin sought was four new corps for coastal defense. Darlan had himself spoken of additional tank sections, but would all this actually happen? The Moroccan ports remained vulnerable, and Juin wanted the matter thrown directly to the German C.A.A., then to Italian armistice authorities, hoping then to move eastward along the coast to beef up Oranie's beaches, and "eventually to the remainder of coastal Algeria and Tunisia, arguing from [previous] approval granted for Morocco." In response, the D.S.A. typically dragged feet in its dealings with the Germans.[94]

In addition to Juin, another Weygand supporter, Murphy, also remained in North Africa, relying on figures the delegate had groomed. In fact, "I had grown to trust some of Weygand's associates as much as I did him...," Murphy declared.[95] But in the run-up to Operation Gymnast, which became TORCH, he refused to give up on Weygand himself as France's potential military leader here. He still considered him popular in French Africa, and associated with tangible rewards that had derived from their agreement. In March 1942, Murphy sent a nephew of Douglas MacArthur to Cannes in order to interest Weygand in becoming top French soldier for Gymnast. Weygand gave a pithy reply: "You do not turn rebel at my age." He also knew how difficult it would be to elude heavy surveillance in order to do so. Nothing daunted, Murphy himself came to Cannes in mid–July to jawbone Weygand concerning a still veiled Allied invasion plan. In that enterprise Weygand wished Murphy well but denying any political aspirations, again demurred. However, the U.S. kept its policies intact, making it easier for Roosevelt to prevail with his particular version of the assault on North Africa. The ground *had* been well prepared by Weygand, and William Langer's conclusions still merit consideration. As Langer put it: "Nothing could be more unjust than to condemn all those who were connected with the Vichy regime or club them all together as collaborationists or traitors." Of no one could that be said more than Weygand, who provided the Americans so much. To Langer, "it would have been perfectly idiotic to cut ourselves off from this vital spring of information." And if the accords had been primordially economic, in order to keep A.F.N. "strong enough to resist aggression," this wasn't how things ended up for the Allies. For "very soon the intelligence possibilities became evident and began to overshadow all other considerations." Thanks to Weygand's cooperation, creation of American vice-consuls had provided the U.S. Johnnys-on-the spot before an invasion that, partly for that reason, worked so well.[96]

While in the South of France, the ex-delegate did admit that he thought of Africa every day, and hadn't gotten it out of his bones. Nor had reciprocal hopes ebbed among the Maghreb faithful — that somehow this beloved proconsul could escape (or had), and would return to them as a leader.[97]

If he could not do so personally, Weygand certainly constituted a significant link to the French group that after his departure, smoothed the path toward a successful American operation in November, 1942. This was the "group of five" of Jacques Lemaigre–Dubreuil, a businessman and newspaper publisher; Colonel Van Hecke, the Fleming who with Weygand's backing had turned North Africa's Chantiers de jeunesse into a military forcing ground; Jacques Tarbé de Saint-Hardouin, assistant secretary-general at Weygand's Délégation headquarters before November 1941; and Lieutenant Henri d'Astier de la Vigerie, a staff officer in Oran. Both Van Hecke and d'Astier would turn Gaullist, but came out of the Weygand hatchery, and/or admired the general. One should also mention Captain André Beaufre, a courageous soldier wounded in the Rif war of the '20s, who worked near Weygand in Algiers during his tenure, but was also en route to Gaullism. Imprisoned from May to November 1941, Beaufre then became a support for the Five, along with General Béthouart, who had been head of the French Armistice Commission in Morocco, commander of army divisions there, and Weygand's new man in the secret service.[98]

Regarding Beaufre, some detractors of Weygand like to lay that arrest completely at his anti–Gaullist door. But the delegate general *had* been on a tightrope in Africa, and proof that he was not simply unjust comes from Beaufre himself. The reason for his arrest was tragi-comic. Beaufre had been drawn into a hasty, unthought-out plan to liberate A.F.N., hatched by a mercurial veteran of World War I and (before flipping) ardent follower of Pétain — Commandant Georges Loustaunau-Lacau. Undoubtedly brilliant, Loustaunau-Lacau was also an unstable, indiscreet Pyreneean, who drew the more grounded Beaufre and Major Léon Faye (later to die in Germany) into this vague plan, whereby the Americans would somehow supply arms. It was a plot the French secret service thankfully foiled before real damage was done. As punishment, Weygand merely wanted to give both Beaufre and Faye disciplinary sanctions, while his secret service purposely allowed Loustaunau to escape back to France. (He had been in North Africa under false papers and name, and they wanted him out, before it reflected badly on them.) However, Vichy insisted on Beaufre's arrest, and Weygand went along. When the two then met after the war — Beaufre having glittered in Tunisia and other campaigns, and ascended the ranks toward general — all was forgiven. Their correspondence became an extensive one. "My opinion," said Beaufre to Louis Guitard, "was that General Weygand was a very winning man of exceptional moral quality, and one who had rendered France immense services." In North Africa he simply hadn't been able to "cross the Rubicon," in a time when that still "posed extremely delicate ethical problems," not to mention practical ones. But "what I remember especially when I think of him," added Beaufre, "is the fashion in which in 1940, he had taken in hand a hopeless situation, in a style, and with a decency at which I could only marvel. It's from that point that my profound esteem for him dates."[99]

One can easily understand why Beaufre and Weygand could develop such a kinship. Beaufre's own memoirs, pithier than Weygand's, but also compelling, reveal another vivid, realistic, yet philosophical French intelligence. Was Beaufre, in fact, a "Gaullist" when he first worked near Weygand under the governor-general in Algiers? In his own view, this over-simplifies, as de Gaulle and the Resistance still constituted a rather vague, far-off movement for whom one could merely cheer. Beaufre's admiration for the soldier the Americans chose over de Gaulle, Giraud, was deeper — as was his esteem for Weygand. Giraud had himself visited Weygand in the south of France June 17, 1942, ready to defer to him as leader of a turnaround in North Africa, and at the least, to get his blessing, which he received. It was Beaufre's planning and connections, along with luck, that then got Giraud out of France in November to meet with Eisenhower at Gibraltar, before he traveled to North Africa. Giraud's sadness at America's inability to see ahead (to the rapid Nazi takeover of both Tunisia and unoccupied France) became his own. In brief, one sees that among influences on this first-class general and military theorist in the making, Weygand and a sometimes naïve, but also brave, intuitive Giraud rank higher than de Gaulle. Patronized by the British, shunned by Vichy, and punished in the way Beaufre himself was by harrowing imprisonments, these Gaullists became, in his view, "intransigent, sectarian, and often embittered...." Which would only intensify after being shut out of TORCH![100]

When that well-organized and thrilling, if too limited, operation occurred in November 1942, Weygand hadn't much freedom of action. Coterminous with news of the landings, November 8, he was informed that he must immediately come to Vichy, and a government plane duly flew him up from Saint-Raphaël on the Riviera. At Vichy he met his son, and seemed openly happy about the Allied invasion, hoping that he had been summoned here for transfer to Algiers (where many still wanted him as French commander). He was adamant, however, that he would go only with a position of real power, and with Pétain's official support. Despite all his former appeasing, even Darlan appeared to be coming belatedly to the right side on a fortuitous visit to Algiers — and this gave Weygand added hope. Some argue that Pétain's fear of taking a plane ready to fly him to North Africa kept him nailed to a France he knew would be punished by the Germans, as indeed it was. Pétain's surface argument, however, made sense as well: that were he to do so, France would be crushed like Poland, and the sufferings of an already much-suffering people would intensify. Some surmise that Pétain wanted Weygand (privately) to go in his stead, but Weygand would not make any unilateral moves. The main thing was that Pétain would have to give approval, as Weygand would go *only* under his orders. His life-long psychology of loyalty held firm; more ominously, he was in fact under heavy surveillance, stemming from the home base in Germany, which for several months had been preparing to pounce on the man they had code-named "Lottermann." It turned out that "Lottermann's" chances of leaving Vichy for Algeria were very low, indeed.

Pétain did make a vague offer to Weygand for him to head the armies *within* France, but Weygand said no to that. He remained at Vichy five days, and kept enjoining the marshal to turn now to the Allies in North Africa — the ground had been well tilled, the much-awaited moment prepared for, and this was the time to move. Resistance to their invasion ought to end, and by a telegram to Darlan, putting the ball in his court (Darlan *also* under American pressure), that soon came about, though not before the deaths of many French soldiers trying to repel the invaders, and an equal amount on the Allied side. Others, meanwhile, tugged at Pétain's sleeves in different directions, while Weygand remained his typical forthright self. *Now*, he argued, was the time for French ships anchored off Toulon to sail for North Africa, or Barcelona, or some port in another neutral country. As in 1940, he wasn't heeded, and two weeks later, with the Germans closing in, the French had to scuttle their ships. It was another potential Weygand legacy that was tragically aborted. Ditto for his idea that French troops in the unoccupied zone be sent immediately to the Alps, the Cévennes, or other defensible regions, thence to become guerilla warriors (using hidden arms depots) on the Allied side. With the Germans massing troops between Occupied and Unoccupied France, coded orders from French Chief of Staff Verneau, eventually to die in Buchenwald, went out to that effect, but were overruled by the collaborationist war minister, General Bridoux; and Weygand blew a fuse. At the same time General Giraud also feared that French metropolitan troops would be cooked. (Giraud had been vainly plumping since his dramatic escape from German captivity to have a Provençal bridgehead for those troops included in Allied invasion plans.)

Responding to that A.F.N. invasion, and scorning Laval's promises to Hitler at Munich and Berchtesgaden, the angered Germans rapidly landed a hundred bombers in Tunisia, then began crossing on November 11 into Unoccupied France, where now only a few undermanned French troops could get away. Had Weygand been heeded, many more might have evaded these Nazi nets, not to mention what remained of France's fine fleet. He wouldn't give up, however, pressing the marshal to broadcast a vigorous protest to Germany, which had ended the armistice agreement for good. When Pétain began doing so, people at Vichy knew that behind the aged marshal was a more vigorous Weygand, and his message was soon cut off.

As noted, the Nazis had been watching "Lottermann" for some time, and Himmler now prevailed with the plan of imprisoning him in the Fatherland. All Weygand learned at the time was that he would be allowed to leave Vichy November 12. Back from Berchtesgaden, Laval — never a fan — assured Weygand that he would be able to depart in safety: who better to know? But Weygand had time for one last wrangle with his nemesis that November 12, vehemently affirming that fighting Germany was now France's *sole* priority; while Laval continued to espouse his policy of collaborationism, considering Nazism a bulwark against Communism in Europe. During testimony at the French High Court of July 31, 1945, Weygand recalled telling Laval: "Sir, you are doing something politically deplorable; you have 95 percent of Frenchmen against you and you have bet on the wrong horse, because Germany is beaten." To which the irrepressible Laval supposedly replied: "Ninety-five percent of Frenchmen — but you're joking! It's 98 percent against me; however, I want to make the happiness of Frenchmen in spite of themselves!"[101]

Weygand had long been on an existential ledge in Africa — trying to prove traditionalist credentials to Vichy (and he had them); but also helping significantly to prepare for the Allied and French turn-around, and first off, by denying the Germans any emendations to the armistice, or further infiltration. He had also insisted on cooperation with the U.S., and even with Britain.[102] However, the game was now up. On that November 12 a government car took him, along with son Jacques, from Vichy, followed by another bearing several French police officers, and supposedly with a destination of the Guéret prefecture. But en route, the car was ambushed and stopped, and an impressive number of German soldiers and civilian personnel burst out with a bevy of machine guns directed at Weygand. An SS officer he had seen following him in the morning told him he was arrested — on Hitler's orders. The French general was then handcuffed and pushed into one of the German cars, and others bearing both soldiers and civilian gun-toters followed. Briefly at a hotel under Gestapo guard, Weygand was then separated from his son, who feared his father would simply be shot; and then came an all-night drive north and east through France to Dijon. From there they pushed on to Germany, where the prisoner was finally taken out at a place near Radolfzell on Lake Constance. He would be incarcerated for the rest of the war.

11

The Long Coda

This first brief leg of Weygand's German imprisonment was not the worst —
though owing to his rank, *none* of it compared to what many were then under-
going in Nazi-occupied Europe; and he could pass the time here listening to
German radio or reading their newspapers, and also begin what turned out to
be the first volume of his memoirs, starting with confusing childhood years that
still perplexed him. When his son and wife were taken back to Vichy, they lodged
protests, trying to effect Weygand's release, and even visiting papal authorities,
but to no avail. Weygand's wife also kept pestering officials to let her go and be
with her husband in Germany. By the time she received an affirmative from the
German consulate in Marseille (January, 1943), the general had been transferred
to Schloss Garlitz, a heavily-guarded country house in Mecklenberg.

Here he and his wife settled into a routine — with him writing his memoirs or reading French classics he was provided, and Renée mainly sewing.
Both, however, got a look at what the Nazis were capable of in wartime, when
he required dental work at the nearby Neuengamme concentration camp,
where the death rate was high. Weygand's customary courage never left him,
as he sent letters of protest virtually every month to German authorities,
demanding his release. Naturally, this angered the Gestapo, and in a freezing
December of 1943 they moved him again across Germany — this time to the
picturesque castle of Itter on a mountain in the Austrian Alps near today's ski
mecca of Kitzbühel. Then it was simply part of Greater Germany.

Here Weygand found himself co-habiting with a congeries of French
notables — Daladier, Léon Jouhaux, a one-time labor leader, General Gamelin,
and former Prime Minister Reynaud, the latter two shunning him from the
start, embittered from the era of their first incarceration and Vichy's Riom
trial of those putatively responsible for the 1940 defeat. They were obviously
preparing now to be on the right side after the war. The Basque tennis star,
Jean Borotra, was there as well. A minister under Vichy who had tried unsuc-
cessfully to reach Algiers in November, 1942, Borotra became a support
system to Weygand here, having known and admired the general since the

early '30s. Borotra was himself known and admired throughout the world. A tennis star of extraordinary panache, he had transfixed audiences everywhere with his unorthodox techniques, pirouettes into the crowds, and constant changing of berets at matches through the '20s and '30s. He had twice won at Wimbledon, come out on the winning side several times in the Davis Cup, won important victories from the U.S. to Australia, and partnered in mixed-doubles events with the great Suzanne Lenglen, until she turned professional. At the same time, Borotra finished a degree at the Ecole Polytechnique, then carried on a successful business career flogging gas pumps, traveling from country to country at a breakneck pace (40 times across the Atlantic, 50,000 kilometers in rickety aircraft by the early 1930s!). To battle the Nazis, Borotra joined an army he could have ducked at 41 (married and with a son), and fought bravely, garnering a second *croix de guerre*, after a first in World War I. He then escaped (on a third try) from German clutches, wanting badly to reach England, where he had always been popular. He knew Churchill, had played tennis with King George VI, and wished to fight on, certain that Britain and its empire would prevail. He even received Defense Minister Weygand's official blessing, and could have made it out as anything but a deserter. Then came the tragedy of Mers-el-Kébir in early July, 1940, and a regretful Borotra changed his mind. On July 12 a fellow Basque, Jean Ybarnegaray, assumed Vichy's Ministry of Youth and Family, and Borotra had long shared Weygand's fears of French youth not being physically fit. The next day he accepted a position under Ybarnegaray as General Commissioner of Education and Sports, where he enacted reforms with characteristic energy, until fired in the spring of 1941. In November 1942 he tried, as noted, to escape to the Allied side in North Africa, was collared by the Gestapo, and deported first to Sachsenhausen, now here. As there was but one Weygand, so there was only one "bounding Basque," as unique as the general he now cared for amidst anti–Weygand feeling around him.[1]

In early 1944 that was compounded by the arrival of Michel Clemenceau, son of a famed father, but emphatically no Tiger, and also a snubber of Weygand. More equitable was Marcel Granger, a Tunisian settler who had been close to Arabs there, then a Resistant handed over by the French Milice to the Gestapo, and after time spent at Dachau, now here as well. Colonel François de la Rocque, founder of the Croix de Feu, but also in the Resistance, and doing poorly after earlier camp stints, added another stripe to an ideologically varied lot. And Weygand silently endured this tense atmosphere, going forward on his memoirs, and producing fine paintings in watercolors; however, even for short walks outside, ice prevailed much of the year, and both he and his wife broke bones while at Itter.

The most balanced portrait of this odd, thrown-together menagerie is provided in a memoir by Augusta Léon-Jouhaux. This French Alsatian was saddened by repetitive rudeness shown not only to Weygand but also his wife, finally inducing Gamelin and Reynaud to bow ever so slightly in her direction when she approached. She found Borotra a prince of a man, Daladier an oddball who in spring stole away to practice nudism in the sun, Reynaud too didactic, ex-ambassador André François-Poncet a help with authorities due to German fluency that she alone could match; and Clemenceau relentlessly vindictive, including to de la Rocque, leading to a mock trial where that Rightist was exonerated of charges Clemenceau made concerning his wartime relations with the Germans. She also trusted Weygand when he told her that he had tried his best in the summer of 1940 to stop the Nazi annexation of Alsace.[2]

François-Poncet was incarcerated here until late November of 1943, then transferred to another prison site just before Weygand's arrival; however, his views on Gamelin and Reynaud are worth citing, offering clues as to why Weygand could never change their minds. The ex-ambassador to Berlin and Rome found Gamelin obsessed by trying to get himself off the strategic hook for the 1940 collapse, placing retrospective blame on soldiers who wouldn't follow his orders, or who lacked morale. François-Poncet called the issue a Nessus' tunic that kept Gamelin on fire, and which he could not discard. "Twenty times a day he repeats himself, declaring to his interlocutors that he missed nothing, that he had done all that one could do, that his orders were irreproachable.... Actually, he was a man who had chosen the wrong vocation. Born into a family of soldiers, he never doubted that he would in his turn become a military man." But in fact, Gamelin "was made to be a professor, judge, diplomat or bishop."[3]

Reynaud was a different kettle of fish, and far more openly egotistical. (Having his female secretary on hand no doubt helped feed that ego.) What we call a Monday morning quarterback, the former prime minister could see nothing positive or necessary in the armistice or Vichy regime. In his diary entries, François-Poncet confirms other estimates of Reynaud at Itter: "He is extraordinarily sure of himself. He is right, and will always be right." And "he lacks respect for others, sensitivity, the ability to examine oneself, and *humanity*." It was quite an indictment of one of Weygand's most sedulous foes.[4]

A less balanced, but equally interesting source on life at Itter is provided by Reynaud himself, and was not available to previous biographers; however, patient decipherings of his tiny, daily scribbles here furnish a contemporary researcher (now able to read them in book form) another damning view of the man himself, thrown into bitter proximity with Weygand.

From the general's arrival, Reynaud pledged not to shake the hand of one who had made France "capitulate" — the term he freely used as an equivalent for armistice. He then enjoined Borotra to have the Weygands eat in their room! In one of his scribbles he was amazed that such an "imbecile" could ever have been promoted to lead the French army, forgetting that he himself had called upon him for the top position in May 1940! Reynaud and his cohort Gamelin were both non–plussed to find Daladier learning that Weygand was indeed patriotic, and emphatically no Pétain. Seeing Daladier and Weygand in conversation angered them, as it did Clemenceau Jr. Verbal jousts on a de Gaulle already showing vengeful colors, and interpretations of what the postwar world would bring fly out in Reynaud's prison journal — by a man who had indeed suffered (not only in wartime imprisonment, but by killing his mistress Hélène de Portes at the time of the armistice in a car accident). However, depicting Weygand as always procuring special treatment here ignores the benefits Reynaud himself derived from Borotra's improvised deck tennis court, or Augusta's cooking enhancements wrung from prison authorities, as well as medical treatment he received for a scratched retina in Innsbruck.[5]

Somehow radios were jigged to pick up heartening news of the Nazis being rolled up, and near the close of the war, the SS began showing nerves, Borotra escaped once amid machine gun fire and was brought back, and on a second try made it out to alert American army authorities. Soon Weygand was in their protective custody, treated with a deference and kindness that turned out to be short-lived, indeed. His trip back to France in early May of 1945 was anything but direct, and nothing like Reynaud's flight home in de Gaulle's private plane. Instead, there were back and forth tergiversations emanating from authorities on high, and when he finally met the prestigious commander of France's First Army in Lindau, found de Lattre in a quandary, pushed by de Gaulle into shunting Weygand onto a plane with Borotra back to Paris — for a new imprisonment! De Lattre's "emotion was visible," but despite his wife's ire, Weygand told the man — slated himself for an early death after fine leadership in Vietnam — to obey. And meanwhile, Granger took Weygand's scrawled memoirs to the general's notary in Paris for safekeeping.[6]

In the capital, Weygand found it downright risible when informed that as a former minister under Vichy, he would be imprisoned and tried as a security risk to the state. But Gaullists and Communists especially wanted his hide, proving, thereby, their own contrastive purity. After several years' imprisonment, Weygand at least wished to get different clothes at his Avénue Friedland apartment, but that wasn't permitted. He was taken to the Conciergerie (did he think of Marie-Antoinette awaiting execution there?), then was to be transferred to the forbidding prison of Fresnes. Jacques Weygand believes that life in a cell there would soon have killed his father; and consequently, brother Edouard fought to have the aged general affected by health problems placed under guard in the Paris hospital of Val-de-Grâce. Acceptance of this request was a lifesaver, and when Weygand was to be transferred elsewhere, both the hospital's director and chief urologist put careers on the line to keep him there. Their obduracy worked on that occasion, and two more to come; and by January, 1946, the new head of the provisional government in France, Félix Gouin, allowed Weygand's stay at this prison-hospital to continue on a legal basis.

De Gaulle would often congratulate himself for treating Weygand without retaliatory rancor — the Weygand he thought had approved a Vichy court's August 1940 verdict on him of death *in absentia*; but in fact, the "constable's" hegemony at war's end wreaked havoc on Weygand, who had already been through a lot. His salary was still not forthcoming, his assets were in judicial hands and bank accounts frozen, so that his wife — who visited him at the hospital each afternoon — was forced to accept largesse from both friends and anonymous sympathizers. Sectors of the press also ganged up, and Weygand was saddened, while also given a repetitive, fatiguing challenge for a man his age — a slew of exhausting hearings where he had to defend himself historically!

The first such challenge occurred when he was summoned to testify in the biggest trial of the era, that of Marshal Pétain, held by the High Court of Justice, which de Gaulle's government had put in place November, 1944, to try top personnel of the Vichy regime.[7] In a period when de Gaulle was a magnet drawing many to his side, unanimity seemed easy to procure; but in fact, the constitution and procedures of this High Court were fought over in Parliament with bitter divisions, especially between Communists and everyone else. The press also kept close watch, commenting plentifully on this High Court of Justice (or Non-Justice, as François Mauriac dubbed it).[8]

Pétain's trial would unfold from July 23 to August 15, 1945, in broiling chambers of the Palais de Justice in Paris, where three magistrates and 24 jurors (drawn from a lottery in the Assembly) were to judge the case, while several lawyers also faced off. These included the egregious Jacques Isorni, whose family had suffered in Vichy's laws of exception against Jews, but who defended Pétain ardently. When Weygand, let out of Val-de-Grâce, marched militarily into the stifling court room on July 31 to testify, he made quite a stir. His deposition and grilling followed those of a once arrested French Communist, and a deportee to a German camp, but he still bowed respectfully in Pétain's direction. Rather than sit, he remained standing like a soldier, if propped up by a cane. Warning the audience he wouldn't be brief,

Marshal Pétain answers charges at his Paris trial, July 30, 1945. Weygand came in to testify the next day, making quite a stir! (Bettmann/CORBIS)

and with adversaries like Reynaud fidgeting, Weygand proceeded to pillory the latter's idea of capitulation versus that of an armistice. There was a world of difference between the two, and for Weygand, this was the major theme of his testimony. He also ridiculed the idea of continuing the fight in North Africa of June 1940, revealing with his usual grasp of facts how badly the French would have fared, and how quickly the Axis would have conquered major swaths of France's empire, greatly affecting England's own fight for survival. Weygand said that one couldn't just improvise naval and land defenses of such huge domains in a couple of weeks: "War isn't an intellectual pastime; war is a matter of strength," as he put it. Questions regarding de Gaulle's wartime correspondence with him (it hadn't come through the right channels, Weygand said), attempts to push him into calling Pétain treasonous, rebuttals from the generalizing Reynaud did not discomfit the general; and as Jules Roy noted, "these people were no match for him." On Wednesday, August 1, the court decided it didn't want him back, then changed its mind, and the Weygand-Reynaud dispute (with a hearing-challenged, bewildered Pétain straining to comprehend) continued.[9]

Rereading notes taken at the trial by its court scribe reveals the aged Weygand as a master at evading traps set by lawyers, jurors, and witnesses, preeminently Reynaud, who comes off as a boring generalist trying to gild his own lily. By contrast, Weygand's deft rejoinders constitute an historian's tour de force; he spoke like the no-nonsense man of culture and depth that he was — relentlessly, impressively trenchant. Questioners didn't broach matters at all chronologically, and the general could find himself now in North Africa of 1941, then back in May 1940, then in the pre–war era, or even in the period when he was in prison and had no impact on policies. None of it fazed him. Questioners tried to pin him down on his reaction to news of a Communist coup June 13, 1940, and he retorted that he and Interior Minister Georges Mandel had procured answers so quickly that this "incident of a moment" was being raised in court only to settle political scores. Staying tough on both Gaullists and English in 1940? It was the sole way to go then, because if Vichy showed it couldn't run its African territories, the Germans would have pounced, and as Weygand cautioned, one couldn't judge the problems of 1940 by 1944 standards. Why had he joined the government in the first place? Well, Reynaud had first called on both him and Pétain, and as for being Vichy's defense minister, a great majority of parliamentarians, now wishing to forget, had voted legally for the regime! On to the Murphy Accords, and before a questioner could skewer him, Weygand shot back: "The Murphy accords are ones I know perfectly, because I made them!"[10]

The Weygand-Reynaud duel truly showed the general to be the greater master both of facts and of language. Weygand also asked pointedly what Reynaud was doing cementing his case by bleating to the press, so that the world's newspapers printed his articles, while court proceedings were still in progress.[11]

In attendance both days, the writer Joseph Kessel was much moved. "One has to admit it," he wrote, "this deposition is of such quality, of such impressive tenor and vigor that one couldn't think of anything else while General Weygand was speaking." Kessel found the scene ultra–dramatic, with Weygand "defending his honor, the honor of the soldier he has been for over a half-century, and one who has known supreme responsibilities." Kessel

considered the deponent's "dignity and pride moving," and also the fact that
"he abdicates not a jot. He regrets nothing." The contrast to Reynaud's spi-
der-like "dialectic" and "feline certitude" was stunning. As Kessel concluded,
"it is rarely given to assembled men to attend such a poignant spectacle." The
defense lawyer Isorni had a similar impression, recalling that even Weygand's
"most bitter adversaries listened religiously." He added that the former prime
minister and commander in chief were equally diminutive — and barely two
meters apart, "railed at each other with mortal courtliness. However, the master was Weygand."[12]

Weygand's own trial for being a security risk to the State, and for the
crime of national indignity, began in the same period. The High Court started
its investigations May 14, 1945, and as it kept reconstituting itself with new
laws and members, the trial grew Kafkaesque — going on and off for three
years, until Weygand was finally acquitted in early May, 1948. In between, he
was summoned on 18 exhausting occasions, with the first hearings at the hospital itself, then mostly at the Luxembourg Palace. The trial might certainly
have ended more expeditiously, but for a Communist coterie which emphatically wanted the general's head. A key figure there was a member of the
court's "Commission of Instruction," Marcel Willard, a lawyer who had joined
the Party in 1923, remaining a member through the period of Stalin's purges,
by now certain. At the Liberation, Willard became Secretary General of the
Justice Ministry, then a senator from 1946 to 1948, co–terminous with Weygand's protracted grilling. What bothered him was that certain jurors would
not consider request of an armistice in June 1940 a criminal act of treason.
Being no soldier, Willard neglected conditions on the ground of that era,
ones Weygand had hardly created. Meanwhile, the general fought back empir-
ically against each sub–accusation, however nonsensical. For example, the
project of bombing Caucasus oil wells early in the war was laid at his door;
but he retorted that the idea had come from the French and British governments, and that by the way, the Nazis *were* using Russian oil for their war
equipment!

Bad apples summoned to tarnish Weygand's past remained true to form:
Gamelin whitewashed his own martial resumé, making his successor of the
eleventh hour the only one who had transgressed. Michel Clemenceau also
piled on, as did the inevitable Reynaud; yet Weygand remained patient and
non–plussed, shredding each accusatory generality with his factual scalpel.
When it came to the period of the African delegation, distinguished career
soldiers sprang to his defense, putting their own promotions at peril. De Lattre de Tassigny was one of them. General de Périer, Weygand's former staff
chief in Algiers, was another, categorically stating that his boss had strongly

opposed Germans and Italians in the empire, built up an army of *revanche* by tugging always at Vichy sleeves, illegally stockpiled arms, and had them manufactured, interned Axis troops trying to enter Tunisia after losses to the English; and in sum, did everything possible to resist the enemy. Weygand also had strong supportive letters from Madame Foch, still alive, and Senator Charles Reibel, an ex-governmental minister.[13] Still, the general had to rely mostly on himself as these years of prosecution drawled by.

Granted provisional freedom in May 1946, which Willard vigorously opposed, Weygand was allowed to regain his rather down-at-heels apartment in Paris' Avénue de Friedland (the Germans had been through his papers here in 1940 and repairs were urgent). But he was still watched by police, his general's status and salary were still not restored, his assets still frozen; and he (and his wife) remained friends in need to the many they knew. Meanwhile, the divided High Court moved from the Luxembourg, earmarked for the Senate, to a mansion in the Rue de Varenne, continuing with proceedings that should have been over — through 1947, and all the way to the acquittal of May 6, 1948. It was springtime then, a season of blossoms and renewal, and after a long climb, Weygand finally recovered his generalship, and salary, not to mention his name.

In response, an irate Willard resigned his position on the Commission of Instruction, followed by other Communist Party jurors, before the High Court closed up shop in the summer of 1949.[14] It had been quite a ride, and de Gaulle's self–congratulatory remarks on all this were exaggerations: Weygand could easily have died back in the Fresnes prison, not to mention from this repetitive courtroom grilling (of a man scarcely in youth's first flush). Nor in his cavalier views on Weygand's treatment, heard intermittently into the '60s, did de Gaulle consider what a long prison term might mean to an old man saved only by his own ability at making a convincing case.

As if all *that* weren't enough, Parliament also decided on its own massive, post–war investigation into France's turmoil between 1933 and 1945 — including the complex etiology of the 1940 catastrophe, and the course of Vichy policy. Here was an investigative committee that still desired Weygand's head, plying him with a plethora of questions, some very general (such as the meaning of treason); and Weygand responded on nine separate occasions, often at three hours a crack, and to late hours for a man around 80. It was bureaucracy triumphant, versus a lone wolf armed only with a patient array of dates, places, and occurrences. The commission was composed of a dozen parliamentarians, and another dozen from other walks of life, including the distinguished Resistance figure Lucie Aubrac. Another man in the Resistance, and for several months in Dachau, Deputy Charles Serre, a lawyer, was *rapporteur général*, or majordomo of proceedings that became drawn-out and super-detailed.

The committee's initial investigations were on the period 1933–1939, and for that swath, Weygand was first summoned July 25, 1947. He launched into an extensive, but never boring historical account of France in the early '30s — discussing his repeated demands for a more mechanized, up-to-date army in an atmosphere of disarmament and growing cuts. He mentioned the issue of the hollow classes, the need to pour money and men into final pacification of the Moroccan highlands, delays in arms manufacturing, and problems with war ministers like Daladier. His testimony was buttressed by quotations from letters he had sent the ministries, and by a close sense of budgetary and bureaucratic reality (complete with statistics), and goes on for some 20 long pages of text. Then came Proustian quizzing, and Weygand's usual aplomb in answering every critique of his past comportment. One deputy demanded why he had given such a sanguine speech on the state of the French army in July 1939, and the general replied that, having cried wolf through the first half of the decade, he had then been retired and out of it, heard of new infusions of money for the army, and did not wish to affect the morale of those now commanding or serving, including Gamelin. He was nonetheless pushed into a critique of that chief of staff, and all he would say was what he had told the commander himself several times in the period — that "I found his organization bad." Gamelin's own deposition in December was more evasive, yet characteristically snide, as when he said (having escaped in time to his flower garden), "*I* wouldn't have been the man of the Armistice."[15]

For the period from 1939 through wartime, Weygand was summoned back before the committee March 8, 1949, then again at the end of that month, twice more in April, '49, once in May, and five times in June of that year, until finally done. Most of the final volume of committee deliberations features questioning of the general, and his responses. He began March 8 with a long deposition on his positions of 1939 through the period of the African delegation; but watching the clock in this night session, he became increasingly elliptical, speaking in terse sentence fragments, and dropping into a dramatic historical present, mirroring his difficult balancing act during the period. Here are samples: "With regard to the enemy: the armistice and nothing but. Good faith on my part toward the Germans? No. I had seen what good German faith was.... Consequently, [my idea was] to hurt them as much as possible, and do everything to aid our allies." The English? Friends, but "I wanted to be master in my house," and preclude a Nazi takeover in French Africa. Ditto for the Gaullists: "no disorders." After all, "their useless boastings had brought me German control commissions [in Morocco], replacing Italian ones. That was quite enough." During this first session of 1949 there was no time for questions.[16]

But in subsequent ones, queries came fast and furious, and the atmosphere was one of circling hunters wanting to finish off their prey, while grudgingly admiring his qualities. To be fair, some were more adversarial than others. Michel Clemenceau, a deputy for Seine et Marne in this period, was predictably difficult, and didn't mind returning to the early '30s, asking again why the general hadn't procured more able soldiers and modern arms for the military. And he elicited the acerbically tragic in his interlocutor: "My life [of the time] was one perpetual struggle: a struggle for military effectives, a struggle for materiel, a struggle in all domains." When prodded on why his measures weren't put into action during the latter half of the decade, Weygand had to remind the deputy that after January 21, 1935, "I was no longer anything." When Clemenceau moved forward to Germany's invasion via the Ardennes of May 1940, Weygand said that French planes could easily have strafed columns of enemy tanks moving through difficult forest terrain toward the Meuse, and that placing French soldiers of middling quality in this sector was an error. One sees that Gamelin should have come under Clemenceau's fire (Weygand being in the Middle East at the time, and having had no part in conceiving military strategy against the Nazi onslaught). But the same ground kept getting re-tramped by such stubborn questioners.[17]

Emile Kahn also revealed himself to be out of Weygand's league when it came to deployments, fortifications, and such. Serre then excoriated the general for participation in Vichy meetings of the fall of 1940, ones where he clearly could not have been! His octogenarian memory needed to be impeccable, while *their* imprecisions, products of a desire to entrap, were subject to no one's rebuke. And when it came to Pétain, Weygand proved again that he would not be a fair-weather witness. Certainly that figure had been secretive in wartime, never explicitly telling Weygand whether North Africa should become a trampoline for a French rebound. But "everyone knew where I was going [there], and the Marshal demonstrated the greatest confidence in me.... Never did I encounter a problem from him when it came to everything I was demanding, or trying to demand, for the French army; nor in my daily jousts with the Germans, and resistance to the armistice commissions." In Weygand's view, the marshal wished to keep him in Africa as long as possible, even at one point proposing a compromise, whereby Weygand would retain civil functions there, but not military ones. The proconsul had retorted that given the nature of North Africa's Muslims, who so respected the sword, this would have gone down badly, and he therefore refused "all the little sweetnesses proffered to keep me there. I was very intransigent, and therefore, was booted out."[18]

Even the late Darlan was treated fairly by a man who admitted he had gotten on "as badly as it was possible to do" with that Vichy powerhouse. To Serre's query, asking whether Darlan had appeased in order to buy time before the Allied comeback, *or* to make France part of the new Nazi order in Europe, Weygand gave a nuanced answer. He prefaced these comments by saying that one couldn't aver anything definitive here; but that perhaps someone like himself, always standing up to Nazi authorities, required the counter–balance of others who didn't. However, all this was "in the domain of hypotheses and feelings, and not of facts."[19]

An ill Lucie Aubrac relayed a series of questions to Kahn, who in turn directed them at Weygand, and one led to a long exchange on the repression of Loustaunau-Lacau's coup attempt, and Beaufre's arrest at Algiers. These soldiers had tried to obtain arms from the Americans in order to raise North Africa against the Nazis; why punish such patriots? Weygand legitimately bristled at the implication that he wasn't equally patriotic. After all, *he* had made the Army of Africa, but with Russia reeling and the Americans not yet in the war, the time wasn't right for these "irresponsible" people to act on their own, risking a Nazi occupation of French North Africa. As he then replied to Serre, they should have come directly to a proconsul they supposedly respected.[20]

Not normally braggadocious, Weygand's ego was coming into play, and he finally felt that he should quote from admiring testimonies made during the High Court's proceedings — from eminent generals (Monsabert, Béthouart, de Lattre, Carpentier, and Navarre, among others, all considering him the key architect of a rejuvenated French army in Africa, and completely for *revanche*). Backed into corners of this legalistic lion's den, a normally modest Weygand also sought in notes he had brought whatever might strengthen his case.[21]

As he neared the close of draining debates with these relentless questioners, he found himself on June 16 faced with the king in that regard, Louis Marin, a Rightist deputy from Meurthe-et-Moselle in Lorraine (since 1905). Marin was also an indefatigable, published philosopher, who would have been at home with Thomas Aquinas. Marin's general nitpicking at Weygand goes on for pages and pages of these published proceedings. On the armistice — ever and again, the armistice — Weygand underlined how keeping the French navy from the Germans was a *sine qua non* for any agreement, along with preservation of the empire. He revealed Hitler's subsequent feeling that he had been comparatively rooked, echoed as well by Churchill. Why then had Hitler made such an agreement? asked Marin. To which Weygand sputtered that Marin was "in the domain of shadows" here, and that one could not answer a question on the Führer's motivations, except hypothetically. Weygand kept wanting to bring Marin back to facts, but the deputy-philosopher repeated the necessity of formulating questions "*in abstracto.*" The general retorted that "I am not a philosopher. I'm an old soldier. I can't treat facts *in abstracto!*" Nothing daunted, Marin continued splitting hairs philosophically on the notions of armistice versus capitulation, and Weygand kept making him look silly; but being a Lorrainer, Marin was not one to back down easily.[22]

When it came to the final go-around, June 30, 1949, Serre emulated Marin's abstractionism, this time concerning the launching of Vichy; and Weygand had to remind him of a defeated country that was in "a frightful state of disorder." The general then sighed that "I will leave your commission with the regret of seeing to what a point you don't understand intellectual honesty!" Temper aroused, and emboldened by his position as the commission's chair, Serre brusquely urged Weygand to "retract your expression!" Weygand said he would do so *pro forma*, all the while saddened by the deep suspicions politicians held toward the military, and the fact that "you view the threat of a coup d'état in every opinion contrary to yours."[23] Saddened he might well have been by all this discord and superficiality; but he continued fighting to the end. When his last appearance drew to a close, Weygand was sent on his way with traditional French courtesy. It had been a long time coming....

One must situate the way authorities under de Gaulle and those who followed dealt with Weygand within a larger atmosphere of *épuration* at war's end, and in the following several years. Rod Kedward has handily summarized the postwar "story" of good, monolithic resistance versus bad, monolithic Vichy, sketching purification pressures emanating from France's Communist Party, treasonous through June 22, 1941, then resurgent at war's end, and numbering almost 400,000 adherents. But de Gaulle's simplistic view of where vice and virtue lay in wartime equally permeated this atmosphere. As Kedward declares, "by the late 1940s the two rival political monopolists of the resistance narrative, de Gaulle and the PCF [French Communists], had fashioned the richly diffused history of resistance into simple mobilizing myths." Many lives, not to mention careers, were destroyed in the process, even if a minority truly merited what they got, and a goodly number of sentences were eventually reduced or altered.[24]

I spoke on the matter in early 2007 with Colonel Serge-Henri Parisot, who at 97 remembered some of the *dramatis personae* tried, like Weygand, for their roles in wartime. Simply restricting ourselves to a clutch of distinguished naval figures, Admiral Derrien was tried behind closed doors and given "criminal reclusion in perpetuity" in May 1944 by a military tribunal in Algiers — this for his inability to repel the German takeover of Bizerte during their occupation of Tunisia (December, 1942). Such a harsh sentence ignored military realities, including Allied caution after TORCH, giving the Nazis time to enter that French protectorate in force. Parisot notes of Derrien, who passed away two years after being sentenced, that "he could do nothing else." As for Tunisia's resident-general Admiral Esteva, at least somewhat protective of Tunisian Jews during wartime, but still faithful to Pétain when the Nazis invaded, he was the first to receive a sentence from the High Court — "perpetual detention" — March 15, 1945. On August 14, 1946, that court issued sentences to three more admirals: Auphan, given "hard labor in perpetuity" (Parisot called the sentence "*ridicule*"); the former hero of Dunkirk and governor-general of Algeria, Admiral Abrial, who received ten years' hard labor, and which Parisot called "unjust"; and Marquis, who got five years' prison. Given that France's armed forces of 1939–1940 contained some five million souls, the impact of these purges broke (at the least) numerous careers. After the fact, and in the way previous Soviet party lines changed, de Gaulle was asking soldiers to have done what had never been demanded in French history: disobey! An eminent military historian, Raoul Girardet, concludes that "the history of the French army during the Second World War reeks of Shakespearian tragedy."[25]

Le grand Charles continued, however, to nurse a special antipathy toward Weygand, partly stemming from competitive egomania, and the need to defeat elders who had been promoted ahead of him. De Gaulle's ambitions knew few bounds, and as he said in 1946, "there has been no moment of my life when I did not have the certitude of ending up one day at the head of France." But along with ego and ambition, one must also factor in a sense of racial or ethnic superiority. In published conversations, Philippe de Gaulle recalled his father discussing one Maxime de Nimal, whose name appeared in one of his old Saint-Cyr bulletins from before 1914, noting that he had gotten the name Weygand from "adoptive parents," and was supposedly the illegitimate son of the Habsburg Emperor Maximilian of Mexico and an Indian woman there. "Without a drop of French blood in his veins," Weygand should never have been given supreme command in 1940, said de Gaulle, adding that "they put an old car jockey on a purebred and asked him to win the Grand Prix!"[26] In a government meeting of the '60s, the French president also provoked laughter by averring that "everything is linked in history. The expedition [to Mexico] put Maximilian in place, General Weygand was Maximilian's progeny, and the armistice of 1940 the progeny of Weygand's nomination as commander in chief!" Alain Peyrefitte recalled a reception later that decade, when de Gaulle declared that Weygand was "either the bastard son of Maximilian of Austria and an Indian, or the product of the insane Empress Charlotte's rape by a Mexican officer." The president said he had discussed the matter with a member of Belgium's royal family, and was more persuaded by "the first version."[27]

No fan of the "Anglo-Saxon" powers through the '60s, de Gaulle's hatred of Weygand partly went back to the delegate general's closeness with wartime U.S. authorities, and pique at their treatment of *him*. In conversations with his son, he would run down Robert Murphy, minimizing the utility of Weygand's wartime accord with that official. De Gaulle also decried the admiration of ambassadors Bullitt and Leahy for Weygand — being "fixated on a backward, stuck-up, capitulating France"; and of course American support for General Giraud, all enhancing his antipathy toward Weygand. And these sources of antipathy never diminished. As Philippe recalls, "when [my father] evoked that era, it was still with much bitterness regarding the Americans." The view that Weygand had helped keep North Africa from the Nazis also angered de Gaulle whenever his son broached the subject.[28]

Weygand's output of books, articles, and prefaces in the post–war era through to the '60s would provoke in de Gaulle a response of damning with faint praise, when they didn't simply infuriate him. In the late '40s, André Malraux mentioned Weygand's writings, including recently published works, and de Gaulle said he could never finish any of the general's books. (Some of those in the late '30s were of course only pamphlet-length.) In 1949 he blew up at the appearance of Weygand's lead article on "Military Traditions — the Voice of Foch" in *Revue historique de l'Armée* (December 4, 1948). Claude Guy remembers him expostulating on that occasion: "Weygand! Weygand! No, it's really frightening, and there's nothing more to derive from this country." Yet de Gaulle neglected to auto-critique his *own* work, especially on World War II — full of vagueness and empty generalizations on the Nazi foe, and exaggerations on how the Resistance had almost solely liberated France. There was a lack of both nuance and gratitude there. One might mention that the first courts he created in Algiers of 1944 and other plans conceived there for the post–war era owed much to Weygand and acolytes, and to the English-speaking powers who had awarded him this base![29]

Later, when Weygand's antipathy circa 1960 to de Gaulle's policy on French Algeria became public, it made the irate president wish to eject him from the army. Nor did Weygand endear himself to the Resistance icon as honorary chairman of an Association to Defend the Memory of Marshal Pétain, wishing to set the record straighter on that controversial figure, and have his remains transferred to Verdun. (It didn't help that one of de Gaulle's great Resistance adherents, "Colonel Rémy," né Gilbert Renault, was a member.) Weygand also responded when figures like Colonel Serge-Henri Parisot requested his court testimony on opposition to de Gaulle's Algerian stance — and which rated Parisot, along with other distinguished figures like Hélie de Saint Marc (who had nearly perished in Buchenwald), extensive prison time in the '60s. The Algerian denouement also cost colonels like Parisot sure–fire promotion to the rank of general. As the French president told Georges Pompidou, "one mustn't soften up adversaries, one must crush them!"[30]

All, however, was not strife for Weygand during this long twilight of his life. He continued to attend Académie meetings and to pour out books, some of which we have already discussed — during the late '40s, '50s, and first half of the '60s. *Forces de la France* (1951) is another of his Burkean romps through the French past, but with emphasis on how fragile this nation had been, and remained. In his introduction Weygand decries not only weakness, but the strong who turn backs on their own strength. Barbarism is always near at hand, says Weygand, and one of his generalizations on French history remains relevant: that when France was strong, it could absorb Roman, Frankish, and other incursions, making its civilization stronger, and more limber. But if, as he put it, one absorbs only out of weakness, mortality is on the horizon. However, in chapters devoted first to the ten centuries preceding the high Middle Ages, then to events like the Hundred Years War, Wars of Religion, the Revolution, et al., he shows how French history, in fact, oscillated between periods of turbulence, and periods when generally a person of strong character (Clovis, Charlemagne, Henri IV, Robespierre, Napoleon) brought the country out of chaos, helping craft a certain coherence. Weygand's last 90 pages treat his own era, with a ringing conclusion on the life of nations as a constant struggle, and on the need to respect and protect the long inheritance. His final line? "Let us not allow the tree of France to be uprooted."[31]

Another history of France, published in 1953, was aimed more at France's youth, and has a simple, sweet literary quality. Again, Weygand's patriotism and humility before past greats he parades through his pages are apparent. He ends with people of his own day who might inspire the young — Jacques Cousteau, explorer of the deep, Albert Schweitzer, doctor extraordinaire in Africa, and Maurice Herzog, first with (Louis Lachenal) to conquer Annapurna, June 3, 1950, despite lack of oxygen, terror in howling snow and ice, and frozen extremities, costing him toes and fingers. Figures like these, following others like Joan of Arc or Molière, collectively made France, and Weygand warns the young to spurn cynicism about possibilities yet remaining to keep the country great.[32]

Everything he did gave more than required, including a book on the

French army in the Académie Française — i.e., those chosen for inclusion in good part due to martial exploits. Weygand first delineates the role of Cardinal Richelieu in creating the Académie after wars of religion and other disorders. With the waning of anarchy, Richelieu wanted a body to set standards in French language and taste, and from its inception in 1635, the Académie gradually opened doors to people of different backgrounds. In Louis XIV's era long wars prevailed, bringing to the fore figures like the Marquis de Dangeau, a courageous noble on the battlefield from the 1660s through to the end of Louis' reign. Dangeau published a journal, which Weygand calls as tasteful and useful on the Sun King's period as the more celebrated memoirs of Saint-Simon. Another aristocratic warrior coming to prominence in that time, then elected to the Académie, was the Marquis de Villars — also courageous, even after severe injuries, and gaining the respect of foes like Marlborough during the War of the Spanish Succession. Weygand admires this Villars, forgiving his apparently large ego and direct manner. For the Enlightenment period, we have a Duc de Richelieu, great-nephew of the Académie's founder, which helped in his election. However, Richelieu also showed his martial mettle during the wars of Polish and Austrian Succession, and the Seven Years' War. Again, all this is military and biographical history characterized by deftness, depth, and insight.

Weygand also shows clearly here whom he dislikes — careerists, credit-takers, and political types, who shone only in the number of meetings they attended (one Old Regime prince making it to 1,244 in his 22 years as an Academician). He also sketches the effect of the Revolution, when quite a number from the Académie were imprisoned or guillotined, and its legal reconstitution remained in abeyance until after 1815. In that Restoration period, Paul-Philippe de Ségur stands out: elected in 1830, but having gained spurs under Napoleon, who valued his bravery and military acumen at Austerlitz, and in Spain, then Russia of 1812, where he was imprisoned. Ségur was too modest to publish his book on that epic invasion, but was pushed, and it became a brisk seller, and a classic. He followed up with other fine historical work, and again had to be impelled to put his name forward for election to the Académie. He then remained a member for some 40 years. As always, Weygand puts readers back in various periods here, whetting historical appetites. One learns less, however, from his more modern parts on marshals like Lyautey, Joffre, Foch, and Juin, who all became Academicians. And Weygand himself? After his refusal to provide an auto-portrait, the series editor asked Marshal Juin to do so, and his extended, laudatory vignette closes out a fine volume.[33]

Weygand also continued to write prefaces for a wide variety of books (as he had done before the war) — his title of general and member of the Académie, and his renown much valued. These prefaces are often remarkable, again whetting readers' appetites, and providing clear summaries of the books' contents or highlights. Predictably, Weygand was a natural for introductions to works on figures like Napoleon. Thus his preface to a book on a Napoleonic aide de camp, General de Marois, shows how prized this function was, and how some of Napoleon's most famous soldiers held the honor; however, the author of this book, using private archives, was now making a quite *obscure* aide de camp better known. In that and other prefaces, Weygand again reveals his identification with the era of Napoleon, and how the Master was a fine designator and delegator, including in his famed Imperial Guard. Weygand felt that historians must still be careful to get things right on this crucial French personage and period.[34]

Predictably, too, he was sought out for prefaces to books on Joan of Arc, where he shows both his vivid patriotism concerning the turnaround she facilitated against the English, and also her uniqueness in Catholic history. There were prefaces as well on other great figures of French military/colonial history, such as Marshal Achille de Saint-Arnaud, where Weygand gives an empathetic sense of what it took to suffer years of torment during the French conquest of Algeria (1840s), then to become France's supreme commander in the Crimea, where Saint-Arnaud perished during the 1850s.[35]

Another alumnus of Algeria in the 1840s, but better known as Paris' military governor during the Franco–Prussian War of 1870, was General Louis Trochu, who rallied and prepared the city for a long German siege. Weygand's preface to a book on this figure again shows empathy for leaders who did their duty in times of great duress. And he salutes the author's research reposing on 50 years of private letters, revealing a Trochu of "generous heart."[36]

Weygand's ability to get one immediately into a new human world is well seen in his preface to a book on General Alfred Malcor, an artillery ace of World War I. On one page Weygand shows the stability of French families and their occupations through many generations. Over 150 years, Malcor's forbears had featured no less than 50 army officers (19 dying in wars), and 18 priests or nuns. His own three sons became officers, too. Weygand salutes Malcor's critiques of ill-conceived offensives during the Great War, and also his courage under fire through to the end, when Foch made him coordinator of artillery corps, and Weygand met this soldier with a "seigneur's mien."[37]

Less enticing is Weygand's preface to a book on Joffre — by a sycophantic biographer who helped ghost-write the marshal's memoirs during the 1920s. Weygand unaccountably accepts Joffre's hype about one more offensive of 1917 that, after over a million French dead, would *surely* have worked had he not been sacked! Generally, he was a good judge of character, but in this case, Weygand's admiration remained misplaced.[38]

He also contributed many prefaces to books on the pre–World War II era, and on that war itself, and one can only sample here. In the preface to a history of German rearmament during the first half of the '30s, the general first gives the reader a handy sketch of steps toward appeasement during the rose-colored '20s — Locarno, the Briand-Kellogg Pact, withdrawal from the Rhineland, etc. Those events still weigh on him, as he salutes this book on the sudden German rebound in the next decade, and how crucial French information-gathering was (and remains) for protection of states from such external threats.[39]

When it comes to World War II, the general's preface to a book on Amiens in the spring of 1940 gives an initial tragic sense of the Picard past as an invasion route. Amiens had suffered badly in the First World War, but bombings and fires of May 1940, and desperate efforts to fight back amidst the loss of thousands of homes, followed by Nazi occupation for four long years, all rouse an obvious sense of poignancy in Weygand. He also contributed fine prefaces to books on Bordeaux of May–June, 1940, swollen by some 800,000 refugees; and on Dunkirk, badly bombed by the Nazis (not to mention by its liberators later in the war). And along with urban or regional tragedies, there were many human ones, such as that of Father Robert Ricard in the port of Brest. Weygand's preface to a book on this relative unknown teaches us much about a sea captain who had found God, then amidst Allied bombing and tenacious Nazi resistance, offered material help and masses to the few remaining in the besieged city, before dying in his underground shelter early in September 1944. The general says he had often seen Father Ricard directing religious retreats near the Weygands' summer home in Brittany during the '30s. A similar personal touch enhances the preface to the memoirs of Marshal Carl Mannerheim, a Finnish war hero who had been in Russia's cavalry before World War I, then met with Weygand and Foch after that conflict, and in 1937 parleyed again with Weygand in Finland. Mannerheim would take a strong role in his country's wartime defense against the Russians, and later, in its liberation from the Nazis. Ever and again, one *learns* from these prefaces, suiting Weygand almost as much as the short story did Somerset Maugham.[40]

He did not shirk more difficult subjects concerning the war years, providing, for example, an introduction to Jacques Mordal's dense book on the Norway campaign preceding the Fall of France. There Weygand surmises that the Russo-Finnish war, ending in onerous peace terms (mid–March, 1940), pressured the Allies to counter possible Russian expansion in Scandinavia. He also notes the enticement of Swedish iron ore, which both the Allies and Nazis coveted. But his preface is clear on the limits of the French-English alliance, and how the two powers dallied on invasion plans, while Hitler scooped them April 9 with a lightning strike into neutral, unprepared Norway. Weygand then shows how the campaign revealed the effects of air bombing, and how the Luftwaffe made a key difference in the Nazi victory. He also discusses the general problem of being a neutral — Norwegian illusions going back to their non–participation in World War I, followed by hopes that things might stay the same again. And he criticizes his own French for ignoring realities, while the British placed their naval forces in great peril, and finally, after a long back and forth battle around Narvik, decided on evacuation. Weygand believes this campaign was full of lessons there was simply no time to digest before France's own invasion and fall. He also contributed a preface to Mordal's book on Narvik alone, and to his co–authored tome (with Admiral Auphan) on the French navy during World War II. Again, Weygand's sadness pervades an introduction to that overview on the French fleet that finally committed suicide in late November 1942. And he conveys admiration for the authors — Auphan definitely brave in the Dunkirk evacuation, and an aid to Weygand's army of Africa while Vichy's naval secretary; and Mordal, who became a military historian after being badly wounded by a mine during the Dunkirk operation.[41]

Concerning the period following cessation of hostilities, Weygand's preface to Maurice Catoire's book on the Direction des Services de l'Armistice (D.S.A.) reiterates how indefatigable one had to be dealing with ever-revisionist Nazi and Italian authorities. And again, the personal intervenes, Weygand having created this service under his own Defense Ministry in June 1940. He also chose General Koeltz to head and staff it, and one of those appointees was Catoire, who spent two years jousting with Axis authorities.[42]

Weygand also prefaced a book on the more controversial Henri Dentz, sent by Vichy to command France's wartime army of the Levant. Following Darlan's lead, General Dentz allowed the Nazis refueling rights there, before fighting and losing in the summer of 1941 to a multi–national group of liberators, including Free French, Australians, and Palestinian Jews like Moshe Dayan (who lost an eye there). In January 1945 Dentz was condemned to death, a sentence de Gaulle commuted to life imprisonment; and he died in prison hospital later that year. Weygand indicates how much he had learned from him when Dentz ran the Information Service in the Levant during Weygand's tenure as high commissioner there in the early '20s. Preoccupied in Africa, he then lost sight of this official in Syria during World War II, but still saw poignancy in an able Alsatian general and administrator coming to such a bad end.[43]

Who *didn't* Weygand know over an enormously long career? His preface to a book on de Lattre de Tassigny, written just after that general's death from cancer in January 1952, shows how he had recognized and promoted talent, appointing "King Jean" to his staff in the early '30s, when he was Inspector General of the Army. Knowing de Lattre's reputation from World War I (four wounds), and from the Rif conflict of the '20s, Weygand also saw for himself the man's maturity and ability to lead. The book notes de Lattre's equal admiration for Weygand.[44]

In addition to prefaces or introductions, there were also published speeches by Weygand, such as at the 1961 induction of the philosopher Jean Guitton into the Académie Française. As usual, Weygand took even this task seriously, and his long retort to Guitton's speech is loving, tasteful, and empathetic. He has that uncanny ability to bring himself and the reader right into

A very old, but still acute General Weygand in his late nineties, with little of a long, constructive life left. To the end, he never made peace with disarray (Hulton-Deutsch Collection/CORBIS).

the regional and familial background that had formed Guitton. Perhaps Weygand was himself imagining what it would have been like to have had as sweet and rational a childhood as did Guitton, with a fine father and mother, and deep provincial roots. However, his sadness intervenes with a remark that many sons of this solid Catholic bourgeoisie were killed off in the Great War. He also feels himself into Guitton's own captivity in a German *oflag* during the next war.[45]

The year 1961 also saw the loss of Weygand's wife, who had become an invalid due to arthritis, deafness, and near blindness. But the general carried on resolutely with his activities to the end of his life. Probably the best window into the personal Weygand of these twilight years comes from a great admirer, Captain Charles Fouvez, who had first met the general in Morocco of the '30s, talking at length with him there. A Belgian in the Foreign Legion, Fouvez was involved in the protectorate's final pacification campaigns. He then got to visit Weygand many times at his home during the '50s, and almost up to his death in the mid-'60s. As Fouvez declares, "I had the most absolute deference toward and respect for his person. Without wishing to idealize him, I considered him one of the most remarkable people of our time, due to his broad outlook, serenity, uprightness, fundamental honesty, and deep faith, as well as the wideness and catholicity of his learning, moral rectitude, and fidelity of his friendships."[46]

Fouvez says he was doubtless the last "Bruxellois" to meet with the general before his death — this on November 18, 1964. He and his wife arrived off the cuff at the Avénue Friedland apartment they knew well — at 10 a.m. They were greeted "with that exquisite urbanity which was one of [Weygand's] dominant characteristics."[47] Though he still had all his buttons, the general showed no interest in making it to 100 years old.

Just about 98 (or more?), Weygand worked his usual late hours on January 20, 1965, trying to keep up with still plentiful correspondence, though aided by a secretary. He then fell and broke a bone in his thigh. Nearing the end, neither leg would keep him aloft anymore. On January 27 he wished to convey regrets to Lady Churchill, concerning the recent death of her eminent husband. Then he passed away during the afternoon of January 28, 1965. Weygand had prescribed his burial for Morlaix in Brittany, beside his wife, but hoped for a mass at the gold-domed church of the Invalides, where the remains of Lyautey, Foch, and of course Napoleon were found.[48] And again, de Gaulle raised hackles against this possibility, which for a general of Weygand's status should have been normal.

The service at Paris' Saint-Philippe du Roule was nonetheless moving, and Jean Laborde, in *L'Aurore* (February 3, 1965), estimated that some 15,000 people of all classes and backgrounds came out. The church filled fast, and it was hard for notables from the military, like generals Beaufre, Koenig, and Gouraud, or from the Académie (André Maurois, Henri Troyat, Marcel Pagnol, among others), to get their seats. Outside, there were some protests against President de Gaulle, but then the moving funeral march of the coffin, accompanied by the hymn of Saint-Cyr, quieted the unruly. In Brittany a service of April 21 was attended by some 2,000, and once again, the crowd was too huge for the church there. Meanwhile, articles criticizing de Gaulle's pettiness had been pouring out in newspapers like *Le Figaro* and *Le Monde*, and in respected journals, such as the *Revue des deux Mondes*.[49]

Le grand Charles' own end was less than six years off. And while Weygand's passing elicited a genuine outpouring of French grief, de Gaulle's (along with the renaming of Paris' Place de l'Etoile as the Place Charles de Gaulle) only revealed the intense divisions in France stemming from 1968 *contestation* against the regime — a new generation's uproar that suddenly impelled the president to court old soldiers, even those who had opposed him on Algeria. And even those who had found his edict against a state funeral service for Weygand at the Invalides out of line.[50]

Weygand had died crowding the very old age of 100, but feeling that he had been granted plenty of time and opportunity to show what he could do. He did not care about the milestone of 100, nor about receiving posthumous honors or monuments, and they were in fact, few and far between. Not many Weygand streets are found around today's France, compared to other major names of French history. But appropriately, there is an Avénue du Général Weygand in Compiègne, where in both world wars of the 20th century, he was on hand for the signing of important — and very different — armistices. He had helped shape or modify content, and even read out terms to the Germans of 1918; and for his role in both these armistices, he should not be blamed. Standing up to a foe always makes one enemies, and in his case, most certainly did. If a person hasn't made enemies in this brief time we have on the planet, then probably, he hasn't done much of significance.

Chapter Notes

Introduction

1. Philip Bankwitz, *Maxime Weygand and Civil-Military Relations in Modern France* (Cambridge, MA: Harvard University Press, 1967).

2. Destremau, *Weygand* (Paris: Perrin, 1989). The earlier biographical studies of Weygand are much less satisfactory. Henry Bordeaux's *Weygand* (Paris: Plon, 1957) is only a sketch, while Guy Raïssac's *Un Soldat dans la tourmente* (Paris: Albin Michel, 1963) is concerned almost solely with the Weygand of World War II and after, devoting only 46 pages to the entire period of his life before and during World War I, and in the inter-war period — that is, up to his early seventies.

3. Jacques Weygand, *Weygand, mon père* (Paris: Flammarion, 1970), 16. General Marcel Bigeard, France's most decorated soldier, highlighted Weygand's courage during World War II in a telephone conversation of November 18, 2006. For a long portrait of Bigeard's fascinating career escaping Nazi imprisonment, participating in the liberation of France, then fighting bravely in French Indochina and Algeria, see Barnett Singer and John Langdon, *Cultured Force: Makers and Defenders of the French Colonial Empire* (Madison: University of Wisconsin Press, 2004), ch. 8. Bigeard has also published over a dozen books, many on his career.

4. Among recent books that explore various strains of resistance, including "Vichy resistance," see Robert Belot's *La Résistance sans de Gaulle* (Paris: Fayard, 2006). Weygand figures prominently there. One should also note the subtlety of Richard Vinen in his *The Unfree French: Life under the Occupation* (New Haven: Yale University Press, 2006). Vinen focuses not only on ordinary life in France of this era, but on ideological variations at Vichy, and again shows how some clearly evolved from Vichy to Resistance (50–51). He also signals that the contrastive purity of de Gaulle has become, quite simply, a myth. And Vinen is truly positive on the wartime role of Weygand (64–66). Also pertinent is the collection of views in Sarah Fishman et al., eds., *France at War: Vichy and the Historians* (tr. David Lake; Oxford: Berg, 2000), especially chapters contributed by French specialists. As one of them, Dominique Veillon, notes, "we are only just beginning to challenge the image of an idyllic Resistance, implacable and pure, which derived its legitimacy from a total and spontaneous condemnation of the Vichy regime from the very outset." *Ibid.*, 174. Veillon and others here show that many resistants operated from a Vichy or pro–Pétain base in roughly the first two years of the regime, then either skirted de Gaulle or, when becoming Gaullists, remained in varying degrees Pétainist at heart. Among many examples cited is the young François Mitterand. Another human example is my dear friend Colonel Serge-Henri Parisot, considered an official resistant ("résistant homologué") by the French government. Yet he too was loyal to Pétain in the early years of the war, though spying on the Germans in Casablanca (at the head of a secret service branch Weygand created), then imprisoned for complicity in Operation TORCH. After that, he participated in the campaigns of Tunisia and Italy, and helped nab key French collaborationists near the end of the war. I have had numerous talks with Parisot, and there is also a recorded interview on his fascinating career at the oral history branch of the Service Historique de l'Armée de Terre, Vincennes.

Chapter 1

1. Joseph A. Capozzoli, "Psychological Relief: An Overview: the Balkan Experience," in Wendy N. Zubenko and Joseph A. Capozzoli, eds., *Children and Disasters: A Practical Guide to Healing and Recovery* (New York: Oxford University Press, 2002), 6.

2. According to John Triseliotis, adopted children "have additional hurdles to overcome connected with their adoption and the construction of their identities. The extra tasks can act

as a stress factor at certain points during childhood ... or in adolescence when they strive to achieve their separateness and find answers to who they are. The same studies equally suggest that many of the problems displayed earlier and in adolescence disappear by the late teens and with time." Which for the most part was Weygand's case as he "found himself," above all, in a military career. Triseliotis, "Identity Formation and the Adopted Person Revisited," in Amal Treacher and Ilan Katz, eds., *The Dynamics of Adoption* (London and Philadelphia: Jessica Kingsley Publishers, 2000), 81–82. C.f. David M. Brodzinsky, Marshall D. Schechter, and Robin Marantz Henig, *Being Adopted: The Lifelong Search for Self* (New York: Doubleday, 1992), on the evolving adoption experience over time. William Feigelman notes the "genealogical bewilderment" of adoptees, which Weygand certainly felt his entire life. But again, this researcher sees a variability in how adopted children react at different times to their predicament, and the results of a large statistical study he undertook "offer confirmation for the theories of adoption positing an identity crisis ordinarily emerging during adolescence [when Weygand affirmed his strong Catholicism and military vocation] with which the adoptee must cope." Feigelman then sees a relative overcoming of insecurities in a majority of those he studied. Feigelman, "Adopted Adults: Comparisons with Persons Raised in Conventional Families," in Harriet E. Gross and Marvin B. Sussman, eds., *Families and Adoption* (New York and London: Haworth Press, 1997), quotations 201 and 220, and see also 220–221. David W. Brodzinsky, Daniel W. Smith, and Anne B. Brodzinsky, in *Children's Adjustment to Adoption: Developmental and Clinical Issues* (Thousand Oaks: SAGE Publications, 1998), note the "confusion, anger, sadness, anxiety, embarrassment, shame" in adopted children (17), but which may then lead to "a variety of coping options" (18). An even more optimistic viewpoint is found in Marvin Olasky, "Adoption is an Act of Compassion," in Andrew Harnack, ed., *Adoption: Opposing Viewpoints* (San Diego: Greenhaven Press, 1995): "There are problems with adoption, to be sure ... but studies show that adoption works well for the vast majority of adopted children.... That's not what anti-adoption propagandists would have us believe though" (25). In Weygand's case, the whole issue is perhaps muddied by a genetic predisposition (on his likeliest father's side) to a military career. If *we* choose to highlight the psychological here, we also pay heed to analyses that try to sort out genetic versus psychological factors in adopted children, such as in Martin Shaw, "Growing Up Adopted," in Philip Bean, ed., *Adoption: Essays in Social Policy,*

Law, and Sociology (London: Tavistock Publications, 1984), chapter 7, and especially 117–118.

3. The best book we now have on the likely background of Weygand is Dominique Paoli, *Maxime ou le secret Weygand* (Brussels: Editions Racine, 2003). Although it reposes on the latest in terms of archival availability, it does stand on the shoulders of a remarkable earlier work on Weygand by a dedicated acolyte: Charles Fouvez, *Le Mystère Weygand: Etude d'un dossier historique au XIXè siècle* (Paris: La Table Ronde, 1967).

4. On Cohen see especially Fouvez, *Le Mystère Weygand,* ch. 6. See also on the Sephardic-Jewish commercial families with whom Cohen conducted business, particularly in Morocco, Daniel J. Schroeter, *Merchants of Essaouira: Urban Society and Imperialism in Southwestern Morocco, 1844–1886* (New York: Cambridge University Press, 1988).

5. Cohen was not the perfect "father figure" alongside Denimal; but there were plenty of pluses here — including his grandchildren (via his first Jewish marriage) to play with Maxime in Provençal summers, as well as aunts and "cousins" on Denimal's side. Raising adopted or, really, any children in a suitable manner partly depends on "marital quality," according to Mark Cummings, Marcie C. Goeke-Morey, and Jessica Raymond in chapter 8 ("Fathers in Family Context: Effects of Marital Quality and Marital Conflict") of Michael E. Lamb, ed., *The Role of the Father in Child Development,* 4th ed. (Hoboken, NJ: John Wiley, 2004). See also the description of "optimal families" in W. Robert Beavers' chapter, "Healthy, Midrange, and Severely Dysfunctional Families," in Froma Walsh, ed., *Normal Family Processes* (New York: Guilford Press, 1982). In "optimal families" children are encouraged to "leave their families not for isolated independence but for other human systems" (47).

6. What Saint-Cyr meant to the young Weygand is best left in his own words of recollection: "After a solitary, joyless childhood and mournful adolescence passed behind lycée walls ... Saint-Cyr, despite its austerity and harshness, and the physical training and work exigencies which filled the day, seemed to me a sort of deliverance...." Maxime Weygand, *Mémoires,* I: *Idéal vécu* (Paris: Flammarion, 1953), 15. Weygand is necessarily less complete than either Destremau or Paoli on the "mysteries" of his childhood, which eluded him, and which also led him on occasion to fudge. In terms of his size, a *Time* magazine article, May 27, 1940, praised Weygand's combativeness and intelligence, despite his putative height of 5' and weight of 120 pounds!

Chapter 2

1. See Eugen Weber's still useful study of *The Nationalist Revival in France, 1905–1914* (Berkeley: University of California Press, 1959). Predictably, Weygand, so loyal to the French army and Catholic Church, was on the anti–Dreyfusard side, according to a number of sources. See, for example, Bertrand Favreau, *Georges Mandel ou la passion de la République 1885–1944* (Paris: Fayard, 1996), 368.

2. For a negative view of Joffre, commanding French forces in World War I, see Singer and Langdon, *Cultured Force*, ch. 4.

3. Liddell Hart expresses this regret in his chapter on Foch in *Reputations, Ten Years After* (Boston: Little, Brown, 1928).

4. Weygand, *Mémoires*, I, part II, ch. 1 for the above.

5. On General de Langle, "I had the time really to observe this man of high distinction, whose proud, noble physiognomy truly reflected his military virtues...." *Ibid.*, 92.

6. Again, he is marvelous on all the old men pushing makeshift trundling devices, and children toddling along, going (as in 1940) goodness knew where. See *ibid.*, 97.

7. For preceding *ibid.*, Part II, through ch. 2.

8. Demands on French generals to help improvise responses to the Germans were rife; for example, Franchet d'Esperey, when asked to use his Fifth Army to help the Ninth in a counterattack: "The answer is immediate. The commander of the Fifth Army does more than simply consent, and thus performs an act of camaraderie in combat that is above all praise." *Ibid.*, 112. As for the heroic General Maunoury, his luck ran out in 1915; when reconnoitering along the front, he was shot in the eye, ending his military service.

9. With Lieutenant-Colonel Devaux at his side, "The night was splendid, all stars lit. Our emotions were so intense that we barely exchanged words." *Ibid.*, 117.

10. End of *ibid.*, part II, ch. 3 for the preceding. Weygand mentions here that, however much Foch pushed others, he himself had suffered losses in his own family of a son and son-in-law just in that initial August of the war.

11. *Ibid.*, 135.

12. On Colonel des Vallières: "Tall, elegant, and with a noble face, he had a remarkable combination of gifts and qualities." Des Vallières would die on the Chemin des Dames in May 1918 and "his death would be a huge loss for the high command." *Ibid.*, 138.

13. And again, Weygand's description of Wilson is priceless: "His physical appearance is too well known for me to dwell on it: two meters tall, lanky and thin: with a face of seductive repugnance, he readily described himself as the ugliest man in England, but he fizzed with wit." Wilson was certainly not the usual Brit, and Weygand remained his friend through the war and its aftermath. *Ibid.*, 145.

14. On all this *ibid.*, end of part II, ch. 4.

15. *Ibid.*, 160.

16. As he put it, "It is appropriate to pay due homage to the valor and tenacity with which the Belgian troops defended a makeshift line of resistance, which they would then hold for four years." *Ibid.*, 162.

17. *Ibid.*, 163.

18. *Ibid.*, 168.

19. *Ibid.*, 169.

20. *Ibid.*, 170.

21. *Ibid.*, 173.

22. As Weygand put it, "And what can one say of the endurance and spirit of sacrifice of the soldiers who fought for weeks under the fire of superior artillery, their feet in water, in trenches that were too shallow, dug into soil that was furnished and gashed with shells, and all too often immixed with dead bodies buried just beneath the earth's surface — the bodies of their comrades in heroism!" *Ibid.*, 177. How much finer such an assessment than Weygand's hero worship of Foch's "unshakeable firmness" — and of Joffre, who appropriated credit for the Marne. *Ibid.*, 180. Mostly a wonderfully integrated, complex person, Weygand also held on to these human talismans. Horne's celebrated book is *The Price of Glory: Verdun 1916* (New York: St. Martin's Press, 1963).

23. Weygand, *Mémoires*, I, end part II, ch. 5 for the preceding.

24. *Ibid.*, 197.

25. Georges Clemenceau was amazed by how ignorant French leadership before World War I had been regarding German firepower. "I have looked through Colonel Foch's work on the principles of war. I saw with utter dismay that there was *not a single word* [his emphasis] in it on the question of armaments. A metaphysical treatise on war! And yet it is not without importance to know if an attack with catapults or with quick-firing guns may call upon us to vary our means of defence." Clemenceau, *Grandeur and Misery of Victory* (tr. F. M. Atkinson; New York: Harcourt, Brace, 1930), 33–34. But then Foch — he might have said the same thing about Joffre — "was by no means rich in subtleties of character...." *Ibid.*, 37.

26. See Weygand, *Mémoires*, I, quotation 206. On Weygand as the one who made Foch more comprehensible, see James Marshall-Cornwall's estimate in his *Foch as Military Commander* (New York: Crane, Russak, 1972): "The combination of Foch and Weygand was quite

remarkable.... Foch entrusted to his chief of staff with complete confidence, the task of translating his jerky and staccato utterances into clear operation orders" (109).

27. Weygand, *Mémoires*, I, 220.

28. *Ibid.*, 222. Joffre was his typical chipper self about French counterattacks which stymied the effect of gas here: "In this way, the consequences of the Germans' unexpected employment of this disloyal weapon were reduced to the proportions of an unpleasant incident of no serious outcome." *The Personal Memoirs of Joffre: Field Marshal of the French Army* (tr. Colonel T. Bentley Mott; New York: Harper and Brothers, 1932), II, 348.

29. Weygand, *Mémoires*, I, 224.

30. The two best books on the German idea of unlimited warfare, where ends justified means, are Modris Eksteins, *Rites of Spring: The Great War and the Birth of the Modern Age* (Boston: Houghton Mifflin, 1989); and especially Isabel V. Hull, *Absolute Destruction: Military Culture and the Practices of War in Imperial Germany* (Ithaca: Cornell University Press, 2005).

31. Weygand, *Mémoires*, I, 229.

32. On Captain Réquin: "Réquin was of small stature, but neatly put together; his physiognomy was fine, and he had a very pleasing expression, though his hair was already nearly white. To much intelligence, Réquin added amiability and tact, but not excluding firmness." Réquin himself was a drawer and painter, having attended the Ecole des Beaux-Arts. *Ibid.*, 250.

33. As he writes, "for all those who took part in those struggles, these names [of villages] speak, for the conquest of all the places they designate cost a lot in sorrow, bravery, and blood." *Ibid.*, 257.

34. *Ibid.*, 264.

35. See *ibid.*, end ch. 3 of Part III for preceding.

36. *Ibid.*, 279. Clemenceau was a more unqualified admirer of Pétain, the soldier, than of Foch or Joffre. "In perilous battles I found [Pétain] tranquilly heroic — that is to say, master of himself. Perhaps without illusions, but certainly without recriminations, he was always ready for self-sacrifice. I have great pleasure in paying him this tribute." Clemenceau, *Grandeur and Misery of Victory*, 36.

37. Joffre's constant blame for these losses on problems like the rainy weather, including in these late September attacks, is discussed in Singer and Langdon, *Cultured Force*, ch. 4, *passim*.

38. As Weygand puts it, "We were forced to recognize that the Germans had prepared their defensive exceptionally well. The organization of their positions was ceaselessly being perfected.... The spirit animating the adversary was particularly aggressive, and never did we attack without submitting to the immediate reaction of a counter-attack." Weygand, *Mémoires*, I, 293; also on that page, the problem of weather combined with German artillery is discussed.

39. Again, an extended discussion of this is found in Singer and Langdon, *Cultured Force*, ch. 4.

40. Weygand, *Mémoires*, I, 299. In his recollections entitled *1914*, but extending into a conclusion on these campaigns of 1915, Sir John French was quite magnanimous to Joffre, but underlined the futility of this entire modus operandi on the Western Front: "As the history of the operations during 1915 will show, this general strategic idea was the foundation of all our efforts throughout that year. It brought about for the British Army the Battles of Neuve Chapelle, Ypres (second), Festubert, and Loos; and for the French other important actions, which, although local successes, did not result in achieving any appreciable advance toward the objectives which the plans sought to attain." Field-Marshal Viscount French of Ypres, *1914* (Boston: Houghton Mifflin, 1919), 349–350. The book is dedicated to David Lloyd George, and also discusses one of his "intimate friends," Winston Churchill, who visited French on the Western Front. (For the latter, see *ibid.*, 308.)

41. Diary entries in Service Historique de l'Armée de Terre (hereafter S.H.A.T.): 1K130: Dépôt Weygand.

42. This comes through intermittently in both Weygand's memoirs and his private diary conserved in the archives.

43. On Joffre and the background to Verdun, see Singer and Langdon, *Cultured Force*, 161–162.

44. Weygand, *Mémoires*, I, 312.

45. "It was impossible not to be won over by General Fayolle," writes Weygand. "Loyalty was painted on his face itself.... He had a wide-ranging intellect that was vivid and very cultivated.... And the years had removed not a jot of his freshness of mind and heart...." Weygand goes on: "Very brave under fire, General Fayolle had the qualities and virtues of a leader. He was loved and revered by those who served at his side." *Ibid.*, 314.

46. As Weygand remembers, "Once again, Parliament was in a fever of great agitation unfavorable to the high command. Against the commander in chief, they invoked the defects of Verdun's defensive organization, cause of the initial German successes...." *Ibid.*, 325. Despite Weygand's attempts to defend Papa Joffre from these insistent politicians, the latter were definitely correct here. Right at this time, General Haig ran into Joffre blowing his top over the direction of operations, then finally simmering

down. As Haig puts it: "I waited calmly till he had finished. His breast heaved and his face flushed! The truth is the poor man cannot argue, nor can he easily read a map." Robert Blake, ed., *The Private Papers of Douglas Haig 1914–1919* (London: Eyre and Spottiswoode, 1952), 154.

47. See Weygand's post-mortem in his *Mémoires*, I, 351. On weather and elements that so compounded the disaster he writes: "Besides, the torrential rains and howling windstorms intervened to slow down the combatants of the Somme, whom one cannot praise too much. The mud had become so fluid and deep that certain isolated men were sucked down into it, without power to get out." Robin Prior and Trevor Wilson, however, explain the military seductions of the region before hostilities began: "Notwithstanding its later evil reputation, the Somme area seemed reasonable campaigning country. Its undulating nature kept the soil well drained and the only swampy areas were around the river banks.... Nor had it yet suffered [before July 1, 1916] the effects of continuous fighting." Prior and Wilson, *The Somme* (New Haven: Yale University Press, 2005), 37. Their thesis is that the political sector ought to share responsibility with military leaders for this unmitigated disaster, causing some 432,000 British casualties and 150,000 dead. But military mistakes kept being compounded, and critiques from General Fayolle about lack of adequate observation and general preparation before artillery barrages and forward charges crescendoed that autumn. See his series of letters to staff commanders, including Foch, of October and November, 1916, in S.H.A.T.: 14N48: Fonds Etat-Major Foch 1916–1919. This file also contains a series of damning letters sent by the peremptory Foch to Haig, urging him to mount attacks on schedule — ones that turned out of course to be very costly.

48. As Weygand recalled: "The end of 1916 found the French government in a state of nervousness and incontestable mistrust towards the High Command." *Mémoires*, I, 356. On the colorful Sarrail and the vicissitudes of Salonika, through to his recall to Paris by Clemenceau in December 1917, see Jan Karl Tannenbaum, *General Maurice Sarrail 1856–1929: The French Army and Left-Wing Politics* (Chapel Hill: University of North Carolina Press, 1974), ch. 4–9. There was much debate in the French Parliament about the Salonika issue.

49. On this see Singer and Langdon, *Cultured Force*, 165–166.

50. This "disgrace of the chiefs" concludes the long part of Weygand's memoirs on 1916 and the Battle of Somme: Weygand, *Mémoires*, I, 305–365.

51. "... his was a clear mind, with straightfor-

ward, logical ideas, and sound, sensible judgment." *Ibid.*, 383.

52. Pierre Miquel considers the Nivelle Offensive, especially occurring after the Verdun holocaust, as France's worst engagement of World War I. Partly, this was due to forbidding, and not well enough examined, terrain. The Chemin des Dames running south to the Aisne was full of rock and forest. As Miquel explains, "Like Swiss cheese, it is filled with holes, huge caverns or 'creutes,' where entire brigades can shelter themselves from shellings. Taking it by storm is a deadly enterprise." So it was for Nivelle's already beleaguered forces trying to overwhelm German defenses. Miquel, *Le Chemin des dames* (Paris: Perrin, 1997), 7. There is a large literature on just why so many soldiers fought so sedulously through to this low point of 1917, when many were starting to question the whole effort. See the recent articles by Edgar Jones, "The Psychology of Killing: The Combat Experience of British Soldiers during the First World War," *Journal of Contemporary History* 41 (April 2006): 229–246, and Alex Watson, "Self-Deception and Survival: Mental Coping Strategies on the Western Front, 1914–1918," in *ibid.*, 269–286. The former discredits the "radical" view of an historical maverick, Niall Ferguson, who felt that soldiers kept fighting so hard because of the joy of killing. The latter article sees soldiers clinging to reassuring superstitions that would minimize risks (in their minds). On the trench experience, there is still nothing better than Robert Graves' masterpiece, *Goodbye to All That*.

53. But at the same time, Weygand did tip his cap, fair as always, to "the very real leadership of General Nivelle." Weygand, *Mémoires*, I, 392. Joffre thought he alone had the keys to the kingdom of victory. As he said: "I repeat ... that if we had had the firmness to renew and amplify the battle [on the Somme] which the winter had interrupted, the Germans would have been crushed.... The men who saved them have a heavy responsibility to bear in the face of History." Joffre, *Personal Memoirs of Joffre*, II, 559.

54. Weygand, *Mémoires*, I, 399. People he saw around these tables included socialists like Albert Thomas, France's Minister of Munitions in 1916–1917, who was, if different ideologically from Weygand, similarly experienced in the scrounging of war materiel for France. One gets a good sense of Thomas's duties from Archives Nationales (hereafter A.N.): 94AP/233: Fonds Albert Thomas. His many lists here include not only munitions, but horses, mules, metals, and the like. And while France's President Poincaré could not attend all conferences, he too was kept abreast of war deployments, with much more

power (including in the military realm) than earlier French presidents of the Republic had had. In S.H.A.T.: 6N6: Fonds Poincaré, one sees detailed, monthly maps of troop detachments deployed on the Western Front (both of the Entente and the Germans), which Poincaré could obviously spread on his desk, noting changes.

55. The issue of how or whether to help Kerensky and the Russians again consumed much time (and many of Weygand's crabbed notes) at a conference opening in London on August 7, 1917, and with Weygand's table drawing again showing the crème de la crème around him (Viscount Alfred Milner, Lloyd George, Arthur Balfour, Lord George Curzon, Lord Edward Derby, Robertson on one side of the table, and on the other side, the French, including Painlevé, Ribot, and Foch). But Weygand also had much to scribble on another potential offensive from Salonika, the Mesopotamia theater, etc. The next day Lloyd George was longwinded on favorite subjects of "overwhelming Austria," developing consensus among the allies for fighting in the Middle East, and more generally, for "unity of forces." See Weygand diary entries in S.H.A.T.: 1K130, August 7, 8, 1917.

56. See, for example, Weygand's diary entry for a meeting he attended June 29, 1917, in S.H.A.T.: 1K130 — on the necessity to "prepare and accelerate the entry into activity of the American army...." His entry for the following day (June 30) in *ibid.* also concerned "Questions Pershing." On August 12 (in *ibid.*) his diary entry contains an estimate of some 7,700,000 horses — this is Weygand the staff man — and partly to see how many could be shunted to the coming Americans. And in *ibid.*, his diary entry of August 29 is indeed on how many thousands of horses to deliver to the Americans, and money realities involved. More ironic, on the brink of the Bolshevik coup, is his entry of August 20, 1917, discussing deliveries of artillery, etc. to the Russians. Even on November 7, in a Weygand entry, Lloyd George was upholding the necessity of informing the Russians about an imminent operation! When, of course, Lenin was about to inflict the famous "ten days that shook the world." In *ibid.*

57. See Lloyd George, *War Memoirs of David Lloyd George* (London: Ivor Nicolson and Watson, 1934), IV, ch. 65, 66, 67. As he put it: "Robertson was terrified of Haig and never dared to utter or mutter a doubt as to his strategy. He himself has admitted that he had serious doubts about Passchendaele...." *Ibid.*, 2341. But Haig kept on with his suicidal attacks. As Lloyd George wrote President Wilson, September 3, 1917: "[Haig] had just captured a small Flemish village and his whole mind was now concentrated on reaching the next hamlet half a kilo-

metre further on.... You feel ... that his mind is stuck in the mud.... His review of a world war is limited by the Passchendaele Ridge a few hundred yards above his front line." *Ibid.*, 2357–2358. And like Joffre, Haig was a first-rate propagandizer, suppressing bad tidings, and hyping the good. "The output of optimistic slosh was at this date at its maximum in quantity and quality. The looms of the victory mills were then working overtime at G.H.Q." *Ibid.*, 2360.

58. On Rapallo see, among others, Alan Palmer, *Victory 1918* (New York: Atlantic Monthly Press, 1998), 143. There he calls it "a curious conference, totally without precedent but with a significant impact on Allied policy for the remainder of the war." Foch felt satisfied enough with his impact in Italy to replace himself there in late November 1917 with the respected General Fayolle. Weygand felt that Foch had done a wonderful job turning the country's war effort around; see his exultant letter sent from Italy to another member of Foch's staff back in Paris, Commandant Fournier, November 19, 1917, in A.N.: 414AP/12: Papiers personnels de Foch. Lettres de personnalités civiles et militaires français.

59. In all, there would be 51 meetings of the Supreme War Council, but owing to the different kinds of people and backgrounds there, it was, as Elizabeth Greenhalgh notes, "an uneven shop." Greenhalgh, *Victory Through Coalition: Britain and France During the First World War* (Cambridge: Cambridge University Press, 2005), 179.

60. The taking of Baghdad and Jerusalem from the Turks gave the British leader a lot of hope in that theater. As he put it, "The name of Baghdad counted for more throughout the Mussulman world than did Passchendaele with all the notoriety it had acquired. Jerusalem meant more to hundreds of millions — Christian and Mussulman alike — than Ostend." *War Memoirs of David Lloyd George*, 2419. Lord Maurice Hankey also confirms the British prime minister's obsession with finishing off the Ottoman Empire in his *The Supreme Command 1914–1918* (London: George Allen and Unwin, 1961), II, ch. 74 (762–774).

61. Haig had real reservations about Foch, and considered him little better than the sacked Joffre! As he put it in a couple of his diary entries of April, 1918: "I found Foch most selfish and obstinate." And: "Foch seems to me unmethodical and takes a 'short view' of the situation. For instance, he does not look ahead and make a forecast of what may be required in a week in a certain area and arrange accordingly." Blake, ed., *Private Papers of Douglas Haig*, 303.

62. See S.H.A.T.: 4N2: Conseil Supérieur de

la Guerre. Section française: Organismes inter-alliés 1917–1918. The carton is dominated by Weygand's correspondence, and his long, detailed, but typically elegant and readable reports on a variety of situations — Belgian use of black troops from Africa, the impact of Japan and China on the war, and of the Russian collapse; and especially, British and French aid to Italy, and extension of fronts in France. All shot through with Weygand's sense that needless human losses were simply no longer permissible. British historians, in particular, have retailed the view that Weygand was merely Foch's "mouthpiece." See, among others, John Grigg, *Lloyd George War Leader 1916–1918* (London: Allen Lane, 2002), who uses the term (285). This is, otherwise, an admirable book. Grigg notes that the British member of the SWC, Sir Henry Wilson, "would have stood out physically in any company on account of his tallness and ugliness." And that "not only was he an intriguer, he was also two-faced, and as time went on more and more of those who had dealings with him [in England] grew to distrust him." Wilson's Francophilia, however, kept him close to Weygand and Foch. As for the SWC's American representative, Bliss, he was the multilingual son of a classics professor and, according to Grigg, "a man of broader outlook than the commander of the AEF" (Pershing). *Ibid.*, quotations 286, 287, 325.

63. "Priestly" is not simply a figure of speech when it comes to Foch. Colonel Serge-Henri Parisot, whose father, General Henri Parisot, served for a long time on Foch's staff, says that Foch was ultra–Catholic, and went to church every day, even in wartime, when possible. Parisot phone interview, August 27, 2006.

64. Oddly, Ludendorff strikes one (from his memoirs) as more caring of lost men in the field than Foch and Joffre. See, especially, parts he devoted to Verdun and the Somme through to the end of 1916 in his *My War Memories 1914–1918* (London: Hutchinson, 1919), I, 239–327.

65. In S.H.A.T.: 1K130, Weygand's March 25, 1918, diary entry is scornful of Clemenceau, noting: "He gave the impression, already felt in London, that he wanted to direct the war by himself.... He is as rash as he is presumptuous."

66. In Weygand, *Mémoires*, I, 482.

67. In *ibid.*, 483. According to Foch, Lord Milner had first talked alone with Clemenceau, and Foch felt that he may have sold the French prime minister the idea of a generalissimo role for the Amiens sector. Ferdinand Foch, *The Memoirs of Marshal Foch* (tr. Colonel T. Bentley Mott; London: William Heinemann, 1931), 299–300. That view has now been confirmed in the latest scholarly biography of Milner, though,

characteristically modest, Milner played down his role here. See J. Lee Thompson, *Forgotten Patriot: A Life of Alfred, Viscount Milner of St. James's and Cape Town, 1854–1925* (Madison, N.J.: Fairleigh Dickinson University Press, 2007), 349. Milner had also apparently helped push Lloyd George toward creation of a Supreme War Council, in order to counter Haig and Robertson. *Ibid.*, 344.

68. After the meeting Lloyd George apparently asked Foch: "And now which must I bet on, Ludendorff or Foch?" To which Foch responded: "You can back me and you will win. For Ludendorff has got to break through our lines, and this he can no longer do." Foch, *Memoirs of Marshal Foch*, 315.

69. Weygand, *Mémoires*, I, 490.

70. John Mosier forcefully argues that only the American intervention, eventually to the tune of some two million fresh soldiers, defeated the Germans; and that all of Foch's strategies could never have done so alone. See Mosier, *The Myth of the Great War: A New Military History of World War I* (New York: HarperCollins, 2001), *passim*.

71. Weygand, *Mémoires*, I, 518.

72. The impatience of major figures in both French and British camps to see the Americans soon make a real difference is found throughout Weygand's notes on this meeting, in S.H.A.T.: 1K130 — "Employment of American forces" the subject heading.

73. A recent book showing the constant, often heated disagreements between Foch and Pétain in the last year or so of the war is Robert A. Doughty's *Pyrrhic Victory: French Strategy and Operations in the Great War* (Cambridge, MA: Belknap Press of Harvard University Press, 2005). See especially Doughty's chapters 8, 9, and 10, with Pétain shown being driven to frequent fits of anger over Foch's dogmatic views. Not to mention the British! For example, General Gough at one point in the spring of 1918 called Foch "amazingly ignorant," adding: "Foch was peremptory, rude, and excited in his manner." In *ibid.*, 438.

74. Kevin D. Stubbs, *Race to the Front: The Materiel Foundations of Coalition Strategy in the Great War* (Westport, CT: Praeger, 2002), 9.

75. Occasionally, Weygand could help break a Foch-Pershing impasse with a suggestion, as occurred (according to Pershing) in a meeting about a month later. See John J. Pershing, *My Experiences in the World War* (New York: Frederick A. Stokes, 1931), II, 78.

76. As Fleming says, "The French repeatedly ordered the Americans to make attacks that were close to suicidal and gave them objectives they could never reach." The result was over 90,000 dead and wounded by the end of August, 1918.

Thomas Fleming, *The Illusion of Victory: America in World War I* (New York: Basic Books, 2003), 265, quotation 266. On Belleau Wood, see Robert B. Asprey, *At Belleau Wood* (Denton, TX: University of North Texas Press, 1996); on Soissons, Douglas V. Johnson II and Rolfe L. Hillman Jr., *Soissons 1918* (College Station, TX: Texas A&M Press, 1999).

77. Edward M. Coffman, *The War to End All Wars: The American Military Experience in World War I* (Madison: University of Wisconsin Press, 1986), quotations 271, 272, and chapter 9 generally. See also Palmer, *Victory 1918*, 206–207. Donald Smythe shows that Pershing and Pétain fundamentally got along on operational issues. See Smythe, *Pershing: General of the Armies* (Bloomington: Indiana University Press, 1986), *passim*.

78. Fleming, *Illusion of Victory*, 268.

79. Pershing, *My Experiences in the World War*, II, quotation 254. As for the weather at the outset of October, "the battle could not be delayed while roads were being built or repaired and supplies brought up. The weather was cold and rainy and not the kind to inspire energetic action on the part of troops unaccustomed to the damp, raw climate." *Ibid.*, 320. In other words, very different from the still-end-of-summer warmth when the Saint-Mihiel operation had begun and worked so well. In a telephone interview with Serge-Henri Parisot, both a long-time military man and a former geographer at Saint-Cyr, his recollection of the Argonne not so long after the battle was of a difficult region for warfare, especially propitious for ambushes from numerous cliffs and defiles. Trees were thick here, and roads for traversing the area too few. Phone conversation with Colonel Serge-Henri Parisot, September 10, 2006. For the effect of the Argonne on President Wilson, see Richard Hofstadter's stirring denouement in his chapter on Wilson in *The American Political Tradition and the Men Who Made It* (New York: A. A. Knopf, 1948). The latest judgment on the Americans in the Meuse-Argonne now, however, blames the Americans themselves. According to Robert H. Ferrell, "The primary reason for the losses in the Meuse-Argonne was the failure of the Wilson administration to mobilize the economy for war." Add to that poor training, lack of requisite weaponry, reluctance to use gas, ineffective artillery and other tactics (some due to Pershing), and this book diminishes French responsibility for these heavy American losses. Ferrell, *America's Deadliest Battle: Meuse-Argonne, 1918* (Lawrence, KS: University Press of Kansas, 2007), quotation 148, and see 148–154 *passim*. Johnson and Hillman seem to concur in their book on Soissons: "So it was that the AEF entered combat for the first time in strength:

partly trained, dubiously led, questionably administered and managed ... and operating under a mixture of doctrines understood by only a few." *Soissons 1918*, 35–36.

80. On the Foch-Pershing quarrel at Bonbon, see Byron Farwell, *Over There: The United States in the Great War 1917–1918* (New York: W. W. Norton, 1999), 234–235. One must, however, note the dissenting view of David Trask — softer on Foch and harder on Pershing's stubborn ideas of American independence, given the spring, 1918 emergency that had been created by Ludendorff's offensives. David E. Trask, *The AEF and Coalition Warmaking, 1917–1918* (Lawrence: University Press of Kansas, 1993). Many argue that Pershing's new army was the first real portent of American world power in the 20th century. See, for example, John S. D. Eisenhower, *Yanks: The Epic Story of the American Army in World War I* (New York: Free Press, 2001). Some future big names were involved in these summer of 1918 battles: Colonel George Marshall, operationally savvy in his late thirties, and George Patton, who could already see the future of tanks, even though as yet, they crawled at about four miles per hour! See also, on changes that would follow this American battle experience in World War I, Jennifer D. Keene, *Doughboys, the Great War, and the Remaking of America* (Baltimore: Johns Hopkins University Press, 2001).

Chapter 3

1. General Weygand, *Le 11 novembre* (Paris: Flammarion, 1958), 22–23, 24.

2. *Ibid.*, 27.

3. *Ibid.*, 29.

4. *Ibid.*, 36; and see Hull, *Absolute Destruction*, *passim*. There has been an historiographical shift on German atrocities of the First World War committed on French and Belgian soil — long dismissed as mostly mythical. Recent work on the subject truly confirms harsh treatment of civilians portending that of the Nazi era. See, for example, Larry Zuckerman, *The Rape of Belgium: The Untold Story of World War I* (New York: New York University Press, 2004); Helen McPhail, *The Long Silence: Civilian Life under the German Occupation of Northern France, 1914–1918* (London: I. B. Tauris, 2001); and John Horne and Alan Kramer, *German Atrocities, 1914: A History of Denial* (New Haven: Yale University Press, 2001). This last work carefully chronicles random murders of thousands of French and Belgian civilians and destruction of some 20,000 homes and buildings. (Near-starvation and torture could also be mentioned.)

5. Weygand, *Le 11 novembre*, quotations 37, 38, 39, 44; and on German wish for "adoucissements," the Bolshevik menace, etc., 45–46. These Foch "no's" were transcribed in Weygand's detailed notes alongside armistice conditions the German delegation kept wishing to alter: in S.H.A.T.: 1K130, written by Weygand just before the final November 11 ceasefire. I have also used here a clear evocation of the armistice in Spencer C. Tucker, *The Great War 1914–1918* (Bloomington: Indiana University Press, 1998), 174–175. While the armistice was signed in the clearing of Rethondes, the actual spot is part of the *commune* of Compiègne, six kilometers from Rethondes. Hence both Rethondes and Compiègne are given as sites of the armistice signing. Partly due to supposedly easy acquiescence to terms of the armistice, Erzberger would pay with his life in 1921; but Klaus Epstein declared that, in fact, he fought hard and patriotically for an agreement that was more favorable to Germany. See Epstein, *Matthias Erzberger and the Dilemma of German Democracy* (Princeton: Princeton University Press, 1959), ch. 11.

6. Weygand, *Le 11 novembre*, quotations 54 (artisans), 56, 57, and for rest of atmosphere painted, 58–61.

7. *Ibid.*, 80–94, quotations 87, 94.

8. *Ibid.*, ch. 6, quotations 97, 98, 108–109. Weygand then adds general commentary from his "today" of the late '50s, contrasting that sacred memory and memorializing to a period when "evasion into sensitivity, indifference, or dilettantism are luxuries our era can no longer afford. This romanticism would lead directly to the ruin of an already shaky society." In fact, "they would like us to believe that a country can remain great without effort, without sacrifices. By learned corruption, they create a youth that is indifferent to the *patrie* and rebellious to what they owe it." Weygand sees in all this the old appeasement of the '30s still much alive. "Some would like to see an experiment and disarm France to see if its self-sacrifice could somehow appease the gods of war still rumbling nearby." To which he contrasts the Great War's gritty soldiers, who — no matter what class they emerged from — gave their all, obeyed, and did what in many cases they didn't want to do. Now? "The rules of the game are: me first..." and, Ortega-like, Weygand lays that to "the extreme, disaggregating individualism which marks our period." We must all go back to the Arch, to the memory, he concludes, of the greatest French sacrifice ever. (*Ibid.*, ch. 7, quotations 117, 118 ["on voudrait ... "], 121, 122 ["l'individualisme..."].) One should also consult Weygand's less passionate, but thorough book (*cum* photos) called *L'Arc de Triomphe de l'Etoile* (Paris: Flammarion, 1960). He is very thorough here on the etiology of arches of triumph going back to the Romans, when battles needed to be major enough (killing at least 5,000 enemy troops and adding significantly to the empire) to qualify! Then came trumpets, treasures, elite prisoners paraded, such as Jugurtha or Vercingetorix, animals for sacrifice, and a procession to Rome's sacred spots. Again, Weygand's patriotism shows through, for example, in the evocation of Vercingetorix, so generous in defeat, so cruelly treated by proud Caesar. He goes on to the arches of France's Louis XIV, including the great one at today's Strasbourg St. Denis subway stop, which became an area of prostitution. Weygand maintained the sacred in his mind through to the end of his life; but many in France gradually let go of it. See *L'Arc de Triomphe, passim*.

9. The study of how the memory of World War I subsequently affected French culture and mores has become a burgeoning field. In France Annette Becker was one of the pioneers in her *Monuments aux morts: Mémoire de la Grande Guerre* (Paris: Errance, 1988), and in the English-speaking world, Jay Winter in his *Sites of Memory, Sites of Mourning: The Great War in European Cultural History* (Cambridge: Cambridge University Press, 1995). More recently we have important studies such as Daniel J. Sherman's *The Construction of Memory in Interwar France* (Chicago: University of Chicago Press, 1999), and Bruno Cabanes' *La Victoire endeuillée: La Sortie de guerre des soldats français 1918–1920* (Paris: Éditions du Seuil, 2004). Memorializing, pilgrimages to great ossuaries, monuments to the dead, naming of children for vanished relatives were mainly an attempt to give meaning to a war hopefully to end war. As Rod Kedward notes, people were putting the question to themselves: "What had it all been for?" See Kedward, *France and the French: A Modern History* (Woodstock, NY: Overlook Press, 2006), 90. A good article on this "memory of the Great War" field is by its *doyen*, Jay Winter: "P vs. C: The Still Burning Anger When the French Talk of the First World War," *Times Literary Supplement*, June 16, 2006, 3–4.

10. Le Général Weygand, *Dans la Nuit Versailles s'éclaire* (Paris: Berger-Levrault, 1959), no pagination. Much of the rest of the book is on the miracle of restoration and electrification at Versailles in the 20th century. And even there, the history-appropriating outsider lavishes his heartfelt gratitude. "What love was necessary to conceal all those kilometers of cables and wires, what careful attention to respect those venerable walls ... what ingenuity and skill to bring to the old chandeliers, candelabras, and *torchères*, new light.... Is that not the most magnificent and respectful homage that one can render to

the Le Vaus, Mansarts, Le Nôtres?" (Unpaginated quotation.)

11. The haggles had obviously started before the Peace Conference. On November 30, 1918, Foch (with Weygand) and Clemenceau arrived in London to meet Lloyd George and other British figures, and to "such a reception as I have never seen accorded to any foreign visitors to our shores." But by their first meeting that evening in Downing Street, the quarrels began, and Lloyd George remembered it as "the first intimation given to the British government that the French intended to secure control over all territory on the left bank of the Rhine." See David Lloyd George, *Memoirs of the Peace Conference* (New Haven: Yale University Press, 1939), I, 77, 78. In a diary entry of December 3, 1918, Weygand quotes Clemenceau and Lloyd George quarreling also about Russian involvement in the coming peace talks, with Clemenceau declaring they could not have representatives in their present condition, and that we should simply "let the Russians cook...." To which Lloyd George replied sharply, noting that "we can't act as if Russia did not exist." No question that "its treachery is certain — but she exists, and one must take that into account, under the threat of great danger." (Both citations in S.H.A.T.: 1K130). There was also wrangling over French insistence on Paris as the site of the Peace Conference (with Lloyd George and President Wilson both initially opposed).

12. Général Weygand, *Mémoires*, II: *Mirages et réalité* (Paris: Flammarion, 1957), quotations 26, 27.

13. But in these extended diary entries from the Peace Conference, he could also be off the cuff, referring on a number of occasions to the Big Four's representatives (Clemenceau, Lloyd George, Wilson, and Orlando) as the four "old women." Sometimes too, he gave in to boredom and drew marvelous portraits of them, and at one point scrawled one of a beautiful, quite unclad woman in these notes. See S.H.A.T.: 1K130 on the "quatre vieilles" — for example, in an entry of March 1919. With the angry stomping off of Orlando, Weygand's entry for April 19, 1919, gives his impression that "this conference is on the road toward disaster." His entry the next day is on President Wilson's putative ignorance of items under discussion, such as the Fiume settlement. In *ibid.*

14. Louis Loucheur, *Carnets secrets 1908–1932* (Brussels: Brepols, 1962), diary entry of April 18, 1919 (77). Clemenceau was not simply hostile to Foch's "guard dog." When Jean Martet, in conversations with the Tiger later in the '20s, said: "You grant some fine qualities to Weygand...," Clemenceau retorted: "It's because Weygand is somebody.... He is a man who must

have had a good many kicks on the behind when he was still in limbo. But he is intelligent and he has a sort of indescribable sombre fire." Jean Martet, *Clemenceau* (tr. Milton Waldman; London and New York: Longman's, Green, 1930), 230. Weygand's utter loyalty to Foch remains evident in his diary entries of the time, along with his view of "the perfidy of these political figures.... " (The latter in S.H.A.T.: 1K130, Weygand entry of May 16, 1919.) Weygand also supported Foch's jousts over issues like the size of Germany's post-war army, expressed in meetings of the French Superior Council for National Defense, which took place at the Elysée, and included the French president, foreign minister, war minister, Pétain, and Foch (as president of the Interallied Committee of Versailles). See on these meetings, S.H.A.T.: 2N5: Etat-Major. Séances du Conseil Supérieur de la Défense Nationale le 19 mars 1920–26 octobre 1923. In his memories of the Peace Conference, Harold Nicolson recalled "Foch striding stockily with Weygand [often] hurrying behind." Nicolson, *Peacemaking 1919* (New York: Grosset and Dunlap, 1965), 153.

15. See Weygand, *Mémoires*, II, ch. 2, and his furious diary entries, increasingly blaming the American tenor of the peace; for example, December 9, 1919, on the U.S.—"the latecomer of the war" who then made "this dream-like treaty without possibility of execution" and without suitable guarantees. Diary entry in S.H.A.T.: 1K130. On the issue of Foch, Clemenceau, and the possibility of a separate Rhineland, the clearest account is in Margaret MacMillan, *Paris 1919: Six Months That Changed the World* (New York: Random House, 2002), ch. 14, 16. According to MacMillan, "Clemenceau always thought he had got the best possible deal for France, and he was right." *Ibid.*, 203. A formerly obdurate André Tardieu agreed in chapter 5 of his *The Truth about the Treaty* (Indianapolis: Bobbs-Merrill, 1921, no translator given). One may also consult the little classic by Jere Clemens King, *Foch Versus Clemenceau: France and German Dismemberment, 1918–1919* (Cambridge, MA: Harvard University Press, 1960). King concludes that Foch's idea of a separate Rhineland could never have worked militarily, given the rise of tanks and aircraft. As he put it, "The failure to appreciate fully the possibilities of the tank and plane was all the more culpable on the part of professional soldier Foch — especially since he had made such a fetish of the attack during 1914–1918" (124). See also on the Foch-Clemenceau rift, appropriate pages of David Sinclair's *Hall of Mirrors* (London: Century, 2001). Particularly valuable on Foch's obsession with the Rhineland are reports by him and others in his files, showing how Rhineland history had included a Roman

occupation and influence, then France's impact during the Revolution; and much affinity with French culture even in the 19th century, partly due to so many Catholics living there. Foch was especially concerned that the post-1918 Rhineland not be Prussianized. See these reports in S.H.A.T.: 4N92: Etat-Major du Maréchal Foch 1918–1919 and Notes de Foch 1920–1926. See also Foch's letters to Clemenceau on the Rhineland problem in S.H.A.T.: 14N50: Fonds Etat-Major Foch: Situation des troupes en Rhenanie. And Weygand's own numerous "go between" letters sent to American and other occupying authorities, attempting to compel German compliance with agreements made, in S.H.A.T.: 4N94: Etat-Major du Maréchal Foch: Comité Militaire Allié de Versailles 1919–1926. And for Foch's activities that year distributing food in Europe (in the path laid out by Herbert Hoover), see S.H.A.T.: 6N290: Fonds Clemenceau: telegram of Stéphen Pichon, Minister of Foreign Affairs, February 26, 1919, to Clemenceau, as well as copies sent to a variety of French ambassadors in Europe. There is a good deal of earlier material here on Hoover's efforts to distribute food in German-occupied areas.

16. Marc Bloch, *Strange Defeat* (tr. Gerard Hopkins; New York: W. W. Norton, 1968), *passim*.

17. See Commandant J. Weygand, *The Role of General Weygand: Conversations with His Son* (tr. J. H. F. McEwen; London: Eyre and Spottiswoode, 1948), ch. 1 (1914–1939), and quotation 22–23. Some Frenchmen were also surprised by what they perceived as American amnesia, and a superiority complex owing to the fact that the U.S. emerged from the war untouched and enriched. See, for example, André Tardieu, *Devant l'obstacle: L'Amérique et nous* (Paris: Emile-Paul Frères, 1929). As he put it: "America says: 'Forget the war!' But the war weighs on Europe, insinuates its poison into its veins, dominates its destiny." *Ibid.*, 278.

18. Weygand's first book on Foch is *Le Maréchal Foch* (Paris: Firmin-Didot, 1929); his second and fuller one is *Foch* (Paris: Flammarion, 1947).

19. C.f. Basil Liddell Hart's estimate: "If Napoleon had a Berthier, Foch had a Weygand — which was better.... Officers who came into close contact with them had the impression that Weygand thought 'Foch' but a little further ahead. And all knew that he brought the organizing power, grasp of detail, and lucidity of expression which were an essential complement to the qualities of his chief." Liddell Hart, *Reputations Ten Years After*, 175–176.

20. Weygand, *Mémoires*, I, 5 and 6.

21. *Ibid.*, 129.

Chapter 4

1. Foch's often-cited view, expressed to the Polish politician Wladyslaw Grabski, was that Weygand "is worth ten divisions." Quoted in (among others) Charles Williams, *The Last Great Frenchman: A Life of General de Gaulle* (London: Little, Brown, 1993), 56.

2. D'Abernon's main post after World War I was as ambassador to Weimar Berlin. See Gaynor Johnson, *The Berlin Embassy of Lord d'Abernon, 1920–1926* (London: Palgrave Macmillan, 2002). In addition to being prime minister (or president of the Council of Ministers) in France, Millerand was also foreign minister, and his papers for this period revolve a good deal around how to deal with Communist Russia — whether to forgive debts, resume commercial ties, and the like. See A.N. 470AP/65: Fonds Millerand, and, more generally, Marjorie Milbank Farrar, *Principled Pragmatist: The Political Career of Alexandre Millerand* (New York: Berg, 1991). She shows Millerand as more obdurate than the British vis-à-vis the Soviets, including the Polish crisis. *Ibid.*, 274–275.

3. As he recalled, "I had never heard praying as I did in Warsaw." Weygand, *Mémoires*, II, 149.

4. *Ibid.*, 152. The acute Lord D'Abernon entirely corroborated this point of view: "Weygand naturally meets with a good deal of jealousy and opposition. Marshal Pilsudski, who is a dangerous conspirator by trade and a Napoleon by ambition but not by capacity, gives [him] rather lukewarm and intermittent support...." D'Abernon letter from Warsaw to Sir Henry Wilson, July 31, 1920, in Keith Jeffery, ed., *The Military Correspondence of Field Marshal Sir Henry Wilson 1918–1922* (London: The Bodley Head, 1985), 192.

5. See in S.H.A.T.: 4N93: Etat-Major du Maréchal Foch: Relations de la France avec la Pologne et les Etats de la Petite Entente 1919–1930, Weygand's letter to Foch of June 6, 1922, enclosing a typically detailed report on Poland's frontiers and what it would take to defend them. The report took account of geography and natural defenses (better, for example, in the south than the north). It drew attention to an eastern frontier with Russia of some 900 kilometers, and a German-Polish frontier that would be especially hard to defend in the controversial Polish Corridor. For this reason he urged Foch to summon Poland's military chief of staff to Paris for discussions on how France might help strengthen Polish defenses; and indeed, such discussions took place during the early fall of 1922.

6. I have used the American edition of Norman Davies, *God's Playground: A History of Poland* (New York: Columbia University Press, 1982), quotation 272–273. Davies also quotes

Lord D'Abernon's fervent estimate of this victory: "If Charles Martel had not checked the Saracen conquest at the Battle of Tours, the interpretation of the Koran would now be taught at the schools of Oxford.... Had Pilsudski and Weygand failed to arrest the triumphant advance of the Soviet Army at the Battle of Warsaw, not only would Christianity have experienced a dangerous reverse, but the very existence of western civilisation would have been imperiled." In *ibid.*, 399–400. C.f. also Pierre Dominique's view that "one of the greatest services General Weygand rendered to the cause of western civilization was what people called the victory of Warsaw in August 1920." Dominique, "Le Général Weygand sauve la Pologne," in Jean-Philippe Sisung and Martin Benoist, eds., *Weygand: Témoignages et documents inédits* (Montsûrs: Editions Résiac, 2006), 63.

7. See Thomas C. Fiddick, *Russia's Retreat from Poland, 1920: From Permanent Revolution to Peaceful Coexistence* (New York: St. Martin's Press, 1990). The earlier book by Norman Davies, *White Eagle, Red Star: The Polish-Soviet War 1919–1920* (New York: St. Martin's Press, 1972) gives a variation — that Trotsky's idea of world revolution was then beginning to give way to the idea of socialism in one country, which of course Stalin would then promote via purges! Despite its promising title, Piotr S. Wandycz and Tomasz Schramm weigh in with a somewhat disappointing article, "Pilsudski et Weygand à la bataille de Varsovie," *Revue d'histoire diplomatique* 115 (2001): 203–212. This is mostly a collection of reprinted primary source letters, where the authors, however, try to place the Polish role clearly above that of Weygand in the preservation of the country from the Russians. Zdzislaw Musialik's *General Weygand and the Battle of the Vistula, 1920* (London: Jozef Pilsudski Institute of Research, 1987) predictably does so as well; this short book is based on a doctoral dissertation. At most, Musialik grants that "Weygand's influence in military and political circles in Paris assured the Poles closer contact with France and her leaders, which given Poland's isolation at that time, was of undeniable moral value" (100) The translation of Andrzej Garlicki's *Josef Pilsudski, 1867–1935*, published in the heady year of 1988, does not even have Weygand in the index! See Garlicki, *Josef Pilsudski, 1867–1935* (tr. John Coutouvidis; Aldershot: Scolar Press, 1995).

8. Martet, *Georges Clemenceau*, 230–231. He went on in conversation with Martet: "He came back [from Poland], didn't swagger, didn't say anything. No one knows what he's doing or where he is. It's rather fine. It isn't that Foch was silly, but his genius was of a good, childish, simple kind. The other had in addition something subtle and deep about him." *Ibid.*, 231.

9. Winston S. Churchill, *The World Crisis* (New York: Scribner's, 1929), V, quotations 282 and 283. Like others of his time, Churchill too was grateful for the stoppage of Russian ambitions here. As he put it, "Russia fell back into Communist barbarism.... The frontiers of Asia and the conditions of the Dark Ages had advanced from the Urals to the Pripet Marshes." But no more advances westward were made. *Ibid.*, 284.

10. Letter of Radcliffe to Sir Henry Wilson, August 18/20, 1920, in Jeffery ed., *Military Correspondence of Field Marshal Sir Henry Wilson*, 196; and Lord Edgar D'Abernon, *An Ambassador at Peace: Pages from the Diary of Viscount D'Abernon* (London: Hodder and Stoughton, 1929), I, 47, 48. See also his grandly-titled book *The Eighteenth Decisive Battle of the World: Warsaw, 1920* (London: Hodder and Stoughton, 1931).

11. One reason Maginot chose Weygand to go abroad: "so that he finally leaves the Foch house where he has sojourned too long." See Marc Sorlot, *André Maginot (1877–1932): L'Homme politique et sa légende* (Metz: Editions Serpenoise, 1995), quotation, 125. Maginot's exact title in this period was Minister of War and of Pensions. On the Ruhr and the press campaign in favor of Weygand, see Stanislaus Jeannesson's monograph, *Poincaré, la France et la Ruhr 1922–1924* (Strasbourg: Presses Universitaires de Strasbourg, 1998): "Most popular newspapers at the end of January [1923] campaigned in favor of Weygand overseeing the operation" (216). In an engaging book, Michael Nolan sees the Ruhr episode of 1923 as the heritage not only of the peace treaty, but also of a long pre-war history of cultural stereotyping: Nolan, *The Inverted Mirror: Mythologizing the Enemy in France and Germany, 1898–1914* (New York: Berghahn Books, 2005), 109–110. As part of the split between former Entente allies, England refused to go along with the French and Belgian occupation. See on this, Martin Thomas, *Britain, France and Appeasement: Anglo-French Relations in the Popular Front Era* (New York: Berg, 1996), ch. 1. And on the period as a whole, Benjamin F. Martin, *France and the Après Guerre 1918–1924* (Baton Rouge: Louisiana State University Press, 1999). On Weygand's attendance at Sir Henry Wilson's funeral in London, see Keith Jeffery, *Field Marshal Sir Henry Wilson: A Political Soldier* (Oxford: Oxford University Press, 2006), 288.

12. See Weygand, *Mémoires*, II, 204; and letter to Foch, April 20, 1923, after ratification of the appointment by Prime Minister and Minister of Foreign Affairs Poincaré. Weygand noted that "it is with great heart-wrenching that I will separate from you.... " In A.N.: 414AP/12. Foch quotation is in Major Charles Bugnet, *Foch*

Speaks (tr. Russell Green; New York: Dial Press, 1929), 122. In conversation at the time with Raymond Recouly, Foch noted of Weygand: "He is not only a great — a very great — general, but he is also an admirable administrator. You may be sure that he will do marvels in Syria and wherever else he is sent." Raymond Recouly, *Foch: My Conversations with the Marshal* (tr. Joyce Davis; New York: D. Appleton, 1929), 295.

13. See for the above (and it is only a sampling of the literature), Nadine Méouchy, et al., *France, Syrie et Liban 1918–1946* (Damascus: Institut Français d'Etudes Arabes de Damas, 2002), appropriate parts; Vincent Cloarec, *La France et la question de la Syrie 1914–1918* (Paris: CNRS Editions, 1998), the best book on how France gained the mandate; William I. Shorrock, *French Imperialism in the Middle East: The Failure of Policy in Syria and Lebanon 1900–1914* (Madison: University of Wisconsin Press, 1976); M. E. Yapp, *The Near East since the First World War: A History to 1995* (London: Longman, 1996), ch. 3; appropriate parts of Efraim and Inari Karsh, *Empires of the Sand: The Struggle for Mastery in the Middle East* (Cambridge, MA: Harvard University Press, 1999); Stephen Longrigg's still-standard *Syria and Lebanon under French Mandate* (Oxford: Oxford University Press, 1958); and Daniel Pipes' spirited account, showing how unwieldy the very notion of "Syria" was — with many definitions of its presumed borders and identity: *Greater Syria: The History of an Ambition* (New York: Oxford University Press, 1990). Unlike "Syria," Lebanon really did have a certain reality and more circumscribed identity since around 1700 under the Ottoman Turks, especially with a much stronger Christian presence (predominately Maronites). See Meir Zamir, *The Formation of Modern Lebanon* (London: Croom Helm, 1985), ch. 1, and K. S. Salibi, *The Modern History of Lebanon* (New York: Praeger, 1965). On one of the key anti-French and pro–Faisal British "meddlers" in the region, see Janet Wallach, *Desert Queen: The Extraordinary Life of Gertrude Bell* (New York: Doubleday, 1996); and more generally, on the bullying of Lloyd George over the Levant by Sharif Hussein of Mecca, then his son Faisal, Eliezer Tauber, *The Arab Movements in World War I* (London: Frank Cass, 1993). One could add memoirs by those like the elegant French general Georges Catroux, helping to solidify the French Mandate over the Levant during its first shaky years before Weygand's arrival: Catroux, *Deux Missions en Moyen-Orient, 1919–1922* (Paris: Plon, 1958).

14. On advice Weygand received, see Weygand, *Mémoires*, II, 208. On budgetary, ethnic, religious, or regional issues Gouraud had dealt with in the Levant, and correspondence on these issues from the Foreign Ministry back home, see S.H.A.T.: 4H44: Haut Commissariat de la République française au Levant: Télégrammes reçus des Affaires Etrangères octobre 1919–juin 1922. See also Centre des Archives d'Outre-Mer (hereafter C.A.O.M.): 1AFFPOL/1422B: Fonds Ministériels: Affaires Politiques: Syrie 1921–1924: Gouraud letter to Prime Minister and Minister of Foreign Affairs, February 6, 1922, on Islamic propaganda and the possible Egyptian and British influence. But the French felt every bit equal to the British as an imperial power, and in the same file there is a radiant report of Maurice Rondet (November 21, 1922), a member of the Conseil Supérieur des Colonies, noting to France's colonial minister that if "our role in this part of the world unfolds according to our will and doctrines, we will have yet another flower in this magnificent crown of civilizing action, and of which no other people in history has more right to be proud."

15. The tragedy of this region, which before World War I had a majority of Christians, is well evoked by the commander of France's under-equipped expeditionary force there, Colonel Edouard Brémond: *La Cilicie en 1919–1920* (Paris: Imprimerie Nationale, 1921). Brémond had real feeling for the Armenians, whose families had been decimated by deportation and widespread murder during World War I.

16. For a handy look at these proconsuls, see Singer and Langdon, *Cultured Force*, ch. 3, 4.

17. Weygand, *Mémoires*, II, 214, and for previous parts on his time in the Levant, 208–214.

18. Weygand called the Alawites "the least evolved population" in the Mandate. *Ibid.*, 215. A good file on pilgrimages both from the Levant, and from other Islamic parts of the French Empire, is C.A.O.M.: 1AFFPOL/924: Fonds Ministériels: Affaires Politiques: Pèlerinages à la Mecque 1928–1936. The file shows how the French kept making it easier and cheaper for pilgrims, but also worked hard on vaccinations against typhus or cholera, quarantine measures, proper identification, certificates of good conduct, and anything else that would smooth the process (given that ports like Beirut were thronged with pilgrims from different parts of Africa). One problem to counter was the possibility of pilgrims being sold into slavery en route (in states like Hedjaz)!

19. Weygand, *Mémoires*, II, 217.

20. As he put it, "it was infuriating not to enjoy either the sea or the mountains." *Ibid.*, 222.

21. *Ibid.*, 224–225.

22. A writer in *El Makattam* (Cairo) noted May 11, 1923, that General Weygand brought quite a major reputation to the Levant "as a soldier and political figure." He had been Poland's

savior, and also played an important role at European conferences following World War I. Another article of that spring, 1923, in Alexandria's *El Bassir*, praised the fact that "never since the beginning of the French occupation have those in revolt been repressed in such an energetic fashion.... General Weygand deserves the sympathy and respect of everyone there." However, *El Qibla*, the Sherifian organ of Mecca, republished a collective lament of Damascus notables (published in *Sada ech Ohi* or *The Echo of the People*), averring that these French who had declared themselves such an improvement were no better than the Turks! But these notables *did* have confidence that General Weygand would bring them justice. Articles quoted and summarized in C.A.O.M.: 1AFFPOL/1422B. Another interesting file has French estimations of the plethora of dailies largely in Beirut and Damascus that almost all exhibited Francophile tendencies, even when published in Arabic. Of course circulations were low, and these newspapers were obviously aimed at a small, educated Arab elite. See C.A.O.M.: 1AFFPOL/2661: Fonds Ministériels: Affaires Politiques: Mandat français sur la Syrie et le Liban 1922–1940....

23. One source of this disorder was succession crises, such as the one following the death of Emir Selim Pasha el Atrash, September 15, 1923, in the Djebel Druz. See an article on this in the *Times* (London), October 6, 1923, cited in C.A.O.M.: 1AFFPOL/1422B. And for previous paragraphs to here, Weygand, *Mémoires*, II, 228–257.

24. A big report from the Service des Renseignements in Beirut (akin to secret service), January 15, 1924, enthused about better transportation and commerce from Syria to cities like Baghdad and Teheran, and even the possibility of products reaching the Caspian Sea. All of it of course spreading French influence as well, and outdoing the British! In C.A.O.M.: 1AFFPOL/1422B. The report noted that Syria as a commercial crossroads went back to the era of Darius and to ancient Roman history. On transportation, and the economy more generally, see also Weygand, *Mémoires*, II, 262–271.

25. *Ibid.*, 296–297.

Chapter 5

1. The term was used for Weygand by Colonel Serge-Henri Parisot, in a phone conversation of February 8, 2006. Meetings of the Conseil Supérieur de la Guerre of this era were dominated by divisions on questions of disarmament, and continuing surveillance of the Germans. See S.H.A.T.: 2N6: Etat-Major: Conseil

Supérieur de la Défense Nationale: Séances du 1 novembre 1923–13 juillet 1928.

2. The mathematician Paul Painlevé was a decidedly pacifistic war minister through much of 1925 and from 1926 to 1929, spreading his views via many talks in France and other countries of Europe, where he was popular, including Germany. Weygand held his feet to the fire when Painlevé made outright errors, as in a letter to him (Weygand's title was Directeur du Centre des Hautes Etudes Militaires) of November 7, 1925, on War Ministry statistics published in the *Journal Officiel*. For the letter, and for many enthusiastic responses to Painlevé speeches promoting peace, see A.N.: 313AP/225: Fonds Paul Painlevé. Painlevé's foil was Raymond Poincaré, unfairly tagged in this period as a warmongering Germanophobe (rather like Weygand). See J. F. V. Keiger's revisionist, and persuasive, biography, *Raymond Poincaré* (Cambridge: Cambridge University Press, 1997).

3. As Weygand recalled, "I found again the Tardieu of old, with his luminous intelligence and dynamism.... An exceptionally gifted man, Tardieu had aroused much jealousy, disappointed many hopes. He ended sadly, diminished by a long illness." Tardieu hadn't fully panned out, but "I was always captivated by the clarity and vivacity of his mind, by his aptitude and energy for work, by the soundness of his relationships; and I keep a faithful and amiable memory of him." Weygand, *Mémoires*, II, 344.

4. See the lavish introduction by Frédéric Guelton to *Le 'Journal' du Général Weygand 1929–1935* (Montpellier: UMR, 1998). Guelton was the first to try to transcribe and publish one part of Weygand's hard-to-understand journal.

5. Again, Weygand's recollected portrait of Maginot is interesting — on a man he considered both politically and militarily sound. "Sergeant Maginot had proven himself on the battlefield and it had cost him physically." Despite his severe wound at Verdun, and with only one good leg, Maginot became a powerful war minister, one of the rare politicians who could help translate Weygand's ideas into reality (and that meant anything but simply the static fortifications for which Maginot would ironically be known). "His lucid and simplifying intelligence, his vigorous, realistic mind protected him from any pacifist illusions; he wanted a strong France, and an army capable of defending it." Weygand, *Mémoires*, II, 347. Sometimes, however, Maginot had to translate Weygand's views into watered-down proposals that would have a chance in parliament. Meanwhile, German military clauses of the treaty remained in a state of "suspension," as Foreign Minister Briand wrote Maginot, March 31, 1931, the same month the Allied Military Committee of Versailles was

abolished in favor of something more anodyne called the Military Section for Study of the Treaties. See S.H.A.T.: 4N95: Etat-Major du Maréchal Foch: Comité militaire allié de Versailles 1927–1930 and Section militaire de l'étude des Traités 1931–1935 (retained in the Foch file despite his death), and including Briand's letter to Maginot.

6. Foch declared that Weygand bought the place near the end of World War I only because his wife was from Brittany; and that it was mere coincidence that it was so near his own spread. See Recouly, *My Conversations with the Marshal*, 298. Son Jacques Weygand was posted to Morocco in this era (early to mid–1930s) during its final era of French pacification; and on it I have a wonderful unpublished manuscript given to me by Serge-Henri Parisot, who was, like Jacques, in the Foreign Legion there at the time. Parisot's Paris-area apartment would remain full of Moroccan swords, rugs, furniture, and the like, and like so many French, he gained a deep appreciation for Berber and Arab culture there.

7. General Max Weygand, *Turenne: Marshal of France* (tr. George B. Ives; Boston and New York: Houghton Mifflin, 1930), quotations 117, 131 (second and third), 137, 152. Weygand's conclusion is a ringing one, and includes a contemporary quotation from La Bruyère that, again, certainly relates to the man Weygand himself wanted to be: "True grandeur is free-mannered, gentle, familiar, popular; it can lose nothing by being seen near at hand; the better one knows it, the more one admires it; it stoops in kindliness to its inferiors and rises without effort to its natural stature." Quoted in Weygand, *Turenne*, 254.

8. Analogies to Churchill keep suggesting themselves. A recent, positive estimate of Churchill's historical work is by Robert Messenger, "Last of the Whigs: Churchill as Historian," *New Criterion* 25 (October 2006): 16–23. He especially lauds Churchill's *The World Crisis* on the Great War.

9. An invitation to André Tardieu from Lyautey and description of proceedings is in Tardieu's papers. The day after the event (June 16, 1932), Weygand wrote Tardieu, apologizing for being too thronged at the event to talk with his esteemed political colleague, and friend. But "I was very deeply touched by your presence and the words you proffered." In A.N.: 324AP/18: Fonds Tardieu.

10. The anecdote on Churchill's visit to Maurois in 1935 is in my *Modern France: Mind, Politics, Society* (Seattle: University of Washington Press, 1980), 106. On Weygand's losing fight to place the Air Ministry under coordinated, unified control, see Frédéric Guelton, "Le Général Weygand et la question des forces aéri-

ennes 1928–1935," *Revue Historique des Armées* 206 (Mars 1997): 31–42. The problems of the War, Marine, Colonies, and Air Ministry were enormous in this period, owing to the industry's youth, rapid-fire demands presented it by competing ministries (war, marine, colonies, and air), mayhem in budgets, competition of manufacturers, which included Renault for motors, a constant need to experiment, a lack of reliable parts, and the list goes on (reminding one of the computer industry's early years!). A fine source on this are the papers of France's air minister for 1931 and nearly two months of 1932: A.N. 130AP/31: Fonds Jacques-Louis Dumesnil. On larger financial and budgetary problems in France (and Europe) of the gathering Depression era, see also the papers of Louis Germain-Martin, budget, then finance minister for the period 1930–1932: A.N. 443AP/11: Fonds Germain-Martin. One of the main budgetary problems for the military was the huge drain from building the Maginot Line in the early '30s of a deepening Depression. See J. E. and H. W. Kaufmann, *The Maginot Line: None Shall Pass* (Westport, CT: Praeger, 1997), 13, on original financial illusions, and Depression realities.

11. See for all this, Weygand, *Mémoires*, II, Part V, ch. 5.

12. As Julian Jackson notes in an authoritative book, Weygand's light mechanized division was unique in its time, created two years before Germany had one. Jackson, *The Fall of France: The Nazi Invasion of 1940* (Oxford: Oxford University Press, 2003), 22.

13. The best book in English on Barthou is Robert J. Young, *Power and Pleasure: Louis Barthou and the Third French Republic* (Montreal: McGill-Queen's University Press, 1991). Weygand quote is in his *Mémoires*, II, 397.

14. See generally Weygand, *Mémoires*, II, Part V, ch. 7. An unfounded rumor in 1934 had it that a troika of Weygand, Chiappe, and Tardieu would take power. See Pierre Pellissier, *6 Février 1934: La République en flammes* (Paris: Perrin, 2000), 215. From within the Conseil Supérieur de la Guerre, Weygand's letters to Pétain (first when Pétain was its vice-president, then war minister), harped on the same themes: lack of adequate materiel for troops, cuts to battalions, poor morale, etc. See typical Weygand letters to Pétain of October 10, 1929, and April 26, 1934, in S.H.A.T.: 7N2294: Inspections du Maréchal Pétain et des généraux membres du C.S.G.: 1920–1939.

15. As Julian Jackson notes, "politicians found Gamelin much more agreeable to deal with than the splenetic and irascible General Weygand, who relished confrontation." Jackson, *Fall of France*, 12. See also on Gamelin, Peter Jackson, *France and the Nazi Menace: Intelli-*

gence and Policy Making 1933–1939 (Oxford: Oxford University Press, 2000), 110–111, drawing attention to his attractive qualities, but concluding: "Gamelin was not a decisive general" (111). The most revisionist study of this French generalissimo, Martin S. Alexander's *The Republic in Danger: Maurice Gamelin and the Politics of French Defence, 1933–1940* (Cambridge: Cambridge University Press, 1993), makes Gamelin putatively as watchful of Germany in the '30s, and as much in favor of military modernization and innovation, as Weygand; but much better at maintaining a civil-military balance than that "reactionary" (a term Alexander uses a number of times, as though it might thereby negate Weygand's talent). Undeniably well researched, the book does not fully persuade (given the many negative assessments of Gamelin by respected military figures of the period). Alexander also paints Gamelin as a victim of political vicissitudes of the decade. Gamelin's own memoirs make him out to be more reasonable than Weygand, dating the "malaise" with his rival from an incendiary disagreement before and during a meeting of the Conseil Supérieur de la Guerre of December, 1933. Gamelin, *Servir* (Paris: Plon, 1946), II, 108, quotation 109.

16. Concerning his legacy, in the fall of 1935, quite a number of Weygand's prized armored fighting vehicles (AFVS) were being manufactured and ordered — some to be highly praised by such as the German panzer general, Heinz Guderian. Weygand had also gotten a heavy subvention from the Finance Ministry for the four coming years, and especially again, to build up crucial branches of materiel like tanks; however, two back-to-back ministers of war (General Maurin and Colonel Fabry) would siphon much of that money into the acquisition of artillery. See Robert Jackson, *The Fall of France: May–June 1940* (London: Barker, 1975), 13–14.

Chapter 6

1. Weygand notes of this Commander Trinquet: "Tall, elegant, and with a severe, purebred face, laced with a scar, in his manner he was a lord both in temperament and allure." Weygand, *Mémoires*, II, 443. In Agadir Weygand also responded to a letter from Tardieu, joking that he was here "without the *Panther*" (a reference to Kaiser Wilhelm II's pre–World War I sabre-rattling there), and nostalgic about "our collaboration.... It was at once interesting, fruitful, and agreeable to work with you. And since ... [his ellipsis] I have had very different [political] collaborators!" In A.N.: 324AP/18.

2. He wrote of the "bustling, laughing, shrieking crowd...." Weygand, *Mémoires*, II, 444.

3. The Vernets were a kind of artistic dynasty, with Carle's son Horace continuing this emphasis on "Orientalism" in his art.

4. General Weygand, *Histoire militaire de Mohammed Aly et de ses fils* (Paris: Imprimerie Nationale, 1936), I, 5.

5. *Ibid.*, 6.

6. *Ibid.*, 9.

7. *Ibid.*, 13.

8. C.f. the priceless descriptions of marauding Moors coming down into Senegal from the Sahara in Pierre Loti, *Le Roman d'un spahi* (Paris: Calmann-Lévy, 1893) — the 35th edition of a very popular novel.

9. Weygand, *Histoire militaire de Mohammed Aly*, I, all ch. 1.

10. *Ibid.*, quote 58.

11. As Weygand notes, "Ibrahim, like his father, was of medium height, with a solid build and a certain tendency to stoutness, characteristic of many 'Orientals' of high condition." (Including Weygand's patron for this project!) "He loved and understood everything having to do with military matters.... And he spoke with equal facility the three languages then essential in the Levant: Turkish, Persian, and Arabic." *Ibid.*, 95.

12. For the preceding see *ibid.*, ch. 3. Weygand had obviously read Machiavelli's *The Prince* carefully, including on that "religious" figure, Cardinal Cesare Borgia, who was obviously much more as well!

13. On ear trophies, *Histoire militaire de Mohammed Aly*, I, 125; and both quotations in *ibid.*, 126.

14. *Ibid.*, 131.

15. *Histoire militaire de Mohammed Aly*, II.

16. *Ibid.*, 16.

17. *Ibid.*, 17.

18. *Ibid.*, 17.

19. *Ibid.*, 21.

20. *Ibid.*, 24.

21. *Ibid.*, quotes 25–26.

22. *Ibid.*, 28. Weygand knew something about the effects of overkill on besieged cities!

23. "Many, such as Captain von Moltke, the future chief of staff under William I, were excellent officers and totally dedicated; but the mechanized training to which they subjected their pupils did not suit the Ottomans. The Turkish soldier lost in this training a part of his native aptitudes, without acquiring the incontestable qualities of the Prussian military." *Ibid.*, 30.

24. Quotations in *ibid.*, 36, 37.

25. *Ibid.*, quotation 38.

26. *Ibid.*, quotations 41, 42.

27. *Ibid.*, 45.

28. "Few terrains lend themselves more easily to defense than the region of Beylan," as

Weygand notes. "From Alexandretta, one climbs toward Beylan, at an altitude of 500 meters, through wooded hills and ravines, which can be held with few men." *Ibid.*, 45.

29. My telephone interview with Colonel Serge-Henri Parisot, August 11, 2006, indicated (from him) that the Israelis could certainly have learned from these older conflicts here.

30. Weygand, *Histoire militaire de Mohammed Aly*, II, 52.

31. "His regular troops ... and acclimated irregulars would have found in the cold and intemperate weather precious allies against an enemy accustomed to the hot climate of the Nile." *Ibid.*, 58.

32. For the preceding see *ibid.*, part III, ch. 1—all on Konia.

33. *Ibid.*, part IV, ch. 1 (on Syria under the Egyptian occupation). The way sheikhs in Palestine incited revolt in that period reminds one of the more recent situation in Iraq or Lebanon. See *ibid.*, 74–75.

34. *Ibid.*, 115.

35. *Ibid.*, see for this Part I, all of ch. 2.

36. See *ibid.*, Part I, through to end of ch. 2.

Chapter 7

1. Maxime Weygand, *Comment élever nos fils?* (Paris: Flammarion, 1937).

2. "Pride easily leads our contemporaries to make *tabula rasa* of the past, and to scorn the experience of their elders...." However, the inheritance might still be frittered away, and telephones, etc., would not make people better, or save young or old from current threats, argued Weygand. *Ibid.*, 5, 6.

3. In his book he cites in his opening chapter the most famous maker of the French obligatory, free, and secular public school of the early 1880s, the anticlerical but patriotic Jules Ferry, who told teachers that what they taught in schools ought to mirror what fathers taught their children at home, including devotion to the *patrie*. See on Ferry my article, "Jules Ferry and the Laic Revolution in French Education," *Paedagogica Historica* 15 (December 1975): 406–425.

4. As he put it: "In its exalted sensibility, the young Germany judges itself a race earmarked for great acts, and as she feels she has suffered from many injustices, she has decided to accomplish these acts without scruples of any sort." *Comment élever nos fils?*, 29. There is debate on how much largely patriotic French teachers (from before 1914) had turned into pacifist educators between 1919 and 1940, having a great effect on French youth. See on this my "From Patriots to Pacifists: The French Primary Schoolteachers, 1880–1940," *Journal of Contemporary History*, 12 (April 1977): 413–434, and the sensible nuancing of Mona Siegel's *The Moral Disarmament of France: Education, Pacifism, and Patriotism, 1914–1940* (Cambridge: Cambridge University Press, 2004).

5. (Paris: Flammarion, 1937). The author is given as Général Weygand de l'Académie Française, and the little book has marching, helmeted soldiers and gunnery on its cover. The book was part of a collection on France of that period, and also included Weygand's *Comment élever nos fils?*, along with books by literary figures like André Maurois.

6. Quotation in Weygand, *La France est-elle défendue?*, 5.

7. A visit in August 1938 to German aircraft factories by France's General Vuillemin, who commanded the French air force, proved unsettling. See Singer, *Modern France*, 112. Vuillemin had already sent Prime Minister Daladier a report on September 27, 1937, concerning the Nazis' air superiority.

8. See background information on the growth of a pre–World War II French navy provided by Charles W. Koburger Jr. in his *The Cyrano Fleet: France and its Navy, 1940–1942* (New York: Praeger, 1989).

9. See Weygand, *La France est-elle défendue?*, 16. One should, however, consult Robert J. Young, *In Command of France: French Foreign Policy and Military Planning, 1933–1940* (Cambridge, MA: Harvard University Press, 1978), which shows that German invasion plans were as uncertain and vacillating as French plans of response.

10. "Sedentary and enriched, the Gauls, Eduens, Bitiurges, Carnutes, Turons, Rèmes let their combative virtues gather moss, [and] their arms and methods made no progress." General Weygand, *Histoire de l'armée française* (Paris: Flammarion, 1961 edition), 11.

11. *Ibid.*, quotations 13, 16.

12. *Ibid.*, 47.

13. *Ibid.*, quote 50.

14. *Ibid.*, 51.

15. *Ibid.*, 52.

16. *Ibid.*, 54.

17. *Ibid.*, quotations 70, 71.

18. *Ibid.*, quotation 73. Again, detail is rich here: "The arms of [French] knights were also heavy and encumbering: the long lance, the shield, the sword, long or shorter.... They went forward in spurs of extravagant form and pony-skin slipper-boots that contributed even more to slow them down" (74). Never truly a snob, Weygand also derided the *hauteur* and sheer inequalities that hampered French efforts: "Contingents were most often constituted not by reason of aptitudes or missions, but with the sole object of taking into account social origins or of respecting susceptibilities" (74).

19. *Ibid.*, 78.

20. A good discussion of these fortified churches is in Nicholas Wright, "French Peasants in the Hundred Years War," *History Today* 33 (June 1983): 38–42.

21. Weygand, *Histoire de l'armée française*, 186.

22. *Ibid.*, quotations 191, 192.

23. *Ibid.*, quotations 211.

24. *Ibid.*, quotations 225.

25. *Ibid.*, 242–245.

26. *Ibid.*, parts IV ("Le Déséquilibre") and V ("La Chute") of ch. 8.

27. *Ibid.*, 322.

28. *Ibid.*, quotation 343, and see ch. 11, parts II and III generally.

29. *Ibid.*, 352, and on Lyautey, 350. Little did Weygand realize that he would soon be playing a major role in that North Africa he had just described, and in the long lineage of its earlier proconsuls. "This multiple life of conqueror, diplomat, administrator, and pioneer progressively marked the soldier of Africa..." and to some degree it would mark Weygand, too. (*Ibid.*, 278.) In a letter of September 8, 2004, to the author, Colonel Serge-Henri Parisot remained idealistic about what he himself had done and learned in French Morocco of the '30s, in wartime there, in Algeria of the '50s, and in the French colonial venture generally: "Far from feeling the least repentance for it, as imbeciles wish, I am on the contrary proud to have (as little as I did), collaborated in this enterprise with a lot of heart."

30. *Ibid.*, 287.

31. *Ibid.*, Part II, ch. 10: "Renaissance Militaire (1872–1890)."

Chapter 8

1. Weygand's often-cited praise for the French army in July 1939 is sometimes considered evidence of his having been on the shelf too long. Other interpretations, however, are possible. As James McMillan puts it in a sensible overview: "Had not General Weygand, in a widely publicized speech at Lille in July 1939, proclaimed that the French army was stronger than at any previous point in its glorious history? That he may well have thought exactly the opposite hardly mattered, since his aim was to reassure the general public." McMillan, *Dreyfus to De Gaulle: Politics and Society in France 1898–1969* (London: Edward Arnold, 1985), 121.

2. Sources for these "war games" preparations in the Levant and for possible use in the Balkans during Weygand's tenure are in S.H.A.T.: 4H272: Commandement supérieur

des troupes du Levant (1er bureau) ... mars 1939–juillet 1941, with a dossier labelled "Mise sur pied, organisation et réinforcement du corps expéditionnaire du Levant mars 1939–juillet 1941"; and in S.H.A.T.: 4H273: Commandement supérieur du Levant (1er bureau) ... Organisation unités et services de l'armée du Levant ... Ordre de bataille ... Encadrement ... Correspondance relative à la situation des effectifs et matériels ... etc. (this carton containing less on the pre–Vichy era than 4H272). A good article on France's (and Weygand's) hopes in the Balkans is Frédéric Guelton, "France, Levant et Balkans 1937–mai 1940: Les Illusions perdues d'une grande stratégie périphérique," *Revue Historique des Armées* 211 (Mars 2002): 107–116; on General Wavell's similar views, see John Connell, *Wavell: Scholar and Soldier* (London: Collins, 1964), 217–218. Bulletins sketching a situation of basic calm in Lebanon and Syria week after week are found in part one of S.H.A.T.: 4H274: Commandement supérieur des troupes du Levant (2ième bureau) ... octobre 1939–juillet 1941. Weygand received these reports from his "second bureau" of the General Staff in the Levant, and a typical one of November 22, 1939, notes of Syria: "The situation is still calm and security is complete." (Was the French mandate underrated, given what has followed in this region, where "calm and security" generally come only as a byproduct of brutal dictatorship?) Other parts of this carton concern different issues Weygand had to deal with, such as arms trafficking and political affairs.

3. Arthur Conte provides a shatteringly negative portrait of Gamelin holed up in his office-bedroom at Vincennes, "playing skillfully at exhibiting the serenity of a great sage." In fact, "he seemed more academic than a thinker ... more of a counselor than a leader." He had gotten his position only because he didn't ruffle the Republic's feathers, but was now "applying himself at being inoffensive to everyone...." His commander in chief of the Northeast Front, General Georges, was dumbfounded by Gamelin's vague, "often contradictory" orders. Conte, *Le 1er janvier 1940* (Paris: Plon, 1977), 99.

4. See Weygand, *Recalled to Service: The Memoirs of General Maxime Weygand of the Académie Française* (tr. E. W. Dickes; London: William Heinemann, 1952), Part One, ch. 1–4. This is a translation of Weygand, *Mémoires, III: Rappelé au service* (Paris: Flammarion, 1950), the only translated volume of the three-volume memoirs. For Weygand's precise, day-to-day movements in the Levant, and his meetings while in Paris, his *journal de marche* is contained in S.H.A.T.: 4H271: Commandement supérieur

des troupes du Levant: Journal de marche de l'E-tat-Major du Commandant en Chef des forces françaises de l'Orient méditerranéen 27 août 1939–15 juillet 1940 (extending into the period of his successor). There are also *journaux de marche* here of the various units that included Indochinese, Malgaches, *zouaves* from North Africa, Senegalese sharpshooters, Foreign Legionnaires, and the like, and which reveal the impact of Weygand's inspection tours.

5. One of the most persuasive indictments of Gamelin is in Nicole Jordan's "Strategy and Scapegoatism: Reflections on the National Catastrophe, 1940," in Joel Blatt, ed., *The French Defeat of 1940: Reassessments* (Providence: Berghahn Books, 1998), 13–38. Jordan renders nonsensical Thomas Christofferson's recent estimate that Weygand (along with Pétain) "were no improvement over Gamelin. Both men were tied to the past...." Thomas Christofferson (with Michael Christofferson), *France during World War II: From Defeat to Liberation* (New York: Fordham University Press, 2006), 28. Christofferson wrongly considers Weygand's strategic ideas as purely "defensive." *Ibid.*, 28. Martin Alexander tries to minimize Gamelin's responsibility for the 1940 disaster by partly, and sensibly, laying the problem to the state of British-French planning and coordination (with Belgium also involved). See the conclusion to Alexander, *Republic in Danger*, and also the older, still influential articles of John C. Cairns: "Great Britain and the Fall of France: A Study in Allied Disunity," *Journal of Modern History* 27 (December 1955): 365–409, and "Along the Road Back to France, 1940," *American Historical Review* 64 (April 1959): 583–603. But Alexander also admits that there is no way of positively revising an estimate of Gamelin as commander in 1940, even though he may try to do so in an upcoming second volume on the generalissimo. On Gamelin's planning, see, among others, Robert Allan Doughty, *The Breaking Point: Sedan and the Fall of France, 1940* (Hamden, CT: Archon Books, 1990), ch. 1; and Don Alexander, "Repercussions of the Breda Variant," *French Historical Studies* 8 (Spring 1974): 459–488.

6. Gamelin's memories of his 9 A.M. meeting May 20 with Weygand are preceded by a nonsensical description of his bedroom at Vincennes, "a real cell, almost monk-like...." On Weygand at the meeting, he recalled snidely: "Not a word coming from the heart. Does this man have one?" But then, "a beaten person [Gamelin] no longer counts, especially when he might embarrass." General Gamelin, *Servir* (Paris: Plon, 1947), III, 435. Gamelin also reproached Weygand for not appearing to recall with suitable gratitude his appointment in the Near East emanating from the ex-commander in

chief. He remembered, too, that Weygand wanted immediately to call the Belgian king, and, never having done so, Gamelin seemed to indicate that it couldn't be done. (*Ibid.*, 437.) Gamelin's wan hesitancies, which made him despised by so many in the army, were obviously compounded by his knowledge of having syphilis in an advanced state. As the son of a general, he may also have been what the French call a *fils à papa*. And he had been Joffre's right-hand man in World War I, not exactly a topflight education. "Abnegation" was Serge-Henri Parisot's term for Weygand's acceptance of the top spot in such dire circumstances. (Phone interview of Parisot, February 13, 2006.) However, a number of others, including Weygand's son, have used it as well. Other, less exalted interpretations of the term "abnegation" are possible, for gossip had it that Weygand was leaving behind a married woman he loved in Beirut! Many were now hoping against hope (with a nostalgic look backward) that this Weygand could somehow redo "the miracle of the Marne" turnaround of 1914. See, for example, Renaud Muselier, *L'Amiral Muselier 1882–1965* (Paris: Perrin, 2000), 99.

7. While in Paris six months earlier, Weygand had written Madame Foch (December 18, 1939) that "each time I make a decision or give an opinion ... I wonder what the Marshal would have thought." In A.N. 414AP/12.

8. On Belgian hesitations about Weygand's adaptive planning, see Roger Keyes, *Outrageous Fortune: The Tragedy of Leopold III of the Belgians 1901–1941* (London: Secker and Warburg, 1984), ch. 21 ("Weygand's Plan"). See also Patrick Turnbull, *Anatomy of a Disaster* (New York: Holmes and Meier, 1978), ch. 5. On Billotte's state of mind, see the account of English C.I.G.S. General Ironside, who managed to meet with him at Lens on May 20, after a harrowing trip over refugee-disorganized country. He found Billotte supine, and "I lost my temper and shook Billotte by the button of his tunic. The man is completely beaten." Ironside's dire call to Weygand that day, advising replacement of Billotte, helped the French commander decide on his trip north. See Edmund Ironside, *The Ironside Diaries 1937–1940* (New York: David McKay, 1962), 321, 322. (The book was edited by Colonel Roderick Macleod and Denis Kelly.) Still perhaps persisting, too, was the feeling of Robert Graves in *Goodbye to All That* that the English should maybe have fought the French in World War I! Or stayed out, as Niall Ferguson broaches most famously in *The Pity of War* (New York: Basic Books, 1999). The confusions and haggling between the allies at this point in the Second World War were intense quite on their own. See, on this, P. M. H.

Bell, *A Certain Eventuality: Britain and the Fall of France* (Farnborough: Saxon House, 1974), *passim*. Meanwhile, *Life's* cover of May 20, 1940, with a picture of Weygand, but as "COMMANDER IN CHIEF OF THE THEATER OF OPERATIONS IN THE EASTERN MEDITERRANEAN," probably raised sales, now that he was the French army's new commander. America's mainstream media had always demonstrated respect for the general. (*Time's* cover featuring Weygand would come out June 3.) Historians still give Lord Gort primary credit for hatching the idea of a cross–Channel retreat from Dunkirk as early as May 19. According to one observer, Gort was "wrestling with his God and his duty at a moment of destiny," and then finally made his decision without consulting Weygand. Quoted in J. R. Colville, *Man of Valour: The Life of Field-Marshal The Viscount Gort* (London: Collins, 1972), 216.

9. On all this one could still consult the old chestnut of Bloch, *Strange Defeat*, and see also Weygand's *Recalled to Service*, Part Two, ch. 1. An article in *Time* (May 27, 1940) on Weygand's new appointment emphasized how he had operated in previous crises, helping to pull Italy out of the drink in World War I, Poland in 1920, and so on.

10. Himself peripatetic during the Battle of Britain, Churchill felt in retrospect that Weygand's first mistake was to have gone impulsively up north; he should have remained at his command post. He did marvel at Weygand's state on returning to Vincennes May 22: "In spite of his physical exertions and a night of travel, he was brisk, buoyant, and incisive. He made an excellent impression upon all." Churchill, *The Second World War* (Boston: Houghton Mifflin, 1949), II, 64. In Churchill's entourage, Lord Ismay, secretary of the Committee of Imperial Defence, noted of Vincennes that "the *Beau Geste* flavour of the old fort was just the same — spahis with white cloaks and long curved swords, on guard duty, and the floors and chairs covered with oriental rugs." But though Weygand's meeting was "short and businesslike," Ismay had his doubts about the plans' feasibility. Hastings Lionel Ismay, *The Memoirs of General Lord Ismay* (New York: Viking Press, 1960), 131. The future General André Beaufre (of whom more in Chapter 10) was very impressed by Weygand, whom he saw up close in this period: "Small and slim, he seemed extremely young although he was actually over seventy. Elegant, well turned out, straight-forward, amiable, but often abrupt and easily crushing, he generated immense energy...." Now, "instead of an ectoplasm, we had a man!" Beaufre, *1940: The Fall of France* (tr. Desmond Flower; New York: A. A. Knopf, 1968), 189, 190.

11. On Arras, see, among others, two old classics — Colonel Adolphe Goutard, *The Battle of France, 1940* (tr. Captain A.R.P. Burgess; New York: Ives Washburn, 1959), 209–221; and Major L. F. Ellis, *The War in France and Flanders 1939–1940* (London: H.M. Stationery Office, 1953), ch. 6 ("Counter-Attack at Arras"). They obviously contain different points of view, Ellis' more admiring of the British effort, and its effect on slowing up the German advance. See also the chapter on "Encirclement" in another classic on the Fall of France, Alistair Horne, *To Lose a Battle, France 1940* (Harmondsworth: Penguin Books, 1979), including Rommel's assessment of Arras, 568–569. And Rommel's own account in B. H. Liddell Hart, ed., *The Rommel Papers* (tr. Paul Findlay; New York: Da Capo Press, 1953), 29–34, and ch. 2 generally ("Closing the Trap").

12. See Michael Glover, *The Fight for the Channel Ports: Calais to Brest 1940: A Study in Confusion* (London: Leo Cooper, 1985), ch. 3, 4, quotation 108.

13. In Brittany in 1970 I met one of those Frenchmen who had remained in England. P. M. H. Bell gives Churchill high marks for following Weygand's advice concerning French departures: "Astonishingly, Churchill's undertaking about equality in the evacuation was fulfilled"; and for the period May 29–June 4, Bell cites British Admiralty statistics showing 139,732 British departures and 139,097 French. Bell, *France and Britain 1900–1940: Entente and Estrangement* (London: Longman, 1996), 238 (quotation), 239. A recent article on the French withdrawal from Dunkirk is Rhiannon Looseley, "Paradise after Hell," *History Today* 56 (June 2006): 32–38 (commissioned by the Franco-British council). Her estimate of French evacuations is in the range of 110,000, and she reminds us that many of those French soon returned after a decent reception in England to fight on in their own country. The classic account of course is still Churchill's. His summation: "There is no doubt that by pressing in all loyalty the Weygand plan ... as long as we did, our dangers, already so grave, were increased. But Gort's decision, in which we speedily concurred, to abandon the Weygand plan and march to the sea, was executed by him and his staff with masterly skill, and will ever be regarded as a brilliant episode in British military annals." Churchill, *Second World War*, II, 98. The best book on Dunkirk — offering at least as much on land battles in the rear as on the maritime evacuation — is now Hugh Sebag-Montefiore, *Dunkirk: Fight to the Last Man* (Cambridge, MA: Harvard University Press, 2006). And on RAF heroism at Dunkirk, the best account is in John Terraine, *The Right of the Line: The Royal Air Force in the European War 1939–1945* (London: Hodder and Stoughton, 1985).

14. See Weygand, *Recalled to Service*, Part Two, ch. 2 and 3 for what precedes; ch. 4 is on "The Battle of France." As Robert Jackson notes of this dire period, "Weygand had ordered his forces to stand and fight to the death, and in many instances the French troops did precisely that." Jackson, *Fall of France*, 139.

15. The great military historian of France, Alistair Horne, confirms this point of view: "That Paris should have capitulated without a struggle, while Warsaw, London, Leningrad and Stalingrad chose to face battle and be devastated, has ever since remained a contentious matter. But by 11 June there would have been little military advantage gained in fighting for Paris." Horne, *Seven Ages of Paris* (New York: A. A. Knopf, 2002), 348.

16. Weygand's account is in *Recalled to Service*, Part Four, ch. 4; and for British recollections of the atmosphere at Briare, see *Memoirs of General Lord Ismay*, ch. 11, and those of the flamboyant, showy Major-General Sir Edward Spears, *Assignment to Catastrophe* (London: William Heinemann, 1954), I, 142–171. Anthony Eden is sympathetic to Weygand's impossible position at Briare in his *The Reckoning: The Memoirs of Anthony Eden, Earl of Avon* (Boston: Houghton Mifflin, 1965). See especially *ibid.*, 134. As for Churchill, he came away sobered from the meeting, writing President Roosevelt ("From Former Naval Person: Personal and Secret") the evening of June 12, asking that he supply France and keep it fighting. Warren F. Kimball, ed., *Churchill and Roosevelt: The Complete Correspondence* (Princeton: Princeton University Press, 1984), I, 44.

17. See Jacques Weygand, *Weygand mon père*, especially ch. 13. On de Gaulle's character, an earlier report from the Ecole de Guerre had noted: "Intelligent officer, cultivated and serious; has brilliance and facility; good deal of worth; unfortunately, spoils incontestable qualities by his excessive assurance, his intolerance for the opinions of others, and his attitude of a king in exile." Quoted in Benjamin F. Martin, *France in 1938* (Baton Rouge: Louisiana State University Press, 2005), 78. De Gaulle's new intransigence marked a kind of divorce from Weygand. Only a short time earlier, "De Gaulle and Weygand were in solidarity during those days of the Dunkirk embarkment, and of skirmishes on the Somme...." François Delpla, *Churchill et les Français* (Ostwald: Editions du Polygone, 2000), 439. Now de Gaulle found himself more at one with Reynaud, but there has been continuing debate on which one first adumbrated the idea of a Breton redoubt. De Gaulle himself would say it was Reynaud. See Raymond Krakovitch, *Paul Reynaud dans la tragédie de l'histoire* (Paris: Tallandier, 1998), 284–285.

18. This rumor and Weygand's fear of a Communist takeover in defenseless Paris are mentioned in many overviews on the period (one of the most stimulating being Richard Vinen's *France, 1934–1970* (New York: St. Martin's Press, 1996)): putative evidence of Weygand, along with others, being "frénétiques de l'antisoviétisme" (in Jean-Louis Crémieux-Brilhac's phrase). Crémieux-Brilhac, *Les Français de l'an 40* (Paris: Gallimard, 1990), I, 226. Perhaps, however, it is time to bring some balance to this problem, and consider certain historians as themselves "frenetic" when discussing those who opposed both Stalin and followers of the Stalinist line in France, such as Thorez (whose situation was whitewashed by Party lies through to the late 1960s — French Communists averring that Thorez *had* remained in France till 1943 and been a "Resistant").

19. On British evacuations see diary entries of Sir Alan Brooke, including those on his own escape, in Alex Danchev and Daniel Todman, eds., *War Diaries 1939–1945: Field Marshal Lord Alanbrooke* (Berkeley: University of California Press, 2001). The tragic hit on the British Cunard liner *Lancastria* showed the difficulties of these evacuations, and Brooke's entry of June 19 (concerning his removal from France beginning the previous evening) noted: "From Ushant we took a very wide sweep out westwards to avoid minefields. We are in a bad way if we should strike a mine, bomb or torpedo, as the whole of the salvage gear is gone to the rescue of survivors of the *Lancastria*." *Ibid.*, 87. On the Highlanders in France, see Saul David, *Churchill's Sacrifice of the Highland Division: France 1940* (London: Brassey's, 1994).

20. For the foregoing see Weygand, *Recalled to Service*, Part Two, II ("The Armistice"), ch. 1 and 2. (Note the odd numbering of "sub-parts" in this memoir.)

21. In a conversation of July 3, 2006, Serge-Henri Parisot summarized that mindset pithily — Weygand wanted to "sauver les meubles" — i.e., save what national furniture he could. Parisot was, at the time, one of those die-hard members of the French Alpine battalions fighting the Italians.

22. Weygand, *Recalled to Service*, 189.

23. On General Frère, a hero in previous campaigns who then died miserably in a German camp during World War II, see Weygand's own book, *Le Général Frère* (Paris: Flammarion, 1949).

24. Weygand, *Recalled to Service*, 242.

25. See *ibid.*, Part Two, II, ch. 3 for armistice hagglings.

26. See William L. Shirer, *The Collapse of the Third Republic* (New York: Simon and Schuster, 1969), ch. 35 on the armistice. Parisot's phone

interview with me on this was February 13, 2006. We are still getting a priori, popular American accounts of the Shirer stamp. For example, William Wiser's *The Twilight Years: Paris in the 1930s* (New York: Carroll and Graf, 2000), swallows Reynaud's intermittent idea of a Breton redoubt, or North African continuation of the war, extrinsic to military realities. And he nonsensically lumps together as "defeatists" Reynaud's mistress of the time, the Countess Hélène de Portes, with Weygand. See Wiser, *Twilight Years*, 257. Weygand knew the realities — that French North Africa had been so stripped of troops for service in the metropole, and so lacked necessary arms, that even a day of fighting there would have been quite miraculous! See Weygand, quoted in Olivier Forcade et al., *Militaires en République 1870–1962: Les Officiers, le pouvoir, et la vie publique en France* (Paris: Publications de la Sorbonne, 1999), 647. Julian Jackson, however, avers that Hitler "offered relatively lenient armistice terms" because he feared France could keep fighting on in North Africa. Jackson, "1940 and the Crisis of Interwar Democracy in France," in Martin S. Alexander, ed., *French History since Napoleon* (London: Arnold, 1999), 223. On the French people and an armistice, Maurice Larkin writes sensibly, noting that some 75 percent of Parisians had abandoned that city before the German arrival, and in the cathedral town of Chartres, only 800 of 23,000 stayed put. Hence the people-clogged roads.... As Larkin writes, "there is no statistical evidence as to how the mass of the population viewed the prospect of an armistice. But all the indicators suggest that most people saw it as the only realistic option open to France." Larkin, *France since the Popular Front: Government and People 1936–1996* (Oxford: Clarendon Press, 1997), 79.

27. Langer, *Our Vichy Gamble* (New York: A. A. Knopf, 1947).

28. Weygand, *En Lisant les mémoires de guerre du Général de Gaulle* (Paris: Flammarion, 1955). General Gamelin also considered "capitulation" and "armistice" as little different. See Gamelin, *Servir*, III, 459. To the end of his mediocre memoirs, he remains vague and snide on the man who replaced him in 1940.

29. Weygand, *En Lisant les mémoires*, quotations 91, and 92 (latter two).

30. For all this see *ibid.*, ch. 5 *passim*, titled "Transport de la Lutte en Afrique du Nord." Last quotation in *ibid.*, 91. De Gaulle has only recently come in for much criticism of his a priori ideas, and later myth-making, particularly in his idiosyncratic war memoirs. As Christopher Lloyd puts it, "History has treated de Gaulle well, partly because of his skill in shaping it as a memorialist who erects his own

monument as an heroic leader...." Lloyd quotes Pierre Lepape on de Gaulle's recollections: "No place for shadows, for doubt.... And no Charles either, who is the greatest missing figure in these memoirs. The Charles who feels, struggles, suffers, thinks is completely devoured by the persona of de Gaulle." Quoted in Christopher Lloyd, *Collaboration and Resistance in Occupied France: Representing Treason and Sacrifice* (Houndmills, England: Palgrave, 2003), 66. First quotation in *ibid.*, 67. De Gaulle's difficulties with Churchill partly stemmed from his relative Anglophobia, even before World War II. See François Kersaudy, *Churchill and de Gaulle* (London: Collins, 1981), ch. 1 ("Francophilia and Anglophobia") — Churchill being the Francophile.

31. A greater figure than either Shirer or de Gaulle also felt that France could have fought on in North Africa. *Providing* that Reynaud had been able to hang on a little longer, which was counter-factual history, Churchill said that his proffered Anglo-French Union (of June 15, 1940), accompanied by his stipulation that the French fleet sail to British ports, would have allowed transfer of the French government to North Africa, a ceasefire in France, and a beguiling series of events: British and French fleets intact, British air forces growing stronger and hitting Italy from Malta, Hitler zooming through Spanish Morocco into French North Africa and breaking himself there, and with possibly too little left for the Battle of Britain or invasion of Russia! Yes, all of France would have been under the Nazi boot, but it would have been worth it. See Churchill, *Second World War*, II, ch. 10. One more curious thesis is that a key reason Weygand and Pétain sought a quick armistice was the fear of a Communist putsch in France. See Georges Vidal, "L'Armée française face au communisme au début des années 1930 jusqu'à 'la débâcle,'" *Historical Reflections* 30 (Summer 2004): 283–309. The author, evidently sympathetic to French Communism, traces this fear of a Communist take-over through the 1930s. Clearly, French Communism, taking orders from Moscow when the latter was allied with Berlin, *was* a problem for France in June, 1940. That it was central to the crafting of an armistice seems, however, to be overblown; quite on their own, and in Paris itself, the Nazis were a sufficient threat to French sovereignty. A conversation with an expert on the Fall of France, John C. Cairns, reinforced the idea that continuing the war in North Africa, much less in Brittany, was simply unfeasible. Cairns also saw Gamelin in much the way I do here. Conversation with Cairns, July 12, 2007.

Chapter 9

1. See Weygand, *Recalled to Service*, 244, and Part Three, ch. 1 *passim*. One must also treat a famous phrase in this period about England being on the rocks, and soon to have "its neck scrunched like a chicken's." Falsely attributed to Weygand by Paul Reynaud, then perpetuated by Churchill, this phrase has made it into too many secondary accounts. See on this, among others, Destremau, *Weygand*, 597–599. Weygand's large correspondence with armistice authorities, and the many tables that show how demands were treated, are found in important files such as S.H.A.T.: 1P54: Vichy: Défense Nationale: Direction des Services de l'Armistice. Section Guerre 1940–1943.

2. See F. Charles-Roux, *Cinq Mois tragiques aux Affaires Etrangères (21 mai–1er novembre 1940)* (Paris: Plon, 1949), 172–178, quotations 173; and Weygand, *Recalled to Service*, 244–245. Whether the letter Huntziger brought to Wiesbaden ever reached Hitler is open to question; but these demands were indeed shelved by the Germans. On the ambassadorial past of André François-Poncet, see his *The Fateful Years: Memoirs of a French Ambassador in Berlin, 1931–1938* (tr. Jacques LeClerq; New York: Harcourt, Brace, 1949) and *Au Palais Farnèse: Souvenirs d'une ambassade à Rome, 1938–1940* (Paris: Fayard, 1961).

3. A good biographical account of Darlan in English is George E. Melton's *Darlan: Admiral and Statesman of France, 1881–1942* (Westport, CT: Praeger, 1998).

4. See Weygand, *Recalled to Service*, 254–256.

5. See S.H.A.T.: 1P4: Vichy: Défense Nationale: Secrétariat Général du Conseil Supérieur de la Défense Nationale ... : Défense des Colonies (1940). Document of Direction des Services de l'Armistice (D.S.A., under Défense Nationale), July 27, 1940.

6. Correspondence between Weygand and the Colonial Secretary, as well as tables on colonial agriculture, infrastructure, etc. is all in S.H.A.T.: 1P4 (with Weygand's emphasis included).

7. See Charles-Roux, *Cinq Mois tragiques aux Affaires Etrangères*, 192–195; and on Mussolini's bombast before the war, indicating a wish to annex areas mentioned, and even French Corsica and Savoy, see François-Poncet, *Au Palais Farnèse*, *passim*. The French ambassador to Italy also discussed Prime Minister Daladier's pre-war rejoinder to Mussolini, averring that France would not surrender even an inch of its territories or empire to the Italians.

8. Letters and telegrams (including quotations) in S.H.A.T.: 1P4.

9. Letter and quotation in *ibid*.

10. Weygand's response, including quotation, in *ibid*.

11. See on all this J. Weygand, *The Role of General Weygand: Conversations with His Son*, 171–172, and Weygand, *Recalled to Service*, 244–246. Weygand says that "I did manage to organize the Ministry of National Defence along certain lines of my own choosing, lay the foundations of the reduced army that we were allowed to maintain in France, encourage the formation of a secret army which was in time to become three times as large as the official force, and make arrangements for the concealment of such stocks of arms as we possessed." In J. Weygand, *The Role of General Weygand: Conversations with his Son*, 170.

12. For this document, see Weygand, *Recalled to Service*, 229–230. On French soul-searching after the defeat Robert O. Paxton's *Vichy France: Old Guard and New Order 1940–1944* (New York: A. A. Knopf, 1972) is still a good introduction.

13. For this period see the heartbreaking squabbles with the Germans and their retorts in *La Délégation française auprès de la Commission Allemande d'Armistice* (Paris: A. Costes, 1947), I (covering June 29–September 29, 1940). German authorities were indefatigable in defending everything they did, sometimes philosophically and historically (citing, for example, mistakes stemming from the Treaty of Versailles, and how the Nazis would be so much fairer!). They also lectured France on its prior decadence, for which it now needed to pay massively; thus the key German negotiator on economic matters, Richard Hemmen, wrote in one missive: "But one must understand in France that the role of the rich is finished, along with their fortunes themselves. The future is to the France that works; [however] she can always appeal to the Führer, and she will always be listened to" (185). On these hagglings one should also consult S.H.A.T.: 1P54. Exhaustive tables showing French demands and Axis responses are found here, as is Weygand's Defense Ministry correspondence with General Huntziger at Wiesbaden, and Huntziger's own epistolary wrangles with the Nazi general Karl-Heinrich von Stulpnagel, president of the German Armistice Commission, especially on ways to increase the size and power of France's armistice army.

14. See Keiger, *France and the World since 1870* (London: Arnold, 2001), 95 — a fine, careful book. None of this activity came easily; as Rivet told Paillole, "I feel pretty well everywhere, except in Weygand, a surly opposition to our projects as simply irritants." Getting "special status" for these agents into legislation was time-consuming, but finally procured. See Paul Paillole's own account, *Services spéciaux*

1935–1945 (Paris: Robert Laffont, 1975), Part Two, quotation 231.

15. See the secret service memoir of Henri Navarre, *Le Temps de vérité* (Paris: Plon, 1979), 80–88. And on the founding and long-term functioning of "TR" under Paillole, Navarre et al., *Le Service des renseignements 1871–1944* (Paris: Plon, 1978), 185–187.

16. See Navarre et al., *Service des renseignements*, 127–135. This is a book Navarre brought together with quite a number of ex-secret service members.

17. On the Alsace-Lorraine issue, and consequent tension between Weygand and Laval, see Charles-Roux, *Cinq Mois tragiques aux Affaires Etrangères*, 308. I also learned about the issue in a phone interview with Serge-Henri Parisot, February 11, 2007. One of Parisot's friends was a "malgré nous" soldier in the German army, and Parisot's secret service helped liberate him at war's end. The two were then apart some 50 years, until they emotionally met again in 2003.

18. Charles-Roux, *Cinq Mois tragiques aux Affaires Etrangères*, 307–313. He himself would have been happy to get out of Vichy, and wished somehow that Weygand could take him to North Africa. Pétain's decree on creation of Weygand's new position in Africa, and later ones of early October 1940, fine-tuning his mission and specifying his pay and remuneration for inspection tours and such, are found in S.H.A.T.: 1P89: Délégation générale du gouvernement en Afrique française puis commandement en chef des forces terrestres en Afrique: Cabinet: J.M.O. (septembre 1940–4 juillet 1942). Pétain's secret "instruction de mission" for Weygand (October 5, 1940) specifies the need to maintain unity in the parts of French Africa not yet taken over by Gaullists, and especially to protect Tunisia, Morocco, and Senegal from Axis incursions. Both military and economic improvement would help in this regard, and so would surveillance of functionaries, as well as propagation of the government message to inhabitants of French Africa by the new delegate general. Parts of these decrees are also found in Weygand's *Recalled to Service*.

19. See Jacques Weygand, *Weygand mon père*, footnote on 281.

Chapter 10

1. Weygand, *Recalled to Service*, 270.

2. Emmanuel Mönick, *Pour Mémoire* (Paris: Firmin-Didot, 1970), 82, 84–85. On the filling out of Weygand's staff, including quotation on Juin in his letter to Huntziger of December 29, 1940, see S.H.A.T.: 1P89. One of his military appointees was Marcel Carpentier, later a distinguished general and commander in French In-

dochina. Another alumnus of Weygand's here, Henri Navarre, became the general who formulated the ill-fated French plan for Dien Bien Phu in 1953–1954!

3. See Jacques Weygand, *Weygand mon père*, 287–288, and Weygand, *Recalled to Service*, 272. Jacques noted that "my father had always liked to save fine, but threatened things from ruin...." (*Weygand mon père*), 287.

4. Jacques Weygand, *Weygand mon père*, 288–290.

5. By the same token, Vichy directives poured out, and needed to be heeded; for example, Pétain's edict of November 10, 1940, regarding censorship for radio listeners (replicating a law for the home territory of October 28) and fines that would apply in the empire; or laws regulating political meetings that applied in both the metropole and abroad. These are found in C.A.O.M.: 1AFFPOL/888: Fonds Ministériels: Affaires Politiques: Mesures intéressant l'ordre et la sécurité publique.

6. Weygand, *Recalled to Service*, 274, on Esteva of Tunisia, and on Noguès, 275–276. See also Louis Berteil, *L'Armée de Weygand* (Paris: Editions Albatros, 1975), 119–120 — on unifying the separate parts of North Africa, and on currencies, 125. As much as he knew how to credit top authorities, and even his pilots, Weygand also had much admiration for what settlers had done here, including when "I flew for the first time over the Mitidja, that masterpiece of French colonisation." Weygand, *Recalled to Service*, 275.

7. Mönick, *Pour Mémoire*, 82. See also Robert O. Paxton, *Parades and Politics at Vichy* (Princeton: Princeton University Press, 1966), 81, and Jacques Weygand, *Weygand mon père*, 282–291. In Weygand's travels, Dakar of course remained a special case — the Senegalese port where recently Gaullist and British forces had been repelled by those of Vichy. Weygand heard via General Huntziger's dealings with two generals on the Nazi General Staff that, had the invaders succeeded and shown that Vichy couldn't defend its colonial holdings, the Germans would have taken over the most economically viable and important of those domains in North Africa — and quickly! Weygand, *Recalled to Service*, 257. His speech on October 29, 1940, to army, navy, and air force personnel based there, was a stirring one, emphasizing clearly that France would definitely come back again in this war. See Maxime Weygand, *Allocution du Général Weygand aux officiers des armées de terre, de mer et de l'air à Dakar, le 29 octobre 1940* (Paris: G. Taupin, no date).

8. The "projet de voyage de M. le Général Weygand dans le département d'Oran" is in C.A.O.M.: 5CAB 1: Cabinets des Gouverneurs

Généraux de l'Algérie: Maxime Weygand (juillet–novembre 1941) et Yves Châtel (novembre 1941–janvier 1943). The file includes a part entitled Dossier relatif au Général Weygand: correspondance 1940–septembre 1942, and another, Rapports des préfets (Situation générale septembre 1941–septembre 1942).

9. See report (including quotation) of Lieutenant-Colonel Liebray, Military Commander of the Territory of Aïn-Sefra, sent to the Governor-General of Algiers, January 7, 1941, on Weygand's tour there. (In *ibid.*)

10. Georges Hirtz, *Weygand: Années 1940–1945: Témoignage* (Gardanne: Esmenjaud, 2003), ch. 3, and quotations 62, 63.

11. *Ibid.*, quotation 63, and on transfer idea, 65.

12. See in C.A.O.M.: 5CAB 1, Prefect of Algiers' note to Governor-General of Algeria, also enclosing a report of March 3 from the Principal Administrator of the Mixed Commune of Palestro sent to him on Weygand's recent visit there. All these reports corroborate Weygand's own stated purpose (to Marshal Pétain) of meeting with every officer, functionary, or notable that he could on these tours, thereby gauging the pulse and needs of France's African domains. Weygand's long, secret report of November 10, 1940, to Pétain (concerning his modus operandi on these tours) is in S.H.A.T.: 1P89. There he also stressed the need for far better transportation in order to hold this vast empire. On *épuration* of personnel, he indicated that care should be taken to avoid creating vacuums.

13. Radio address in S.H.A.T.: 1P35: Vichy: Défense Nationale: Organisation du commandement et plans de défense de l'Afrique du Nord ... novembre 1940–septembre 1942. Some parts of Africa received these radio addresses in a scratchy, intermittent manner; hence Weygand believed that personal tours were a necessary supplement.

14. In C.A.O.M.: 5CAB 1. Besides corresponding, Weygand met with Nogues on two early Moroccan tours — one of October 19–22 and a longer one of November 25–December 3, 1940. His precise *journal de marche*, but with lacunae, is contained in S.H.A.T.: 1P89.

15. Much detail on these meetings is in C.A.O.M.: 5CAB 1. On the difficulties of French companies producing vegetable oils for home use, soap, etc., see William A. Hoisington Jr., *The Assassination of Jacques Lemaigre Dubreuil: A Frenchman between France and North Africa* (London: RoutledgeCurzon, 2005), *passim*. For companies such as the one in which Lemaigre played an important role, North Africa was a lifeline, and those who were able to do so moved operations there from occupied France. For precise agendas of public functions, which sometimes ate up an en-

tire day for Weygand, see C.A.O.M.: 1CM27: Gouvernement général de l'Algérie: Délégation générale du gouvernement en Algérie: Cabinet Militaire: Correspondance de la Délégation ... Fête de Jeanne d'Arc mai 1941 ... etc. There are detailed agendas not only for the Joan of Arc festival in Algiers, May 10–May 11, 1941, but also for others, such as the Fête du Travail et de la Concorde Sociale of May 1, where Weygand arrived at the Algiers Cathedral promptly at 8:30 A.M. The Algiers synagogue on the Rue Volland was also involved in the day's ceremonies, as were Protestants, and Weygand had other duties later in the day. On the importance of Joan of Arc for Vichy, including in the empire, see Eric T. Jennings, "Reinventing Jeanne: The Iconology of Joan of Arc in Vichy Schoolbooks, 1940–44," *Journal of Contemporary History* 29 (October 1994): 711–734; and on other aspects of Vichy ideology in the empire, his *Vichy in the Tropics: Pétain's National Revolution in Madagascar, Guadeloupe, and Indochina, 1940–1944* (Stanford: Stanford University Press, 2001).

16. All of the above is in C.A.O.M.: 5CAB 1, including on issue of military reports, Weygand's directive of March 12, 1941.

17. All in *ibid.*

18. General A. S. Van Hecke, *Les Chantiers de la jeunesse au secours de la France (Souvenirs d'un soldat)* (Paris: Nouvelles Editions Latines, 1970), 88–89, quotation 99.

19. C.A.O.M.: 5CAB 33: Cabinets des Gouverneurs Généraux de l'Algérie: Rapports sur le moral de l'armée, synthèses hebdomadaires, rapports bi-mensuels, activité indigène, etc. (Juin–septembre 1941 and août–octobre 1941): Report, among others here, July 23, 1941, from Chef du B.C.T. de la Délégation Générale du Gouvernement en Afrique Française to Cabinet du Gouverneur Général on propaganda, etc., both in Algeria, and in Tunisia and Morocco.

20. This particular report is in *ibid.*: Général de Corps d'Armée Beynet, Etat-Major 2ième Bureau, 19ième Région, August 9, 1941: "Aperçu d'Ensemble."

21. These are in C.A.O.M.: 5CAB 22: Cabinets des Gouverneurs Généraux de l'Algérie: Bulletins mensuels d'information et de documentation sur la situation politique et les faits intéressants l'ordre social ... Correspondance diverse 1939–1941....

22. In *ibid.*

23. In *ibid.*

24. These circulars and reports are in C.A.O.M.: 5CAB 1.

25. Case's book is *French Opinion on War and Diplomacy during the Second Empire* (Philadelphia: University of Pennsylvania Press, 1954).

26. Report of September 26, 1941, by Prefect of Algiers in C.A.O.M.: 5CAB 1.

27. See reports in C.A.O.M.: 1AFFPOL/917: Fonds Ministériels: Affaires Politiques: Ministère de la Guerre: Deuxième Bureau: Section des Affaires Musulmanes: Bulletins mensuels des renseignements sur les pays musulmans 1940–1941. These reports were based on reports of the French African "second bureaus" under Weygand's purview.

28. See Charles de Gaulle's own, rather unchronological, account in *War Memoirs: The Call to Honour 1940–1942* (tr. Jonathan Griffin; New York: Viking Press, 1958), 173, 174 (including quotation).

29. See, among others on this, Berteil, *Armée de Weygand*, 59–61. There is still much debate on double-dealing perpetrated by Canaris at the head of the Abwehr, the Nazis' foreign intelligence service, and particularly on his wartime contacts with the British. The latest estimate (in English) is quite sympathetic: Richard Bassett, *Hitler's Spy Chief: The Wilhelm Canaris Mystery* (London: Weidenfeld and Nicolson, 2005).

30. On Boisson, including his later punishment by Gaullists, see Pierre Ramognino, *L'Affaire Boisson: Un Proconsul de Vichy en Afrique* (Paris: Les Indes Savantes, 2006); William I. Hitchcock, "Pierre Boisson, French West Africa, and the Postwar *Epuration*: A Case from the Aix Files," *French Historical Studies* 24 (Spring 2001): 305–341; and the older, passionate defense of Daniel Chenet, *Qui a sauvé l'Afrique* (Paris: L'E-lan, 1949). On his dealings with West African dissidents, Gaullists, and/or Freemasons, see Ruth Ginio, *French Colonialism Unmasked: The Vichy Years in French West Africa* (Lincoln: University of Nebraska Press, 2006), 25–30, 83. See also C.A.O.M.: 1AFFPOL/888 for Pétain's laws abolishing "secret associations," and for Boisson's following suit — for example, with the December 1940 dissolution of "La Fraternité Africaine" in Côte d'Ivoire, a society affiliated with the Grand Orient lodge. See *ibid.* for Boisson correspondence on sums collected from dissolutions of secret societies, and directed to the colonial ministry's branch for those who had suffered in the war. On "Menées Antinationales" in A.O.F., the archival file C.A.O.M.: 1AFFPOL/883: Fonds Ministériels: Affaires Politiques: Affaires Diplomatiques: Menées Antinationales" section is rather disappointing. On the Germans permitting Boisson's arms build-up in West Africa (as a quid pro quo for dependability), see, among others, Norman J. W. Goda, *Tomorrow the World: Hitler, Northwest Africa, and the Path toward America* (College Station, TX: Texas A&M University Press, 1998), 36–43, 83, and Martin Thomas, *The French Empire at War 1940–45* (Manchester: Manchester University Press, 1998), quotation 83–84; Nancy Ellen Lawler estimates that about a fifth of the

125,000-man army in A.O.F. was composed of "Europeans legally or illegally transferred from the Armistice Army" (of France). Lawler, *Ivoirien Tirailleurs of World War II* (Athens, OH: Ohio University Press, 1992), 133. On Weygand's tours in French West Africa, see his *journal de marche* in S.H.A.T.: 1P89. His second tour there lasted a week and a half (December 14–December 24).

31. The telegram along with many others is in C.A.O.M.: 1TEL/692: Fonds Ministériels: Télégrammes Départ: A.O.F. (janvier–mai 1941). For correspondence between Boisson and the Colonial Ministry on permits to transport explosives or acquire hunting rifles, see C.A.O.M.: 1AFFPOL/635: Fonds Ministériels: Affaires Politiques: Organisation administration de l'Afrique Occidentale Française 1940–1942....

32. See C.A.O.M.: 1TEL/737: Fonds Ministériels: Alger: Délégué général. Télégrammes Départ (29 novembre 1940–12 novembre 1942). Arrivée (19 octobre 1940–9 novembre 1942). (Délégué et divers.) The latter part ("Arrivée") contains Weygand's telegrams cited. Weygand's correspondence with the Direction des Carburants, and thence the Colonial Ministry, regarding a North African conference (July 1941) on peanut oil as fuel is also included here. See, for example, telegram from Direction des Carburants to Weygand of June 3, 1941, a telegram Weygand then sent on to the Colonial Ministry. The peanut oil fuel would be especially useful for the French merchant marine in North Africa. (Note that this file persists after the period when the "general delegation" was altered.) Weygand also corresponded with Boisson on the necessity of frontier security, and propaganda, including via the airwaves. In part that propaganda was necessary to counter Islamic propaganda emanating from points as far as Turkey, and encouraged by the Germans themselves. See on this, C.A.O.M.: 1AFFPOL/1421: Fonds Ministériels: Affaires Politiques, dossier 10 (Affaires Musulmanes Vichy 1941–42–43).

33. For the Mandate, see the beautiful evocation of Jewish life under the French in Syrian Aleppo in Haim Sabato, *Aleppo Tales: A Tapestry of Tradition and Faith* (tr. Philip Simpson; New Milford, CT: Toby Press, 2004).

34. See Pierre Hebey, *Alger 1898: La grande vague antijuive* (Paris: NiL Éditions, 1996).

35. Berteil, *Armée de Weygand*, 128. On abrogation of the Crémieux decree, a Deuxième Bureau report from its Muslim Section, December 18, 1940, noted that "Muslim indigenous people in the main, express their satisfaction [with it]." In C.A.O.M.: 1AFFPOL/917. On cancellation of the Crémieux decree and

Peyrouton's role in it, see also Benjamin Stora's chapter in Shmuel Trigano, ed., *L'Identité des Juifs en Algérie: Une Expérience originale de la modernité* (Paris: Alliance Israélite Universelle, 1999), 23. On Pétain's pressure (seen in a letter to Weygand of October 5, 1940, noting that "the Jewish question in 'AFN' is to be regulated..."), see Henri Msellati, *Les Juifs d'Algérie sous le régime de Vichy: 10 juillet 1940–3 novembre 1943* (Paris: L'Harmattan, 1999), 65. See also Norbert Bel Ange, *Quand Vichy internait ses soldats juifs d'Algérie: Bedeau, sud Oranais, 1941–1943* (Paris: L'Harmattan, 2006), 32, including Weygand quotation. On Jacques Doriot's Parti Populaire Français, and its hopes of expelling the Jews from Algeria, see Robert Attal, *Regards sur les Juifs d'Algérie* (Paris: L'Harmattan, 1996), 94. Doriot was an ex–French Communist who turned into an active Nazi collaborator on the extreme Right.

36. Destremau, *Weygand*, 669.

37. Michael R. Marrus and Robert O. Paxton, *Vichy France and the Jews* (New York: Basic Books, 1981); Susan Zuccotti, *The Holocaust, the French, and the Jews* (New York: Basic Books, 1993).

38. Attal, *Regards sur les Juifs d'Algérie*, 94–96, and Bel Ange, *Quand Vichy internait ses soldats juifs* (on Bedeau in the Southern Oranais), *passim*. For a view that describes the comparative mildness of these camps, see Roger Bensadoun, *Les Juifs de la République en Algérie et au Maroc: Chroniques et mémoires d'autre temps*...(Clamecy: Publisud, 2003), 133.

39. See among others on this, Michael Curtis, *Verdict on Vichy: Power and Prejudice in the Vichy France Regime* (New York: Arcade Publishing, 2002), 80–81, and Zuccotti, *The Holocaust, the French, and the Jews*, 56–57.

40. See Zuccotti, *The Holocaust, the French, and the Jews*, 57–60.

41. See Msellati, *Juifs d'Algérie sous le régime de Vichy*, 68 and ch. 2 *passim* on all this; and Joëlle Allouche-Benayoun and Doris Bensimon, *Les Juifs d'Algérie: Mémoires et identités plurielles* (Paris: Editions Stavit, 1998), 286.

42. See, for example, Msellati, *Juifs d'Algérie sous le régime de Vichy*, 100–103.

43. See André Chouraqui, *L'Amour fort comme la mort: Une autobiographie* (Paris: Robert Laffont, 1990), and on Weygand, 235.

44. Joëlle Bahloul, *The Architecture of Memory: A Jewish-Muslim Household in Colonial Algeria, 1937–1962* (tr. Catherine du Peloux Ménagé; Cambridge: Cambridge University Press, 1996), quotations 116, and on food situation, 117.

45. On the yellow-star order in Algeria, see Msellati, *Juifs d'Algérie sous le régime de Vichy*, 88, and for putative number ordered, Bensadoun, *Juifs de la République en Algérie et au Maroc*, 108. On the yellow star in mainland France, see Serge Klarsfeld, *L'Etoile des Juifs* (Paris: L'Archipel, 1992). On the U.G.I.A. and notables selected, Msellati, *Juifs d'Algérie sous le régime de Vichy*, 69 and Benayoun and Bensimon, *Juifs d'Algérie*, 286–287.

46. See also on the penniless exodus of Jews from many other Muslim countries, Malka Hillel Shulewitz, ed., *The Forgotten Millions: The Modern Jewish Exodus from Arab Lands* (London: Cassell, 1999) and Shmuel Trigano, ed., *L'Exclusion des Juifs des pays arabes* (Paris: Pardès, 2003), showing that concepts like *jihad*, and open hatred, made the French small potatoes by comparison.

47. See on this, Michael M. Laskier, *The Alliance Israélite Universelle and the Jewish Communities of Morocco: 1862–1962* (Albany: SUNY Press, 1983), 165–171. More obtained citizenship in the protectorate of Tunisia before World War II.

48. On Thabault see *ibid.*, 182–183, and his own recollections of "Le Maroc à l'heure du Vichyisme," in *Les Nouveaux Cahiers* (Winter 1975–1976): 16–20. Sent back to France during the war, Thabault worked in Bourges and wrote a classic book on how secular schools and other institutions of modernization had promoted people in his own French village, making life happier there. The book was published near the end of the war, before Thabault's transfer back to the Morocco he loved in 1945, and it later came out in English as *Education and Change in a Village Community: Mazières-en-Gâtine, 1848–1914* (tr. Peter Tregear; New York: Schocken Books, 1971).

49. See, for example, David Cohen, *Passion marocaine: Mémoires* (Paris: Editions Biblioeurope, 1996), by a man who grew up in Meknès (which in the late 1920s had 8,000 Jews); Jacques Dahan, *Regard d'un Juif marocain sur l'histoire contemporaine de son pays* (Paris: L'Harmattan, 1995), which mentions the ousting of his father from his customs position during World War II, but reveals much admiration for French administrators, including Noguès; Hanania Alain Amar, *Une Jeunesse juive au Maroc* (Paris: L'Harmattan, 2001), again showing the tepid manner in which racial laws were applied to the Jews in her parents' wartime Morocco; and for the relatively decent situation in the great city of Casablanca (built up by the French), Abraham Serafaty (with Mikhaël Elbaz), *L'Insoumis: Juifs, Marocains et rebelles* (Paris: Desclée de Brouwer, 2001), ch. 2. Robert Assaraf's books on the subject also point to moderation in Noguès and his French administration, and the sultan's mainly benevolent attitude as well. See Assaraf, *Une Certaine Histoire des Juifs au Maroc 1860–1999* (Paris: Gawsewitch, 2005), ch. 17, 18; and his *Mohammed V et les Juifs au Maroc à l'époque de*

Vichy (Paris: Plon, 1997). Born in Rabat in 1936, Assaraf is an example of someone who embraced French culture, benefiting by subsequent education at Paris' elite Ecole de Sciences Politiques.

50. Phone interview with Orli K., December 15, 2006. Another interview with Sarah C., Tel Aviv, May 2002, indicated a fine life for her parents and then, after the war, for herself in Algeria's Oran under the French. They later had to run to Paris. Ultimately leaving Paris, where she and her husband, a lawyer of Moroccan Jewish background, had had a well-off situation, she found a little of the insouciance and beauty of her old life in French North Africa by the Mediterranean — this time in Israel.

51. Useful memoirs include Irene Awret, *Days of Honey: The Tunisian Boyhood of Rafael Uzan* (New York: Schocken Books, 1984), quotation 168, and ch. 22–24 generally; and Albert Hayat, *Ihasra: Souvenances* (Paris: Albert Hayat, 1993) — see 190–192 on Jewish relationship with *bey* and impact of Jewish statute. The best monograph on the subject is Daniel Carpi, *Between Mussolini and Hitler: The Jews and the Italian Authorities in France and Tunisia* (Hanover: University Press of New England, 1994), noting that Resident-General Esteva "did not approve of the institution of a racist antisemitic constitution in Tunisia" and that "the Jews of Tunisia enjoyed a more privileged status than their coreligionists in the area under Vichy administration, in both France and North Africa." *Ibid.*, 207.

52. A nuanced assessment of Jewish affinity for French Communism is in William B. Cohen and Irwin M. Wall, "French Communism and the Jews," in Frances Malino and Bernard Wasserstein, eds., *The Jews in Modern France* (Hanover: University Press of New England, 1985), noting: "The Communism of the mid-1930s was patriotic, nationalist, and Jacobin; it supported the Popular Front ... and emphasized the need to hold the line against Fascism. Under these circumstances it was natural for Jews to be attracted to Communism." *Ibid.*, 86. What the authors skirt is the Popular Front's attitude to defense and defense industries, given the menacing colossus across the Rhine; and especially the terrific flips induced by a Stalinist party line that changed to collaboration with Nazism in August 1939. The authors leap directly here from the Popular Front to the impact of the 1940 defeat. Some who argue that Weygand relished the imposition of anti–Semitic measures in North Africa lack objectivity; for example, a Gaullist hagiographer, Paul-Marie de la Gorce, in his *De Gaulle* (Paris: Perrin, 1999), 406–407.

53. Esther Benbassa, *The Jews of France: A History from Antiquity to the Present* (tr. M. B. DeBevoise; Princeton: Princeton University Press, 1999), 170.

54. The foregoing letters — and there are many more — as well as incidents are all in C.A.O.M.: 5CAB 1.

55. Letters and reports (including others of the sort) in *ibid.*

56. Berteil, *Armée de Weygand*, 26, 88–89, 98–99, 127. Weygand also worked on Vichy authorities, including the marshal himself, to procure assistance for families of Muslim prisoners of war, or of those who had perished in the conflict. See, for example, his letter of July 17, 1941, to Pétain on this, in S.H.A.T.: 1P89.

57. The preceding is all in S.H.A.T.: 1P34: Vichy: Défense Nationale: Mission et pouvoirs du Général Weygand, délégué du gouvernement pour l'AFN et l'AOF (juillet 1941); organisation de l'armée d'armistice en Afrique (septembre 1940–janvier 1942); rapport du secrétariat de coordination sur la production économique de l'Afrique française, la protection de l'AFN contre une attaque maritime et les possibilités de reconquête des territoires dissidents (mai 1941) ... Procès-verbaux de séances des conférences minières africaines tenues sous la présidence du Général Weygand (avril–septembre 1941).... Attaque et défense de Dakar (septembre–décembre 1940) ... trafic maritime et régime douanier ... janvier 1940–octobre 1942, etc. It should be noted that Weygand was every bit as urgent in his dealings with supreme military commanders below him in Morocco, Algeria, and Tunisia, and with the High Commissioner in French West Africa. From them too, he wanted everything "yesterday" — reports on materiel, troop needs, and the like. His telegrams flew out copiously, containing warnings even on any slackening of sartorial standards in his African military! See S.H.A.T.: 1P93: Délégation générale en Afrique française: Courrier Départ: 9 décembre 1940–18 janvier 1941. Weygand's brisk telegrams were often sent simultaneously to the "génésupers" of Tunisia, Morocco, and Algeria.

58. All of the foregoing is in *ibid.* Another file at Vincennes has a number of interesting studies, showing long-held, as well as current, German colonial ambitions, especially in French North Africa. These are in S.H.A.T.: 1P33: Vichy: Défense Nationale: Bulletins quotidiens d'information du secrétariat d'Etat aux colonies reçus par le secrétariat de coordination etc... (1939–1941). A typical part is entitled "Etudes sur l'importance militaire des colonies (février–mars 1941)," noting the riches particularly of French Morocco. There are a number of studies here, and long ones, showing the importance of these colonial domains for national defense in France. Inventories of roads, railways, products, and so on again convey "richness" — and would have to the Germans as well. There are charts of munitions and where they were putatively stored

in French Africa, and then documents showing *German* interest in those French colonial holdings, such as a resumé of an article in *Das Reich* of September 1, 1940, by Friedrich A. Eck, on France's accomplishments in North Africa. The man even wanted to claim German origins in Lyautey! Vichy correspondence on all this, including by French armistice delegation personnel, and unsigned documents, like "Les Menaces du colonialisme allemand," pointing to pre–1939 German wishes for *lebensraum* in French and British imperial domains, show French concerns here. The Vichy Service de Presse analyzed German articles and books on these themes through 1941, summarizing their content as "German colonial claims." Yet as Weygand's tenure drew to a close in North Africa, Darlan kept underplaying the Germans and overplaying the English as a threat. For example, in a report stamped "very secret" of September, 1941, Darlan's sympathies are clear in a discussion of French Morocco. The report notes: "Morocco is coveted by the Germans and Anglo-Saxons...." But it concludes that, again, defenses should be oriented against the English. The latter in S.H.A.T.: 1P35.

59. See report on Conférence Minière Africaine (under Weygand presidency) March 28–April 1 (of some 70 pages), and a subsequent one of similar length in S.H.A.T.: 1P34.

60. Weygand, *Recalled to Service*, 293.

61. Bankwitz, *Maxime Weygand and Civil-Military Relations in France*, 345–346 (quotations on those pages). An observer at Vichy in early June 1941 noted that Weygand "was on the Marshal's left; I felt him boiling like a racehorse wanting to jump and Darlan had hardly finished before General Weygand took the offensive...." J. Berthelot, quoted in Charles Williams, *Pétain* (London: Little, Brown, 2005), 385. See also *Time*'s article, "Weygand v. Darlan," June 16, 1941. And the revisionist views of Melton in *Darlan*, 112, and *passim*—i.e., that Darlan himself was buying time.

62. For the notes deriving from this conference see the general file of S.H.A.T.: 1P36: Vichy: Défense Nationale: Contribution financière de l'Afrique du Nord aux dépenses militaires de la metropole ... Equipements défensifs de l'AFN (mars 1941–février 1942) ... Procès-verbaux de la conférence Nord-africaine des vins et alcools (septembre 1941) (dossier three)....

63. These reports or letters of March 15 and October 27, 1941, the latter specifically addressed to M. the Admiral of the Fleet, Minister of National Defense, are in *ibid*.

64. All of the above in S.H.A.T.: 1P34. Weygand also appends pages of precise statistics to shore up his usual arguments.

65. All in S.H.A.T.: 1P35.

66. Hirtz, *Weygand: Témoignage*, 93–94;

Jacques Weygand, *Weygand mon père*, 297. The latter provides "exact" numbers in a footnote: 55,000 rifles, 4,000 automatic arms, 210 mortars, 26,000,000 cartridges, 52 diverse items, 6,000 trucks and light trucks. Jacques Weygand, *Weygand mon père*, 297, and see also his father's own description and inventorying of stockpiled items kept from German surveillance in an article of 1955, translated as "The Reconstruction of the Army of Africa 1940–1941," in the document collection *France under the German Occupation 1940–1944* (tr. Philip W. Whitcomb; Stanford: Stanford University Press, 1959), II, 761–775. On Nazi limitations forced on the metropolitan army, versus conditions of the army and its materiel in French North Africa, see Paxton, *Parades and Politics at Vichy*, 41–43, 47–48.

67. With Navarre. Chrétien was Colonel Serge-Henri Parisot's boss, and Parisot found him a good one, and thought it interesting that to nettle Vichy, Chrétien took the code name of "Israël." Phone interview with Colonel Serge-Henri Parisot, January 19, 2007. He also had high praise for the legendary Paul Paillole, who became his boss later in the war.

68. Jacques Weygand, *Weygand mon père*, 295; and see also Berteil, *Armée de Weygand*, 73, and on Axis intelligence agents, 108: "Intelligent, subtle, disposing of much money, they infiltrated everywhere...."

69. See S.H.A.T.: 9P81: Vichy Etat-Major: Divisions puis régions militaires: 19ième région militaire (Armée Armistice) y compris Territoires du Sud — especially part four (3ième Bureau: Correspondance 'départ' aôut–décembre 1940: Contrôle des unités, des matériels et armement par la sous-délégation italienne....) This carton contains Vinaz' letter of November 20, 1940, in both Italian and French, addressed to Commandant Bourgeois Etat-Major 19ième Région (Algeria).

70. On the very morrow of Weygand's dismissal in late November 1941, the Nazis began wearing uniforms in Casablanca, as well as in towns like Meknès, and the local population was truly shocked. See *deuxième bureau* report of December 15, 1940 (on the month of November), in its Muslim Affairs Section, in C.A.O.M.: 1AFFPOL/917.

71. See Navarre, *Temps des vérités*, 97–99.

72. The most thorough secondary source on these German colonial ambitions is Chantal Metzger, *L'Empire colonial français dans la stratégie du Troisième Reich (1936–1945)* (Brussels: Peter Lang, 2002), I.

73. Parisot's unpublished manuscript, which he provided me, was written at the end of 1942 when he was under house arrest in Eastern Morocco, for having colluded with the Allied

invasion of North Africa. (Quotations are taken from it.) He went on to join the renewed French war effort in Tunisia and in Italy, and one of his intelligence coups to come was helping capture Joseph Darnand, head of the "Milice." Some of the material here has been used in different form in my "'Casablanca' in its Time — and Ours," *Contemporary Review* 139 (October 2005): 233–237. See also François Broche, *L'Armée française sous l'Occupation: La dispersion* (Paris: Presses de la Cité, 2002), 485–488 (Annèxe ll: Les services secrets en Afrique du Nord) and General Marie-Emile Béthouart, *Cinq Années d'espérance: Mémoires de guerre 1939–1945* (Paris: Plon, 1968), 113–116. For Morocco, there is also a thesis covering some of this ground, arriving late in the day for this author: Guillet Thibault, "Le Renseignement au Maroc 1940–1942," Ecole Spéciale Militaire de Saint-Cyr, 1998. Boisson's persistent cat-and-mouse game with Axis authorities also continued, as he kept denying them consular rights in French West Africa.

74. Robert Murphy, *Diplomat among Warriors* (Garden City, NY: Doubleday, 1964), 68.

75. Childs' account is in his *Let the Credit Go: The Autobiography of J. Rives Childs* (New York: K. S. Giniger, 1983), ch. 12–17, but the entire book makes fine reading. Admiral Leahy, who had to be super-careful in spy-ridden Vichy, felt that Weygand "probably was the best soldier in France.... He had no confidence whatever in either the promises or purposes of Nazi Germany — which was more than could be said for many of the men of Vichy." William D. Leahy, *I Was There* (New York: Whittlesey House, 1950), 58.

76. Murphy, *Diplomat among Warriors*, 73.

77. Irwin Wall has, however, castigated Murphy in over-simplified American terms that nonetheless indicate why he and Weygand could get along: "Robert Murphy, of German-Irish and devoutly Catholic background, displayed sympathy for assorted right-wing politicians and schemers who permeated the Vichy regime.... Murphy inveighed against the Popular Front, held Blum responsible for French unpreparedness in 1940, and blamed Vichy antisemitism on the large number of Jews in the French Communist party." Such over-simplifying historians might do well to concede that the period under discussion was more complex, including militarily, than that of their own youths on U.S. campuses of the '60s. Wall, *The United States and the Making of Postwar France, 1945–1954* (Cambridge: Cambridge University Press, 1991), 21, 22. See also Mönick, *Pour Mémoire*, 86–99.

78. Murphy, *Diplomat among Warriors*, 78, 82; Thomas, *French Empire at War*, 83–84 (quotation 83); Hoisington Jr., *Assassination of Jacques Lemaigre Dubreuil*, 63; and Mönick, *Pour Mémoire*, 103–104.

79. Metzger, *Empire colonial français*, I, 323. See also William A. Hoisington Jr., *The Casablanca Connection: French Colonial Policy, 1936–1943* (Chapel Hill: University of North Carolina Press, 1984), 196–206 *passim*.

80. See James J. Dougherty, *The Politics of Wartime Aid: American Economic Assistance to France and French Northwest Africa, 1940–1946* (Westport, CT: Greenwood Press, 1978), 30, and report of Otto Abetz, September 16, 1941, in Abetz, *Pétain et les Allemands: Mémorandum d'Abetz sur les rapports franco-allemands* (Paris: Editions Gaucher, 1948), 118. What later became this book was written as a long memorandum in July 1943 by Abetz, incorporating some previous documents. It was later found in German archives. (No translator given for the book.)

81. For the foregoing, see Pierre Darcourt, *Armée d'Afrique: La Revanche des drapeaux* (Paris: La Table Ronde, 1972), 48–49; François Lehideux, *De Renault à Pétain: Mémoires* (Paris: Pygmalion/Gérard Watelet, 2001), 224, 292–294, 347–348; Hervé Coutau-Bégarie and Claude Huan, eds., *Lettres et notes de l'Amiral Darlan* (Paris: Economica, 1992), 402 — a collection derived from often illegible archival sources; and Hirtz, *Weygand: Témoignage*, 91. Lehideux' book has a sympathetic preface from the historian Emmanuel Le Roy-Ladurie. Some have posited that Darlan had caved in to Weygand's firmness on the Paris Protocols in June 1941, hoping to use it against him at the appropriate time. Darlan had also taken over France's Service de Renseignements and "purified" it in a way Weygand couldn't approve. See Jean-Paul Cointet, *Histoire de Vichy* (Paris: Plon, 1996), 198–199, 218. On Goering's mistrust of Weygand, Patrick Facon, *Vichy Londres-Alger 1940–1944* (Paris: Pygmalion/Gérard Watelet, 1998), 216.

82. Leahy, *I Was There*, 58–59. Also see, among others, Darcourt, *Armée d'Afrique*, 49; Cointet, *Histoire de Vichy*, 219; and Van Hecke, *Chantiers de la jeunesse*, 112–113. Darlan's quotation is in *Lettres et notes de l'Amiral Darlan*, 406 — from a handwritten note he wrote at the time of Weygand's fall, which also decried the "mediocrity of his entourage, the general's imprudent words, and his political pin-pricks toward the German armistice commission...." *Ibid.*, 406. Jacques Weygand contrasts the sloppy, thin, poorly-armed military of North Africa when his father arrived, with the army he left in place: "A year after coming here, to this same General Huntziger down for the centenary festival of *tirailleurs* and *spahis*, he could show off a totally renewed army, the genesis of what would soon become the Expeditionary Corps in Italy, then the First French Army." Jacques Weygand, *Weygand mon père*, 293. Meanwhile, Dar-

lan now began allowing the German army a series of favors, departing considerably from the armistice; while Pétain complained that nothing was being done in return about the many prisoners of war in Germany, the ironclad demarcation line in France, etc. See Abetz, *Pétain et les Allemands*, 119, 123.

83. See Jacques Weygand, *Weygand mon père*, 297–301. On the distribution of coffee, Weygand's Directeur de Ravitaillement (within the Governor-General's office) had stipulated to prefects that all inhabitants of Algeria would receive monthly allotments of 250 grams — made up of 40 percent coffee and 60 percent substitutes (from dates, acorns and other nuts). Alternatively, one could have 100 grams of pure coffee. And these edicts applied to everyone over three years old! They are found in C.A.O.M.: 1CM27. Even Darlan conceded to Benoist-Méchin, in a letter of November 23, 1941, that too much change from Weygand's period in North Africa would be a bad thing. *Lettres et notes de l'Amiral Darlan*, 428–429.

84. See Jacques Weygand, *Weygand mon père*, 324–327, quotation 327. Vichy apparently took notice of admiring notices in foreign journals concerning Weygand's forced departure. See, for example, article in the Spanish review of international politics, *Mundo*, of November, 1941, saluting the energy and acumen of Weygand in keeping a vast French empire together during his period as delegate. The article is summarized by Vichy authorities, in C.A.O.M.: 1AFFPOL/ 635.

85. In C.A.O.M.: 5CAB 1.

86. All in *ibid*.

87. Letter of Prefect of Algiers to Châtel, Governor-General of Algeria, January 23, 1942, in *ibid*.

88. In *ibid*.

89. All of the above correspondence on Algeria is in *ibid*.; and for evidence of similar pro-Weygand feeling in Morocco and Tunisia, see report of *deuxième bureau* Muslim Affairs Section (part labeled "Aperçu d'ensemble") of December 15, 1940, in C.A.O.M.: 1AFFPOL/917. According to this report, Muslims missed both the prestigious man of the sword, and the man of reforms.

90. In S.H.A.T.: 1P35.

91. Letter and documents in *ibid*.

92. In *ibid*.

93. Maréchal [Alphonse] Juin, *Mémoires* (Paris: Fayard, 1959), I, 39–44, quotations 39, 41.

94. Letter to Darlan of August 1942, in S.H.A.T.: 1P35. Parisot's unpublished memoir notes how the French armistice authorities in North Africa were often dilatory — talking the talk, but not walking the walk — with the German armistice commission. He also said (in a conversation of June 26, 2006) that he preferred dealing with bigger fish like Juin, rather than with lower-level bureaucrats (this in support of Juin's "czar" idea). For earlier material in paragraph, see S.H.A.T.: 1P85: Vichy: Délégation générale du gouvernement en Afrique française, puis commandement en chef des forces en Afrique 1 mars–18 juin, 1942. On the need for cables and other telegraphic equipment, Juin to Darlan, March 5 and March 21, 1942; on North African manufacture of batteries, generators, etc., Juin's secret note of April 1, 1942; on lack of fuel, Juin to Secrétaire Général Permanent, Algiers, April 7, 1942, and earlier report of March 24, 1942; on his need to maintain centralized control in North Africa, Juin to War Ministry, Vichy, June 1, 1942; and on the need to bring more materials to Bizerte, etc., for upgraded defenses, Juin to Estéva, June 11, 1942 (after his inspection tour of Tunisia earlier in the month): all in S.H.A.T.: 1P85. Juin's vigorous leadership in A.F.N. is also seen in the plethora of telegrams he sent military authorities and residents-general such as Noguès of Morocco, concerning numerous transfers of military personnel and materiel, asking for their advice, but also retaining the final word on where to deploy. These are found in S.H.A.T.: 1P87: Vichy: Délégation générale du gouvernement en Afrique française, puis commandement en chef des forces en Afrique: Cabinet: Télégrammes "Départ" janvier–septembre 1942.

95. Murphy, *Diplomat among Warriors*, 95.

96. See William Langer, *Our Vichy Gamble* (1947; reprint, Hamden, CT: Archon Books, 1965), chapter X and quotations 387, 388. De Gaulle? Not mainstream enough until the very eve of the 1942 invasion; and "everywhere he had the reputation of being a man personally vain and ambitious, self-centered and almost impossible to deal with." *Ibid.*, 394.

97. See, for example, a police report of September 21, 1942, from the department of Constantine, sent to Algeria's governor-general, and noting: "Rumor has it in the European and indigenous populations that General Weygand has supposedly left France and passed into dissidence." And in an earlier letter from Weygand at Grasse to Châtel, January 27, 1941, he says that "no day passes where my thoughts do not go toward Africa, and [especially] toward those Algerian reforms to which I had become so attached!" Both in C.A.O.M.: 5CAB 1.

98. The best material on Lemaigre Dubreuil and the Five is now in English: Hoisington Jr., *Assassination of Jacques Lemaigre Dubreuil*, ch. 3, 4.

99. Beaufre's quotations in Louis Guitard, *Lettre sans malice à François Mauriac* (Paris:

Aubanel, 1966), Appendix VI ("L'Opinion du Général Beaufre sur le Général Weygand"), 281–282. The clearest account of Loustaunau-Lacau's inchoate plan, and its infiltration by the French secret service in North Africa, is in Navarre, *Temps des vérités*, 106–108. Loustaunau's later career in the Resistance is a fascinating one. See his own *Mémoires d'un Français rebelle, 1914–1948* (Paris: Robert Laffont, 1948) and, by a famous associate, Marie-Madeleine Fourcade, *Noah's Ark* (tr. Kenneth Morgan; London: Allen and Unwin, 1973).

100. General André Beaufre, *Mémoires 1920–1940–1945* (Paris: Presses de la Cité, 1965), *passim*, and quotation 450. Beaufre reproduces some of his later exchange of letters (and Weygand's replies) when he and the general repaired their relationship after the war. (*Ibid.*, 443–448). In the run-up to TORCH, President Roosevelt took a Churchillian role, overwhelming preferences of some of his generals for an Operation Sledgehammer into France. See Rick Atkinson, *An Army at Dawn: The War in North Africa 1942–1943* (New York: Henry Holt, 2002), 1–32. On the relationship of Roosevelt and de Gaulle, see Raoul Aiglon, *Roosevelt and de Gaulle: Allies in Conflict: a Personal Memoir* (New York: Free Press, 1988). Ironically, Roosevelt helped free the French empire in North Africa, then became a key voice against that empire's maintenance. See Wm. Roger Louis, *Imperialism at Bay 1941–1945: The United States and the Decolonisation of the British Empire* (Oxford: Oxford University Press, 1977), 27–28. On Giraud's visit to Weygand, see General Henri Giraud, *Mes Evasions* (Paris: René Julliard, 1946), 147–149, where apparently Weygand openly declared his hatred for Laval and Darlan, and their policies. On Giraud versus de Gaulle, Serge Henri-Parisot summarized pithily why *le grand Charles* ultimately prevailed: Giraud "was only a soldier. And against him was ranged a politician...." Phone interview with Parisot, January 18, 2007. Loustaunau-Lacau was no fan either of a de Gaulle sitting comfortably in London while other Gaullists took dangerous chances in France. But he also registered serious disappointment with Weygand, who had not gone along with his North African coup attempt, refusing to burn bridges. See Loustaunau-Lacau, *Mémoires d'un Français rebelle*, 226–227, 249–251. Part of his critique of the aged Weygand reminds one of Jean Dutourd's oedipal viewpoint in his classic *The Taxis of the Marne* (tr. Harold King; New York: Simon and Schuster, 1957).

101. See Cointet, *Histoire de Vichy*, 275, and, for the words putatively exchanged between Laval and Weygand, *Procès du Maréchal Pétain: texte intégral: d'après les notes prises par le greffier de la Haute Cour de justice* (Nîmes: Lacour,

1997), 141, also cited in Cointet, *Pierre Laval* (Paris: Fayard, 1993), 416. See too, Hirtz, *Weygand Témoignage*, 149–150 (based on conversations after the war with Weygand on his state of mind at the time), as well as Weygand's own memoirs on this exchange.

102. While in Africa, Weygand worried always about British vulnerability, including on the high seas. In his diary entry of April 15, 1941, he noted that England was losing some 500,000 tons of shipping per month, and called the situation "very critical." In S.H.A.T.: 1K130.

Chapter 11

1. On Borotra, the latest biography is Daniel Amson, *Borotra: De Wimbledon à Vichy* (Paris: Editions Tallandier, 1999). In English, there is a book by Sir John Smyth, *Jean Borotra, the Bounding Basque: His Life of Work and Play* (London: Paul, 1974). For Borotra's association with Lenglen (herself a French winner at Wimbledon from 1919 through 1925), see Richard Holt, *Sport and Society in Modern France* (London: Macmillan, 1981), 178–179.

2. See Augusta Léon-Jouhaux, *Prison pour hommes d'état 1943–1945* (Paris: Denoël/Gonthier, 1973), *passim*. On the dining arrangement of Weygand, Borotra, and de la Rocque at one table, Gamelin, Clemenceau, and Reynaud at another, see, among others, Paul Reynaud, *In the Thick of the Fight* (tr. James D. Lambert; London: Cassell, 1955), 571. Reynaud's character portrait of Weygand here was of a man who was "thoughtless, hot-headed and violent," but who had also shown wartime courage vis-à-vis Laval and Darlan, and in opposing Germany's occupation of the south of France in November 1942 (589).

3. André François-Poncet, *Carnets d'un captif* (Paris: Fayard, 1952), 40–41 (diary entry of September 9, 1943), and quotation 77–78 (diary entry November 19, 1943).

4. *Ibid.*, 67, and see also 32, 52. By contrast, the ex-ambassador considered Borotra far and away the nicest (and least political) person here (79).

5. See Paul Reynaud, *Carnets de captivité 1941–1945* (Paris: Fayard, 1997), 303 ("capitulation"), 304 (on Weygand the "imbecile"), and *passim* through 366. Daladier's newfound respect for Weygand, now that they were together, contrasts with his earlier views, such as in a diary entry of November 22, 1941, concerning the delegate's ouster from Algeria: "[Weygand] is at bottom just an African proconsul who succeeded in making a good name for himself with the Americans and the British, and in creating illusions about himself in the minds of French

patriots; in sum, he's a Prefect masquerading as a General." In Edouard Daladier, *Prison Journal 1940–1945* (tr. Arthur D. Greenspan; Boulder, CO: Westview Press, 1995), 97.

6. Weygand note quoted by Jacques Weygand, *Weygand mon père*, 409; and on the memoirs taken for safekeeping, Léon-Jouhaux, *Prison pour hommes d'état*, 165. De Gaulle knew de Lattre's feelings for Weygand, and therefore had instructed him as follows: "General Weygand is obviously one of those people who must be brought to Paris in conditions that preclude any *éclat*. I must give you this order whatever personal sentiments you may have kept in his regard. It is an affair of State." De Gaulle's telegram marked "Secret" is in his *Lettres notes et carnets: Juin 1943–mai 1945* (Paris: Plon, 1983), 404–405. There is no date, but the editors have inserted "after March 31, 1945" in brackets.

7. There had been different versions of a "High Court" in France since July 23, 1789, and previous spectacular trials in its history. See Raymond Lindon and Daniel Amson, *La Haute Cour 1789–1987* (Paris: Presses Universitaires de France, 1987).

8. The best book on how the High Court functioned in this divisive era is by the man who became its president, Louis Noguères, *La Haute Cour de la libération 1944–1949* (Paris: Les Editions de Minuit, 1965). The son of a judge, Noguères was himself a lawyer, and a parliamentarian of 1940 who would not grant Pétain extended powers. He had then become part of the Resistance (as did his son).

9. See Jules Roy, *The Trial of Marshal Pétain* (tr. Robert Baldick; New York: Harper and Row, 1968), quotations 90, 93; Jacques Weygand, *Weygand mon père*, 415–424.

10. *Procès du Maréchal Pétain: texte intégral*, 142, 144, 145.

11. *Ibid.*, 154. Four of Reynaud's articles in translation appeared, among many other places, in the *New York Times*, including one of August 1, 1945, with much quotation from his old telegrams to and from Churchill et al.; but with typical inability to distinguish between armistice and capitulation. Reynaud also takes credit for pushing the British on more evacuation of French soldiers at Dunkirk, and keeping the operation going until June 4, omitting Weygand's role here. A sensible article from Paris by Harold Callender in the *New York Times* (July 29, 1945) holds that culpability in the Pétain trial ought to include other powers who had appeased in the '30s, including the U.S. It also stressed that Roosevelt's recognition of and relationship with Vichy helped prepare the way for the successful invasion of North Africa, and the road to France's liberation.

12. See Joseph Kessel, *Jugements derniers: le procès Pétain, le procès de Nuremberg* (Etrépilly, France: C. de Bartillat, 1995), quotations 58, 62, 63, 65, taken from Kessel's diary entries of August 1 and 2, 1945; and Jacques Isorni, *Mémoires: 1911–1945* (Paris: Robert Laffont, 1984), I, 461.

13. Weygand's principal lawyer, Maître Baudelot, asked for Madame Foch's letter, and she was happy to provide it. See Weygand's letter of thanks to Madame Foch, November 21, 1945, in A.N. 414AP/12, and also Senator Charles Reibel's forthright letter of recommendation in the same file — mystified that Weygand was being accused for his political stance, when Reibel had never (in a long association going back to 1920) heard him make political comments. General de Périer's deposition on Weygand for the High Court of Justice is in S.H.A.T.: 1P89.

14. On Willard's actions see Noguères, who had to deal with his obstructionism, in *La Haute Cour de la libération*, Part III, ch. 1. Willard's own book, *La Défense accuse*, came out in a new edition of 1951 (Paris: Editions Sociales, 1951), with a simplistic preface on the derailing of postwar *épuration* and return of collaborationists. Written before World War II, the book features admiring chapters on the Bolsheviks, French Communist deputies, the Hungarian Stalinist Rakosi, etc. One reason Weygand's trial had lasted so long was a jury contingent that favored the Left, especially Socialists and Communists, who constituted a dominant force in the French Assembly of that era. Thus the juror pool of July 1946 included 25 Communists, 21 Socialists, and 25 from the centrist Mouvement républicain populaire; but only a handful from each of the other parties. See Noguères, *La Haute Cour de la libération*, 141.

15. Charles Serre, ed., *Assemblée Nationale. Rapport fait au nom de la commission chargée d'enquêter sur les événements survenus en France de 1933 à 1945* (Paris: Imprimerie Nationale, 1951), I, 231–247, Weygand quotation 248; and II, 531–534, quotation by Gamelin 531.

16. *Ibid.*, VI, 1547–1576, quotations 1571.

17. *Ibid.*, VI, quotations 1599, 1600.

18. *Ibid.*, VI, quotations 1617, 1635.

19. *Ibid.*, VI, 1622.

20. *Ibid.*, VI, quotation 1642, 1643.

21. *Ibid.*, VI, 1650–1651.

22. *Ibid.*, VI, quotations 1822.

23. *Ibid.*, VI, all quotations 1927.

24. Kedward, *France and the French*, 313–317, quotations 313, 317. Kedward's earlier books include *Resistance in Vichy France: A Study of Ideas and Motivation in the Southern Zone, 1940–1942* (Oxford: Oxford University Press, 1978); *Occupied France: Collaboration and Resistance,*

1940–1944 (Oxford: Blackwell, 1985); and *In Search of the Maquis: Rural Resistance in Southern France, 1942–1944* (Oxford: Oxford University Press, 1993). Another informed analyst of the complexity of these issues is John F. Sweets in his *Choices in Vichy France: The French under Nazi Occupation* (New York: Oxford University Press, 1986).

25. See François Broche, *L'Armée française sous l'Occupation: Le Rassemblement* (Paris: Presses de la Cité, 2003), 387–393. Girardet quoted there, 393. My telephone conversation with Parisot on this subject was on January 6, 2007. See also Claude d'Abazac-Epezy's chapter on "épuration" in the French army, in Marc Olivier Baruch et al., *Une Poignée de misérables; L'Epuration de la société française après la Second Guerre Mondiale* (Paris: Fayard, 2003). The army was most broken in the period 1946–1949.

26. First quotation on de Gaulle's sense that he would make it to the top in Max Gallo, *De Gaulle: Le Premier des Français* (Paris: Robert Laffont, 1998), 29. This was expressed in a speech he gave at Bayeux. For the rest, Philippe de Gaulle, *De Gaulle, mon père: Entretiens avec Michel Tauriac* (Paris: Plon, 2003), 103 (quoted), 104.

27. Alain Peyrefitte, *C'était de Gaulle* (Paris: Gallimard, 2002), 1111 (second anecdote in footnote).

28. Philippe de Gaulle, *De Gaulle, mon père,* 282–283, 309, quotations respectively on 282, 283. De Gaulle's simplistic views on the Americans of wartime take no account of their own distinctions, expressed by figures like Leahy, such as between the slippery, overly "ambitious" Darlan, and Weygand, the honorable soldier. See Eric Roussel, *Charles de Gaulle* (Paris: Gallimard, 2002), 257. Over and over, one can cite examples of Gaullist hypocrisy when it came to Weygand's achievements in North Africa. For example, de Gaulle telegraphed General Juin — from Algiers, July 25, 1944 — that he wanted General Marcel Carpentier transferred immediately to be his chief of staff for his "Army B." Carpentier had been at Weygand's side in the late '30s, then his assistant in Algiers from February 1941 (head of the Third Bureau); then Juin's staff head in 1943–1944, and de Lattre's later in 1944! But such Weygand alumni were simply taken, never credited. See de Gaulle's telegram to Juin in his *Lettres notes et carnets: Juin 1943–mai 1945,* 270.

29. Claude Guy, *En écoutant de Gaulle: Journal 1946–1949* (Paris: Bernard Grasset, 1996), 335, 336, and quotation 459. See on de Gaulle's falsification of the historical record Nicolas Tenzer, *La Face cachée du Gaullisme* (Paris: Hachette, 1998). Jacques Isorni, whose own family had experienced anti–Jewish laws of exception in the war, nonetheless found this postwar de Gaulle "envious, full of spite and rancor...." Isorni, *Mémoires,* I, 231. And Paul Paillole, the great spymaster during the war, resigned rather than serve under *le grand Charles.*

30. De Gaulle quoted in Robert Rocca, ed., *Le Petit Livre rouge du Général* (Paris: Editions de la Pensée Moderne, 1968), 100. Later chairmen of the board of the Association to Defend the Memory of Marshal Pétain included Borotra and François Lehideux (see Henry Rousso, *The Vichy Syndrome: History and Memory in France Since 1944* [tr. Arthur Goldhammer; Cambridge, MA: Harvard University Press, 1991], 43–46). Its current head, General Jacques Le Groignec, has written a series of books on what he considers the falsification of wartime French history, most recently, *Réplique aux diffamateurs de la France 1940–1944* (Paris: Nouvelles Editions Latines, 2006) and *Philippique contre des mémoires gaulliens* (Paris: Nouvelles Editions Latines, 2004). See also his passionate *Pétain et de Gaulle* (Paris: Nouvelles Editions Latines, 1998). In the latter he quotes a number of people who found de Gaulle extremely two-faced and secretive, including Weygand himself ("[De Gaulle] is really one of the most secretive men I have ever known.") *Ibid.,* 239. (Of course he said the same of Pétain!) Le Groignec was a product of the wartime Army of Africa, commanding a squadron of Spitfires against the Nazis, then fighting after the war in Indochina and Algeria, before becoming French Commander of Air Defenses (1970–1974). Hélie de Saint-Marc's great autobiography (with Laurent Beccaria) is *Mémoires: Les Champs de braises* (Paris: Perrin, 1995), and there is also a recent DVD titled "Servir?" on his fascinating life. On de Gaulle's antipathy to Weygand over the Algerian viewpoint, see his letter to Prime Minister Michel Debré, October 24, 1959: "General Weygand recently made a very disagreeable declaration on Algeria, which the press widely diffused." The President informed Debré that he should warn the 90-year-old general to "conform to the rules of military discipline." If Weygand desired "complete liberty of expression," then he must retire from the service, or go into the reserves. De Gaulle, *Lettres notes et carnets: Juin 1958–décembre 1960* (Paris: Plon, 1985) (vol. 8), 274–275.

31. Weygand, *Forces de la France: Vocation de la France* (Paris: Boivin, 1951), quotation 181.

32. Weygand, *Et que vive la France* (Paris: La Colombe, 1953). As the author says, "Let us leave those who like putting on slippers by the fire the task of shrugging shoulders, denigrating great actions and saying: what good are they? In reality, the only ones worthy of the name 'men' are those who know how to put their strength

at the service of their heart and intelligence."
Ibid., 172.

33. General Weygand, *L'Armée à l'Académie* (Paris: Wesmael-Charlier, 1962).

34. Examples of Weygand prefaces to books on Napoleon include the one to Colonel Gaston Gillot's *Un Aide de camp de Napoléon: Le Général de Marois* (Paris: Editions du Conquistador, 1957); Commandant Henry Lachouque's *Napoléon et la garde impériale* (Paris: Bloud and Gay, 1956), a book he considers a masterpiece; and Renée Deburat's *Napoléon et les manuels d'histoire* (Paris: Editions André Lavaud, 1956).

35. Examples of Weygand prefaces to books on Joan of Arc, lamenting the decline of both patriotism and religiosity in his own France, include those to X. de la Rochefordière, *Sainte Jehanne d'Arc: Secours permanent de la France* (Paris: Les Editions de l'Ecole, 1957) and Renée Grisel, *Présence de Jeanne d'Arc* (Paris: Nouvelles Editions Latines, 1956); and on Saint-Arnaud, Louis de Charbonnières, *Une grande figure: Saint-Arnaud: Maréchal de France* (Paris: Nouvelles Editions Latines, 1960). In his preface to this book, Weygand likens the difficulties encountered in Algeria during the 1840s to those still confronting France there at the end of the 1950s.

36. Weygand preface to Jean Brunet-Moret, *Le Général Trochu 1815–1896* (Paris: Les Editions Haussmann, 1955), quotation 8.

37. Weygand preface to Colonel Roger Malcor, *Idéal de chef: Le Général Alfred Malcor 1853–1937* (Paris: La Colombe, 1956), 7, quotation 10.

38. Weygand preface to General Marie-Alphonse Desmazes, *Joffre: La victoire du caractère* (Paris: Nouvelles Editions Latines, 1955).

39. Preface to Georges Castellan, *Le Réarmement clandestin du Reich 1930–1935: Vu par le 2è bureau de l'Etat-Major français* (Paris: Plon, 1954).

40. Weygand prefaces to Pierre Vasselle, *La Tragédie d'Amiens (mai–juin 1940)* (Amiens: Léveillard, 1952); L. G. Planes and Robert Dufourg, *Bordeaux capitale tragique! Et la base navale de Bordeaux-Le Verdon mai–juin 1940* (Paris: Editions Médicis, 1956); Albert Chatelle, *Dunkerque ville ardente mai–juin 1940* (Paris: Ozanne, 1950); Charles Jenger and Henry Marsille, *Victime du siège de Brest: Robert Ricard:*

Capitaine de frégate et Jésuite 1883–1944 (Paris: Editions du Conquistador, 1959); and Carl Gustave Mannerheim, *Les Mémoires du Maréchal Mannerheim 1882–1946* (tr. Jean-Louis Perret; Paris: Hachette, 1952).

41. Weygand prefaces to: Jacques Mordal, *La Campagne de Norvège* (Paris: Editions Self, 1949), second edition of Mordal, *Narvik* (Paris: Presses de la Cité, 1960), and Admiral Gabriel Auphan and Mordal, *La Marine française pendant la seconde guerre mondiale* (Paris: Hachette, 1958). The English translation of the latter quickly came out as *The French Navy in World War II* (tr. A. C. J. Sabalot; Annapolis: United States Naval Institute, 1959).

42. Weygand preface to Maurice Catoire, *La Direction des Services de l'Armistice à Vichy* (Paris: Berger-Levrault, 1955).

43. Weygand preface to General André Laffargue, *Le Général Dentz, Paris 1940–Syrie 1941* (Paris: Les Iles d'Or, 1954). An article in *Time* on Dentz' signature of capitulation at Acre, July 14, 1941, noted that he resembled a "provincial druggist in uniform." (*Time,* July 21, 1941.)

44. Weygand preface to Louis Chaigne, *Jean de Lattre: Maréchal de France* (Paris: Fernand Lanore, 1952). On de Lattre's admiration for Weygand, and lessons learned from him, 83–87.

45. Jean Guitton, *Discours de réception à l'Académie Française et réponse du Général Weygand* (Paris: Editions Montaigne, 1962).

46. Fouvez, *Le Mystère Weygand*, 14.

47. *Ibid.*, 12.

48. See *ibid.*, 225–226.

49. A good source (really an anthology) on the atmosphere of Weygand's funeral service in Paris and burial in Morlaix, and including articles critical of de Gaulle, is *Dernier hommage du CEPEC à son président d'honneur le Général Weygand* (Paris: Centre d'Etudes Politiques et Civiques, 1965).

50. De Gaulle simply believed that one couldn't honor such a general with a national service at this sacred place. As ex-commander in chief, Weygand had already been treated leniently enough — so Philippe de Gaulle recalls his father saying. After the war he had (eventually) retained a regular army salary and "all the privileges and material advantages due his rank." But a service at the Invalides? There de Gaulle drew the line. Philippe de Gaulle, *De Gaulle, mon père,* 104.

Bibliography

I. *Archival Sources*

(For more detailed descriptions of contents in each number given here, or parts used in *fonds*, see Notes.)

A. Service Historique de l'Armée de Terre

1K130: Dépôt Weygand.

3K10: Interview Colonel Serge-Henri Parisot (Histoire Orale).

4H44: Haut Commissariat de la République au Levant: Télégrammes Affaires Etrangères....

4H271, 4H272, 4H273, 4H274: Commandement supérieur des troupes du Levant ... 1939–1941.

2N5, 2N6: Etat-Major. Conseil Supérieur de la Défense Nationale: Séances (1920–1923) ... (1923–1928).

4N2: Conseil Supérieur de la Guerre. Section française: Organismes interalliés 1917–1918.

4N92, 4N93, 4N94, 4N95: Etat-Major du Maréchal Foch....

6N6: Fonds Poincaré.

6N290: Fonds Clemenceau.

7N2294: Inspections Conseil Supérieur de Guerre: 1920–1939.

14N48, 14N50: Fonds Etat-Major Foch.

1P4: Vichy: Secrétariat de Défense Nationale.

1P33, 1P34, 1P35, 1P36: Vichy: Défense Nationale: Dossiers concernant l'empire français.

1P54: Vichy: Défense nationale: Section des Services de l'Armistice.

1P85, 1P87, 1P89, 1P93: Vichy: Délégation générale du gouvernement en Afrique française/ Commandement en chef des forces en Afrique.

9P181: Vichy: Etat-Major: Divisions puis régions militaires: 19ième région militaire (Armée Armistice) 1940–1942 [Algeria].

B. Centre des Archives d'Outre–Mer

5CAB 1, 5CAB 22, 5CAB 33: Cabinets des Gouverneurs Généraux de l'Algérie (1940–1943).

1AFFPOL/635: Fonds Ministériels: Affaires Politiques: Organisation administration de l'Afrique Occidentale Française 1940–1942....

1AFFPOL/883: Fonds Ministériels: Affaires Politiques: Section on "Menées Antinationales."

1AFF/POL888: Fonds Ministériels: Affaires Politiques: Mesures intéressant l'ordre et la sécurité publique (1940–1942).

1AFFPOL/917: Fonds Ministériels: Affaires Politiques: Bulletins mensuels ... sur les pays musulmans 1940–1941.

1AFFPOL/924: Fonds Ministériels: Affaires Politiques: Pèlerinages à la Mecque ... Afrique et Levant.

1AFFPOL/1421: Fonds Ministériels: Affaires Politiques: Dossier 10: Affaires Musulmanes: Vichy 1941–42–43.

1AFFPOL/1422B: Fonds Ministériels: Affaires Politiques: Syrie 1921–1924.

1CM27: Gouvernement général de l'Algérie: Délégation générale du gouvernement en Algérie: Cabinet Militaire: Correspondance ... 1940–1941.

1TEL/692: Fonds Ministériels: Télégrammes Départ: A.O.F. (1941).

1TEL/737: Fonds Ministériels: Alger: Délégué général. Télégrammes Départ ... Arrivée (1940–1942).

C. Archives Nationales

414AP: Fonds Foch.
94AP: Fonds Albert Thomas.
470AP: Fonds Millerand.
313AP: Fonds Paul Painlevé.
324AP: Fonds Tardieu.
130AP: Fonds Jacques-Louis Dumesnil.
443AP: Fonds Germain-Martin.

II. Books and Articles

Abetz, Otto. *Pétain et les Allemands: Mémorandum d'Abetz sur les rapports franco–allemands*. Paris: Editions Gaucher, 1948.

Aglion, Raoul. *Roosevelt and de Gaulle: Allies in Conflict: A Personal Memoir*. New York: The Free Press, 1988.

Alexander, Don. "Repercussions of the Breda Variant." *French Historical Studies* 8 (Spring 1974): 459–488.

Alexander, Martin S. *The Republic in Danger: General Maurice Gamelin and the Politics of French Defence, 1933–1940*. Cambridge: Cambridge University Press, 1992.

Allouche-Benayoun, Joëlle, and Doris Bensimon. *Les Juifs d'Algérie: Mémoires et identités plurielles*. Paris: Editions Stavit, 1998.

Amson, Daniel. *Borotra: De Wimbledon à Vichy*. Paris: Editions Tallandier, 1999.

Asprey, Robert B. *At Belleau Wood*. Denton: University of North Texas Press, 1996.

Atkinson, Rick. *An Army at Dawn: The War in North Africa 1942–1943*. New York: Henry Holt, 2002.

Attal, Robert. *Regards sur les Juifs d'Algérie*. Paris: L'Harmattan, 1996.

Bahloul, Joëlle. *The Architecture of Memory: A Jewish-Muslim Household in Colonial Algeria, 1937–1962*. Tr. Catherine du Peloux Ménagé. Cambridge: Cambridge University Press, 1996.

Bankwitz, Philip. *Weygand and Civil-Military Relations in Modern France*. Cambridge: MA.: Harvard University Press, 1967.

Baruch, Marc Olivier, et al. *Une Poignée de misérables: L'Epuration de la société française après la Seconde Guerre Mondiale*. Paris: Fayard, 2003.

Bassett, Richard. *Hitler's Spy Chief: The Wilhelm Canaris Mystery*. London: Weidenfeld and Nicolson, 2005.

Baudouin, Paul. *The Private Diaries (March 1940 to January 1941) of Paul Baudouin*. Tr. Charles Petrie. London: Eyre & Spottiswoode, 1948.

Beaufre, André. *Mémoires 1920–1940–1945*. Paris: Presses de la Cité, 1965.

_____. *1940: The Fall of France*. Tr. Desmond Flower. New York: A. A. Knopf, 1968.

Beavers, W. Robert. "Healthy, Midrange, and Severely Dysfunctional Families." In Froma Walsh, ed. *Normal Family Processes*. New York: Guilford Press, 1982.

Becker, Annette. *Monuments aux morts: Mémoire de la Grande Guerre*. Paris: Errance, 1988.

Bel Ange, Norbert. *Quand Vichy internait ses soldats juifs d'Algérie: Bedeau, sud Oranais, 1941–1943*. Paris: L'Harmattan, 2006.

Bell, P. M. H. *A Certain Eventuality: Britain and the Fall of France*. Farnborough, Hants.: Saxon House, 1974.

_____. *France and Britain 1900–1940: Entente and Estrangement*. London: Longman, 1996.

Belot, Robert. *La Résistance sans de Gaulle*. Paris: Fayard, 2006.

Benbassa, Esther. *The Jews of France: A History from Antiquity to the Present*. Tr. M. B. DeBevoise. Princeton: Princeton University Press, 1999.

Bensadoun, Roger. *Les Juifs de la République en Algérie et au Maroc: Chroniques et mémoires d'autre temps....* Clamecy: Publisud, 2003.

Berteil, Louis. *L'Armée de Weygand*. Paris: Editions Albatros, 1975.

Béthouart, Marie-Emile. *Cinq Années d'espérance: Mémoires de guerre 1939–1945*. Paris: Plon, 1968.

Blake, Robert, ed. *The Private Papers of Douglas Haig 1914–1919*. London: Eyre and Spottiswoode, 1952.

Blatt, Joel, ed. *The French Defeat of 1940: Reassessments*. Providence: Berghahn Books, 1998.

Bloch, Marc. *Strange Defeat*. Tr. Gerard Hopkins. New York: W. W. Norton, 1968.

Bordeaux, Henri. *Weygand*. Paris: Plon, 1957.

Brémond, Edouard. *La Cilicie en 1919–1920*. Paris: Imprimerie Nationale, 1921.

Broche, François. *L'Armée française sous l'Occupation: La Dispersion*. Paris: Presses de la Cité, 2002.

_____. *L'Armée française sous l'Occupation: Le Rassemblement*. Paris: Presses de la Cité, 2003.

Brodzinsky, David M., Marshall D. Schechter, and Robin Marantz Henig. *Being Adopted: The Lifelong Search for Self*. New York: Doubleday, 1992.

_____, Smith, Daniel W., and Anne B. Brodzinsky. *Children's Adjustment to Adoption: Developmental and Clinical Issues*. Thousand Oaks: SAGE Publications, 1998.

Bugnet, Charles. *Foch Speaks*. Tr. Russell Green. New York: Dial Press, 1929.

Cabanes, Bruno. *La Victoire endeuillée: La Sortie de guerre des soldats français 1918–1920*. Paris: Editions du Seuil, 2004.

Capozzoli, Joseph A. "Psychological Relief: An Overview: The Balkan Experience." In Wendy N. Zubenko and Joseph A. Capozzoli, eds. *Children and Disasters: A Practical Guide to Healing and Recovery*. New York: Oxford University Press, 2002.

Cairns, John C. "Along the Road Back to France, 1940." *American Historical Review* 64 (April 1959): 583–603.

_____. "Great Britain and the Fall of France: A Study in Allied Disunity." *Journal of Modern History* 27 (December 1955): 365–409.

Case, Lynn M. *French Opinion on War and Diplomacy During the Second Empire*. Philadelphia: University of Pennsylvania Press, 1954.

Catroux, Georges. *Deux Missions en Moyen-Orient, 1919–1922*. Paris: Plon, 1958.

Charles-Roux, F. *Cinq Mois tragiques aux Affaires Etrangères (21 mai–1er novembre 1940)*. Paris: Plon, 1949.

Chenet, Daniel. *Qui a sauvé l'Afrique*. Paris: L'Elan, 1949.

Childs, J. Rives. *Let the Credit Go: The Autobiography of J. Rives Childs*. New York: K. S. Giniger, 1983.

Chouraqui, André. *L'Amour fort comme la mort: Une autobiographie*. Paris: Robert Laffont, 1990.

Christofferson, Thomas R. *France During World War II: From Defeat to Liberation*. New York: Fordham University Press, 2006.

Churchill, Winston S. *The Second World War* (Boston: Houghton Mifflin, 1949), II.

_____. *The World Crisis*. New York: Scribner's, 1929, V.

Clemenceau, Georges. *Grandeur and Misery of Victory*. Tr. F. M. Atkinson. New York: Harcourt, Brace, 1930.

Coffman, Edward M. *The Regulars: The American Army, 1898–1941*. Cambridge, MA: Belknap Press of Harvard University Press, 2004.

_____. *The War to End All Wars: The American Military Experience in World War I*. Madison: University of Wisconsin Press, 1986.

Cohen, William B., and Irwin M. Wall. "French Communism and the Jews." In Frances Malino and Bernard Wasserstein, eds. *The Jews in Modern France*. Hanover: University Press of New England, 1985.

Cointet, Jean-Paul. *Histoire de Vichy*. Paris: Plon, 1996.

_____. *Pierre Laval*. Paris: Fayard, 1993.

Colville, J. R. *Man of Valour: The Life of Field-Marshal The Viscount Gort*. London: Collins, 1972.

Connell, John. *Wavell: Soldier and Scholar*. London: Collins, 1964.

Conte, Arthur. *Le 1er janvier 1940*. Paris: Plon, 1977.

Coutau-Bégarie, Hervé, and Claude Huan, eds. *Lettres et notes de l'Amiral Darlan*. Paris: Economica, 1992.

Crémieux-Brilhac, Jean-Louis. *Les Français de l'an 40*. Paris: Gallimard, 1990, I.

Cummings, Mark, Marcie C. Goeke-Morey, and Jessica Raymond. "Fathers in Family Context: Effects of Marital Quality and Marital Conflict." In Michael E. Lamb, ed. *The Role of the Father in Child Development*. Hoboken, NJ: John Wiley and Sons, 2004.

Curtis, Michael. *Verdict on Vichy: Power and Prejudice in the Vichy France Regime*. New York: Arcade Publishing, 2002.

D'Abernon, Edgar. *An Ambassador of Peace: Pages from the Diary of Viscount D'Abernon*. 2 vols. London: Hodder and Stoughton, 1929.

_____. *The Eighteenth Decisive Battle of the World: Warsaw, 1920*. London: Hodder and Stoughton, 1931.

Daladier, Edouard. *Prison Journal 1940–1945*. Tr. Arthur D. Greenspan. Boulder, CO: Westview Press, 1995.

Danchev, Alex, and Daniel Todman, eds. *War Diaries, 1939–1945: Field Marshal Lord Alanbrooke*. Berkeley: University of California Press, 2001.

Darcourt, Pierre. *Armée d'Afrique: La Revanche des drapeaux*. Paris: La Table Ronde, 1972.

David, Saul. *Churchill's Sacrifice of the Highland Division: France 1940*. London: Brassey's, 1994.

Davies, Norman. *God's Playground: A History of Poland*. New York: Columbia University Press, 1982.

_____. *White Eagle, Red Star: The Polish-Soviet War 1919–1920*. New York: St. Martin's Press, 1972.

Davies, Peter. *France and the Second World War: Occupation, Collaboration and Resistance*. London: Routledge, 2001.

La Délégation française auprès de la Commission Allemande d'Armistice. Paris: A. Costes, 1947, I.

Delpla, François. *Churchill et les Français*. Ostwald: Editions du Polygone, 2000.

Dernier hommage du CEPEC à son président d'honneur le Général Weygand. Paris: Centre d'Etudes Politiques et Civiques, 1965.

Destremau, Bernard. *Weygand*. Paris: Perrin, 1989.

Dougherty, James A. *The Politics of Wartime Aid: American Economic Assistance to France and French Northwest Africa, 1940–1946*. Westport, CT: Greenwood Press, 1978.

Doughty, Robert A. *The Breaking Point: Sedan and the Fall of France, 1940*. Hamden, CT: Archon Books, 1990.

_____. *Pyrrhic Victory: French Strategy and Operations in the Great War.* Cambridge, MA: Belknap Press of Harvard University Press, 2005.

Dutourd, Jean. *The Taxis of the Marne.* Tr. Harold King. New York: Simon and Schuster, 1957.

Eden, Anthony. *The Reckoning: The Memoirs of Anthony Eden, Earl of Avon.* Boston: Houghton Mifflin, 1965.

Eisenhower, John S. D. *Yanks: The Epic Story of the American Army in World War I.* New York: Free Press, 2001.

Eksteins, Modris. *Rites of Spring: The Great War and the Birth of the Modern Age.* Boston: Houghton Mifflin, 1989.

Ellis, L. F. *The War in France and Flanders 1939–1940.* London: H.M. Stationery Office, 1953.

Epstein, Klaus. *Matthias Erzberger and the Dilemma of German Democracy.* Princeton: Princeton University Press, 1959.

Facon, Patrick. *Vichy Londres-Alger 1940–1944.* Paris: Pygmalion/Gérard Watelet, 1998.

Farrar, Marjorie Milbank. *Principled Pragmatist: The Political Career of Alexandre Millerand.* New York: Berg, 1991.

Farwell, Byron. *Over There: The United States in the Great War 1917–1918.* New York: W. W. Norton, 1999.

Favreau, Bertrand. *Georges Mandel ou la passion de la République 1885–1944.* Paris: Fayard, 1996.

Feigelman, William. "Adopted Adults: Comparisons with Persons Raised in Conventional Families." In Harriet E. Gross and Marvin B. Sussman, eds. *Families and Adoption.* New York: Haworth Press, 1997.

Ferguson, Niall. *The Pity of War.* New York: Basic Books, 1999.

Ferrell, Robert H. *America's Deadliest Battle: Meuse-Argonne, 1918.* Lawrence: University Press of Kansas, 2007.

Fiddick, Thomas C. *Russia's Retreat from Poland, 1920: From Permanent Revolution to Peaceful Coexistence.* New York: St. Martin's Press, 1990.

Fishman, Sarah, et al., eds. *France at War: Vichy and the Historians.* Oxford: Berg, 2000.

Fleming, Thomas J. *The Illusion of Victory: America in World War I.* New York: Basic Books, 2003.

Foch, Ferdinand. *The Memoirs of Marshal Foch.* Tr. Colonel T. Bentley Mott. London: William Heinemann, 1931.

Forcade, Olivier, et al. *Militaires en République 1870–1962: Les Officiers, le pouvoir, et la vie publique en France.* Paris: Publications de la Sorbonne, 1999.

Fourcade, Marie-Madeleine. *Noah's Ark.* Tr. Kenneth Morgan. London: Allen and Unwin, 1973.

Fouvez, Charles. *Le Mystère Weygand: Etude d'un dossier historique du XIXè siècle.* Paris: La Table Ronde, 1967.

France under the German Occupation 1940–1944. Tr. Philip W. Whitcomb. Stanford: Stanford University Press, 1959, II.

François-Poncet, André. *Au Palais Farnèse: Souvenirs d'une ambassade à Rome, 1938–1940.* Paris: Fayard, 1961.

_____. *Carnets d'un captif.* Paris: Fayard, 1952.

_____. *The Fateful Years: Memoirs of a French Ambassador in Berlin, 1931–1938.* Tr. Jacques LeClerq. New York: Harcourt, Brace, 1949.

French, John. *1914.* Boston: Houghton Mifflin, 1919.

Funk, Arthur Layton. *The Politics of TORCH: The Allied Landings and the Algiers Putsch 1942.* Lawrence: University Press of Kansas, 1974.

Garlicki, Andrzej. *Josef Pilsudski, 1867–1935.* Tr. John Coutouvidis. Aldershot: Scolar Press, 1995.

Gallo, Max. *De Gaulle: Le Premier des Français.* Paris: Robert Laffont, 1998.

Gamelin, Maurice. *Servir.* Paris: Plon, 1946, 1947, II, III.

Gandin, Robert. *Darlan—Weygand—Cunningham: Artisans de la victoire 1939–1944.* Paris: Nouvelles Editions Latines, 1977.

Gaulle, Charles de. *Lettres notes et carnets: Juin 1943–mai 1945.* Paris: Plon, 1983.

_____. *Lettres notes et carnets: Juin 1958–décembre 1960.* Paris: Plon, 1985.

_____. *War Memoirs: The Call to Honour 1940–1942.* Tr. Jonathan Griffin. New York: Viking Press, 1958.

Gaulle, Philippe de. *De Gaulle, mon père: Entretiens avec Michel Tauriac.* Paris: Plon, 2003.

Ginio, Ruth. *French Colonialism Unmasked: The Vichy Years in French West Africa.* Lincoln: University of Nebraska Press, 2006.

Giraud, Henri. *Mes Evasions.* Paris: René Julliard, 1946.

Glover, Michael. *The Fight for the Channel Ports: Calais to Brest 1940: A Study in Confusion.* London: Leo Cooper, 1985.

Goda, Norman J. W. *Tomorrow the World: Hitler, Northwest Africa, and the Path toward America.* College Station: Texas A&M University Press, 1998.

Gorce, Paul-Marie de la. *De Gaulle.* Paris: Perrin, 1999.

Goutard, Adolphe. *The Battle of France, 1940.* Tr. Captain A. R. P. Burgess. New York: Ives Washburn, 1959.

Greenhalgh, Elizabeth. *Victory Through Coalition: Britain and France During the First World War.* Cambridge: Cambridge University Press, 2005.

Grigg, John. *Lloyd George, War Leader 1916–1918.* London: Allen Lane, 2002.

Guelton, Frédéric. "France, Levant et Balkans 1937–mai 1940: Les Illusions perdues d'une grande stratégie périphérique." *Revue Historique des Armées* 211 (Mars 2002): 107–116.

_____. "Le Général Weygand et la question des forces aériennes 1928–1935." *Revue Historique des Armées* 206 (Mars 1997): 31–42.

Guitard, Louis. *Lettre sans malice à François Mauriac.* Paris: Aubanel, 1966.

Guitton, Jean. *Discours de réception à l'Académie Française et réponse du Général Weygand.* Paris: Editions Montaigne, 1962.

Guy, Claude. *En écoutant de Gaulle: Journal 1946–1949.* Paris: Bernard Grasset, 1996.

Hankey, Maurice. *The Supreme Command 1914–1918.* London: George Allen and Unwin, 1961, II.

Hebey, Pierre. *Alger 1898: La grande vague antijuive.* Paris: NiL Editions, 1996.

Hirtz, Georges. *Weygand: Années 1940–1945: Témoignage.* Gardanne: Esmenjaud, 2003.

Hitchcock, William I. "Pierre Boisson, French West Africa, and the Postwar *Epuration*: A Case from the Aix Files." *French Historical Studies* 24 (Spring 2001): 305–341.

Hofstadter, Richard. *The American Political Tradition and the Men Who Made It.* New York: A. A. Knopf, 1948.

Hoisington, William A, Jr. *The Assassination of Jacques Lemaigre Dubreuil: A Frenchman Between France and North Africa.* London: RoutledgeCurzon, 2005.

_____. *The Casablanca Connection: French Colonial Policy, 1936–1943.* Chapel Hill: University of North Carolina Press, 1984.

Horne, Alistair. *The Price of Glory: Verdun 1916.* New York: St. Martin's Press, 1963.

_____. *Seven Ages of Paris.* New York: A. A. Knopf, 2002.

_____. *To Lose a Battle: France, 1940.* Harmondsworth, Eng.: Penguin Books, 1979.

Horne, John, and Alan Kramer. *German Atrocities, 1914: A History of Denial.* New Haven: Yale University Press, 2001.

Hull, Isabel V. *Absolute Destruction: Military Culture and the Practices of War in Imperial Germany.* Ithaca: Cornell University Press, 2005.

Ironside, Edmund. *Time Unguarded: The Ironside Diaries 1937–1940.* New York: David McKay, 1962.

Ismay, Lionel Hastings. *The Memoirs of General Lord Ismay.* New York: Viking Press, 1960.

Isorni, Jacques. *Mémoires: 1911–1945.* Paris: Robert Laffont, 1984, I.

Jackson, Julian. *The Fall of France: The Nazi Invasion of 1940.* Oxford: Oxford University Press, 2003.

_____. "1940 and the Crisis of Interwar Democracy in France." In Martin S. Alexander, ed. *French History Since Napoleon.* London: Arnold, 1999.

Jackson, Peter. *France and the Nazi Menace: Intelligence and Policy Making 1933–1939.* Oxford: Oxford University Press, 2000.

Jackson, Robert. *The Fall of France: May–June 1940.* London: Barker, 1975.

Jackson, W. G. F. *Alexander of Tunis as Military Commander.* London: B. T. Batsford, 1971.

Jeannesson, Stanislaus. *Poincaré, la France et la Ruhr 1922–1924.* Strasbourg: Presses Universitaires de Strasbourg, 1998.

Jeffery, Keith. *Field Marshal Sir Henry Wilson: A Political Soldier.* Oxford: Oxford University Press, 2006.

_____, ed. *The Military Correspondence of Field Marshal Sir Henry Wilson 1918–1922.* London: The Bodley Head, 1985.

Jennings, Eric T. "Reinventing Jeanne: The Iconology of Joan of Arc in Vichy Schoolbooks, 1940–1944." *Journal of Contemporary History* 29 (October 1994): 711–734.

_____. *Vichy in the Tropics: Pétain's National Revolution in Madagascar, Guadeloupe, and Indochina, 1940–1944.* Stanford: Stanford University Press, 2001.

Joffre, Joseph. *The Personal Memoirs of Joffre, Field Marshal of the French Army.* Tr. Colonel T. Bentley Mott. New York: Harper and Brothers, 1932, II.

Johnson, Douglas V., II, and Rolfe L. Hillman, Jr. *Soissons 1918.* College Station: Texas A&M Press, 1999.

Johnson, Gaynor. *The Berlin Embassy of Lord d'Abernon, 1920–1926.* London: Palgrave Macmillan, 2002.

Jones, Edgar. "The Psychology of Killing: The Combat Experience of British Soldiers during the First World War." *Journal of Contemporary History* 41 (April 2006): 229–246.

Juin, Alphonse. *Mémoires.* Paris: Fayard, 1959, I.

Karsh, Efraim and Inari. *Empires of the Sand: The Struggle for Mastery in the Middle East.* Cambridge, MA: Harvard University Press, 1999.

Kaufmann, J. E. and H. W. *The Maginot Line: None Shall Pass.* Westport, CT: Praeger, 1997.

Kedward, H. R. *France and the French: A Modern History.* Woodstock, NY: Overlook Press, 2006.

_____. *In Search of the Maquis: Rural Resistance in Southern France, 1942–1944.* Oxford: Oxford University Press, 1993.

_____. *Occupied France: Collaboration and Resistance, 1940–1944.* Oxford: Blackwell, 1985.

_____. *Resistance in Vichy France: A Study of Ideas and Motivation in the Southern Zone, 1940–1942.* Oxford: Oxford University Press, 1978.

Keene, Jennifer D. *Doughboys, the Great War, and the Remaking of America.* Baltimore: Johns Hopkins University Press, 2001.

Keiger, J. F. V. *France and the World since 1870.* London: Arnold, 2001.

_____. *Raymond Poincaré.* Cambridge: Cambridge University Press, 1997.

Kersaudy, François. *Churchill and de Gaulle.* London: Collins, 1981.

Kessel, Joseph. *Jugements derniers: le procès Pétain, le procès de Nuremberg.* Etrepilly, France: C. de Bartillat, 1995.

Keyes, Roger. *Outrageous Fortune: The Tragedy of Leopold III of the Belgians 1901–1941.* London: Secker and Warburg, 1984.

Kimball, Warren F., ed. *Churchill and Roosevelt: The Complete Correspondence.* Princeton: Princeton University Press, 1984, I.

King, Jere Clemens. *Foch Versus Clemenceau: France and German Dismemberment, 1918–1919.* Cambridge, MA: Harvard University Press, 1960.

Klarsfeld, Serge. *L'Etoile des Juifs*. Paris: L'Archipel, 1992.

Koburger, Charles W., Jr. *The Cyrano Fleet: France and Its Navy, 1940–1942*. New York: Praeger, 1989.

Krakovitch, Raymond. *Paul Reynaud dans la tragédie de l'histoire*. Paris: Tallandier, 1998.

Langer, William. *Our Vichy Gamble*. New York: A. A. Knopf, 1947.

Larkin, Maurice. *France Since the Popular Front: Government and People 1936–1996*. Oxford: Clarendon Press, 1997.

Laskier, Michael M. *The Alliance Israélite Universelle and the Jewish Communities of Morocco: 1862–1962*. Albany: SUNY Press, 1983.

Lawler, Nancy Ellen. *Ivoirien Tirailleurs of World War II*. Athens: Ohio University Press, 1992.

Leahy, William D. *I Was There*. New York: Whittlesey House, 1950.

Le Groignec, Jacques. *Pétain et de Gaulle*. Paris: Nouvelles Editions Latines, 1998.

_____. *Philippique contre des mémoires gaulliens*. Paris: Nouvelles Editions Latines, 2004.

_____. *Réplique aux diffamateurs de la France 1940–1944*. Paris: Nouvelles Editions Latines, 2006.

Lehideux, François. *De Renault à Pétain: Mémoires*. Paris: Pygmalion/Gérard Watelet, 2001.

Léon-Jouhaux, Augusta. *Prison pour hommes d'état 1943–1945*. Paris: Denoël/Gonthier, 1973.

Liddell Hart, Basil H. *Reputations, Ten Years After*. Boston: Little, Brown, 1928.

_____, ed. *The Rommel Papers*. Tr. Paul Findlay. New York: Da Capo Press, 1953.

Lindon, Raymond, and Daniel Amson. *La Haute Cour 1789–1987*. Paris: Presses Universitaires de France, 1987.

Lloyd, Christopher. *Collaboration and Resistance in Occupied France: Representing Treason and Sacrifice*. Houndmills, Eng.: Palgrave, 2003.

Lloyd George, David. *Memoirs of the Peace Conference*. New Haven: Yale University Press, 1939, I.

_____. *War Memoirs of David Lloyd George*. London: Ivor Nicolson and Watson, 1934, IV.

Longrigg, Stephen H. *Syria and Lebanon Under French Mandate*. Oxford: Oxford University Press, 1958.

Looseley, Rhiannon. "Paradise After Hell." *History Today* 56 (June 2006): 32–38.

Loti, Pierre. *Le Roman d'un spahi*. Paris: Calmann-Lévy, 1893.

Loucheur, Louis. *Carnets secrets 1908–1932*. Brussels: Brepols, 1962.

Louis, Wm. Roger. *Imperialism at Bay 1939–1945: The United States and the Decolonization of the British Empire*. Oxford: Oxford University Press, 1977.

Loustaunau-Lacau, Georges. *Mémoires d'un Français rebelle 1914–1948*. Paris: Robert Laffont, 1948.

Ludendorff, Erich. *My War Memories 1914–1918*. London: Hutchinson, 1919, I.

MacMillan, Margaret. *Paris 1919: Six Months That Changed the World*. New York: Random House, 2002.

Marshall-Cornwall, James. *Foch as Military Commander*. New York: Crane, Russak, 1972.

Martet, Jean. *Clemenceau*. Tr. Milton Waldman. London: Longman's, Green, 1930.

Martin, Benjamin F. *France and the Après Guerre 1918–1924*. Baton Rouge: Louisiana State University Press, 1999.

_____. *France in 1938*. Baton Rouge: Louisiana State University Press, 2005.

McMillan, James. *Dreyfus to de Gaulle: Politics and Society in France 1898–1969*. London: Edward Arnold, 1985.

McPhail, Helen. *The Long Silence: Civilian Life Under the German Occupation of Northern France, 1914–1918*. London: I. B. Tauris, 2001.

Melton, George E. *Darlan: Admiral and Statesman of France, 1881–1942*. Westport, CT: Praeger, 1998.

Méouchyetal, Nadine, et al. *Syrie et Liban 1918–1946.* Damascus: Institut Français d'Etudes Arabes de Damas, 2002.

Messenger, Robert. "Last of the Whigs: Churchill as Historian." *The New Criterion* 25 (October 2006): 16–23.

Metzger, Chantal. *L'Empire colonial français dans la stratégie du Troisième Reich (1936–1945).* Brussels: Peter Lang, 2002, I.

Miquel, Pierre. *Le Chemin des dames.* Paris: Perrin, 1997.

Mönick, Emmanuel. *Pour Mémoire.* Paris: Firmin-Didot, 1970.

Mosier, John. *The Myth of the Great War: A New Military History of World War I.* New York: HarperCollins, 2001.

Msellati, Henri. *Les Juifs d'Algérie sous le régime de Vichy: 10 juillet 1940–3 novembre 1943.* Paris: L'Harmattan, 1999.

Murphy, Robert. *Diplomat among Warriors.* Garden City, NY: Doubleday, 1964.

Muselier, Renaud. *L'Amiral Muselier 1882–1965.* Paris: Perrin, 2000.

Musialik, Zdzislaw. *General Weygand and the Battle of the Vistula, 1920.* London: Jozef Pilsudski Institute of Research, 1987.

Navarre, Henri, et al. *Le Service des renseignements 1871–1944.* Paris: Plon, 1978.

_____. *Le Temps de vérité.* Paris: Plon, 1979.

Nicolson, Harold. *Peacemaking 1919.* New York: Grosset and Dunlap, 1965.

Noguères, Louis. *La Haute Cour de la libération 1944–1949.* Paris: Les Editions de Minuit, 1965.

Nolan, Michael. *The Inverted Mirror: Mythologizing the Enemy in France and Germany, 1898–1914.* New York: Berghahn Books, 2005.

North, John, ed. *The Alexander Memoirs 1940–1945.* New York: McGraw-Hill, 1961.

Olasky, Marvin. "Adoption Is an Act of Compassion." In Andrew Harnack, ed. *Adoption: Opposing Viewpoints.* San Diego: Greenhaven Press, 1995.

Paillole, Paul. *Services spéciaux 1935–1945.* Paris: Robert Laffont, 1975.

Palmer, Alan. *Victory 1918.* New York: Atlantic Monthly Press, 1998.

Paoli, Dominique. *Maxime ou le secret Weygand.* Brussels: Editions Racine, 2003.

Paxton, Robert O. *Parades and Politics at Vichy.* Princeton: Princeton University Press, 1966.

_____. *Vichy France: Old Guard and New Order 1940–1944.* New York: A. A. Knopf, 1972.

_____, and Michael R. Marrus *Vichy France and the Jews.* New York: Basic Books, 1981.

Pellissier, Pierre. *6 Février 1934: La République en flammes.* Paris: Perrin, 2000.

Pershing, John J. *My Experiences in the World War.* New York: Frederick A. Stokes, 1931.

Peyrefitte, Alain. *C'était de Gaulle.* Paris: Gallimard, 2002.

Pipes, Daniel. *Greater Syria: The History of an Ambition.* New York: Oxford University Press, 1990.

Porch, Douglas. *The Path to Victory: The Mediterranean Theater in World War II.* New York: Farrar, Straus, Giroux, 2004.

Prior, Robin, and Trevor Wilson. *The Somme.* New Haven: Yale University Press, 2005.

Procès du Maréchal Pétain: texte intégral: d'après les notes prises par le greffier de la Haute Cour de justice. Nîmes: Lacour, 1997.

Raïssac, Guy. *Un Soldat dans la tourmente.* Paris: Albin Michel, 1963.

Ramognino, Pierre. *L'Affaire Boisson: Un Proconsul de Vichy en Afrique.* Paris: Les Indes Savantes, 2006.

Recouly, Raymond. *Foch: My Conversations with the Marshal.* Tr. Joyce Davis. New York: D. Appleton, 1929.

Reynaud, Paul. *Carnets de captivité 1941–1945.* Paris: Fayard, 1997.

_____. *In the Thick of the Fight.* Tr. James D. Lambert. London: Cassell, 1955.

Rocca, Robert, ed. *Le Petit Livre rouge du Général.* Paris: Editions de la Pensée Moderne, 1968.

Roussel, Eric. *Charles de Gaulle.* Paris: Gallimard, 2002.

Rousso, Henry. *The Vichy Syndrome: History and Memory in France since 1944*. Tr. Arthur Goldhammer. Cambridge, MA: Harvard University Press, 1991.

Roy, Jules. *The Trial of Marshal Pétain*. Tr. Robert Baldick. New York: Harper and Row, 1968.

Sabato, Haim. *Aleppo Tales: A Tapestry of Tradition and Faith*. Tr. Philip Simpson. New Milford, CT: Toby Press, 2004.

Saint Marc, Hélie de. *Mémoires: Les Champs de braises*. Paris: Perrin, 1995.

Salibi, K. S. *The Modern History of Lebanon*. New York: Praeger, 1965.

Schroeter, Daniel J. *Merchants of Essaouira: Urban Society and Imperialism in Southwestern Morocco, 1844–1886*. New York: Cambridge University Press, 1988.

Sebag-Montefiore, Hugh. *Dunkirk: Fight to the Last Man*. Cambridge, MA: Harvard University Press, 2006.

Serre, Charles, ed. *Assemblée Nationale. Rapport fait au nom de la commission chargée d'enquêter sur les événements survenus en France de 1933 à 1945*. Paris: Imprimerie Nationale, 1951, I, II, VI.

Shaw, Martin. "Growing Up Adopted." In Philip Bean, ed. *Adoption: Essays in Social Policy, Law, and Sociology*. London: Tavistock Publications, 1984.

Sherman, Daniel J. *The Construction of Memory in Interwar France*. Chicago: University of Chicago Press, 1999.

Shirer, William L. *The Collapse of the Third Republic*. New York: Simon and Schuster, 1969.

Shorrock, William I. *French Imperialism in the Middle East: The Failure of Policy in Syria and Lebanon 1900–1914*. Madison: University of Wisconsin Press, 1976.

Siegel, Mona L. *The Moral Disarmament of France: Education, Pacifism, and Patriotism, 1914–1940*. Cambridge: Cambridge University Press, 2004.

Sinclair, David. *Hall of Mirrors*. London: Century, 2001.

Singer, Barnett. "'Casablanca' in its Time — and Ours." *Contemporary Review* 139 (October 2005): 233–237.

_____. "From Patriots to Pacifists: The French Primary Schoolteachers, 1880–1940." *Journal of Contemporary History* 12 (April 1977): 413–434.

_____. *Modern France: Mind, Politics, Society*. Seattle: University of Washington Press, 1980.

_____, and John Langdon. *Cultured Force: Makers and Defenders of the French Colonial Empire*. Madison: University of Wisconsin Press, 2004.

Sisung, Jean-Philippe, and Martin Benoist, eds. *Weygand: Témoignages et documents inédits*. Montsûrs: Editions Résiac, 2006.

Smyth, John. *Jean Borotra, the Bounding Basque: His Life of Work and Play*. London: Paul, 1974.

Smythe, Donald. *Pershing: General of the Armies*. Bloomington: Indiana University Press, 1986.

Sorlot, Marc. *André Maginot (1877–1932): L'Homme politique et sa légende*. Metz: Editions Serpenoise, 1995.

Spears, Edward. *Assignment to Catastrophe*. 2 vols. London: William Heinemann, 1954.

Stubbs, Kevin D. *Race to the Front: The Materiel Foundations of Coalition Strategy in the Great War*. Westport, CT: Praeger, 2002.

Sweets, John F. *Choices in Vichy France: The French under Nazi Occupation*. New York: Oxford University Press, 1986.

Tannenbaum, Jan Karl. *General Maurice Sarrail 1856–1929: The French Army and Left-Wing Politics*. Chapel Hill: University of North Carolina Press, 1974.

Tardieu, André. *Devant l'obstacle: L'Amérique et nous*. Paris: Editions Emile-Paul Frères, 1929.

_____. *The Truth about the Treaty*. Indianapolis: Bobbs-Merrill, 1921.

Tauber, Eliezer. *The Arab Movements in World War I*. London: Frank Cass, 1993.

Tenzer, Nicolas. *La Face cachée du Gaullisme.* Paris: Hachette, 1998.

Terraine, John. *The Right of the Line: The Royal Air Force in the European War 1939–1945.* London: Hodder and Stoughton, 1985.

Thomas, Martin. *Britain, France and Appeasement: Anglo-French Relations in the Popular Front Era.* New York: Berg, 1996.

_____. *Empires of Intelligence: Security Services and Colonial Disorder After 1914.* Berkeley: University of California Press, 2007.

_____. *The French Empire at War 1940–45.* Manchester: Manchester University Press, 1998.

Thompson, J. Lee. *Forgotten Patriot: A Life of Alfred, Viscount Milner of St. James's and Cape Town, 1854–1925.* Madison, NJ: Fairleigh Dickinson University Press, 2007.

Trask, David E. *The AEF and Coalition Warmaking, 1917–1918.* Lawrence: University Press of Kansas, 1993.

Trigano, Shmuel, ed. *L'Identité des Juifs en Algérie: Une Expérience originale de la modernité.* Paris: Alliance Israélite Universelle, 1999.

Triseliotis, John. "Identity Formation and the Adopted Person Revisited." In Amal Treacher and Ilan Katz, eds. *The Dynamics of Adoption.* London: Jessica Kingsley Publishers, 2000.

Tucker, Spencer C. *The Great War 1914–1918.* Bloomington: Indiana University Press, 1998.

Turnbull, Patrick. *Anatomy of a Disaster.* New York: Holmes and Meier, 1978.

Van Hecke, A. S. *Les Chantiers de la jeunesse au secours de la France (Souvenirs d'un soldat).* Paris: Nouvelles Editions Latines, 1970.

Vidal, Georges. "L'Armée française face au communisme au début des années 1930 jusqu'à 'la débâcle.'" *Historical Reflections* 30 (Summer 2004): 283–309.

Vinen, Richard. *France, 1934–1970.* New York: St. Martin's Press, 1996.

_____. *The Unfree French: Life under the Occupation.* New Haven: Yale University Press, 2006.

Wall, Irwin M. *The United States and the Making of Postwar France, 1945–1954.* Cambridge: Cambridge University Press, 1991.

Wallach, Janet. *Desert Queen: The Extraordinary Life of Gertrude Bell.* New York: Doubleday, 1996.

Wandycz, Piotr S., and Tomasz Schramm. "Pilsudski et Weygand à la bataille de Varsovie." *Revue d'histoire diplomatique* 115 (2001): 203–212.

Watson, Alex. "Self-Deception and Survival: Mental Coping Strategies on the Western Front, 1914–1918." *Journal of Contemporary History* 41 (April 2006): 269–286.

Weber, Eugen. *The Nationalist Revival in France, 1905–1914.* Berkeley: University of California Press, 1959.

Weygand, Jacques. *The Role of General Weygand: Conversations with His Son.* Tr. J. H. F. McEwen. London: Eyre and Spottiswoode, 1948.

_____. *Weygand mon père.* Paris: Flammarion, 1970.

Willard, Marcel. *La Défense accuse.* Paris: Editions Sociales, 1951.

Williams, Charles. *The Last Great Frenchman: A Life of General de Gaulle.* London: Little, Brown, 1993.

_____. *Pétain.* London, Little, Brown, 2005.

Winter, Jay. *Sites of Memory, Sites of Mourning: The Great War in European Cultural History.* Cambridge: Cambridge University Press, 1995.

Wiser, William. *The Twilight Years: Paris in the 1930s.* New York: Carroll and Graf, 2000.

Wright, Nicholas. "French Peasants in the Hundred Years War." *History Today* 33 (June 1983): 38–42.

Yapp, M. E. *The Near East since the First World War: A History to 1995.* London: Longman, 1996.

Young, Robert J. *In Command of France: French Foreign Policy and Military Planning, 1933–1940.* Cambridge, MA: Harvard University Press, 1978.

_____. *Power and Pleasure: Louis Barthou and the Third French Republic*. Montreal: McGill-Queen's University Press, 1991.

Zamir, Meir. *The Formation of Modern Lebanon*. London: Croom Helm, 1985.

Zuccotti, Susan. *The Holocaust, the French, and the Jews*. New York: Basic Books, 1993.

Zuckerman, Larry. *The Rape of Belgium: The Untold Story of World War I*. New York: New York University Press, 2004.

III. Works by Maxime Weygand (Cited)

Allocution du Général Weygand aux officiers des armées de terre, de mer et de l'air à Dakar, le 29 octobre 1940. Paris: G. Taupin, no date.

L'Arc de Triomphe de l'Etoile. Paris: Flammarion, 1960.

L'Armée à l'Académie. Paris: Wesmael-Charlier, 1962.

Comment élever nos fils? Paris: Flammarion, 1937.

Dans la Nuit Versailles s'éclaire. Paris: Berger-Levrault, 1959.

En lisant les mémoires de guerre du Général de Gaulle. Paris: Flammarion, 1955.

Et que vive la France. Paris: La Colombe, 1953.

Foch. Paris: Flammarion, 1947.

Forces de la France: Vocation de la France. Paris: Boivin, 1951.

La France est-elle défendue? Paris: Flammarion, 1937.

Le Général Frère. Paris: Flammarion, 1949.

Histoire de l'armée française. Paris: Flammarion, 1938.

Histoire militaire de Mohammed Aly et de ses fils. 2 vols. Paris: Imprimerie Nationale, 1936.

Le 'Journal' du Général Weygand 1929–1935. Montpellier: UMR, 1998. (Ed. Frédéric Guelton).

Le Maréchal Foch. Paris: Firmin-Didot, 1929.

Mémoires. I: *Idéal vécu*. Paris: Flammarion, 1953.

Mémoires. II: *Mirages et réalité*. Paris: Flammarion, 1957.

Mémoires. III: *Rappelé au service*. Paris: Flammarion, 1950.

Le 11 novembre. Paris: Flammarion, 1958.

Recalled to Service: The Memoirs of General Maxime Weygand of the Académie Française. Tr. E. W. Dickes. London: William Heinemann, 1952.

Turenne: Marshal of France. Tr. George B. Ives. Boston: Houghton Mifflin, 1930.

Works with Prefaces or Introductions by Maxime Weygand (Cited)

Auphan, Gabriel, and Jacques Mordal. *La Marine française pendant la seconde guerre mondiale*. Paris: Hachette, 1958.

Brunet-Moret, Jean. *Le Général Trochu 1815–1896*. Paris: Les Editions Haussmann, 1955.

Castellan, Georges. *Le Réarmement clandestin du Reich 1930–1935: Vu par le 2è bureau de l'Etat-Major français*. Paris: Plon, 1954.

Catoire, Maurice. *La Direction des Services de l'Armistice à Vichy*. Paris: Berger-Levrault, 1955.

Chaigne, Louis. *Jean de Lattre: Maréchal de France*. Paris: Fernand Lanore, 1952.

Charbonnières, Louis de. *Une grande figure: Saint-Arnaud, Maréchal de France*. Paris: Nouvelles Editions Latines, 1960.

Chatelle, Albert. *Dunkerque ville ardente mai–juin 1940*. Paris: Ozanne, 1950.

Deburat, Renée. *Napoléon et les manuels d'histoire*. Paris: Editions André Lavaud, 1956.

Demazes, Marie-Alphonse. *Joffre: la victoire du caractère*. Paris: Nouvelles Editions Latines, 1955.

Gillot, Gaston. *Un Aide de camp de Napoléon: Le Général de Marois*. Paris: Editions du Conquistador, 1957.

Grisel, Renée. *Présence de Jeanne d'Arc.* Paris: Nouvelles Editions Latines, 1956.

Jenger, Charles, and Henry Marsille. *Victime du siège de Brest: Robert Ricard: Capitaine de frégate et Jésuite 1883–1944.* Paris: Editions du Conquistador, 1959.

Lachouque, Henry. *Napoléon et la garde impériale.* Paris: Bloud and Gay, 1956.

Laffargue, André. *Le Général Dentz, Paris 1940–Syrie 1941.* Paris: Les Iles d'Or, 1954.

Malcor, Roger. *Idéal de chef: Le Général Alfred Malcor 1853–1937.* Paris: La Colombe, 1956.

Mannerheim, Carl Gustave. *Les Mémoires du Maréchal Mannerheim 1882–1946.* Tr. Jean-Louis Perret. Paris: Hachette, 1952.

Mordal, Jacques. *La Campagne de Norvège.* Paris: Editions Self, 1949.

———. *Narvik.* Paris: Presses de la Cité, 1960.

Planes, L. G., and Dufourg, Robert. *Bordeaux capitale tragique! Et la base navale de Bordeaux-Le Verdon mai–juin 1940.* Paris: Editions Médicis, 1956.

Rochefordière, X. de la. *Sainte Jehanne d'Arc: Secours permanent de la France.* Paris: Les Editions de l'Ecole, 1957.

Vasselle, Pierre. *La Tragédie d'Amiens (mai–juin 1940).* Amiens: Léveillard, 1952.

Articles in newspapers or magazines, and/or personal interviews
have not been listed; see Notes.

Index